D0933030

PSY-FI ONE

**An Anthology of Psychology
in Science Fiction**

Edited by
*Kenneth B. Melvin,
Stanley L. Brodsky,
and Raymond D. Fowler, Jr.*

Random House New York

First Edition

9 8 7 6 5 4 3 2 1

Copyright © 1977 by Random House, Inc.

All rights reserved under International and Pan-American Copyright Conventions. No part of this book may be reproduced in any form or by any means, electronic or mechanical, including photocopying, without permission in writing from the publisher. All inquiries should be addressed to Random House, Inc., 201 East 50th Street, New York, N.Y. 10022. Published in the United States by Random House, Inc., and simultaneously in Canada by Random House of Canada Limited, Toronto.

Library of Congress Cataloging in Publication Data

Main entry under title:

Psy fi one: an anthology of psychology in science fiction.

    Includes index.
    1. Science fiction, American. I. Melvin, Kenneth B. II. Brodsky, Stanley L., 1939–
III. Fowler, Raymond D., 1930– IV. Title: Psychology in science fiction.
PZ1.P957 [PS648.S3]   813'.0876   76-56825
ISBN 0-394-30576-0

Manufactured in the United States of America. Composed by Datagraphics, Phoenix, Arizona. Printed and bound by R. R. Donnelley & Sons, Co., Crawfordsville, Ind.

Cover art: Stanislaw Fernandes

Since this page cannot legibly accommodate all the copyright notices, the pages following constitute an extension of the copyright page.

acknowledgments

JAMES RANSOM, "Fred One," from *The Best from Fantasy and Science Fiction,* 1965, 14th series, pp. 239–251. Copyright © 1964, Mercury Press, Inc. First published in *The Magazine of Fantasy and Science Fiction.* By permission of the author and his agents, Raines & Raines.

DANIEL KEYES, "Flowers for Algernon," from *Fantasy and Science Fiction,* April 1959, *16,* pp. 5–30. Reprinted by permission of the author and the author's agent, Robert P. Mills, Ltd.

JAMES MCCONNELL, "Learning Theory," from *Psychology in the WRY* by Robert A. Baker, pp. 66–81. New York: Van Nostrand Reinhold, 1963. Reprinted by permission of the author.

PHILIP JOSÉ FARMER, "How Deep the Grooves," from *Down in the Black Gang* by Philip José Farmer, pp. 205–215. New York: Signet, 1971. Reprinted by permission of the author and his agents, Scott Meredith Literary Agency, Inc., 845 Third Avenue, New York, N.Y. 10022.

ROBERT SILVERBERG, "In the House of Double Minds," from *Vertex,* 1974, *2,* pp. 30–33, 56–59. Copyright © 1974 by Mankind Publishing Co., Inc. Reprinted by permission of the author.

NORMAN SPINRAD, "All the Sounds of the Rainbow," from *Vertex,* 1973, *1,* pp. 18–23, 76–79, 92–93. Reprinted by permission of the author and his agents, Scott Meredith Literary Agency, Inc., 845 Third Avenue, New York, N.Y. 10022.

PAUL COREY, "If You're So Smart," from *New Writings in SF 9* by E. J. Carnell, pp. 55–68. New York: Bantam Books, 1972. Copyright © by John Carnell for "New Writings in SF 9." Reprinted by permission of the E. J. Carnell Literary Agency, London.

LARRY EISENBERG, "The Executive Rat," from *Worlds of Science Fiction,* November–December 1972, pp. 146–153. Copyright © by Universal Publishing & Distributing Corp. Reprinted by permission of the author.

ROBERT SHECKLEY, "Love, Incorporated," from *Playboy Book of Science Fiction and Fantasy,* pp. 47–60. Copyright © 1964 by Robert Sheckley. Reprinted by permission of the Sterling Lord Agency, Inc.

JOHN BRUNNER, "Such Stuff," from *Eighth Annual Edition of the Year's Best Science Fiction* by J. Merril, pp. 73–90. New York: Dell. Copyright © 1962 by Fantasy and Science Fiction. Reprinted by permission of Paul R. Reynolds, Inc., 599 Fifth Avenue, New York, N.Y. 10017.

LARRY EISENBERG, "The Baby," from *Galaxy Science Fiction,* March 1974, *34,* pp. 127–133. Copyright © 1974 by Universal Publishing & Distributing Corp. Reprinted by permission of the author.

HOWARD FAST, "The First Men," from *Fantasy and Science Fiction,* February 1960, *17,* pp. 5–30. Copyright © by Howard Fast. Reprinted by permission of Paul R. Reynolds, Inc., 599 Fifth Avenue, New York, N.Y. 10017.

KEITH LAUMER, "Placement Test," from *Nine by Laumer* by Keith Laumer, pp. 91–118. New York: Berkeley, 1967. Copyright © 1964 by Ziff-Davis Publishing Company. Reprinted by permission of Robert P. Mills, Ltd.

RAY BRADBURY, "The Man in the Rorschach Shirt," from *Playboy,* October 1966, pp. 82, 84, 92, 210–211. Copyright 1966 by Ray Bradbury. Reprinted by permission of Harold Matson Co., Inc.

NORMAN SPINRAD, "It's a Bird! It's a Plane!" from *The Last Hurrah of the Golden Horde* by Norman Spinrad, pp. 171–179. Garden City: Doubleday, 1970. Reprinted by permission of the author and his agents, Scott Meredith Literary Agency, Inc., 845 Third Avenue, New York, N.Y. 10022.

URSULA K. LE GUIN, "The Diary of the Rose," from *Future Power* by Jack Dann and Gardner R. Dozois, pp. 1–23. New York: Random House, 1976. Reprinted by permission of the author and the author's agent, Virginia Kidd.

ALBERT TEICHNER, "Christlings," from *Orbit 10* by D. Knight, pp. 118–132. New York: G. P. Putnam's Sons, 1972. Reprinted by permission of the author.

GRAHAME LEMAN, "Conversational Mode," from *Best Science Fiction for 1972* by F. Pohl, pp. 98–112. New York: Ace Books, 1972. Copyright © 1972 by John Carnell for "New Writings in SF 20." Reprinted by permission of the author and E. J. Carnell Literary Agency.

STANLEY BRODSKY, "A Touch of Sanity," from *The Worm Runner's Digest,* Winter 1970–1971, pp. 99–100. Reprinted by permission of the author.

ROBY JAMES, "Care." An original story written with love especially for this book.

STANLEY L. BRODSKY and KENNETH B. MELVIN, "Psy-Fi," from *Human Behavior,* January 1975, pp. 65–68. Reprinted by permission of the authors.

ACKNOWLEDGMENT

Bernice J. Melvin

preface

"You can't teach a pig to sing. It only annoys the pig and wastes your time."
This pessimistic thought of Lazarus Long, alias Robert Heinlein, underlies the
teaching practices of a substantial segment of higher education. The high
achievers, the people who want to learn anyway, are taught the melodies, with
the instructors taking great pleasure in their sweet songs. The students who
aren't interested, who don't learn, why they are the pigs! The reason they don't
learn is that pigs can't sing anyway. A circular reasoning process applies, much
like Ambrose Bierce's astute observation that the absence of functional wings
presents no handicap to the ostrich since the ostrich can't fly anyway.

We see this process of pig making as a toxic transformation. Unknowingly,
unwittingly, professors all too often turn into the evil queen of Snow White,
carrying along under their sweeping black robes poisoned apples cleverly
disguised as lectures and texts. One bite, and fertile minds and lovely thoughts
go to rest for 100 years or one semester, whichever comes first in students'
subjective time. The student blames the instructor for not being stimulating;
the unaware instructor blames the sleeping student for not paying attention.
This process, which Ryan calls "Blaming the Victim," has its fulfillment when
the victim accepts the belief that he can't sing. The essence of the Blaming the
Victim syndrome is illustrated in a Zero Mostel piece, in which Mostel plays
a Southern senator investigating the beginnings of World War II. "What," he
blusters, "was Pearl Harbor doing out there in the middle of the Pacific
Ocean?"

Behind the student's notebook or text in the classes in which he is pig-
transformed, is a Robert Heinlein science fiction book, or a Marvel comic, or
a *Mad* or *National Lampoon.* Those of us who sometimes feel sucked into the
second-order transformation—from our mirror image of handsome prince or
princess into wicked witch of the podium—become aware that the comic or
paperback novel represents a spontaneous, joyous learning by the student of
things he wishes to learn on his terms. How do we cause our terms to meet?

One solution is to sneak copies of *The Hulk* and *Guardians of the Galaxy*
onto our lecterns, so that we should meet on the students' terms. A second
solution is the one presented by this book: to bring together some science-
fiction stories that say something meaningful about psychology; add introductory comments that are about one-half fun, one-fourth substance, and
one-fourth real spaghetti sauce; and to hope to hear some sweet songs.

We are not at liberty to reveal our own secret identities at this time. We
appear in many forms and many names when humanity needs us. However,
the next time there is a near disaster and some ordinary person performs
extraordinary feats to save others, look carefully at the heroes. Note that they

appear publicly just that once and seem to vanish, and that nobody suspects anything else. 'Nuff said.

Oh yes, the identities of which we *can* speak. To the outside observer we are psychology-teacher types, who compose the full membership of the West Alabama flying psychologist science fiction writers club. "Psychologists are so boring," one of our friends observed, "all they talk about is flying."

Our friend was wrong. We talk about singing as well. Confucius wrote that to hear is to forget, to see is to remember, and to do is to understand. The purpose of this book is to let the reader see and do psychology as we see and do, with singing, with belly laugh, and with the allure of an intriguing science mystery story yet to be solved.

contents

introduction

Today, psychologists can teach a person to control voluntarily his heart rate or the alpha rhythms of his brain. Psychological research has established the fact that we need to dream and, in fact, make up for lost dreams. We now have computers printing out psychodiagnostic statements based on psychological tests. And experimenters have transferred a simple memory from one animal to another.

This is reality. It is also the stuff of science fiction a mere twenty years ago. What will psychologists be doing twenty years from now? Who will use psychology, and for what ends?

Most of our stories concern this future psychology. Others could take place now (but have not). These tales vary, covering a range from learning to testing, from IQ to dreams, and from conditioned love to computer psychotherapy. Along with diversity of topic, there is variation in style and approach. Our selections display the adventure, the humor, and even the horror of many possible psychological realities. And included are some deft implications as to where psychology might be heading.

Our stories have aspects in common, also. All of them involve some type of psychological technique (even though the protagonist may be from a related discipline, psychiatry, for example). They are primarily science fiction, with a dash of fantasy. Best of all, they are fine reading.

We hope that students of psychology will find this book a valuable companion to their introductory text. These stories should heighten interest in psychology, and, we hope, increase the motivation to learn more about the subject. Further, we feel that they are fine examples of science fiction: reading them is not a chore, but a delight. In addition, the introduction to each section introduces some new material, some comments on the section topic, and sets the stage for the stories to follow. Each story has an introduction to help the student look for psychological themes, facts, principles, and problems.

Why should science fiction stories help to teach psychology? Well, for one thing, they provide vivid examples of psychological techniques and principles. Secondly, such stories stretch the imagination and are thought provoking. As we see fictional characters conditioning love or programming psychotherapy by computer, we see the extension of psychological principles and techniques —and may well want to consider the problems which may follow. In fiction, we may feel more deeply about the humans who are in these situations, since these writers are expert in getting us to identify with their characters. (We defy anyone to read "Flowers for Algernon" without getting a "lump in the throat.") So we hope that our stories may sensitize the reader to the human problems that may be cured (or aggravated) by the psychology of today, and tomorrow.

Conditioning, Learning, and Memory

Throughout life, the human being is a learning organism. We learn crawling and dancing, the meaning of words, the abstractions of science—the morals of our culture as well as the skills of the criminal, the symptoms of neurosis as well as the social graces.

Most psychologists define *learning* as a relatively permanent change in behavior resulting from experience or practice. This learning process has been studied on many levels, ranging from the classical conditioning of flatworms to the complexities of concept formation in humans. In the former example, the worms were repeatedly given a light followed by electric shock. While at first the worms twitched only to the shock, after training, the light also would make them twitch. Contrast this basic form of learning with, for example, the abstract reasoning and concept formation required to learn calculus.

First let us look at the more basic types of learning, specifically, operant and classical conditioning. Many of the principles determining classical conditioning were discovered by the Russian physiologist Ivan Pavlov. (Does the name Pavlov ring a bell?) In this procedure, a neutral stimulus (one that initially does not elicit the to-be-learned response) is paired with a stimulus that elicits a response, and soon the neutral stimulus elicits the response. For example, Pavlov paired a bell with meat powder, a stimulus which elicited salivation in dogs. After repeated presentations, the dogs salivated to the bell. Classical conditioning is important to us in terms of the ways we acquire emotional responses. We may also show conditioned salivation with the sight of a steak, but more importantly, respond with fear or anger to other stimuli through conditioning. In Huxley's classic science fiction novel *Brave New World,* children selected to be laborers were given books and flowers, followed by loud noises and electric shocks. As a character in the novel logically puts it, ". . . this batch of infants will be safe from books and botany all their lives." Conditioning techniques, however, can be used for more beneficial purposes. For example, phobias have been cured by gradually associating the feared object, such as a cat or snake, with a pleasurable and competing response, such as relaxation.

Another basic form of learning is termed instrumental learning or operant conditioning. Unlike classical conditioning, here reward (or reinforcement) depends on the organism's response. Our behavior is established in the manner in which, for example, we work to receive pay or change our social behavior to obtain approval.

Until recently, it was thought that this type of learning was limited to responses of the skeletal muscles, such as raising an arm. However, experimenters have shown that autonomic functions such as blood pressure, rate of saliva production, body temperature, and the production of urine can be operantly conditioned. Normally, we receive little information or feedback following changes in these functions: we cannot normally see, touch, or hear changes in our blood pressure, and thus most of us are not clearly conscious of it. When we use our skeletal muscles, however, it is much easier to find out how these muscles are operating, since we can combine several sensory impressions. Reach for your pen and you see your hand move, feel the impact of your fingers as they touch it, and sense the muscle response involved.

Through the work of Neal Miller and other researchers, the use of biofeedback instrumentation to provide a person information about physiological events within his or her body has proven effective in modifying such events. In typical biofeedback training, the person gets information through machines which pick up and amplify internal bodily signals, translating them into stimuli such as tones and lights. In a matter of hours, the trainee can learn to control voluntarily this bodily function and dispense with the machine. Before this technique was discovered, there were certain people, like yogis, who performed such feats, but it took years of self-training. Now we can make people into "instant yogis" through biofeedback training.

This biofeedback technique has promise in the treatment of medical and psychological problems. For example, chronically anxious patients have been taught to relax by controlling a tone that rises when the frontalis (forehead) muscle contracts and falls when it relaxes. People have learned to control heart irregularities (premature ventricular contractions) through heart-rate biofeedback. They first learn to speed or slow the heart, then to maintain the rate within normal limits. Other research is in progress, including training persons with high blood pressure to control this ailment.

A not uncommon theme in fantasy and science fiction has been the "superhero." As we gain more and more control over our bodies, we will be superior to most humans a decade ago. We may not fly like Superman, or bounce bullets off bracelets with the agility of Wonder Woman, yet we are beginning to develop powers even they do not possess.

More typical in both basic and applied psychology, however, is the operant conditioning of voluntary responses. Quite a few years ago, B. F. Skinner reported that he had taught pigeons to play Ping-Pong. While the practical application of this feat is nil (who wants a bunch of pigeons cluttering up a Ping-Pong table?), the power of operant techniques was clearly shown. Today, therapeutic techniques based on operant conditioning, often called behavior modification, are widely used with a variety of human problems. For example, mentally retarded children have been taught to dress and feed themselves by rewarding closer and closer approximations of the desired behavior (shaping). Behavior modification is also used in toilet training, in token economies in mental hospitals, and in conjunction with programmed learning, to give a few more instances.

Fifteen years ago, some of the above examples of conditioning and learning would have been considered science fiction. One wonders what science fiction of today will be reality fifteen years from now. Perhaps the following stories will give us a hint.

1. Fred One

James Ransom

One problem of psychological research is the interaction of subjects with the experimenter. The experimenter must be careful not to let any bias influence the subjects' responses. If so, human subjects may try to conform with the experimental hypothesis, except for those who show the "screw you" effect. Of course this problem is lessened with subhuman organisms such as the rat.

Or is it? In James Ransom's fantasy, we meet "Fred One," who is not only highly intelligent, but is also one of the psychologist's favorite subjects —a laboratory rat. Through the rat's-eye view of Fred One, we may learn something about learning experiments, the world of subjects, and perhaps the motivation of experimenters. So imagine you are a rat, and let Fred One show you the world of the lab.

Before you go, here are a few things to think about and look for on your journey. Food, water, shock escape, and sex are emphasized as rewards for rat learning—yet researchers have successfully used other incentives. What are some of these? Our protagonist is certainly curious; but what about normal laboratory rats? How did one researcher in this story control for the rat's sense of smell in a learning experiment? Can you think of a better method? What about the motivations of the researchers? Admittedly, Fred One's perception, as his vision, may be a bit distorted here.

In this fantasy, the author has the rats communicating with each other through language. While psychologists do not typically talk to their rats, they have recently been talking to chimps—and getting an answer. In the 1960s, Beatrice and Allen Gardner taught Washoe, a young female chimpanzee, a sign language used by the deaf. Washoe went on to construct rudimentary sentences, such as "come-gimme-sweet," and to ask questions. Other chimps, as well as other nonhuman primates, have followed in Washoe's footsteps (or should we say pawprints?).

One further thought—rats and college students have been the favorite subjects of learning experiments. What are the advantages and disadvantages of this practice? And how else are rats like college students?

Night falls in clinical laboratories much the same as elsewhere. Shadows lengthen across tabletops. The furnace clears its heavy throat and rumbles complacently into being. Lights flash on and off and feet shuffle about, kicking wheeled buckets of Roccal disinfectant, as the mops flick back and forth in the corridors quelling outbreaks of infectious riot like so many horses swatting flies. Long silences now—and darkness fitful with cold instrumental luminosities and the bewhiskered questing in confinement of a thousand tiny noses.

In Room 17B—Experimental Psychology: Erwin Allen, Ph.D.—a rack of twelve cages on a wheeled flat has been rolled to the center of the floor from Breeding and Procurement in the subcellar. Each cage contains eight rats, mostly all white with pink tails and eyes but some of them brindled and a few "pintos" with rakish patches of black and brown in saddle or eye-shield distribution. Six of the cages are tagged "M" and six "F"—for male and female, which is to be the significant point of differentiation among the animals. No other differences are of interest—nor, indeed, would further differentiation be possible in the present state of these particular experimenters' knowledge of these particular rats. Among the rats themselves, however, individual differences are widely acknowledged.

The twelve cages are stacked up in three piles of four, like a cluster of apartment dwellings newly erected in the center of town. In the uppermost compartment of one pile a brindled male upright along the grill-work sidesteps neatly to the corner, completing an unsatisfactory surveillance of the dim laboratory, and hustles across drowsing bodies to a crouched white resting easily on all fours in the centermost corner of the three stacks of life.

"Fred One?"

"What is it?" the white murmurs softly, as if not to wake whatever sleepers there may be among them.

"I can't see anything yet. Are you Fred One?"

"Yes."

"I'm Fred Three, but I guess I'm Two if that's all right. I don't think there's a Two in any of the cages."

"Did you try to find out?"

"Yes. Hell, I'm not bucking for anything."

"All right, you're Two, then. What does it look like out there?"

"I can't see. Just a bare lab, for all I can tell. I lost track of the turns on the way up and I'm not sure which side of the building we're on now. Maybe the moon will help."

"Or the sun, of course."

"No, I doubt if the sun will help." Fred Three—now Fred Two—flicked his whiskers in a fierce gesture and threw himself down on all fours at a discreet distance from One. "I've heard of you," he said.

Fred One gave a mental shrug and glanced with fleeting concern at Two crouched nervously alert among the shredded headlines of the nest. One of those bitter ones, he concluded—or rather Twos, he corrected himself with that scrupulous linguistic honesty that was more a source of annoyance to him than of pride and comfort. He would have to work on Two if he expected to be any good to the others, and there wasn't much time. One had calculated the orientation of the windows from the apparent slant of the wind against them, and he knew that the moon would soon give sufficient light to enable them to make out the contours of the equipment.

"Can you smell anything, Two?"

"Just the water."

"Nothing else?"

"No food. Just water."

"Well, all labs have water, Two."

"I know. They use it to wash out the test tubes."

"Well, they do."

"Fred One on my last design was one of their test tubes."

Fred One nodded in a pleasant way to acknowledge the gibe and to say that he knew well enough the cruel uses to which water could be put in certain types of experiments.

"How many of these designs have you been on, Two?"

"This is my fourth."

"It's my twenty-third. Some of them were not so bad."

Fred Two crouched closer at the sleeve-plucking insistence of his curiosity.

"Tell me about the one where you stretched the learning curve up into the superior adult human range," he said.

"That was a long time ago." Fred One shook his head, annoyed at the pleasure any reference to this exploit always gave him. That had been a first-rate design and it had caught him at the full tilt of his powers—or Powers, he giggled, remembering with strange pleasure Edith Powers and her soft clean hands lifting him into the maze to show her skeptical colleagues what a smart rat could do with adequate "reinforcement," they called it—the adroit manipulation of challenge and reward. Like geniuses of all times and species, Fred One was not above day-dreaming, and his fondest reverie always found him loose at night in the stacks of the library scratching through the files of the *Journal of Comparative & Physiological Psychology* for Lister & Powers: "Positive Reinforcement and Escalated Obstacle Frustration in a Group of Sexually Deprived Inbred Male Rats." Sexually deprived! Fred One knew their attitude and no longer bewailed it: a rat is cheese, disease, and procreation, or the occasional object of a terrier's hunt. But why even mention such a meaningless form of deprivation when deprivation was the cage itself? Oh, he did not mean the absence of freedom—to starve or to be caught and killed. He meant the cage of idleness—to be stacked in a corner of the subcellar and fed and watered but never again . . . rewarded? No—challenged. It had not been the tidbits at the goal that drew his racing feet along the corridors of the Lister Maze—he had sometimes barely managed to choke them down. It was the peering girl and her ticking stopwatch, and the triumphant flourish as she depressed the stem when he saw through a clumsy lure and went on to beat his best time. Fred One had bitterly resented not being chosen for the next design—phase II of the same experiment—in which an entire colony of twelve cages was kept for six weeks in an enriched environment with toys, light, and plenty of mazes. There was one toy in particular that he dearly wished he could get his hands on—*paws* on!—a clockwork thing that you . . . But no matter, and no matter either that all of the rats in that experiment were later sacrificed and their brains spun down for cerebrocortical cholinesterase determinations. If Fred One had news for the world it was that none of his kind expected not to be sacrificed, and if he had more news it was that he would go on being sexually deprived until *Rattus rattus* was no more IF ONLY THEY WOULD LET HIM LEARN!

"What's the matter, One?" Fred Two crouched closer still, glancing about nervously for the source of One's unease.

"Nothing, it's all right. I was just thinking . . . Do you like cheese, Two?"

"Not much. I like grain. I like—"

"Grain, then. I remember one of these designs where all we were asked to do was express a preference for any of several kinds of food. Grain was one of the choices. We were in individual cages, I recall, and after we had made our selections the various foods were distributed over the metal flooring and the food each of us had chosen was defended with an electric charge. You could do one of three things: brave the charge and get to your favorite food; avoid that food and settle for something a bit less to your liking; or try to plot the field and learn to get to your preferred food without receiving a shock. I was Fred One for the first time."

"Yeah?"

"Well, what do you think we did?"

"I don't know. What are these shocks like?"

"They're not pleasant. You can stand it."

"Well, I don't know. I guess it would depend."

"No."

"Well, what, then?"

"We sized it up and passed the word. Every one of us chose a food we didn't like and let them defend that. So we just relaxed with our 'second choices' and had a nice vacation for about two weeks."

This story was almost more than Fred Two could stand. Feeling vaguely grumpy at what he felt to be too much success, Fred One turned his mind away in search of better things while Two glinted and snarled and swayed from side to side in staccato paroxysms of joy. "Oh, oh, that's rich!" he gasped over and over, and more than once started up as if to nudge the others in the nest and then drew back, unwilling yet to interrupt pleasure with the effort of sharing it. Fred One waited between convulsions for the opportunity to make his point.

"And they—and they—oh, ho-ho-ho!" Fred Two exulted, triumphant with the vision of his hated testers carefully observing and writing things down and drawing con-con-*conclusions* from the cautious behavior of Fred One and the other rats.

"The point, Two, is that—"

"Oh, ho-ho-ho—"

"Two!"

"Yes, One." Two subsided with effort, and gazed happily at Fred One with renewed admiration and confidence.

"The *point,* Two, is that these things are not necessarily the end of the world *as long as we cooperate.*"

"I know the system, One."

"These are intelligent people, trying to do a good job. They're all right."

"If you say so, One."

"We only have to keep our heads and look sharp. If it gets tough, we just try to save as many as we can."

"I know. You tell me what to do and I'll do it."

"I don't know what to do because I have no idea what the design is. Are you sure no one has heard anything?"

"Nothing, One. Every cage has at least a Four, and each one has called the roll. Nobody knows anything."

"These things don't just start on somebody's inspiration, you know. They have weeks of conferences, get preliminary approval from the department chief, then the Dean—the money has to be okayed, the time, the physical facilities, us, the research assistants and technicians all have to be lined up. You'd think—"

"Excuse me, One. I'm sure. Nothing."

"All right. Then we depend on our first sight of the equipment. Some of it you can see. Some of it—chemicals, food, machine oil—you can smell. I'll need you for that."

"I know."

One was sure that Two did know, and hoped he also knew that the subject was delicate. Lured beyond the bounds of judgment by the taunt that her "brilliant" rat was simply following a scent, Edith Powers had paralyzed the nerves inside his nose with a cotton swab soaked in a dilute solution of trichloroacetic acid that had not been dilute enough, and he had never quite regained the ability to make out presences in the dark. What was worse, she had spilled the stock bottle near the cage and then rushed to open a window before trapping the fumes in a towel, so that a gust of wind blew the greedy stuff into his eyes and he now saw reality through a pane of frosted glass. He didn't blame her and he wished the others wouldn't—it had been her pride in him, he was sure, that had made her do it. But it was awkward all the same, especially since part of his job depended upon being able to convince the others that they were in the hands of intelligent people.

It was a job that was difficult enough at times, One admitted. Word had gotten around lately about a nonesterified fatty acid study in the medical school in which an inexperienced laboratory assistant had fed lino*lenic* instead of linoleic acid in the final phase of an experiment and six weeks of semi-starvation (fourteen of twenty rats had developed nephritis and died) ended in "no result." (That experiment should have been confined in the first place, One was sure, to fatty acids showing geometric isomerism, since the negligible effects of arachidonic withdrawal had already been sufficiently demonstrated by Harper and others at Bethesda.)

But in the meantime the night was passing, Two was waiting, and the moon was coming. What would it show? One had uneasy feelings about this design. He thought he had heard of Erwin Allen, Ph.D., but something about the name bothered him. A visiting professor? If he turned out to be a young fellow, just starting out, that in itself could be a bad thing. Or if he were over thirty and still assistant prof that could be even worse. Some of these chaps eagerly approaching their first work or beginning to flounder in mid-career could be dangerous, especially if they were on warning from the chief to produce something. One definitely knew of a case where a sick rat was stuffed in a lunch bag to suffocate and a healthy one substituted so a meaningless sleeping pill could be reported out as harmless to laboratory animals. But Allen? For some reason the name was associated in One's mind with sleep deprivation and exhaustion time studies—the bane of the laboratory animal's life and the all-too-frequent cause of his untimely death. The classic example was Koprowski & Moore (1951). In that experiment forty rats were slotted in treadmills tilted into water in such a way that they could stay out of the water only by walking uphill. At the same time they could get air only by working a complicated spring mechanism at the top of the hill with their noses. As time went on and the rats got tired, they became confused about how the spring mechanism worked. The frequency of successful manipulations (rhinipulations?) of the spring was automatically recorded, and the treadmills were stopped in different series for ten minutes per hour, five minutes, three minutes, and one minute per hour. All of the rats ultimately drowned, and One supposed the data were used to support somebody's idea about coffee breaks in business and industry. The design itself, however—so it seemed to One—left a great deal to be desired. After all, it was not the business of business and industry to work people until they drowned. Those animals should have been kept alive and checked carefully over a period of months to determine if there were any lasting ill effects of prolonged fatigue. If he had his way, he would repeat that experiment, taking care this time to—

One clapped a mental paw over his racing thoughts and peered guiltily at

Two as if to make certain that he had not been talking to himself. What was he thinking! *Would* he repeat such a barbaric experiment if he had the authority? He knew he would not. And yet—

And yet he had not quite told Two all of what had happened on that happy occasion of the defended choices. Anything—but comfort most of all—gets dull after a while. One had found himself looking with mounting intellectual greed at a dish of gritty stuff he knew he hated. Surely there must be a way to get at it. Vague fragments of conversation overheard in a dozen labs had finally clicked into place and he had determined to try an experiment of his own. One night he had collected tiny shavings of newspaper from the place where he hid his droppings and rubbed them vigorously against a bakelite water container attached to the bars of the cage. One by one, in a line pointing toward the forbidden dish, he had let them fall slowly to the floor. Suddenly he let one drop and it fell like lead—and he had located the outermost limits of the charged field. All night he worked furiously, and by dawn had cleared a narrow winding path hedged on both sides by bits of paper. Gaily he made his way back and forth from the dish to his bed, piling up the hateful gritty stuff—for no other reason than to sit gloating beside it when the technician checked the cages in the morning.

The immediate result had been most gratifying. Oh, the head-scratching and the clipboard-clutching and the *attention* he had received! One laughed once, as he often did, thinking of that morning—but then immediately sobered, as he always did, and acknowledged his full personal responsibility for what followed. The simple design was immediately reshuffled beyond their powers (Edith!) of divination, the voltage was increased, and three of the older rats making a break for it across a loaded field had gone into ventricular fibrillation and died.

They should have died hereafter!—a great human king had once proclaimed.

No, One. You have taken as the touchstone of your behavior the minimization—to paraphrase Pauling—of murine misery, and that is—

"Yes, Two?"

A flurry of nerve impulses nearby in the nest wrenched One away from his contemplations.

"One, I think the moon is coming!"

It was true. The first rays had fallen on the far wall, and soon would sweep the tables clean of their mystery. One would then know what Erwin Allen (*Allen?*) and his co-workers had in store for the colony. Two raced to the bars, squeaking messages to all of the Fours in the other cages as the colony came to life. The females, One knew, would begin briskly to move shredded papers about into little hollows—as if the act of preparing to nourish nonexistent young would protect them from harm. The males would watch their Fours, scuttling out of the way as the Fours moved importantly back and forth inside the bars peering for data. Two did the same thing, skillfully maintaining his own vigilance while at the same time cocking his whiskers to receive signals from his lieutenants in the other cages. The moon slowly swelled with borrowed heat and floated upward until One could almost feel its light like fingers on his blinking lids.

"One, they see a computer!" Two scampered to headquarters and then back to his forward post, trembling with excitement.

One pricked up his whiskers. "What kind?"

"Large—I see it now—at least, it *looks* like a computer."

"What does it say on the front panel, Two?"

"I can't make it out! Oh, God! Wires! One, it's electricty again! Wires leading to cages!"

"How many cages? Calm down, Two."

"I don't know—they're all over the floor! There must be a hundred of them!" One got up slowly and made his way to the grillwork. Two crouched beside him, starting to snivel. "One, I don't think I'd like those shocks! My feet are tender! I was raised in a cage!"

"Be quiet, we were all raised in cages." With gruff sympathy he nudged Two with his nose and pressed against the grillwork, vainly trying to see. "Tell them to be quiet." Two swallowed hard against the resistance of the dry membranes inside his mouth and throat and ran along the grill croaking orders. With the comfortable habit of obedience the rats fell silent except for one voice on the far side of the flat.

"Is that a Four? What's he saying?"

Two ran to the extreme corner of the cage and exchanged a relay of messages, reporting back over his shoulder as the reply came in.

"Pile of papers or magazines on a desk . . ."

"That'll be it."

". . . journals, it looks like."

"Bound volumes?"

"Unbound . . ."

"Recent, then. What journals?"

". . . can't see the titles . . ."

"The top one?"

". . . getting it. *The Journal* . . . *of the* . . . *Institute* . . ."

"Of what? What institute?" One came alert.

". . . of *Radio Eng*—"

"Radio Engineers! The I.R.E.!" One tensed and held his breath as the name Allen circled widely into the vortex of his bottomless memory. Brusquely he called Two and nudged him roughly to attention. "Now you describe that equipment, Two. It must be light enough—I can feel it."

"C-Cages, One, like I said."

"How big?"

"Large—larger than this one—room for m-maybe forty rats in each one."

"What else?"

"This big thing—computer thing—only I've seen com-p-puters and this one has these . . . wires!"

"What about the wires?"

"They run out of this big thing, One—all over the front of it—"

Fred One lowered his voice to almost a whisper. "All right, now listen—this is very important: Do you see any *buttons*?"

"B-Buttons, One?"

"Buttons! In the cages!"

Two scrambled away, calling to the Fours on the lower most tiers to describe the inside of the cages, and came back, momentarily forgetful of his anxieties under the prodding of reinforced admiration. "One, you've got something? Yes! Each cage has these but—"

"By God, Two, we're all right!" One laughed and reached blindly with a paw as if to ruffle the hair on Two's head the way he remembered seeing a young experimenter do to his visiting son. He grinned fiercely and made a swooping infinity sign with his tail.

"W-Whuh—"

"It's a branching 709!"

"What's a—"

"A teaching machine, you idiot!" THIS IS THE CULMINATION!—One almost screamed it as the name Allen tilted and fell. Four hundred thousand from HEW to develop a self-organizing mathetics logosystem with wash-ahead and subsequence—Burkhaalter circuits with looping impedance—and the "let the machine do it" answer to the problem of programming ahead of the superior students. "Why Can't Johnny Read Sanskrit?"—Abel & Forbes, *J. Res. Soc. Am. 33, 1962. Because he hasn't got a 709!*

So it had come. This was what he had been building for—training for—being "deprived" for . . . Deprived? One slammed shut the steel valves of memory but it was too late. Now he remembered . . . It had not been her clumsiness that day in the lab that had spilled the acid and blinded him, it had been Alan Lister and their sudden reaching for each other and her breathless, "Yes, Alan! Oh, yes! Yes!"—and then the swirling and shouting in each others' arms while he lunged at the grillwork, squeaking, "Edith! Edith!" and *then* the acid and the haze forever before his eyes and the sleepless nights thinking about her and Alan Lister squirming together in their warm nest of shredded newspapers. But no matter now, Edith! Take your Alan—I have mine!

The cages were in a furor as the word went down that Fred One was excited about something. It didn't matter. They would be all right. They could scamper about in the way rats were expected to do, dropping feces whenever they felt like it. They would be his backdrop, the baseline of his accomplishment, the abscissa to his rocketing ordinate, the muted accompaniment to his virtuoso improvisations. Two would take care of them, order them about. It was what they liked. They were the rats. Cheese, disease, and procreation. Shucking off the last shred of his vanishing guilt he regretted no longer his inability to smell them or see them. Ugly scampering things with their naked tails! Fred One was going to join his own! Life was short, and rats were cheap, but a liberated brain can outrun the stars and the 709 had better be ready. Fred One chuckled, imagining the first-frame programmers groping downward to rat level: things in twos reward with food; threes, water; fives, pain. And now you and the computer are on your own. Well, then, what about multiples—or even cubes—of two, three, five? Would he leap to thirty—the first multiple of all three? Or why go in that direction at all? Fred One could do square root and nobody knew it. A self-organizing system was bound to take him at least that far. He leaned against the grill, brushing aside Two's eager questions and blinking through frosted corneas at the huge black friend. How much farther would it take him? How far was there to go? One caught his breath and whistled loudly through his nose at the sudden thought that in effect he would be programming his own system . . . a self-organizing computer responded at *and beyond* the level of the input and *made no distinction between rats and men!*

Fred One began to tremble. It was better than that. If the computer was organized to stay ahead of him, One was in effect teaching, then learning, teaching, then learning—as fast as the circuits could function. There was—simply and at last—no limit any more.

Fred One slumped against the grill, smiling. What did they want—his beloved colleagues with their white coats and pipes and grubby politicking after grants? The beta$_2$ chain of isovaleryl? The coefficient of weightlessness in the Enders neutrino? Well, they should have it! They were good people, and had held him gently. What did they call it—serendipity? Would they accept a breakthrough—would they recognize one—from a rat and a computer? Probably not. Probably not.

But Fred One would die knowing.

And the computer would remember . . .

2. flowers for Algernon

Daniel Keyes

Psychologists and educators have long searched for ways to improve learning and memory, with some success. But what if we could find a way that was quick, with dramatic results? Think of the advantages of this, especially for those persons of below-average intelligence, the "mentally retarded." And what about the problems? The following story should illustrate some of these.

Retardation is a persistent and moving phenomenon which comes especially to the attention of psychologists. While the term "retardation" has some popular acceptance, psychologists consider it to refer to a wide spectrum of behavior deficits. Typically, retardation is indicated when intellectual functioning is below normal and social adjustment, learning ability, or both, are impaired. Scores on an individually administered intelligence test of less than 68–70 are one indicator of mental retardation. Yet some who are labeled retarded aren't! Racial bias in tests, situational factors, and limited behavior samples may lead to false signals of retardation. Even with accurate diagnoses, the term "retardate" produces a panoply of secondary negative reactions. If the child was not at a severe disadvantage before, he can count on being damned now. Yet the promise of psychological acceleration of intellectual abilities attracts and beckons us.

In this classic story, Daniel Keyes tells us the story of Charlie and Algernon, a mental retardate and a mouse whose capacities to learn and remember are drastically altered through psychosurgery (the use of neurosurgical procedures to treat behavioral disorders). Psychology and related disciplines now have developed ways of surgically producing increases in anger, thirst, sexual endurance, and various types of emotionality. Given the background of psychosurgery, it is a technique which should be marked "handle with care." For example, during the 1950s, about 50,000 psychotic patients received prefrontal lobotomies, a technique which involves cutting the nerve fibers that connect the frontal lobes of the brain with the thalamus. Whereas the beneficial effects of this drastic treatment were quite variable, the patients often wound up hollow shells of their former selves, with blunted emotions and impaired reasoning.

More recently, psychosurgery has been focused on the limbic system, the area of the brain heavily involved in emotional and motivational behavior. While psychosurgery seems more appropriate for emotional than intellectual problems, perhaps other techniques, or a combination of psychosurgery and other techniques, might increase intelligence.

As you read the story of Charlie, there are some things you should note. First of all, two projective tests of personality, the Rorschach test and the Thematic Apperception Test, are given to Charlie Gordon. Is this an appropriate use of this sort of test? One standard measure of learning ability in mice and men has been the maze. It is used separately in this story; however, mazes are found on some of our best-known and most valid intelligence tests. Finally, "sleep learning" is portrayed in this story. It sounds good, but research has indicated that it is not too efficient.

progris riport 1—martch 5, 1965

Dr. Strauss says I shud rite down what I think and evrey thing that happins to me from now on. I dont know why but he says its importint so they will see if they will use me. I hope they use me. Miss Kinnian says maybe they can make me smart. I want to be smart. My name is Charlie Gordon. I am 37 years old. I have nuthing more to rite now so I will close for today.

progris riport 2—martch 6

I had a test today. I think I faled it. And I think maybe now they wont use me. What happind is a nice young man was in the room and he had some white cards and ink spilled all over them. He sed Charlie what do yo see on this card. I was very skared even tho I had my rabits foot in my pockit because when I was a kid I always faled tests in school and I spillled ink to.

I told him I saw a inkblot. He said yes and it made me feel good. I thot that was all but when I got up to go he said Charlie we are not thru yet. Then I dont remember so good but he wantid me to say what was in the ink. I dint see nuthing in the ink but he said there was picturs there other pepul saw some picturs. I couldnt see any picturs. I reely tryed. I held the card close up and then far away. Then I said if I had my glasses I coud see better I usally only ware my glases in the movies or TV but I said they are in the closit in the hall. I got them. Then I said let me see that card agen I bet Ill find it now.

I tryed hard but I only saw the ink. I told him maybe I need new glases. He rote something down on a paper and I got skared of faling the test. I told him it was a very nice inkblot with littel points all around the edges. He looked very sad so that wasnt it. I said please let me try agen. Ill get in a few minits becaus Im not so fast somtimes. Im a slow reeder too in Miss Kinnians class for slow adults but I'm trying very hard.

He gave me a chance with another card that had 2 kinds of ink spilled on it red and blue.

He was very nice and talked slow like Miss Kinnian does and he explaned it to me that it was a *raw shok*. He said pepul see things in the ink. I said show me where. He said think. I told him I think a inkblot but that wasn't rite eather. He said what does it remind you—pretend something. I closed my eyes for a long time to pretend. I told him I pretend a fowntan pen with ink leeking all over a table cloth.

I dont think I passed the *raw shok* test.

Dr Strauss and Dr Nemur say it dont matter about the inkblots. They said that maybe they will still use me. I said Miss Kinnian never gave me tests like that one only spelling and reading. They said Miss Kinnian told that I was her bestist pupil in the adult nite school becaus I tryed the hardist and I reely wantid to lern. They said how come you went to adult nite scool all by yourself Charlie. How did you find it. I said I asked pepul and sumbody told me where I shud go to lern to read and spell good. They said why did you want to. I told them becaus all my life I wantid to be smart and not dumb. But its very hard to be smart. They said you know it will probly be tempirery. I said yes. Miss Kinnian told me. I dont care if it herts.

Later I had more crazy tests today. The nice lady who gave it to me told me the name and I askcd her how do you spellit so I can rite it my progris riport. THEMATIC APPERCEPTION TEST. I dont know the frist 2 words but I know what *test* means. You got to pass it or you get bad marks. This test lookd easy becaus I coud see the picturs. Only this time she dint want me to tell her the picturs. That mixed me up. She said make up storys about the pepul in the picturs.

I told her how can you tell storys about pepul you never met. I said why shud I make up lies. I never tell lies any more becaus I always get caut.

She told me this test and the other one thc raw-shok was for getting personality. I laffed so hard. I said how can you get that thing from inkblots and fotos. She got sore and put her picturs away. I don't carc. It was sily. I gess I faled that test too.

Later some men in white coats took me to a difernt part of the hospitil and gave me a game to play. It was like a race with a white mouse. They called the mouse Algernon. Algernon was in a box with a lot of twists and turns like all kinds of walls and they gave me a pencil and a paper with lines and lots of boxes. On one side it said START and on the other end it said FINISH. They said it was *amazed* and that Algernon and me had the same *amazed* to do. I dint see how we could have the same *amazed* if Algernon had a box and I had a paper but I dint say nothing. Anyway there wasnt time because the race started.

One of the men had a watch he was trying to hide so I wouldnt see it so I tryed not to look and that made me nervus.

Anyway that test made me feel worser than all the others because they did it over 10 times with different *amazeds* and Algernon won every time. I dint know that mice were so smart. Maybe thats because Algernon is a white mouse. Maybe white mice are smarter than other mice.

progris riport 4—Mar 8

Their going to use me! Im so excited I can hardly write. Dr Nemur and Dr Strauss had a argament about it first. Dr Nemur was in the office when Dr Strauss brot me in. Dr Nemur was worryed about using me but Dr Strauss told him Miss Kinnian rekemmended me the best from all the people who she was teaching. I like Miss Kinnian becaus shes a very smart teacher. And she said Charlie your going to have a second chance. If you volenteer for this experament you mite get smart. They dont know if it will be perminint but theirs a chance. Thats why I said ok even when I was scared because she said it was an operashun. She said dont be scared Charlie you done so much with so little I think you deserv it most of all.

So I got scaird when Dr. Nemur and Dr. Strauss argud about it. Dr. Strauss said I had something that was very good. He said I had a good *motorvation*. I never even knew I had that. I felt proud when he said that not every body with an eye-q of 68 had that thing. I dant know what it is or where I got it but he said Algernon had it too. Algernons *motorvation* is the cheese they put in his box. But it cant be that because I didn't eat any cheese this week.

Then he told Dr Nemur something I dint understand so while they were talking I wrote down some of the words.

He said Dr. Nemur I know Charlie is not what you had in mind as the first of your new brede of intelek** (coudnt get the word) superman. But most people of his low ment ** are host** and uncoop** they are usually dull apath** and hard to reach. He has a good natcher hes intristed and eager to please.

Dr Nemur said remember he will be the first human beeng ever to have his intelijence tripled by surgicle meens.

Dr. Strauss said exakly. Look at how well hes lerned to read and write for his low mental age its as grate an acheve** as you and I lerning einstines therey of **vity without help. That shows the inteness motorvation. Its comparat** a tremen** achev** I say we use Charlie.

I dint get all the words but it sounded like Dr Strauss was on my side and like the other one wasnt.

Then Dr Nemur nodded he said all right maybe your right. We will use Charlie. When he said that I got so exited I jumped up and shook his hand for being so good to me. I told him thank you doc you wont be sorry for giving me a second chance. And I mean it like I told him. After the operashun Im gonna try to be smart. Im gonna try awful hard.

progris riport 5—Mar 10

Im skared. Lost of the nurses and the people who gave me the tests came to bring me candy and wish me luck. I hope I have luck. I got my rabits foot and my lucky penny. Only a black cat crossed me when I was comming to the hospitil. Dr Strauss says dont be supersitis Charlie this is science. Anyway Im keeping my rabits foot with me.

I asked Dr Strauss if Ill beat Algernon in the race after the operashun and he said maybe. If the operashun works Ill show that mouse I can be as smart as he is. Maybe smarter. Then Ill be abel to read better and spell the words good and know lots of things and be like other people. I want to be smart like other people. If it works perminint they will make everybody smart all over the wurld.

They dint give me anything to eat this morning. I dont know what that eating has to do with getting smart. Im very hungry and Dr. Nemur took away my box of candy. That Dr Nemur is a grouch. Dr Strauss says I can have it back after the operashun. You cant eat befor a operashun . . .

progress report 6—Mar 15

The operashun dint hurt. He did it while I was sleeping. They took off the bandijis from my head today so I can make a PROGRESS REPORT. Dr. Nemur who looked at some of my other ones says I spell PROGRESS wrong and told me how to spell it and REPORT too. I got to try and remember that.

I have a very bad memary for spelling. Dr Strauss says its ok to tell about all the things that happin to me but he says I should tell more about what I feel and what I think. When I told him I dont know how to think he said try. All the time when the bandijis were on my eyes I tryed to think. Nothing happened. I dont know what to think about. Maybe if I ask him he will tell me how I can think now that Im suppose to get smart. What do smart people think about. Fancy things I suppose. I wish I knew some fancy things alredy.

progress report 7—mar 19

Nothing is happining. I had lots of tests and different kinds of races with Algernon. I hate that mouse. He always beats me. Dr. Strauss said I got to play those games. And he said some time I got to take those tests over again. Those inkblots are stupid. And those pictures are stupid too. I like to draw a picture of a man and a woman but I wont make up lies about people.

I got a headache from trying to think so much. I thot Dr Strauss was my frend but he dont help me. He dont tell me what to think or when Ill get smart.

Miss Kinnian dint come to see me. I think writing these progress reports are stupid too.

progress report 8—Mar 23

Im going back to work at the factory. They said it was better I shud go back to work but I cant tell anyone what the operashun was for and I have to come to the hospitil for an hour evry night after work. They are gonna pay me mony every month for learning to be smart.

Im glad Im going back to work because I miss my job and all my frends and all the fun we have there.

Dr Strauss says I shud keep writing things down but I dont have to do it every day just when I think of something or something speshul happins. He says dont get discoridged because it takes time and it happins slow. He says it took a long time with Algernon before he got 3 times smarter than he was before. Thats why Algernon beats me all the time because he had that operashun too. That makes me feel better. I could probly do that *amazed* faster than a reglar mouse. Maybe some day Ill beat him. That would be something. So far Algernon looks smart perminent.

Mar 25 (I dont have to write PROGRESS REPORT on top any more just when I hand it in once a week for Dr Nemur. I just have to put the date on. That saves time)

We had a lot of fun at the factery today. Joe Carp said hey look where Charlie had his operashun what did they do Charlie put some brains in. I was going to tell him but I remembered Dr Strauss said no. Then Frank Reilly said what did you do Charlie forget your key and open your door the hard way. That made me laff. Their really my friends and they like me.

Sometimes somebody will say hey look at Joe or Frank or George he really pulled a Charlie Gordon. I dont know why they say that but they always laff. This morning Amos Borg who is the 4 man at Donnegans used my name when he shouted at Ernie the office boy. Ernie lost a packige. He said Ernie for godsake what are you trying to be a Charlie Gordon. I dont understand why he said that.

Mar 28 Dr Strauss came to my room tonight to see why I dint come in like I was suppose to. I told him I dont like to race with Algernon any more. He said I dont have to for a while but I shud come in. He had a present for me. I thot it was a little television but it wasnt. He said I got to turn it on when I go to sleep. I said your kidding why shud I turn it on when Im going to sleep. Who ever herd of a thing like that. But he said if I want to get smart I got to do what he says. I told him I dint think I was going to get smart and he puts his hand on my sholder and said Charlie you dont know it yet but your getting smarter all the time. You wont notice for a while. I think he was just being nice to make me feel good because I dont look any smarter.

Oh yes I almost forgot. I asked him when I can go back to the class at Miss Kinnians school. He said I wont go their. He said that soon Miss Kinnian will come to the hospitil to start and teach me speshul.

Mar 29 That crazy TV kept up all night. How can I sleep with something yelling crazy things all night in my ears. And the nutty pictures. Wow. I don't know what it says when Im up so how am I going to know when Im sleeping.

Dr Strauss says its ok. He says my brains are lerning when I sleep and that will help me when Miss Kinnian starts my lessons in the hospitil (only I found out it isn't a hospitil its a labatory.) I think its all crazy. If you can get smart when your sleeping why do people go to school. That thing I don't think will work. I use to watch the late show and the late late show on TV all the time and it never made me smart. Maybe you have to sleep while you watch it.

progress report 9—April 3

Dr Strauss showed me how to keep the TV turned low so now I can sleep. I don't hear a thing. And I still dont understand what it says. A few times I play it over in the morning to find out what I lerned when I was sleeping and I don't think so. Miss Kinnian says Maybe its another langwidge. But most times it sounds american. It talks faster than even Miss Gold who was my teacher in 6 grade.

I told Dr. Strauss what good is it to get smart in my sleep. I want to be smart when Im awake. He says its the same thing and I have two minds. Theres the *subconscious* and the *conscious* (thats how you spell it). And one dont tell the other one what its doing. They dont even talk to each other. Thats why I dream. And boy have I been having crazy dreams. Wow. Ever since that night TV. The late late late show.

I forgot to ask him if it was only me or if everybody had those two minds.

(I just looked up the word in the dictionary Dr Strauss gave me. The word is *subconscious. adj. Of the nature of mental operations yet not present in consciousness; as, subconscious conflict of desires.)* There's more but I still dont know what it means. This isnt a very good dictionary for dumb people like me.

Anyway the headache is from the party. My friends from the factery Joe Carp and Frank Reilly invited me to go to Muggsys Saloon for some drinks. I don't like to drink but they said we will have lots of fun. I had a good time.

Joe Carp said I should show the girls how I mop out the toilet in the factory and he got me a mop. I showed them and everyone laffed when I told that Mr. Donnegan said I was the best janiter he ever had because I like my job and do it good and never miss a day except for my operashun.

I said Miss Kinnian always said Charlie be proud of your job because you do it good.

Everybody laffed and we had a good time and they gave me lots of drinks and Joe said Charlie is a card when hes potted. I dont know what that means but everybody likes me and we have fun. I cant wait to be smart like my best friends Joe Carp and Frank Reilly.

I dont remember how the party was over but I think I went out to buy a newspaper and coffe for Joe and Frank and when I came back there was no one their. I looked for them all over till late. Then I dont remember so good but I think I got sleepy or sick. A nice cop brot me back home Thats what my landlady Mrs Flynn says.

But I got a headache and a big lump on my head. I think maybe I fell but Joe Carp says it was the cop they beat up drunks some times. I don't think so. Miss Kinnian says cops are to help people. Anyway I got a bad headache and Im sick and hurt all over. I dont think Ill drink anymore.

April 6 I beat Algernon! I dint even know I beat him until Burt the tester told me. Then the second time I lost because I got so exited I fell off the chair before I finished. But after that I beat him 8 more times. I must be getting smart to beat a smart mouse like Algernon. But I dont *feel* smarter.

I wanted to race Algernon some more but Burt said thats enough for one day. They let me hold him for a minit. Hes not so bad. Hes soft like a ball of cotton. He blinks and when he opens his eyes their black and pink on the eges.

I said can I feed him because I felt bad to beat him and I wanted to be nice and make friends. Burt said no Algernon is a very specshul mouse with an operashun like mine, and he was the first of all the animals to stay smart so long. He told me Algernon is so smart that every day he has to solve a test to get his food. Its a thing like a lock on a door that changes every time Algernon goes in to eat so he has to lern something new to get his food. That made me sad because if he couldnt lern he would be hungry.

I don't think its right to make you pass a test to eat. How would Dr Nemur like it to have to pass a test every time he wants to eat. I think Ill be friends with Algernon.

April 9 Tonight after work Miss Kinnian was at the laboratory. She looked like she was glad to see me but scared. I told her dont worry Miss Kinnian I not smart yet and she laffed. She said I have confidence in you Charlie the way you struggled so hard to read and right better than all the others. At werst you will have it for a littel wile and your doing somthing for science.

We are reading a very hard book. Its called *Robinson Crusoe* about a man who gets merooned on a dessert Iland. Hes smart and figers out all kinds of things so he can have a house and food and hes a good swimmer. Only I feel sorry because hes all alone and has no frends. But I think their must be somebody else on the iland because theres a picture with his funny umbrella looking at footprints. I hope he gets a frend and not be lonly.

April 10 Miss Kinnian teaches me to spell better. She says look at a word and close your eyes and say it over and over until you remember. I have lots of truble with *through* that you say *threw* and *enough* and *tough* that you dont say *enew* and *tew.* You got to say *enuff* and *tuff.* Thats how I use to write it before I started to get smart. Im confused but Miss Kinnian says theres no reason in spelling.

Apr 14 Finished *Robinson Crusoe.* I want to find out more about what happens to him but Miss Kinnian says thats all there is. *Why.*

Apr 15 Miss Kinnian says Im lerning fast. She read some of the Progress Reports and she looked at me kind of funny. She says Im a fine person and Ill show them all. I asked her why. She said never mind but I shouldnt feel bad if I find out everybody isnt nice like I think. She said for a person who god gave so little to you done more then a lot of people with brains they never even used. I said all my friends are smart people but there good. They like me and they never did anything that wasnt nice. Then she got something in her eye and she had to run out to the ladys room.

Apr 16 Today, I lerned, the *comma,* this is a comma (,) a period, with a tall, Miss Kinnian, says its important, because, it makes writing, better, she said, somebody, could lose, a lot of money, if a comma, isnt, in the, right place, I dont have, any money, and I dont see, how a comma, keeps you, from losing it,

Apr 17 I used the comma wrong. Its punctuation. Miss Kinnian told me to look up long words in the dictionary to lern to spell them. I said whats the difference if you can read it anyway. She said its part of your education so now on Ill look up all the words Im not sure how to spell. It takes a long time to write that way but I only have to look up once and after that I get it right.

You got to mix them up, she showed? me" how. to mix! them (and now; I can! mix up all kinds" of punctuation, in! my writing? There, are lots! of rules? to lern; but Im gettin'g them in my head.

One thing I like about, Dear Miss Kinnian: (thats the way it goes in a business letter if I ever go into business) is she, always gives me' a reason" when —I ask. She's a gen'ius! I wish I cou'd be smart" like her;

(Punctuation, is; fun!)

April 18 What a dope I am! I didn't even understand what she was talking about. I read the grammar book last night and it explanes the whole thing. Then I saw it was the same way as Miss Kinnian was trying to tell me, but I didn't get it.

Miss Kinnian said that the TV working in my sleep helped out. She and I reached a plateau. Thats a flat hill.

After I figured out how puncuation worked, I read over all my old Progress Reports from the beginning. Boy, did I have crazy spelling and punctuation! I told Miss Kinnian I ought to go over the pages and fix all the mistakes but she said, "No, Charlie, Dr. Nemur wants them just as they are. That's why he let you keep them after they were photostated, to see your own progress. You're coming along fast, Charlie."

That made me feel good. After the lesson I went down and played with Algernon. We don't race any more.

April 20 I feel sick inside. Not sick like for a doctor, but inside my chest it feels empty like getting punched and a heartburn at the same time. I wasn't going to write about it, but I guess I got to, because its important. Today was the first time I ever stayed home from work.

Last night Joe Carp and Frank Reilly invited me to a party. There were lots of girls and some men from the factory. I remembered how sick I got last time I drank too much, so I told Joe I didn't want anything to drink. He gave me a plain coke instead.

We had a lot of fun for a while. Joe said I should dance with Ellen and she would teach me the steps. I fell a few times and I couldn't understand why because no one else was dancing besides Ellen and me. And all the time I was tripping because somebody's foot was always sticking out.

Then when I got up I saw the look on Joe's face and it gave me a funny feeling in my stomack. "He's a scream," one of the girls said. Everybody was laughing.

"Look at him. He's blushing. Charlie is blushing."

"Hey, Ellen, what'd you do to Charlie? I never saw him act like that before."

I didn't know what to do or where to turn. Everyone was looking at me and laughing and I felt naked. I wanted to hide. I ran outside and I threw up. Then I walked home. It's a funny thing I never knew that Joe and Frank and the others liked to have me around all the time to make fun of me.

Now I know what it means when they say "to pull a Charlie Gordon." I'm ashamed.

progress report 11

April 21 Still didn't go into the factory. I told Mrs. Flynn my landlady to call and tell Mr. Donnegan I was sick. Mrs. Flynn looks at me very funny lately like she's scared.

I think it's a good thing about finding out how everybody laughs at me. I thought about it a lot. It's because I'm so dumb and I don't even know when

I'm doing something dumb. People think it's funny when a dumb person can't do things the same way they can.

Anyway, now I know I'm getting smarter every day. I know punctuation and I can spell good. I like to look up all the hard words in the dictionary and I remember them. I'm reading a lot now, and Miss Kinnian says I read very fast. Sometimes I even understand what I'm reading about, and it stays in my mind. There are times when I can close my eyes and think of a page and it all comes back like a picture.

Besides history, geography and arithmetic, Miss Kinnian said I should start to learn foreign languages. Dr. Strauss gave me some more tapes to play while I sleep. I still don't understand how that conscious and unconscious mind works, but Dr. Strauss says not to worry yet. He asked me to promise that when I start learning college subjects next week I wouldn't read any books on psychology—that is, until he gives me permission.

I feel a lot better today, but I guess I'm still a little angry that all the time people were laughing and making fun of me because I wasn't so smart. When I become intelligent like Dr. Strauss says, with three times my IQ of 68, then maybe I'll be like everyone else and people will like me.

I'm not sure what an I.Q. is. Dr. Nemur said it was something that measured how intelligent you were—like a scale in the drugstore weighs pounds. But Dr. Strauss had a big argument with him and said an I.Q. didn't weigh intelligence at all. He said an I.Q. showed how much intelligence you could get, like the numbers on the outside of a measuring cup. You still had to fill the cup up with stuff.

Then when I asked Burt, who gives me my intelligence test and works with Algernon, he said that both of them were wrong (only I had to promise not to tell them he said so). Burt says that the I.Q. measures a lot of different things including some of the things you learned already, and it really isn't any good at all.

So I still don't know what I.Q. is except that mine is going to be over 200 soon. I didn't want to say anything, but I don't see how if they don't know *what* it is, or *where* it is—I don't see how they know *how much* of it you've got.

Dr. Nemur says I have to take a *Rorshach Test* tomorrow. I wonder what *that* is.

April 22 I found out what a Rorshach is. It's the test I took before the operation—the one with the inkblots on the pieces of cardboard.

I was scared to death of those inkblots. I knew the man was going to ask me to find the pictures and I knew I couldn't. I was thinking to myself, if only there was some way of knowing what kind of pictures were hidden there. Maybe there weren't any pictures at all. Maybe it was just a trick to see if I was dumb enough to look for something that wasn't there. Just thinking about that made me sore at him.

"All right, Charlie," he said, "you've seen these cards before, remember?"

"Of course I remember."

The way I said it, he knew I was angry, and he looked surprised. "Yes, of course. Now I want you to look at this. What might this be? What do you see on this card? People see all sorts of things in these inkblots. Tell me what it might be for you—what it makes you think of."

I was shocked. That wasn't what I had expected him to say. "You mean there are no pictures hidden in those inkblots?"

He frowned and took off his glasses. "What?"

"Pictures. Hidden in the inkblots. Last time you told me everyone could see them and you wanted me to find them too."

He explained to me that the last time he had used almost the exact same words he was using now. I didn't believe it, and I still have the suspicion that he misled me at the time just for the fun of it. Unless—I don't know any more —could I have been *that* feeble-minded?

We went through the cards slowly. One looked like a pair of bats tugging at something. Another one looked like two men fencing with swords. I imagined all sorts of things. I guess I got carried away. But I didn't trust him any more, and I kept turning them around, even looking on the back to see if there was anything there I was supposed to catch. While he was making his notes, I peeked out of the corner of my eye to read it. But it was all in code that looked like this:

$$WF + A \qquad DdF - Ad \text{ orig.} \qquad WF - A$$
$$SF + obj$$

The test still doesn't make sense to me. It seems to me that anyone could make up lies about things that they didn't really imagine? Maybe I'll understand it when Dr. Strauss lets me read up on psychology.

April 25 I figured out a new way to line up the machines in the factory, and Mr. Donnegan says it will save him ten thousand dollars a year in labor and increased production. He gave me a $25 bonus.

I wanted to take Joe Carp and Frank Reilly out to lunch to celebrate, but Joe said he had to buy some things for his wife, and Frank said he was meeting his cousin for lunch. I guess it'll take a little time for them to get used to the changes in me. Everybody seems to be frightened of me. When I went over to Amos Borg and tapped him, he jumped up in the air.

People don't talk to me much any more or kid around the way they used to. It makes the job kind of lonely.

April 27 I got up the nerve today to ask Miss Kinnian to have dinner with me tomorrow night to celebrate my bonus.

At first she wasn't sure it was right, but I asked Dr. Strauss and he said it was okay. Dr. Strauss and Dr. Nemur don't seem to be getting along so well.

They're arguing all the time. This evening I heard them shouting. Dr. Nemur was saying that it was *his* experiment and *his* research, and Dr. Strauss shouted back that he contributed just as much, because he found me through Miss Kinnian and he performed the operation. Dr. Strauss said that some-day thousands of neuro-surgeons might be using his technique all over the world.

Dr. Nemur wanted to publish the results of the experiment at the end of this month. Dr. Strauss wanted to wait a while to be sure. Dr. Strauss said Dr. Nemur was more interested in the Chair of Psychology at Princeton than he was in the experiment. Dr. Nemur said Dr. Strauss was nothing but an oppor-tunist trying to ride to glory on *his* coattails.

When I left afterwards, I found myself trembling. I don't know why for sure, but it was as if I'd seen both men clearly for the first time. I remember hearing Burt say Dr. Nemur had a shrew of a wife who was pushing him all the time to get things published so he could become famous. Burt said that the dream of her life was to have a big shot husband.

April 28 I don't understand why I never noticed how beautiful Miss Kinnian really is. She has brown eyes and feathery brown hair that comes to the top of her neck. She's only thirty-four! I think from the beginning I had the feeling that she was an unreachable genius—and very, very old. Now, every time I see her she grows younger and more lovely.

We had dinner and a long talk. When she said I was coming along so fast I'd be leaving her behind, I laughed.

"It's true, Charlie. You're already a better reader than I am. You can read a whole page at a glance while I can take in only a few lines at a time. And you remember every single thing you read. I'm lucky if I can recall the main thoughts and the general meaning."

"I don't feel intelligent. There are so many things I don't understand."

She took out a cigarette and I lit it for her. "You've got to be a *little* patient You're accomplishing in days and weeks what it takes normal people to do in a lifetime. That's what makes it so amazing You're like a giant sponge now, soaking things in. Facts, figures, general knowledge. And soon you'll begin to connect them, too. You'll see how different branches of learning are related. There are many levels, Charlie, like steps on a giant ladder that take you up higher and higher to see more and more of the world around you.

"I can see only a little bit of that, Charlie, and I won't go much higher than I am now, but you'll keep climbing up and up, and see more and more, and each step will open new worlds that you never even knew existed." She frowned. "I hope . . . I just hope to God—"

"What?"

"Never mind, Charles. I just hope I wasn't wrong to advise you to go into this in the first place."

I laughed. "How could that be? It worked, didn't it? Even Algernon is still smart."

We sat there silently for a while and I knew what she was thinking about as she watched me toying with the chain of my rabbit's foot and my keys. I didn't want to think of that possibility any more than elderly people want to think of death. I *knew* that this was only the beginning. I knew what she meant about levels because I'd seen some of them already. The thought of leaving her behind made me sad.

I'm in love with Miss Kinnian.

progress report 12

April 30 I've quit my job with Donnegan's Plastic Box Company. Mr. Donnegan insisted it would be better for all concerned if I left. What did I do to make them hate me so?

The first I knew of it was when Mr. Donnegan showed me the petition. Eight hundred names, everyone in the factory, except Fanny Girden. Scanning the list quickly, I saw at once that hers was the only missing name. All the rest demanded that I be fired.

Joe Carp and Frank Reilly wouldn't talk to me about it. No one else would either, except Fanny. She was one of the few people I'd known who set her mind to something and believed it no matter what the rest of the world proved, said or did—and Fanny did not believe that I should have been fired. She had been against the petition on principle and despite the pressure and threats she'd held out.

"Which don't mean to say," she remarked, "that I don't think there's something mighty strange about you, Charlie. Them changes. I don't know. You used to be a good, dependable, ordinary man—not too bright maybe, but honest. Who knows what you done to yourself to get so smart all of a sudden. Like everybody around here's been saying, Charlie, it's not right."

"But how can you say that, Fanny? What's wrong with a man becoming intelligent and wanting to acquire knowledge and understanding of the world around him?"

She stared down at her work and I turned to leave. Without looking at me, she said: "It was evil when Eve listened to the snake and ate from the tree of knowledge. It was evil when she saw that she was naked. If not for that none of us would ever have to grow old and sick, and die."

Once again, now, I have the feeling of shame burning inside me. This intelligence has driven a wedge between me and all the people I once knew and loved. Before, they laughed at me and despised me for my ignorance and dullness; now, they hate me for my knowledge and understanding. What in God's name do they want of me?

They've driven me out of the factory. Now I'm more alone than ever before. . . .

May 15 Dr. Strauss is very angry at me for not having written any progress reports in two weeks. He's justified because the lab is now paying me a regular salary. I told him I was too busy thinking and reading. When I pointed out that writing was such a slow process that it made me impatient with my poor handwriting, he suggested I learn to type. It's much easier to write now because I can type seventy-five words a minute. Dr. Strauss continually reminds me of the need to speak and write simply so people will be able to understand me.

I'll try to review all the things that happened to me during the last two weeks. Algernon and I were presented to the *American Psychological Association* sitting in convention with the *World Psychological Association.* We created quite a sensation. Dr. Nemur and Dr. Strauss were proud of us.

I suspect that Dr. Nemur, who is sixty—ten years older than Dr. Strauss —finds it necessary to see tangible results of his work. Undoubtedly the result of pressure by Mrs. Nemur.

Contrary to my earlier impressions of him, I realize that Dr. Nemur is not at all a genius. He has a very good mind, but it struggles under the spectre of self-doubt. He wants people to take him for a genius. Therefore it is important for him to feel that his work is accepted by the world. I believe that Dr. Nemur was afraid of further delay because he worried that someone else might make a discovery along these lines and take the credit from him.

Dr. Strauss on the other hand might be called a genius, although I feel his areas of knowledge are too limited. He was educated in the tradition of narrow specialization; the broader aspects of background were neglected far more than necessary—even for a neuro-surgeon.

I was shocked to learn the only ancient languages he could read were Latin, Greek and Hebrew, and that he knows almost nothing of mathematics beyond the elementary levels of the calculus of variations. When he admitted this to me, I found myself almost annoyed. It was as if he'd hidden this part of himself in order to deceive me, pretending—as do many people I've discovered—to be what he is not. No one I've ever known is what he appears to be on the surface.

Dr. Nemur appears to be uncomfortable around me. Sometimes when I try to talk to him, he just looks at me strangely and turns away. I was angry at first when Dr. Strauss told me I was giving Dr. Nemur an inferiority complex. I thought he was mocking me and I'm oversensitive at being made fun of.

How was I to know that a highly respected psychoexperimentalist like Nemur was unacquainted with Hindustani and Chinese? It's absurd when you consider the work that is being done in India and China today in the very field of his study.

I asked Dr. Strauss how Nemur could refute Rahajamati's attack on his method if Nemur couldn't even read them in the first place. That strange look on Strauss' face can mean only one of two things. Either he doesn't want to tell Nemur what they're saying in India, or else—and this worries me—Dr. Strauss doesn't know either. I must be careful to speak and write clearly and simply so people won't laugh.

May 18 I am very disturbed. I saw Miss Kinnian last night for the first time in over a week. I tried to avoid all discussions of intellectual concepts and to keep the conversation on a simple, everyday level, but she just stared at me blankly and asked me what I meant about the mathematical variance equivalent in Dorbermann's *Fifth Concerto.*

When I tried to explain she stopped me and laughed. I guess I got angry, but I suspect I'm approaching her on the wrong level. No matter what I try to discuss with her, I am unable to communicate. I must review Vrostadt's equations on *Levels of Semantic Progression.* I find I don't communicate with people much any more. Thank God for books and music and things I can think about. I am alone at Mrs. Flynn's boarding house most of the time and seldom speak to anyone.

*May*20 I would not have noticed the new dishwasher, a boy of about sixteen, at the corner diner where I take my evening meals if not for the incident of the broken dishes.

They crashed to the floor, sending bits of white china under the tables. The boy stood there, dazed and frightened, holding the empty tray in his hand. The catcalls from the customers (the cries of "hey, there go the profits!" . . . *"Mazeltov!"* . . . and "well, *he* didn't work here very long . . ." which invariably seem to follow the breaking of glass or dishware in a public restaurant) all seemed to confuse him.

When the owner came to see what the excitement was about, the boy cowered as if he expected to be struck. "All right! All right, you dope," shouted the owner, "don't just stand there! Get the broom and sweep that mess up. A broom . . . a broom, you idiot! It's in the kitchen!"

The boy saw he was not going to be punished. His frightened expression disappeared and he smiled as he came back with the broom to sweep the floor. A few of the rowdier customers kept up the remarks, amusing themselves at his expense.

"Here, sonny, over here there's a nice piece behind you . . ."

"He's not so dumb. It's easier to break 'em than wash 'em!"

As his vacant eyes moved across the crowd of onlookers, he slowly mirrored their smiles and finally broke into an uncertain grin at the joke he obviously did not understand.

I felt sick inside as I looked at his dull, vacuous smile, the wide, bright eyes of a child, uncertain but eager to please. They were laughing at him because he was mentally retarded.

And I had been laughing at him too.

Suddenly I was furious at myself and all those who were smirking at him. I jumped up and shouted, "Shut up! Leave him alone! It's not his fault he can't understand! He can't help what he is! But he's still a human being!"

The room grew silent. I cursed myself for losing control. I tried not to look at the boy as I walked out without touching my food. I felt ashamed for both of us.

How strange that people of honest feelings and sensibility, who would not take advantage of a man born without arms or eyes—how such people think nothing of abusing a man born with low intelligence. It infuriated me to think that not too long ago I had foolishly played the clown.

And I had almost forgotten.

I'd hidden the picture of the old Charlie Gordon from myself because now that I was intelligent it was something that had to be pushed out of my mind. But today in looking at that boy, for the first time I saw what I had been. *I was just like him!*

Only a short time ago, I learned that people laughed at me. Now I can see that unknowingly I joined with them in laughing at myself. That hurts most of all.

I have often reread my progress reports and seen the illiteracy, the childish naïveté, the mind of low intelligence peering from a dark room, through the keyhole at the dazzling light outside. I see that even in my dullness I knew I was inferior, and that other people had something I lacked—something denied me. In my mental blindness, I thought it was somehow connected with the ability to read and write, and I was sure that if I could get those skills I would automatically have intelligence too.

Even a feeble-minded man wants to be like other men.

A child may not know how to feed itself, or what to eat, yet it knows of hunger.

This then is what I was like. I never knew. Even with my gift of intellectual awareness, I never really knew.

This day was good for me. Seeing the past more clearly, I've decided to use my knowledge and skills to work in the field of increasing human intelligence levels. Who is better equipped for this work? Who else has lived in both worlds? These are my people. Let me use my gift to do something for them.

Tomorrow, I will discuss with Dr. Strauss how I can work in this area. I may be able to help him work out the problems of widespread use of the technique which was used on me. I have several good ideas of my own.

There is so much that might be done with this technique. If I could be made into a genius, what about thousands of others like myself? What fantastic levels might be achieved by using this technique on normal people? On *geniuses?*

There are so many doors to open. I am impatient to begin.

progress report 13

May 23 It happened today. Algernon bit me. I visited the lab to see him as I do occasionally, and when I took him out of his cage, he snapped at my hand. I put him back and watched him for a while. He was unusually disturbed and vicious.

May 24 Burt, who is in charge of the experimental animals, tells me that Algernon is changing. He is less cooperative; he refuses to run the maze any more; general motivation has decreased. And he hasn't been eating. Everyone is upset about what this may mean.

May 25 They've been feeding Algernon, who now refuses to work the shifting-lock problem. Everyone identifies me with Algernon. In a way we're both the first of our kind. They're all pretending that Algernon's behavior is not necessarily significant for me. But it's hard to hide the fact that some of the other animals who were used in this experiment are showing strange behavior.

Dr. Strauss and Dr. Nemur have asked me not to come to the lab any more. I know what they're thinking but I can't accept it. I am going ahead with my plans to carry their research forward. With all due respect to both these fine scientists, I am well aware of their limitations. If there is an answer, I'll have to find it out for myself. Suddenly, time has become very important to me.

May 29 I have been given a lab of my own and permission to go ahead with the research. I'm onto something. Working day and night. I've had a cot moved into the lab. Most of my writing time is spent on the notes which I keep in a separate folder, but from time to time I feel it necessary to put down my moods and thoughts from sheer habit.

I find the *calculus of intelligence* to be a fascinating study. Here is the place for the application of all the knowledge I have acquired.

May 31 Dr. Strauss thinks I'm working too hard. Dr. Nemur says I'm trying to cram a lifetime of research and thought into a few weeks. I know I should rest, but I'm driven on by something inside that won't let me stop. I've got to find the reason for the sharp regression in Algernon. I've got to know *if* and *when* it will happen to me.

June 4

LETTER TO DR. STRAUSS (*copy*)

Dear Dr. Strauss:

Under separate cover I am sending you a copy of my report entitled, "The Algernon-Gordon Effect: A Study of Structure and Function of Increased Intelligence," which I would like to have published.

As you see, my experiments are completed. I have included in my report all of my formulae, as well as mathematical analysis in the appendix. Of course, these should be verified.

Because of its importance to both you and Dr. Nemur (and need I say to myself, too?) I have checked and rechecked my results a dozen times in the hope of finding an error. I am sorry to say the results must stand. Yet for the sake of science, I am grateful for the little bit that

I here add to the knowledge of the function of the human mind and of the laws governing the artificial increase of human intelligence.

I recall your once saying to me that an experimental *failure* or the *disproving* of a theory was as important to the advancement of learning as a success would be. I know now that this is true. I am sorry, however, that my own contribution to the field must rest upon the ashes of the work of two men I regard so highly.

Yours truly,
Charles Gordon

June 5 I must not become emotional. The facts and the results of my experiments are clear, and the more sensational aspects of my own rapid climb cannot obscure the fact that the tripling of intelligence by the surgical technique developed by Drs. Strauss and Nemur must be viewed as having little or no practical applicability (at the present time) to the increase of human intelligence.

As I review the records and data on Algernon, I see that although he is still in his physical infancy, he has regressed mentally. Motor activity is impaired; there is a general reduction of glandular activity; there is an accelerated loss of coordination.

There are also strong indications of progressive amnesia.

As will be seen by my report, these and other physical and mental deterioration syndromes can be predicted with significant results by the application of my formula.

The surgical stimulus to which we were both subjected has resulted in an intensification and acceleration of all mental processes. The unforeseen development, which I have taken the liberty of calling the *Algernon-Gordon Effect*, is the logical extension of the entire intelligence speed-up. The hypothesis here proven may be described simply in the following terms: Artificially increased intelligence deteriorates at a rate of time directly proportional to the quantity of the increase.

I feel that this, in itself, is an important discovery.

As long as I am able to write, I will continue to record my thoughts in these progress reports. It is one of my few pleasures. However, by all indications, my own mental deterioration will be very rapid.

I have already begun to notice signs of emotional instability and forgetfulness, the first symptoms of the burnout.

June 10 Deterioration progressing. I have become absent-minded. Algernon died two days ago. Dissection shows my predictions were right. His brain had decreased in weight and there was a general smoothing out of cerebral convolutions, as well as a deepening and broadening of brain fissures.

I guess the same thing is or will soon be happening to me. Now that it's definite, I don't want it to happen.

I put Algernon's body in a cheese box and buried him in the backyard. I cried.

June 15 Dr. Strauss came to see me again. I wouldn't open the door and I told him to go away. I want to be left to myself. I am touchy and irritable. I feel the darkness closing in. It's hard to throw off thoughts of suicide. I keep telling myself how important this journal will be.

It's a strange sensation to pick up a book you enjoyed just a few months ago and discover you don't remember it. I remembered how great I thought John Milton was, but when I picked up *Paradise Lost* I couldn't understand it at all. I got so angry I threw the book across the room.

I've got to try to hold on to some of it. Some of the things I've learned. Oh, God, please don't take it all away.

June 19 Sometimes, at night, I go out for a walk. Last night, I couldn't remember where I lived. A policeman took me home. I have the strange feeling that this has all happened to me before—a long time ago. I keep telling myself I'm the only person in the world who can describe what's happening to me.

June 21 Why can't I remember? I've got to fight. I lie in bed for days and I don't know who or where I am. Then it all comes back to me in a flash. Fugues of amnesia. Symptoms of senility—second childhood. I can watch them coming on. It's so cruelly logical. I learned so much and so fast. Now my mind is deteriorating rapidly. I won't let it happen. I'll fight it. I can't help thinking of the boy in the restaurant, the blank expression, the silly smile, the people laughing at him. No—please—not that again. . . .

June 22 I'm forgetting things that I learned recently. It seems to be following the classic pattern—the last things learned are the first things forgotten. Or is that the pattern? I'd better look it up again. . . .

I re-read my paper on the *Algernon-Gordon Effect* and I get the strange feeling that it was written by someone else. There are parts I don't even understand.

Motor activity impaired. I keep tripping over things, and it becomes increasingly difficult to type.

June 23 I've given up using the typewriter. My coordination is bad. I feel I'm moving slower and slower. Had a terrible shock today. I picked up a copy of an article I used in my research. Krueger's *Uber psychische Ganzheit,* to see if it would help me understand what I had done. First I thought there was something wrong with my eyes. Then I realized I could no longer read German. I tested myself in other languages. All gone.

June 30 A week since I dared to write again. It's slipping away like sand through my fingers. Most of the books I have are too hard for me now. I get angry with them because I know that I read and understood them just a few weeks ago.

I keep telling myself I must keep writing these reports so that somebody will know what is happening to me. But it gets harder to form the words and remember spellings. I have to look up even simple words in the dictionary now and it makes me impatient with myself.

Dr. Strauss comes around almost every day, but I told him I wouldn't see or speak to anybody. He feels guilty. They all do. But I don't blame anyone. I knew what might happen. But how it hurts.

July 7 I don't know where the week went. Todays Sunday I know because I can see through my window people going to church. I think I stayed in bed all week but I remember Mrs. Flynn bringing food to me a few times. I keep saying over and over I've got to do something but then I forget or maybe its just easier not to do what I say I'm going to do.

I think of my mother and father a lot these days. I found a picture of them with me taken at a beach. My father has a big ball under his arm and my mother is holding me by the hand. I dont remember them the way they are in the picture. All I remember is my father drunk most of the time and arguing with mom about money.

He never shaved much and he used to scratch my face when he hugged me. My Mother said he died but Cousin Miltie said he heard his dad say that my father ran away with another woman. When I asked my mother she slapped me and said my father was dead. I dont think I ever found out the truth but I dont care much. (He said he was going to take me to see cows on a farm once but he never did. He never kept his promises. . . .)

July 10 My landlady Mrs. Flynn is very worried about me. She says the way I lay around all day and dont do anything I remind her of her son before she threw him out of the house. She said she doesn't like loafers. If Im sick its one thing, but if Im a loafer thats another thing and she won't have it. I told her I think Im sick.

I try to read a little bit every day, mostly stories, but sometimes I have to read the same thing over and over again because I don't know what it means. And its hard to write. I know I should look up all the words in the dictionary but its so hard and Im so tired all the time.

Then I got the idea that I would only use the easy words instead of the long hard ones. That saves time. I put flowers on Algernons grave about once a week. Mrs Flynn thinks Im crazy to put flowers on a mouses grave but I told her that Algernon was special.

July 14 Its sunday again. I dont have anything to do to keep me busy now because my television set is broke and I dont have any money to get it fixed.

(I think I lost this months check from the lab. I dont remember)

I get awful headaches and asperin doesn't help me much. Mrs. Flynn knows Im really sick and she feels very sorry for me. Shes a wonderful woman whenever someone is sick.

July 22 Mrs. Flynn called a strange doctor to see me. She was afraid I was going to die. I told the doctor I wasn't too sick and I only forget sometimes. He asked me did I have any friends or relatives and I said no I don't have any. I told him I had a friend called Algernon once but he was a mouse and we used to run races together. He looked at me kind of funny like he thought I was crazy. He smiled when I told him I used to be a genius. He talked to me like I was a baby and he winked at Mrs. Flynn. I got mad and chased him out because he was making fun of me the way they all used to.

July 24 I have no more money and Mrs Flynn says I got to go to work somewhere and pay the rent because I havent paid for two months. I dont know any work but the job I used to have at Donnegans Box Company. I dont want to go back because they all knew me when I was smart and maybe they'll laugh at me. But I dont know what else to do to get money.

July 25 I was looking at some of my old progress reports and its very funny but I cant read what I wrote. I can make out some of the words but they dont make sense.

Miss Kinnian came to the door but I said go away I dont want to see you. She cried and I cried too but I wouldnt let her in because I didn't want her to laugh at me. I told her I didnt like her any more. I told her I didnt want to be smart any more. Thats not true. I still love her and I still want to be smart but I had to say that so shed go away. She gave Mrs. Flynn money to pay the rent. I dont want that. I got to get a job.

Please . . . please let me not forget how to read and write. . . .

July 27 Mr. Donnegan was very nice when I came back and asked him for my old job of janitor. First he was very suspicious but I told him what happened to me then he looked very sad and put his hand on my shoulder and said Charlie Gordon you got guts.

Everybody looked at me when I came downstairs and started working in the toilet sweeping it out like I used to. I told myself Charlie if they make fun of you dont get sore because you remember their not so smart as you once thot they were. And besides they were once your friends and if they laughted at you that doesnt mean anything because they liked you too.

One of the new men who came to work there after I went away made a nasty crack he said hey Charlie I hear your a very smart fella a real quiz kid. Say something intelligent. I felt bad but Joe Carp came over and grabbed him by the shirt and said leave him alone you lousy cracker or I'll break your neck.

I didnt expect Joe to take my part so I guess hes really my friend.

Later Frank Reilly came over and said Charlie if anybody bothers you or trys to take advantage you call me or Joe and we will set em straight. I said thanks Frank and I got choked up so I had to turn around and go into the supply room so he wouldnt see me cry. Its good to have friends.

July 28 I did a dumb thing today I forgot I wasnt in Miss Kinnians class at the adult center any more like I used to be. I went in and sat down in my old seat in the back of the room and she looked at me funny and she said Charles. I dint remember she ever called me that before only Charlie so I said hello Miss Kinnian Im redy for my lesin today only I lost my reader that we was using. She startid to cry and run out of the room and everybody looked at me and I saw they wasnt the same pepul who use to be in my class.

Then all of a suddin I remembered some things about the operashun and me getting smart and I said holy smoke I reely pulled a Charlie Gordon that time. I went away before she come back to the room.

Thats why Im going away from New York for good. I dont want to do nithing like that agen. I dont want Miss Kinnian to feel sorry for me. Evry body feels sorry at the factery and I dont want that eather so Im going someplace where nobody knows that Charlie Gordon was once a genus and now he cant even reed a book or rite good.

Im taking a cuple of books along and even if I cant reed them Ill practise hard and maybe I wont forget everything I lerned. If I try reel hard maybe Ill be a littel bit smarter than I was before the operashun. I got my rabits foot and my luky penny and maybe they will help me.

If you ever reed this Miss Kinnian dont be sorry for me Im glad I got a second chanse to be smart becaus I lerned a lot of things that I never even new were in this world and Im grateful that I saw it all for a littel bit. I dont know why Im dumb agen or what I did wrong maybe its because I dint try hard enuff. But if I try and practis very hard maybe Ill get a littl smarter and know what all the words are. I remember a littel bit how nice I had a feeling with the blue book that has the torn cover when I red it. Thats why Im gonna keep trying to get smart so I can have that feeling agen. Its a good feeling to know things and be smart. I wish I had it rite now if I did I would sit down and reed all the time. Anyway I bet Im the first dumb person in the world who ever found out something importent for science. I remember I did somthing but I dont remember what. So I gess its like I did it for all the dumb pepul like me.

Goodbye Miss Kinnian and Dr. Strauss and evreybody. And P.S. please tell Dr Nemur not to be such a grouch when pepul laff at him and he would have more frends. Its easy to make frends if you let pepul laff at you. Im going to have lots of frends where I go.

P.P.S. Please if you get a chanse put some flowrs on Algernons grave in the bak yard. . . .

3. learning theory

James McConnell

Our next author, James McConnell, is an experimental psychologist and the editor of a journal called The Worm Runner's Digest *(the serious portion of this journal is called* The Journal of Biological Psychology*). If "rat runners" experiment with rats what do "worm runners" do? You guessed it! McConnell started out with a lowly cross-eyed flatworm, the planarian. While not noted for its intellect, the planarian has one outstanding ability: you can cut it in half and the head will grow a new tail. More surprising, the tail grows a new head.*

McConnell and his associates first taught the worms a conditioned response—to twitch to a light paired with an electric shock. They then cut these educated worms in half and let them regenerate. When tested for memory, the former tails remembered at least as well as the heads. This finding not only led to some jokes on where we do our thinking, but a good deal of scientific head scratching. It also helped to lead to the search for the "memory molecule."

Some psychologists assume that memory is due to changes in brain proteins, since proteins are the basic chemical building blocks of neurons. A modification of this theory involves changes in RNA, which forms proteins. If one adopts a "protein" theory of learning, it follows that memory in the form of protein molecules can be extracted from one brain and injected into a second brain. Presto, instant learning! Such memory transfer experiments have been conducted with positive findings; however, there have been numerous failures to replicate what seems to be a delicate and elusive phenomenon.

An example of a memory transfer experiment done by McConnell and associates is one in which untrained planaria (no fastidious feeders, they) were fed chopped up trained planaria. Soon after dinner, the cannibalistic worms displayed the knowledge of the worms they had devoured. Some overenthusiastic students pointed out that this result indicates a more efficient use for aging, knowledge-crammed professors. While we cannot generalize from worm to man quite that easily, these discoveries stimulated further research. A varied array of psychologists, biochemists, and others have gone on to investigate the chemical transfer of learning by injecting the brain extract of one animal (e.g., the mouse) into the brain of another, with mixed success and failure. In any event, James McConnell has not only written science fiction, but has helped to discover science facts which resemble the "far-out" conjectures of science fiction.

But we digress. "Learning Theory" presents some basic psychological techniques from the point of view of the subject—a somewhat sophisticated point of view, we might add, since the subject is himself a psychologist.

Note the types of apparatus which are used to study learning. In the Skinner box, the subject is free from distractions, yet how might this apparatus restrict his behavior? Note when the subject is rewarded intermittently—what does this procedure make him do? In the ordinary maze, the human subject learns about as fast as the rat. However, when the maze is reversed to a mirror image of itself, our human subject solves it in two trials. How can you explain this un-ratlike learning? In the jumping stand situation, you might notice that two sources of motivation are mixed together, and that jumping is rewarded or punished, depending on the correctness of the response (a type of discrimination learning). This apparatus is generally no longer used in psychological research—you may have some ideas why this is so after reading "Learning Theory."

"It's better to be wanted for murder than not to be wanted at all."
Marty Winch (via Don Lewis)

I am writing this because I presume He wants me to. Otherwise He would not have left paper and pencil handy for me to use. And I put the word "He" in capitals because it seems the only thing to do. If I am dead and in hell, then this is only proper. However, if I am merely a captive somewhere, then surely a little flattery won't hurt matters.

As I sit here in this small room and think about it, I am impressed most of all by the suddenness of the whole thing. At one moment I was out walking in the woods near my suburban home. The next thing I knew, here I was in a small, featureless room, naked as a jaybird, with only my powers of rationalization to stand between me and insanity. When the "change" was made (whatever the change was), I was not conscious of so much as a momentary flicker between walking in the woods and being here in this room. Whoever is responsible for all of this is to be complimented—either He has developed an instantaneous anesthetic or He has solved the problem of instantaneous transportation of matter. I would prefer to think it the former, for the latter leads to too much anxiety.

Yes, there I was walking through the woods, minding my own business, studiously pretending to enjoy the outing so that I wouldn't mind the exercise too much, when the transition took place. As I recall, I was immersed in the problem of how to teach my class in Beginning Psychology some of the more abstruse points of Learning Theory when the transition came. How far away and distant life at the University seems at the moment! I must be forgiven if now I am much more concerned about where I am and how to get out of here than about how freshmen can be cajoled into understanding Hull or Tolman.

Problem One. Where am I? For an answer, I can only describe this room. It is about twenty feet square, some twelve feet high, with no windows, but with what might be a door in the middle of one of the walls. Everything is of a uniform gray color, and the walls and ceiling emit a fairly pleasant achromatic light. The walls themselves are of some hard material which might be metal since it feels slightly cool to the touch. The floor is of a softer, rubbery material that yields a little when I walk on it. Also, it has a rather "tingly" feel to it, suggesting that it may be in constant vibration. It is somewhat warmer than the walls, which is all to the good since it appears I must sleep on the floor.

The only furniture in the room consists of what might be a table and what passes for a chair. They are not quite that, but they can be made to serve this purpose. On the table I found the paper and the pencil. No, let me correct myself. What I call paper is a good deal rougher and thicker than I am used to, and what I call a pencil is nothing more than a thin round stick of graphite which I have sharpened by rubbing one end of it on the table.

And that is the sum extent of my surroundings. I wish I knew what He has done with my clothes. The suit was an old one, but I am worried about the walking boots. I was very fond of those boots—not because of any sentimental attachment nor because they had done me much good service, but rather because they were quite expensive and I would hate to lose them.

The problem still remains to be answered, however, as to just where in the hell I am—if not in hell itself!

Problem Two is a knottier one—why am I here? Were I subject to paranoid tendencies, I would doubtless come to the conclusion that my enemies had kidnapped me. Or perhaps that the Russians had taken such an interest in my research that they had spirited me away to some Siberian hideout and would soon appear to demand either cooperation or death. Sadly enough, I am too reality oriented. My research was highly interesting to me, and perhaps to a few other psychologists who like to dabble in esoteric problems of animal learning, but it was scarcely startling enough to warrant such attention as kidnapping.

So I am left as baffled as before. Where am I, and why?

And who is He?

2

I have decided to forego all attempts at keeping this diary according to "days" or "hours." Such units of time have no meaning in my present circumstances, for the light remains constant all the time I am awake. The human organism is not possessed of as neat an internal clock as some of the lower species. Far too many studies have shown that a human being who is isolated from all external stimulation soon loses his sense of time. So I will merely indicate breaks in the narrative and hope that He will understand that if He wasn't bright enough to leave me with my wristwatch, He couldn't expect me to keep an accurate record.

Nothing much has happened since I began this narrative, except that I have slept, been fed and watered, and have emptied my bladder and bowels. The food was waiting on the table when I awoke last time. I must say that He had little of the gourmet in Him. Protein balls are not my idea of a feast royal. However, they will serve to keep body and soul together (presuming, of course, that they *are* together at the moment). But I must object to my source of liquid refreshment. The meal made me very thirsty and I was in the process of cursing Him and everybody else when I noticed a small nipple which had appeared in the wall while I was asleep. At first I thought that perhaps Freud was right after all, and that my libido had taken over control of my imagery. Experimentation convinced me, however, that the thing was real, and that it is my present source of water. If one sucks on the thing, it delivers a slightly cool and somewhat sweetish flow of liquid. But really, it's a most undignified procedure. It's bad enough to have to sit around all day in my birthday suit. But for a full professor to have to stand on his tiptoes and suck on an artificial nipple in order to obtain water is asking a little too much. I'd complain to the Management if only I knew to whom to complain!

Following eating and drinking, the call to nature became a little too strong to ignore. Now, I was adequately toilet-trained with indoor plumbing, and the absence of same is most annoying. However, there was nothing much to do but choose a corner of the room and make the best of a none-too-pleasant situation. (As a side-thought, I wonder if the choosing of a corner was in any way instinctive?) However, the upshot of the whole thing was my learning what is probably the purpose of the vibration of the floor. For the excreted material disappeared through the floor not too many minutes later. The process was a gradual one. Now I will be faced with all kinds of uncomfortable thoughts concerning what might possibly happen to me if I slept too long!

Perhaps this is to be expected, but I find myself becoming a little paranoid after all. In attempting to solve my *Problem Two,* why I am here, I have begun to wonder if perhaps some of colleagues at the University are not using me as the subject in some kind of experiment. It would be just like them to dream up some fantastic kind of "human-in-isolation" experiment and use me as a pilot observer. You would think that they'd have asked my permission first. However, perhaps it's important that the subject not know what's happening to him. If so, I have one happy thought to console me. If any of them are responsible for this, they'll have to take over the teaching of my classes for the time being. And how they hate teaching Learning Theory to freshmen!

You know, this place seems dreadfully quiet to me.

3

Suddenly I have solved two of my problems. I know both where I am and who He is. And I bless the day I got interested in the perception of motion.

I should say to begin with that the air in this room seems to have more than the usual concentration of dust particles. This didn't seem particularly noteworthy until I noticed that most of them seemed to pile up along the floor against one wall in particular. For a while I was sure that this was due to the ventilation system—perhaps there was an out-going air duct there where this particular wall was joined to the floor. However, when I went over and put my hand to the floor there, I could feel no breeze whatsoever. Yet even as I held my hand along the dividing line between the wall and the floor, dust motes covered my hand with a thin coating. I tried this same experiment everywhere else in the room to no avail. This was the only spot where the phenomenon occurred, and it occurred along the entire length of this one wall.

But if ventilation was not responsible for the phenomenon, what was? All at once there popped into my mind some calculations I had made back when the rocket boys had first proposed a manned satellite station. Engineers are notoriously naive when it comes to the performance of a human being in most situations, and I remembered that the problem of the perception of the satellite's rotation seemingly had been ignored by the slip-stick crowd. They had planned to rotate the doughnut-shaped satellite in order to substitute centrifugal force for the force of gravity. Thus the outer shell of the doughnut would appear to be "down" to anyone inside the thing. Apparently they had not realized that man is at least as sensitive to angular rotation as he is to variations in the pull of gravity. As I figured the problem then, if a man aboard the doughnut moved his head as much as three or four feet outwards from the center of the doughnut, he would have become fairly dizzy! Rather annoying it would have been, too, to have been hit by a wave of nausea every time one sat down in a chair. Also, as I pondered the problem, it became apparent that dust particles and the like would probably show a tendency to move in a direction opposite to the direction of the rotation, and hence pile up against any wall or such that impeded their flight.

Using the behavior of the dust particles as a clue, I then climbed atop the table and leapt off. Sure enough, my head felt like a mule had kicked it by the time I landed on the floor. My hypothesis was confirmed.

So I am aboard a spaceship!

The thought is incredible, but in a strange way comforting. At least now I can postpone worrying about heaven and hell—and somehow I find the idea of being in a spaceship much more to the liking of a confirmed agnostic. I suppose I owe my colleagues an apology—I should have known they would never have put themselves in a position where they might have to teach freshmen all about learning!

And, of course, I now know who "He" is. Or rather, I know who He *isn't*, which is something else again. Surely, though, I can no longer think of Him as being human. Whether I should be consoled at this or not, I have no way of telling.

I still have no notion of *why* I am here, however, nor why this alien chose to pick me of all people to pay a visit to His spaceship. What possible use could I be? Surely if He were interested in making contact with the human race, He would have spirited away a politican. After all, that's what politicans are for! Since there has been no effort made to communicate with me, however, I must reluctantly give up any cherished hopes that His purpose is that of making contact with *genus homo*.

Or perhaps He's a galactic scientist of some kind, a biologist of sorts, out gathering specimens. Now, that's a particularly nasty thought. What if He turned out to be a psychologist, interested in cutting me open eventually to see what makes me tick? Will my innards be smeared over a glass slide for scores of youthful Hims to peer at under a microscope? Brrrr! I don't mind giving my life to Science, but I'd rather do it a little at a time.

If you don't mind, I think I'll go do a little repressing for a while.

4

Good God! I should have known it! Destiny will play her little tricks, and all jokes have their cosmic angles. He is a *psychologist!* Had I given it due consideration, I would have realized that whenever you come across a new species, you worry about behavior first, physiology second. So I have received the ultimate insult—or the ultimate compliment. I don't know which. I have become a specimen for an alien psychologist!

This thought first occurred to me when I awoke after my latest sleep (which was filled, I must admit, with most frightening dreams). It was immediately obvious that something about the room had changed. Almost at once I noticed that one of the walls now had a lever of some kind protruding from it, and to one side of the lever, a small hole in the wall with a container beneath the hole. I wandered over to the lever, inspected it for a few moments, then accidentally depressed the thing. At once there came a loud clicking noise, and a protein ball popped out of the hole and fell into the container.

For just a moment a frown crossed my brow. This seemed somehow so strangely familiar. Then, all at once, I burst into wild laughter. The room had been changed into a gigantic Skinner Box! For years I had been studying animal learning by putting white rats in a Skinner Box and following the changes in the rats' behavior. The rats had to learn to press the lever in order to get a pellet of food, which was delivered to them through just such an apparatus as is now affixed to the wall of my cell. And now, after all of these years, and after all of the learning studies I had done, to find myself trapped like a rat in a Skinner Box! Perhaps this was hell after all, I told myself, and the Lord High Executioner's admonition to "let the punishment fit the crime" was being followed.

Frankly, this sudden turn of events has left me more than a little shaken.

5

I seem to be performing according to theory. It didn't take me long to discover that pressing the lever would give me food some of the time, while at other times all I got was the click and no protein ball. It appears that approximately every twelve hours the thing delivers me a random number of protein balls—the number has varied from five to fifteen so far. I never know ahead of time how many pellets—I mean protein balls—the apparatus will deliver, and it spews them out intermittently. Sometimes I have to press the lever a dozen times or so before it will give me anything, while at other times it gives me one ball for each press. Since I don't have a watch on me, I am never quite sure when the twelve hours have passed, so I stomp over to the lever and press it every few minutes when I think it's getting close to time to be fed. Just like my rats always did. And since the pellets are small and I never get enough of them, occasionally I find myself banging away on the lever with all the compulsion of a stupid animal. But I missed the feeding time once and almost starved to death (so it seemed) before the lever delivered food the next time. About the only consolation to my wounded pride is that at this rate of starvation, I'll lose my bay window in short order.

At least He doesn't seem to be fattening me up for the kill. Or maybe he just likes lean meat.

6

I have been promoted. Apparently He in His infinite alien wisdom has decided that I'm intelligent enough to handle the Skinner-type apparatus, so I've been promoted to solving a maze. Can you picture the irony of the situation? All of the classic Learning Theory methodology is practically being thrown in my face in mockery. If only I could communicate with Him! I don't mind being subjected to tests nearly as much as I mind being underestimated. Why, I can solve puzzles hundreds of times more complex than what He's throwing at me. But how can I tell Him?

7

As it turns out, the maze is much like our standard T-mazes, and is not too difficult to learn. It's a rather long one, true, with some 23 choice points along the way. I spent the better part of half an hour wandering through the thing the first time I found myself in it. Surprisingly enough, I didn't realize the first time out what I was in, so I made no conscious attempt to memorize the correct turns. It wasn't until I reached the final turn and found food waiting for me that I recognized what I was expected to do. The next time through the maze my performance was a good deal better, and I was able to turn in a perfect performance in not too long a time. However, it does not do my ego any good to realize that my own white rats could have learned the maze a little sooner than I did.

My "home cage," so to speak, still has the Skinner apparatus in it, but the lever delivers food only occasionally now. I still give it a whirl now and again, but since I'm getting a fairly good supply of food at the end of the maze each time, I don't pay the lever much attention.

Now that I am very sure of what is happening to me, quite naturally my thoughts have turned to how I can get out of this situation. Mazes I can solve without too much difficulty, but how to escape is apparently beyond my intellectual capacity. But then, come to think of it, there was precious little chance for my own experimental animals to get out of my clutches. And assuming that I am unable to escape, what then? After He has finished putting me through as many paces as He wishes, where do we go from there? Will he treat me as I treated most of my non-human subjects—that is, will I get tossed into a jar containing chloroform? "Following the experiment, the animals are sacrificed," as we so euphemistically report in the scientific literature. This doesn't appeal to me much, as you can imagine. Or maybe if I seem particularly bright to Him, He may use me for breeding purposes, to establish a colony of His own. Now, that might have possibilities . . .

Oh, damn Freud anyhow!

8

And damn Him, too! I had just gotten the maze well learned when He upped and changed things on me. I stumbled about like a bat in the sunlight for quite some time before I finally got to the goal box. I'm afraid my performance was pretty poor.

9

Well, it wasn't so bad after all. What He did was just to reverse the whole maze so that it was a mirror image of what it used to be. Took me only two trials to discover the solution. Let Him figure that one out if He's so smart!

10

My performance on the maze reversal must have pleased Him, because now He's added a new complication. And again I suppose I could have predicted the next step if I had been thinking along the right direction. I woke up a few hours ago to find myself in a totally different room. There was nothing whatsoever in the room, but opposite me were two doors in the wall—one door a pure white, the other jet black. Between me and the doors was a deep pit, filled with water. I didn't like the looks of the situation, for it occurred to me right away that He had devised a kind of jumping-stand for me. I had to choose which of the doors was open and led to the food. The other door would be locked. If I jumped at the wrong door, and found it locked, I'd fall in the water. I needed a bath, that was for sure, but I didn't relish getting it in this fashion.

While I stood there watching, I got the shock of my life. I mean it quite literally. The bastard had thought of everything. When I used to run rats on jumping stands, to overcome their reluctance to jump, I used to shock them. He's following exactly the same pattern. The floor in this room is wired but good. I howled and jumped about and showed all the usual anxiety behavior. It took me less than two seconds to come to my senses and make a flying leap at the white door, however.

You know something? That water is ice-cold.

11

I have now, by my own calculations, solved no fewer than 87 different problems on the jumping stand, and I'm getting sick and tired of it. One time I got angry and just pointed at the correct door—and got shocked for not going ahead and jumping. I shouted bloody murder, cursing Him at the top of my voice, telling Him if He didn't like my performance, He could damn well lump it. All He did, of course, was to increase the shock.

Frankly, I don't know how much longer I can put up with this. It's not that the work is difficult. But rather that it seems so senseless, so useless. If He were giving me half a chance to show my capabilities, I wouldn't mind it. I suppose I've contemplated a thousand different ways of escaping, but none of them is worth mentioning. But if I don't get out of here soon, I shall go stark raving mad!

12

For almost an hour after it happened, I sat in this room and just wept. I realize that it is not the style of our culture for a grown man to weep, but there are times when cultural taboos must be forgotten. Again, had I thought much about the sort of experiments He must have had in mind, I most probably could have predicted the next step. Even so, I most likely would have repressed the knowledge.

One of the standard problems which any learning psychologist is interested in is this one—will an animal learn something if you fail to reward him for his performance? There are many theorists, such as Hull and Spence, who believe that reward (or "reinforcement" as they call it) is absolutely necessary for learning to occur. This is mere stuff and nonsense, as anyone with a grain of sense knows, but nevertheless the "reinforcement" theory has been dominant in the field for years now. We fought a hard battle with Spence and Hull, and actually had them with their backs to the wall at one point, when suddenly they came up with the concept of "secondary reinforcement." That is, anything associated with a reward takes on the ability to act as a reward itself. For example, the mere sight of food would become a reward in and of itself —almost as much as a reward, in fact, as is the eating of the food. The *sight* of food, indeed! But nonetheless, it saved their theories for the moment.

For the past five years now, I have been trying to design an experiment that would show beyond a shadow of a doubt that the *sight* of a reward was not sufficient for learning to take place. And now look at what has happened to me!

I'm sure that He must lean towards Hull and Spence in his theorizing, for earlier today, when I found myself in the jumping stand room, instead of being rewarded with my usual protein balls when I made the correct jump, I discovered . . .

I'm sorry, but it is difficult to write about even now. For when I made the correct jump and the door opened and I started toward the food trough, I found it had been replaced with a photograph. A calendar photograph. You know the one. Her name, I think, is Monroe.

I sat on the floor for almost an hour weeping afterwards. For five whole years I have been attacking the validity of the secondary reinforcement theory, and now I find myself giving Him evidence that the theory is correct! For I cannot help "learning" which of the doors is the correct one to jump through. I refuse to stand on the apparatus and have the life shocked out of me, and I refuse to pick the wrong door all the time and get an icy bath time after time. It just isn't fair! For He will doubtless put it all down to the fact that the mere *sight* of the photograph is functioning as a reward, and that I am learning the problems merely to be able to see Miss What's-her-name in her bare skin!

Oh, I can just see Him now, sitting somewhere else in this spaceship, gathering in all the data I am giving Him, plotting all kinds of learning curves, chortling to Himself because I am confirming all of His pet theories. I just wish . . .

13

Almost an hour has gone by since I wrote the above section. It seems longer than that, but surely it's been only an hour. And I have spent the time in deep thought. For I have discovered a way out of this place, I think. The question is, dare I do it?

I was in the midst of writing that paragraph about His sitting and chortling and confirming his theories, when it suddenly struck me that theories are born of the equipment that one uses. This has probably been true throughout the history of all science, but perhaps most true of all in psychology. If Skinner had never invented his blasted box, if the maze and the jumping stand had not been developed, we probably would have entirely different theories of learning today than we now have. For if nothing else, the type of equipment that one uses drastically reduces the type of behavior that one's subjects can show, and one's theories have to account only for the type of behavior that appears in the laboratories.

It follows from this also that any two cultures that devise the same sort of experimental procedures will come up with almost identical theories.

Keeping all of this in mind, it's not hard for me to believe that He is an iron-clad reinforcement theorist, for He uses all of the various paraphernalia that they use, and uses it in exactly the same way.

My means of escape is therefore obvious. He expects from me confirmation of all His pet theories. Well, He won't get it any more! I know all of His theories backwards and forwards, and this means I know how to give Him results that will tear his theories right smack in half!

I can almost predict the results. What does any learning theorist do with an animal that won't behave properly, that refuses to give the results that are predicted? One gets rid of the beast, quite naturally. For one wishes to use only healthy, normal animals in one's work, and any animal that gives "unusual" results is removed from the study but quickly. After all, if it doesn't perform as expected, it must be sick, abnormal, or aberrant in one way or another . . .

There is no guarantee, of course, what method He will employ to dispose of my now annoying presence. Will He "sacrifice" me? Or will He just return me to the "permanent colony?" I cannot say. I know only that I will be free from what is now an intolerable situation. The chance must be taken.

Just wait until He looks at His results from now on!

II

FROM: Experimenter-in-Chief, Interstellar Labship PSYCH-145
TO: Director, Bureau of Science

Thlan, my friend, this will be an informal missive. I will send the official report along later, but I wanted to give you my subjective impressions first.

The work with the newly discovered species is, for the moment, at a standstill. Things went exceeding well at first. We picked what seemed to be a normal, healthy animal and smattered it into our standard test apparatus. I may have told you that this new species seemed quite identical to our usual laboratory animals, so we included a couple of the "toys" that our home animals seem to be fond of—thin pieces of material made from woodpulp and a tiny stick of graphite. Imagine our surprise, and our pleasure, when this new specimen made exactly the same use of the materials as have all of our home colony specimens. Could it be that there are certain innate behavior patterns to be found throughout the universe in the lower species?

Well, I merely pose the question. The answer is of little importance to a Learning Theorist. Your friend Verpk keeps insisting that the use of these "toys" may have some deeper meaning to it, and that perhaps we should investigate further. At his insistence, then, I include with this informal missive the materials used by our first subject. In my opinion, Verpk is guilty of gross anthropomorphism, and I wish to have nothing further to do with the question. However, this behavior did give us hope that our newly discovered colony would yield subjects whose performance would be exactly in accordance with standard theory.

And, in truth, this is exactly what seemed to be the case. The animal solved the Bfian Box problem in short order, yielding as beautiful data as I have ever seen. We then shifted it to maze, maze-reversal and jumping stand problems, and the results could not have confirmed our theories better had we rigged the data. However, when we switched the animal to secondary reinforcement problems, it seemed to undergo a strange sort of change. No longer was its performance up to par. In fact, at times it seemed to go quite berserk. For part of the experiment, it would perform superbly. But then, just as it seemed to be solving whatever problem we set it to, its behavior would subtly change into patterns that obviously could not come from a normal specimen. It got worse and worse, until its behavior departed radically from that which our theories predicted. Naturally, we knew then that something had happened to the animal, for our theories are based upon thousands of experiments with similar subjects, and hence our theories must be right. But our theories hold only for normal subjects, and for normal species, so it soon became apparent to us that we had stumbled upon some abnormal type of animal.

Upon due consideration, we returned the subject to its home colony. However, we also voted almost unanimously to request from you permission to take steps to destroy the complete colony. It is obviously of little scientific use to us, and stands as a potential danger that we must take adequate steps against. Since all colonies are under your protection, we therefore request permission to destroy it in toto.

I must report, by the way, that Verpk's vote was the only one which was cast against this procedure. He has some silly notion that one should study behavior as one finds it. Frankly, I cannot understand why you have seen fit to saddle me with him on this expedition, but perhaps you have your reasons.

Verpk's vote notwithstanding, however, the rest of us are of the considered opinion that this whole new colony must be destroyed, and quickly. For it is obviously diseased or some such—as reference to our theories has proven. And should it by some chance come in contact with our other colonies, and infect our other animals with whatever disease or aberration it has, we would never be able to predict their behavior again. I need not carry the argument further, I think.

May we have your permission to destroy the colony as soon as possible, then, so that we may search out yet other colonies and test our theories against other healthy animals? For it is only in this fashion that science progresses.

Respectfully yours,
Iowyy

II

Physiological and Perceptual Processes

As pervasive and important as learning is to us, this capacity is based on, and structured by, our physiology and anatomy. In fact, all behavior is mediated in some way by physical structures and physiological processes. Since heredity heavily influences anatomy and physiology, the science of genetics is important in understanding behavior.

However, genes do not act directly on behavior; they regulate the production of proteins, which in turn are responsible for the structure and enzymatic functions of an organism. For example, phenylketonuria (PKU), a disease characterized by severe mental deficiency, results from defects at a single gene locus. Such defects lead to an overproduction of phenylpyruvic acid and thus brain damage as an infant. Fortunately, now this problem can be diagnosed, then prevented through the proper diet.

A more complex example of the effects of heredity on behavior is seen in schizophrenia, a severe form of behavior disturbance characterized by disordered thinking, hallucinations, and delusions. Although environmental factors are important, the propensity to become schizophrenic seems strongly influenced by heredity. Research has shown, for example, that if an identical twin develops schizophrenia, the chances are at least even that his twin will become schizophrenic. With fraternal twins, however, only 9 to 15 percent will both become schizophrenic. Since identical twins are genetically identical, and fraternal twins are genetically no more similar than ordinary brothers or sisters, this difference indicates a genetic component.

Typically, the question is not whether or not our genetic inheritance influences behavior, but to what degree. In certain areas of psychology, this is a very controversial question. Arthur Jensen's proposition that racial differences in intelligence are inherited has generated a heated scientific (and sometimes not-so-scientific) debate. Another researcher, the noted ethologist Konrad Lorenz, holds that man is innately aggressive, a view that has been attacked aggressively by other scientists. With the recent discovery of the roles of DNA and RNA in genetic transmission, behavior genetics promises to be a significant area in psychology.

Areas of interest more traditional for the physiological psychologist than behavioral genetics are the glandular and nervous systems. Within the nervous system, psychologists have focused their research energies on the brain. Some of the resulting discoveries would have been science fiction twenty-five years ago; indeed, they resemble it even today. One such discovery was made by James Olds, who found that rats would press a bar to receive electrical stimulation in certain areas of the lower brain. After noting that hungry rats would neglect food to receive these shocks, sometimes pressing the bar over 5,000 times an hour, Olds maintained that there is a "pleasure center" in the brain. Other researchers have confirmed similar effects in humans. While so far no brain-stimulation addicts have been reported, one wonders about the future. For a science fiction account of the possibility, read Larry Niven's novella *Death by Ecstasy*. Here there are pushers who deal in brain stimulation, stimulation addicts, and overdoses.

Shortly after Olds's discovery, Joseph Kamiya found that human subjects could control their brain waves and, thus, their mental states. He set up circuitry which translated alpha waves, as measured by an electroencephalograph, into a tone. As long as the subject kept the tone on, he was producing alpha waves (the alpha state is pleasant and relaxed). This technique is a form of biofeedback training. Since Kamiya's early work, researchers have found that other types of brain waves can be self-controlled.

Other recent research on the brain tells us some fascinating facts about memory. During electrical stimulation of certain association areas in the temporal lobes, vivid memories may be brought to consciousness. The person relives actual events from long ago, such as childhood experiences. These events may be ones the subject has long forgotten, at least without the aid of electrical stimulation.

In the occipital lobe of the brain lie centers crucial for vision. When the visual cortex is stimulated electrically, the person reports seeing spots or flashes of light. Research based on this phenomenon holds some promise for the induction of artificial vision for blind persons. In one experiment, a number of electrodes were implanted in the visual cortex of two blind subjects. On stimulation of a pattern of electrodes, the blind person sensed visual patterns. Although a crude approximation of real sight, it is a start. What develops from this research in the future is science fiction today.

Two other basic areas of psychology deal with sensation and perception. Through the senses we receive our knowledge of the world: they are our gateways to the mind. We see, hear, and hurt; we are warm or cold, feel the roughness of jagged scrap iron and the sleek sensuousness of silk. Yet these raw sensory impressions are not what we experience; rather they are modified by our previous information and thought processes. Thus the role of perception is to organize and interpret sensations.

From the beginnings of scientific psychology, researchers have studied sensation and perception. One controversial question asked more frequently today is: Can there be perception without the stimulation of a sense organ (or at least a known sense organ)? Extrasensory perception (ESP) has been studied in psychological laboratories with varying results. Many psychologists remain unconvinced of the validity of this phenomenon, but it appears that more of them accept it as an object of scientific study. Although psychologists have been slow to accept ESP, it has long been a staple of science fiction. For two such examples, turn to "Such Stuff" (page 136) and/or "If You're So Smart" (page 104). The former story has other things to tell us about psychology and is thus in the section on emotion and motivation; however, it also deals with sensation and perception. The same is true of "The Man in the Rorschach Shirt" (page 210). While we put it in the area of personality, it too has something to say about perception.

We leave you now as you sense black marks on white paper, and perceive sentences, words, and four thought-provoking stories.

4. how deep the grooves

Philip José Farmer

All mad-scientist stories must have two ingredients. The level of scientific discovery has to extend beyond existing knowledge, and the result has to be dramatic and at least a bit bizarre. Without both elements the story becomes mundane.

For example, suppose that Dr. Frankenstein's remarkable discovery was tooth transplants. While it might be incredible for his time, it simply is not the stuff that mad-scientist stories are made of. After all, who can picture a tooth that has been brought back to life, turning on its creator or being chased down the street by an angry mob with torches? Just think if Dr. Jeckyl were alive today. He might have submitted an article to the Journal of Comparative and Physiological Psychology *on the chemical stimulation of rage in mammals. His classic experiment might then have gone unnoticed, or worse yet, been rejected by the editors because of his small sample.*

The traditional mad scientist has usually been a loner, with perhaps only one faithful research assistant. In Farmer's story, however, he is sanctioned by what seems to be a "mad society." Of course, scientists have always served "mad" as well as "sane" societies. For example, Hitler had his rocket and nuclear scientists, as did Roosevelt. But then, perhaps the author is pointing out a significant trend. As behavioral scientists find more effective ways to change behavior, totalitarian governments no doubt will be more likely to use these scientists and their techniques to control behavior. Shades of 1984!

Like Dr. Frankenstein, Dr. Carroad unwittingly releases powerful and unknown forces in which creation becomes destruction. This process, along with a "socko" ending and some startling ideas about fate and determinism, come together in a story that lingers on for a long time in one's mind —like the "groovy" melody of a familiar record.

Note that Dr. Carroad is an expert on electroencephalographic (EEG) research. At present, the EEG machine is used to amplify the tiny electrical potentials emitted by the brain and present them in written form. With the EEG machine, scientists can detect epilepsy and brain tumors, and identify stages of sleep. Recently, researchers at Stanford University have demonstrated that brain waves induced by viewing nude photographs appear to reveal a person's sexual preferences. That is, females typically showed a stronger brainwave response to male nudes than female nudes, and the reverse was true for male subjects. Is this technique mind reading by machine, or shall we have to wait for a Dr. Carroad? Would a perfected mind-reading technique be beneficial to humanity? The story shows some possible uses.

Always in control of himself, Doctor James Carroad lowered his voice.

He said, "You will submit to this test. We must impress the Secretary. The fact that we're willing to use our own unborn baby in the experiment will make the impression a deeper one."

Doctor Jane Carroad, his wife, looked up from the chair in which she sat. Her gaze swept over the tall lean figure in the white scientist's uniform and the two rows of resplendent ribbons and medals on his left chest. She glared into the eyes of her husband.

Scornfully, she said, "You did not want this baby. I did, though now I wonder why. Perhaps, because I wanted to be a mother, no matter what the price. Not to give the State another citizen. But, now we're going to have it, you want to exploit it even before it's born, just as . . ."

Harshly, he said, "Don't you know what such talk can lead to?"

"Don't worry! I won't tell anyone you didn't desire to add to the State. Nor will I tell anybody how I induced you to have it!"

His face became red, and he said. "You will never again mention that to me! Never again! Understand?"

Jane's neck muscles trembled, but her face was composed. She said, "I'll speak of that, to you, whenever I feel like it. Though, God knows, I'm thoroughly ashamed of it. But I do get a sour satisfaction out of knowing that, once in my life, I managed to break down that rigid self-control. I made you act like a normal man, one able to forget himself in his passion for a woman. Doctor Carroad the great scientist of the State, really forgot himself then."

She gave a short brittle laugh and then settled back in the chair as if she would no longer discuss the matter.

But he would not, could not, let her have the last word. He said, "I only wanted to see how it felt to throw off all restraints. That was all—an experiment. I didn't care for it; it was disgusting. It'll never happen again."

He looked at his wristwatch and said, "Let's go. We must not make the Secretary wait."

She rose slowly, as if the eight months' burden was at last beginning to drain her strength.

"All right. But I'm submitting our baby to this experiment only under protest. If anything happens to it, a potential citizen . . ."

He spun around. "A written protest?"

"I've already sent it in."

"You little fool! Do you want to wreck everything I've worked for?"

Tears filled her eyes.

"James! Does the possible harm to our baby mean nothing to you? Only the medals, the promotions, the power?"

"Nonsense! There's no danger! If there were, wouldn't I know it? Come along now!"

But she did not follow him through the door. Instead, she stood with her face against the wall, her shoulders shaking.

A moment later, Jason Cramer entered. The young man closed the door behind him and put his arm around her. Without protest, she turned and buried her face in his chest. For a while, she could not talk but could only weep.

Finally, she released herself from his embrace and said, "Why is it, Jason, that every time I need a man to cry against, James is not with me but you are?"

"Because he is the one who makes you cry," he said. "And I love you."

"And James," she said, "loves only himself."

"You didn't give me the proper response, Jane. I said I loved you."

She kissed him, though lightly, and murmured, "I think I love you. But I'm not allowed to. Please forget what I said. I mean it."

She walked away from him. Jason Cramer, after making sure that he had no lipstick on his face or uniform, followed her.

Entering the laboratory, Jane Carroad ignored her husband's glare and sat down in the chair in the middle of the room. Immediately thereafter, the Secretary of Science and two Security bodyguards entered.

The Secretary was a stocky dark man of about fifty. He had very thick black eyebrows that looked like pieces of fur pasted above his eyes. He radiated the assurance that he was master, in control of all in the room. Yet, he did not, as was nervously expected by James Carroad and Jason Cramer, take offense because Jane did not rise from the chair to greet him. He gave her a smile, patted her hand, and said, "Is it true you will bear a male baby?"

"That is what the tests indicate," she said.

"Good. Another valuable citizen. A scientist, perhaps. With its genetic background . . ."

Annoyed because his wife had occupied the center of the stage for too long, Doctor James Carroad loudly cleared his throat. He said, "Citizens, honored Secretary, I've asked you here for a demonstration because I believe that what I have to show you is of utmost importance to the State's future. I have here the secret of what constitutes a good, or bad, citizen of the State."

He paused for effect, which he was getting, and then continued, "As you know, I—and my associates, of course—have perfected an infallible and swift method whereby an enemy spy or deviationist citizen may be unmasked. This method has been in use for three years. During that time, it has exposed many thousands as espionage agents, as traitors, as potential traitors."

The Secretary looked interested. He also looked at his wristwatch. Doctor Carroad refused to notice; he talked on at the same pace. He could justify any amount of time he took, and he intended to use as much as possible.

"My Department of Electroencephalographic Research first produced the devices delicate enough to detect the so-called rho waves emanated by the human brain. The rho or semantic waves. After ten years of hard work, I correlated the action of the rho waves in a particular human brain with the action of the individual's voice mechanisms. That meant, of course, that we had a device which mankind has long dreamed of. A—pardon the term— mind-reading machine."

Carroad purposely avoided scientific terminology. The Secretary did have a Ph.D. in political science, but he knew very little of any biological science.

Jason Cramer, at a snap of the fingers by Carroad, wheeled a large round shining machine to a spot about two feet in front of Jane. It resembled a weird metallic antelope, for it had a long flexible neck at the end of which was an oval and eyeless head with two prongs like horns. These pointed at Jane's skull. On the side of the machine—Cervus III—was a round glass tube. The oscilloscope.

Carroad said, "We no longer have to attach electrodes to the subject's head. We've made that method obsolete. Cervus' prongs pick up rho waves without direct contact. It is also able to cut out 99.99 percent of the 'noise' that had hampered us in previous research."

Yes, thought Jane, *and why don't you tell them that it was Jason Cramer who made that possible, instead of allowing them to think it was you?*

At that moment, she reached the peak of her hate for him. She wished that the swelling sleeper within her was not Carroad's but Cramer's. And, wishing that, she knew that she must be falling in love with Cramer.

Carroad's voice slashed into her thoughts.

"And so, using the detected rho waves, which can be matched against definite objective words, we get a verbal picture of what is going in the subject's mind at the conscious level."

He gave an order to Cramer, and Cramer twisted a dial on the small control board on the side of Cervus.

"The machine is now set for semantic relations," Carroad said.

"Jane!" he added so sharply that she was startled. "Repeat this sentence after me! Silently!"

He then gave her a much-quoted phrase from one of the speeches of the Secretary himself. She repressed her scorn of him because of his flattery and dutifully concentrated on thinking the phrase. At the same time, she was aware that her tongue was moving in a noiseless lockstep with the thoughts.

The round tube on the side of Cervus glowed and then began flashing with many twisting threads of light.

"The trained eye," said Carroad, "can interpret those wave-forms. But we have a surprise for you to whom the patterns are meaningless. We have perfected a means whereby a technician with a minimum of training may operate Cervus."

He snapped his fingers. Cramer shot him a look; his face was expressionless, but Jane knew that Cramer resented Carroad's arrogance.

Nevertheless, Cramer obeyed; he adjusted a dial, pushed down on a toggle switch, rotated another dial.

A voice, tonelessly and tinnily mechanical, issued from a loud-speaker beneath the tube. It repeated the phrase that Carroad had given and that Jane was thinking. It continued the repetition until Cramer, at another fingersnap from Carroad, flicked the toggle switch upward.

"As you have just heard," said Carroad triumphantly, "we have converted the waveforms into audible representations of what the subject is thinking."

The Secretary's brows rose like two caterpillars facing each other, and he said, "Very impressive."

But he managed to give the impression that he was thinking, Is that all?

Carroad smiled. He said, "I have much more. Something that, I'm sure, will please you very much. Now, as you know, this machine—my Cervus— is exposing hundreds of deviationists and enemy agents every year.

"Yet, this is *nothing!*"

He stared fiercely at them, but he had a slight smile on the corners of his lips. Jane, knowing him so well, could feel the radiance of his pride at the fact that the Secretary was leaning forward and his mouth was open.

"I say this is nothing! Catching traitors after they have become deviationist is locking the garage after the car has been stolen. What if we had a system of control whereby our citizens would be *unable* to be anything but unquestioningly loyal to the State?"

The Secretary said, "Aah!"

"I knew you would be far from indifferent," said Carroad.

Carroad pointed a finger downwards. Cramer, slowly, his jaws set, twisted the flexible neck of Cervus so that the pronged head pointed directly at Jane's distended stomach. He adjusted controls on the board. Immediately the oscilloscope danced with many intricate figures that were so different from the previous forms that even the untutored eyes of the Secretary could perceive the change.

"Citizens," said Carroad, "for some time after we'd discovered the rho waves in the adult and infant, we searched for their presence in the brain of the unborn child. We had no success for a long time. But that was not because the rho waves did not exist in the embryo. No, it was because we did not have delicate enough instruments. However, a few weeks ago, we succeeded in building one. I experimented upon my unborn child, and I detected weak traces of the rho waves. Thus, I demonstrated that the ability to form words is present, though in undeveloped form, even in the eight-month embryo.

"You're probably wondering what this means. This knowledge does not enable us to make the infant or the unborn speak any sooner. True. But what it does allow us to do is . . ."

Jane, who had been getting more tense with every word, became rigid. Would he allow this to be done to his own son, his own flesh and blood. Would he permit his child to become a half-robot, an obedient slave to the State, incapable in certain fields of wielding the power of free will? The factor that most marked men from the beasts and the machine?

Numbly, she knew he would.

". . . to probe well-defined areas in the undeveloped mind and there to stamp into it certain inhibitory paths. These inhibitions, preconditioned reflexes, as it were, will not, of course, take effect until the child has learned a language. And developed the concepts of citizen and State.

"But, once that is done, the correlation between the semantic waves and the inhibitions is such that the subject is unable to harbor any doubts about the teachings of the State. Or those who interpret the will of the State for its citizens.

"It is not necessary to perform any direct or physical surgery upon the unborn. The reflexes will be installed by Cervus III within a few minutes. As you see, Cervus cannot only receive; it can also transmit. Place a recording inside that receptacle beneath the speaker, actuate it, and, in a short time, you have traced in the grooves of the brain—if you will pardon an unscientific comparison—the voice of the State."

There was a silence. Jane and Cramer were unsuccessful in hiding their revulsion, but the others did not notice them. The Secretary and his bodyguards were staring at Carroad.

After several minutes, the Secretary broke the silence. "Doctor Carroad, are you sure that this treatment will not harm the creative abilities of the child? After all, we might make a first-class citizen, in the political sense, out of your child. Yet, we might wreck his potentialities as a first-class scientist. If we do that to our children, we lose out in the technological race. Not to mention the military. We need great generals, too."

"Absolutely not!" replied Carroad, so loudly and flatly that the Secretary was taken aback. "My computations, rechecked at least a dozen times, show there is no danger whatsoever. The only part of the brain affected, a very small area, has nothing to do with the creative functions. To convince you, I am going to perform the first operation upon my own son. Surely, I could do nothing more persuasive than that."

"Yes," said the Secretary, stroking his massive chin. "By the way, can this be done also to the adult?"

"Unfortunately, no," said Carroad.

"Then, we will have to wait a number of years to determine if your theory is correct. And, if we go ahead on the assumption that the theory is correct, and treat every unborn child in the country, we will have spent a tremendous amount of money and time. If you are not correct . . ."

"I can't be wrong!" said Carroad. His face began to flush, and he shook. Then, suddenly, his face was its normal color, and he was smiling.

Always in control, thought Jane. *Of himself and, if circumstances would allow, of everybody.*

"We don't have to build any extra machines," said Carroad. "A certain amount will be built, anyway, to detect traitors and enemies. These can be used in hospitals, when not in use elsewhere, to condition the unborn. Wait. I will show you how simple, inexpensive, and swift the operation is."

He gestured to Cramer. Cramer, the muscles twitching at the corners of his mouth, looked at Jane. His eyes tried desperately to tell her that he had to obey Carroad's orders. But, if he did, would he be understood, would he be forgiven?

Jane could only sit in the chair with a face as smooth and unmoving as a robot's and allow him to decide for himself without one sign of dissent or consent from her. What, after all, could either do unless they wished to die?

Cramer adjusted the controls.

Even though Jane knew she would feel nothing, she trembled as if a fist were poised to strike.

Bright peaks and valleys danced on the face of the oscilloscope. Carroad, watching them, gave orders to Cramer to move the prongs in minute spirals. When he had located the area he wished, he told Cramer to stop.

"We have just located the exact chain of neurons which are to be altered. You will hear nothing from the speaker because the embryo, of course, has no language. However, to show you some slight portion of Cervus' capabilities, Cramer will stimulate the area responsible for the rho waves before we begin the so-called inhibiting. Watch the 'scope. You'll see the waves go from a regular pulse into a wild dance."

The cyclopean eye of the oscilloscope became a field of crazed lines, leaping like a horde of barefooted and wire-thin fakirs on a bed of hot coals.

And a voice boomed out, *"Nu'sey! Nu'sey! Wanna d'ink!"*

Jane cried out, "God, what was that?"

The Secretary was startled; Cramer's face paled; Carroad was frozen.

But he recovered quickly, and he spoke sharply. "Cramer, you must have shifted the prongs so they picked up Jane's thoughts."

"I—I never touched them."

"Those were not my thoughts," said Jane.

"Something's wrong," said Carroad, needlessly. "Here. I'll do the adjusting."

He bent the prongs a fraction, checked the controls, and then turned the power on again.

The mechanical voice of Cervus spoke again.

"What do you mean? What're you saying? My father is not crazy! He's a great scientist, a hero of the State. What do you mean? Not any more?"

The Secretary leaped up from the chair and shouted above Cervus' voice, "What is this?"

Carroad turned the machine off and said, "I—I don't know."

Jane had never seen him so shaken.

"Well, find out! That's your business!"

Carroad's hand shook; one eye began to twitch. But he bent again to the adjustment of the dials. He directed the exceedingly narrow beam along the area from which the semantic waves originated. Only a high-pitched gabble emerged from the speaker, for Carroad had increased the speed. It was as if he were afraid to hear the normal rate of speech.

Jane's eyes began to widen. A thought was dawning palely, but horribly, on the horizon of her mind. If, by some intuition, she was just beginning to see the truth . . . But no, that could not be.

But, as Carroad worked, as the beam moved, as the power was raised or lowered, so did the voice, though always the same in tone and speed, change in phrase. Carroad had slowed the speed of detection, and individual words could be heard. And it was obvious that the age level of the speaker was fluctuating. Yet, throughout the swiftly leaping sentences, there was a sameness, an identity of personality. Sometimes, it was a baby just learning the language. At other times, it was an adolescent or young boy.

"Well, man, what is it?" bellowed the Secretary.

The mysterious voice had struck sparks off even his iron nerves.

Jane answered for her husband.

"I'll tell you what it is. It's the voice of my unborn son."

"Jane, you're insane!" said Carroad.

"No, I'm not, though I wish I were."

"God, he's at the window!" boomed the voice. *"And he has a knife! What can I do? What can I do?"*

"Turn that off until I get through talking," said Jane. "Then, you can listen again and see if what I'm saying isn't true."

Carroad stood like a statue, his hand extended towards the toggle switch but not reaching it. Cramer reached past him and flicked the switch.

"James," she said, speaking slowly and with difficulty. "You want to make robots out of everyone. Except, of course, yourself and the State's leaders. But what if I told you that you don't have to do that? That Nature and God or whatever you care to call the Creator, has anticipated you? And done so by several billion years?

"No don't look at me that way. You'll see what I mean. Now, look. The only one whose thoughts you could possibly have tapped is our son. Yet, it's impossible for an unborn baby to have a knowledge of speech. Nevertheless, you heard thoughts, originated by a boy, seeming to run from the first years of speech up to those of an adolescent. You have to admit that, even if you don't know what it means.

"Well, I do."

Tears running down her cheeks, choking, she said, "Maybe I see the truth where you don't because I'm closer to my baby. It's part of me. Oh, I know you'll say I'm talking like a silly woman. Maybe. Anyway, I think that what we've heard means that we—all of humanity without exception—*are* machines. Not steel and electrical robots, no, but still machines of flesh, engines whose behavior, motives, and very thoughts, conscious or unconscious, spring from the playing of protein tapes in our brains."

"What the hell are you talking about?" said Carroad.

"If I'm right, we are in hell," she said. "Through no fault or choice of ours. Listen to me before you shut your ears because you don't want to hear, can't hear.

"Memories are not recordings of what has happened in our past. Nor do we act as we will. We speak and behave according to our 'memories,' which are not recorded *after* the fact. They're recorded *before* the fact. Our actions are such because our memories tell us to do such. Each of us is set like a clockwork doll. Oh, not independently, but intermeshed, working together, synchronized as a masterclock or masterplan decrees.

"And, all this time, we think we are creatures of free will and chance. But we do not know there isn't such a thing as chance, that all is plotted and foretold, and we are sliding over the world, through time, in predetermined grooves. We, body and mind, are walking recordings. Deep within our cells, a molecular needle follows the grooves, and we follow the needle.

"Somehow, this experiment has ripped the cover from the machine, showed us the tape, stimulated it into working long before it was supposed to."

Suddenly, she began laughing. And, between laughing and gasping, she said, "What am I saying? It can't be an accident. If we have discovered that we're puppets, it's because we're supposed to do so."

"Jane, Jane!" said Carroad. "You're wild, wild! Foolish woman's intuition! You're supposed to be a scientist! Stop talking! Control yourself!"

The Secretary bellowed for silence, and, after a minute, succeeded. He said, "Mrs. Carroad, please continue. We'll get to the bottom of this."

He, too, was pale and wide-eyed. But he had not gotten to his position by refusing to attack.

She ordered Cramer to run the beam again over the previous areas. He was to speed up the process and slow down only when she so directed.

The result was a stream of unintelligibilities. Occasionally, when Cramer slowed Cervus at a gesture from Jane, it broke into a rate of speech they could understand. And, when it did, they trembled. They could not deny that they were speeding over the life thoughts of a growing male named James Carroad, Junior. Even at the velocity at which they traveled and the great jumps in time that the machine had to make in order to cover the track quickly, they could tell that.

After an hour, Jane had Cramer cut off the voice. In the silence, looking at the white and sweating men, she said, "We are getting close to the end? Should we go on?"

Hoarsely, the Secretary shouted, "This is a hoax! I can prove it must be! It's impossible! If we carry the seeds of predeterminism within us, and yet, as now, we discover how to foresee what we shall do, why can't we change the future?"

"I don't know, Mr. Secretary," said Jane. "We'll find out—in time. I can tell you this. If anyone is preset to foretell the future, he'll do so. If no one is, then the problem will go begging. It all depends on Whoever wound us up."

"That's blasphemy!" howled the Secretary, a man noted for his belligerent atheism. But he did not order the voice to stop after Jane told Cramer to start the machine up again.

Cramer ran Cervus at full speed. The words became a staccato of incomprehensibility; the oscilloscope, an almost solid blur. Flickers of blackness told of broad jumps forward, and then the wild intertwined lightning resumed.

Suddenly, the oscilloscope went blank, and the voice was silent.

Jane Carroad said, "Backtrack a little, Jason. And then run it forward at normal speed."

James Carroad had been standing before her, rigid, a figure seemingly made of white metal, his face almost as white as his uniform. Abruptly, he broke into fluidity and lurched out of the laboratory. His motions were broken; his shouts, broken also.

"Won't stay to listen . . . rot . . . mysticism . . . believe this . . . go insane! Mean . . . no control . . . no control . . ."

And his voice was lost as the door closed behind him.

Jane said, "I don't want to hear this, Jason. But . . ."

Instantly, the voice boomed, *"God, he's at the window! And he has a knife! What can I do? What can I do? Father, father, I'm your son! He knows it, he knows it, yet he's going to kill me. The window! He's breaking it! Oh, Lord, he's been locked up for nineteen years, ever since he shot and killed my mother and all those men and I was born a Caesarean and I didn't know he'd escape and still want to kill me, though they told me that's all he talked about, raving mad, and . . ."*

5. in the house of double minds

Robert Silverberg

There is a form of epilepsy in which abnormal electrical activity begins on one side of the brain and spreads to the other side, producing intense seizures. A technique for the reduction of such seizures involves cutting the corpus callosum, the bundle of fibers connecting the cerebral hemispheres of the brain. These split-brain patients can function almost normally; however, laboratory tests reveal some striking differences between the functions of the two hemispheres. The dominant, left hemisphere is specialized for language, logic, and mathematics. The nondominant, right hemisphere can only comprehend very simple language. However, it seems to have well-developed nonverbal abilities, such as spatial relations, patterning, and music.

In the normal person, the two hemispheres interact to produce integrated behavior. With the split-brain person, however, the two hemispheres may actually conflict. One example of this was seen during the assembly of a geometric puzzle. Here, the right hemisphere was superior, since the task involved spatial perception. When the split-brain person was instructed to put together the puzzle, the dominant left hemisphere attempted to do so using the right hand. However, progress was made only with the left hand, which is controlled by the right hemisphere. Then the right hand would take over and succeed in messing up the puzzle. It finally got to the point where the left hand would grab the right and try to prevent it from participating.

After a split-brain operation, patients may be said to possess two brains and even two separate "consciousnesses." For example, it appears that the

two hemispheres can experience two different emotions at the same time.
With Robert Silverberg, we enter a world in which normal children have
their brains split. They then learn to explore and exploit their new capaci-
ties to the fullest, with remarkable and sometimes tragic results. In the
house of double minds, you experience with the protagonist what it might
be like to have two brains.

Now they bring in the new ones, this spring's crop of ten-year-olds—six
boys, six girls—and leave them with me in the dormitory room that will be
their home for the next dozen years. The room is bare, austere, with black slate
floors and rough brick walls, furnished for the time being with cots and
clothes-cabinets and little more. The air is chill and the children, who are
naked, huddle in discomfort.

"I am Sister Mimise," I tell them. "I will be your guide and counselor in
the next twelve months of your new life in the House of Double Minds."

I have lived in this place for eight years, since I was fourteen, and this is
the fifth year that I have had charge of the new children. If I had not been
disqualified by my left-handedness, this is the year I would have been graduated into full oraclehood, but I try not to dwell on that. Caring for the children
is a rewarding task in itself. They arrive scrawny and frightened, and slowly
they unfold, they blossom, they ripen, they grow toward their destinies. Each
year there is some special one for me, some favorite, in whom I take particular
joy. In my first group, four years ago, it was long-legged, laughing Jen, she who
is now my lover. A year later it was soft beautiful Jalil, and then Timas, who
I thought would become one of the greatest of all oracles, but after two years
of training Timas cracked and was culled. And last year bright-eyed Runild,
impish Runild, my pet, my darling boy, more gifted even than Timas and, I
fear even less stable. I look at the new ones, wondering who will be special
among them for me this year.

The children are pale, slender, uneasy; their thin nude bodies look more
than naked because of their shaven skulls. As a result of what has been done
to their brains they move clumsily today. Their left arms often dangle as
though they have entirely forgotten them, and they tend to walk in a shuffling
sidewise motion, dragging their left legs a little. These problems soon will
disappear. The last of the operations in this group was performed only two
days ago, on the short, wide-shouldered girl whose breasts have already begun
to grow. I can see the narrow red line marking the place where the surgeon's
beam sliced through her scalp to sever the hemispheres of her brain.

"You have been selected," I say in a resonant formal tone, "for the highest
and most sacred office in our society. From this moment until you reach
adulthood your lives and energies will be consecrated to the purpose of attain-

ing the skills and wisdom an oracle must have. I congratulate you on having come so far."

And I envy you.

I do not say that part aloud.

I feel envy and pity both. I have seen the children come and go, come and go. Out of each year's dozen, one or two usually die along the way of natural causes or accidents. At least three go insane under the terrible pressure of the disciplines and have to be culled. So only about half the group is likely to complete the twelve years of training, and most of those will prove to have little value as oracles. The useless ones will be allowed to remain, of course, but their lives will be meaningless. The House of Double Minds has been in existence for more than a century; there are at present just one hundred forty-two oracles in residence, seventy-seven women and sixty-five men, of whom all but about forty are mere drones. A thin harvest out of some twelve hundred novices since the beginning.

These children have never met before. I call upon them to introduce themselves. They give their names in low, self-conscious voices, eyes downcast. A boy named Divvan asks, "Will we wear clothes soon?"

Their nakedness disturbs them. They hold their thighs together and stand at odd storklike angles, keeping apart from one another, trying to conceal their undeveloped loins. They do this because they are strangers. They will forget their shame before long. As the months pass they will become closer than brothers and sisters.

"Robes will be issued this afternoon," I tell him. "But clothing ought not to be important here, and you need have no reason to wish to hide your bodies." Last year when this same point arose—it always does—the mischievous boy Runild suggested that I remove my own robe as a gesture of solidarity. Of course I did, but it was a mistake; the sight of a mature woman's body was more troubling to them than even their own bareness.

Now it is the time for the first exercises, so that they may learn the ways in which the brain operation has altered the responses of their bodies. At random I choose a girl named Hirole and ask her to step forward, while the rest form a circle around her. She is tall and fragile-looking and it must be torment to her to be aware of the eyes of all the others upon her.

Smiling, I say gently, "Raise your hand, Hirole."

She raises one hand.

"Bend your knee."

As she flexes her knee, there is an interruption. A wiry naked boy scrambles into the room, fast as a spider, wild as a monkey, and bursts into the middle of the circle, shouldering Hirole aside. Runild again! He is a strange and moody and extraordinarily intelligent child, who, now that he is in his second year at the House, has lately been behaving in a reckless, unpredictable way. He runs around the circle, seizing several of the new children briefly, putting his face close to theirs, staring with crazy intensity into their eyes. They are terrified of him. For a moment I am too astonished to move. Then I go to him and seize him.

He struggles ferociously. He spits at me, hisses, claws my arms, makes thick wordless grunting sounds. Gradually I get control of him. In a low voice I say, "What's wrong with you, Runild? You know you aren't supposed to be in here!"

"Let me go."

"Do you want me to report this to Brother Sleel?"

"I just want to see the new ones."

"You're frightening them. You'll be able to meet them in a few days, but you're not allowed to upset them now." I pull him toward the door. He continues to resist and nearly breaks free. Eleven-year-old boys are amazingly strong, sometimes. He kicks my thigh savagely: I will have purple bruises tonight. He tries to bite my arm. Somehow I get him out of the room, and in the corridor he suddenly goes slack and begins to tremble, as though he has had a fit that now is over. I am trembling too. Hoarsely I say, "What's happening to you, Runild? Do you want to be culled the way Timas and Jurda were? You can't keep doing things like this! You—"

He looks up at me, wild-eyed, and starts to say something, and stifles it, and turns and bolts. In a moment he is gone, a brown naked streak vanishing down the hallway. I feel a great sadness: Runild was a favorite of mine, and now he is going insane, and they will have to cull him. I should report the incident immediately, but I am unable to bring myself to do it, and, telling myself that my responsibility lies with the new ones, I return to the dorm room.

"Well!" I say briskly, as if nothing unusual had happened. "He's certainly playful today, isn't he! That was Runild. He's a year ahead of you. You'll meet him and the rest of his group a little later. Now, Hirole—"

The children, preoccupied with their own altered state, quickly grow calm; they seem much less distressed by Runild's intrusion than I am. Shakily I begin again, asking Hirole to raise a hand, to flex a knee, to close an eye. I thank her and call a boy named Mulliam into the center of the circle. I ask him to raise one shoulder above the other, to touch his hand to his cheek, to make a fist. Then I pick a girl named Fyme and instruct her to hop on one foot, to put an arm behind her back, to kick one leg in the air.

I say, "Who can tell me one thing that was true of every response?"

Several of them answer at once, "It was always the right side! The right eye, the right hand, the right leg—"

"Correct." I turn to a small, dark-visaged boy named Bloss and ask, "Why is that? Do you think it's just coincidence?"

"Well," he says, "everybody here is right-handed, because left-handers aren't allowed to become oracles, and so everybody tended to use the side that he—"

Bloss falters, seeing heads shaking all around the circle.

Galaine, the girl whose breasts have begun to sprout, says, "It's because of the operation! The right side of our brains doesn't understand words very well, and it's the Right that controls the left side of the body, so when you tell us in words to do something, only our Left understands and moves the muscles it controls. It gets the jump on the Right because the Right can't speak or be spoken to."

"Very good, Galaine. That's it exactly."

I let it sink in. Now that the connections between the two halves of their brains have been cut, the Rights of these children are isolated, unable to draw on the skills of the language center in the Left. They are only now realizing what it means to have half a brain rendered illiterate and inarticulate, to have their Left respond as though it is the entire brain, activating only the muscles it controls most directly.

Fyme says, "Does that mean we won't ever be able to use our left sides again?"

"Not at all. Your Right isn't paralyzed or helpless. It just isn't very good at using words. So your Left is quicker to react when I give a verbal instruction. But if the instruction isn't phrased in words, the Right will be able to take control and respond."

"How can you give an instruction that isn't in words?" Mulliam asks.

"In many ways," I say. "I could draw a picture, or make a gesture, or use some sort of symbol. I'll show you what I mean by going through the exercises again. Sometimes I'll give the instructions in words, and sometimes by acting them out. When I do that, imitate what you see. Is that clear?"

I wait a moment to allow the sluggish word-skills of their Rights to grasp the scheme.

Then I say, "Raise a hand."

They lift their right arms. When I tell them to bend a knee, they bend their right knees. But when I wordlessly close my left eye, they imitate me and close their left eyes. Their Rights are able to exert muscular control in a normal way when the instructions are delivered nonverbally; but when I use words, the Left alone perceives and acts.

I test the ability of their Lefts to override the normal motor functions of their Rights by instructing them verbally to raise their left shoulders. Their Rights, baffled by my words, take no action, forcing their Lefts to reach beyond a Left's usual sphere of dominance. Slowly, with great difficulty, a few of the children manage to raise their left shoulders. Some can manage only a mere twitch. Fyme, Bloss, and Mulliam, with signs of struggle evident on their faces, are unable to budge their left shoulders at all. I tell the entire group to relax, and the children collapse in relief, sprawling on their cots. There is nothing to worry about, I say. In time they will all regain full motor functions in both halves of their bodies. Unless they are driven insane by the split-brain phenomena, that is, but no need to tell them that.

"One more demonstration for today," I announce. This one will show them in another way how thoroughly the separation of the hemispheres affects the mental processes. I ask Gybold, the smallest of the boys, to seat himself at the testing table at the far end of the room. There is a screen mounted on the table; I tell Gybold to fix his eyes on the center of the screen, and I flash a picture of a banana on the left side of the screen for a fraction of a second.

"What do you see, Gybold?"

"I don't see anything, Sister Mimise," he replies, and the other children gasp. But the "I" that is speaking is merely Gybold's Left, which gets its visual information through his right eye; that eye did indeed see nothing. Meanwhile Gybold's Right is answering my question in the only way it can: the boy's left hand gropes among several objects lying on the table hidden behind the screen, finds the banana that is there, and triumphantly holds it up. Through sight and touch Gybold's Right has prevailed over its wordlessness.

"Excellent," I say. I take the banana from him and, drawing his left hand behind the screen where he is unable to see it, I put a drinking-glass into it. I ask him to name the object in his hand.

"An apple?" he ventures. I frown, and quickly he says, "An egg? A pencil?"

The children laugh. Mulliam says, "He's just guessing!"

"Yes, he is. But which part of Gybold's brain is making the guesses?"

"His Left," Galaine cries. "But it's the Right that knows it's holding a glass."

They all shush her for giving away the secret. Gybold pulls his hand out from under the screen and stares at the glass, silently forming its name with his lips.

I put Herik, Chith, Simi, and Clane through related experiments. Always the results are the same. If I flash a picture to the right eye or put an object in the right hand, the children respond normally, correctly naming it. But if I transmit information only to the left eye or the left hand, they are unable to use words to describe the objects their Rights see or feel.

It is enough for now. The children are silent and have withdrawn into individual spheres of privacy. I know that they are working things out within their minds, performing small self-devised experiments, testing themselves, trying to learn the full extent of the changes the operation has brought about. They glance from one hand to another, flex fingers, whisper little calculations. They should not be allowed to look inward so much, not at the beginning. I take them to the storeroom to receive their new clothing, the simple gray monastic robes that we wear to set us apart from the ordinary people of the city. Then I turn them free, sending them romping into the broad fields of soft green grass behind the dormitory, to relax and play. They may be oracles in the making; but they are also, after all, ten-year-old children.

It is my afternoon rest period. On my way through the dark cool corridors to my chamber I am stopped by Brother Sleel, one of the senior oracles. He is a white-haired man, tall and of powerful build, and his blue eyes work almost independently of one another. Constantly scanning his surroundings in restless separate searches. Sleel has never been anything but warm and kind to me, and yet I have always been afraid of him, I suppose more out of awe for his office than out of fear for the man himself. Really I feel timid with all the oracles, knowing that their minds work differently from mine and that they see things in me that I may not see myself. Sleel says, "I saw you having difficulties with Runild in the hall this morning. What was happening?"

"He wandered into my orientation meeting. I asked him to leave."

"What was he doing?"

"He said he wanted to see the new children. But of course I couldn't let him bother them."

"And he started to fight with you?"

"He made some trouble. Nothing much."

"He was fighting with you, Mimise."

"He was rather unruly," I admit.

Sleel's left eye stares into mine. I feel a chill. It is the oracle-eye, the all-seeing one. Quietly he says, "I saw you fighting with him."

I look away from him. I study my bare feet. "He wouldn't leave. He was frightening the new ones. When I tried to lead him from the room he jumped at me, yes. But he didn't hurt me and it was all over in a moment. Runild is high-spirited, Brother."

"Runild is a troubled child," Sleel says heavily. "He is disturbed. He is becoming wild, like a beast."

"No, Brother Sleel." How can I face that terrible eye? "He has extraordinary gifts. You know—surely you must know—that it takes time for one like him to settle down, to come to terms with—"

"I've had complaints from his counselor, Voree. She says she hardly knows how to handle him."

"It's only a phase. Voree's had responsibility for him only a couple of weeks. As soon as she—"

"I know you want to protect him, Mimise. But don't let your love for the boy cloud your judgment. I think this is Timas happening all over again. It's an old, old pattern here, the brilliant novice who is unable to cope with his changes, who—"

"Are you going to cull him?" I blurt.

Sleel smiles. He takes both my hands in his. I am engulfed by his strength, by his wisdom, by his power. I sense the unfathomable flow of perception from his mystic right to his calm, analytic Left. He says, "If Runild gets any worse, I'll have to. But I want to save him. I like the boy. I respect his potential. What do you suggest we do, Mimise?"

"What do *I*—"

"Tell me. Advise me."

The senior oracle is playing a little game with me, I suppose. Shrugging, I say, "Obviously Runild's trying to gain attention through all these crazy pranks. Let's try to reach him and find out what he really wants, and perhaps there'll be some way we can give it to him. I'll speak to Voree. I'll talk to his sister, Kitrin. And tomorrow I'll talk to Runild. I think he trusts me. We were very close last year, Runild and I."

"I know," Sleel says gently. "Very well; see what you can do."

Still later that afternoon, as I cross the central courtyard, Runild erupts from the second-year house and rushes up to me. His face is flushed, his bare chest is shiny with sweat. He clings to me, pulls me down to this height, looks me in the eye. His eyes have already begun to stray a little; one day they may be like Sleel's.

I think he wants to apologize for his invasion of my group. But all he manages to say is: "I am sorry for you. You wanted so much to be one of us." And he runs off.

To be one of them. Yes. Who does not long to dwell in the House of Double Minds, living apart from the noise and chaos of the world, devoting oneself to oracular contemplation and the service of mankind? My mother's father's sister was of that high company, and in early girlhood I was taken to visit her. How awesome it was to stand in the presence of her all-knowing Right, to feel the flood of warmth and understanding that emanated from her wise eyes. It was my dream to join her here, a dream doubly thwarted, for she died when I was eight, and by then the fact of my left-handedness was irremediably established.

Left-handers are never selected to undergo the oracle-making operation. The two halves of our brains are too symmetrical, too ambidextrous: we have speech centers on both sides, most of us left-handers, and so we are not likely to develop those imbalances of cerebral powers that oracles must have. Right-handers, too, are born with symmetrically functioning brains, each hemisphere developing independently and duplicating the operations of the other. But by the time they are two years old, their Lefts and Rights are linked in a way that gives them a shared pool of skills, and therefore each half is free to develop its own special capabilities, since the gifts of one half are instantly available to the other.

At the age of ten this specializing process is complete. Language, sequential thought, all the analytic and rational functions, center in the Left. Spacial perception, artistic vision, musical skill, emotional insight, center in the Right. The brain's left side is the scientist, the architect, the general, the mathematician. The brain's right side is the minstrel, the sculptor, the visionary, the dreamer. Normally the two halves operate as one. The Right experiences a flash of poetic intuition, the Left clothes it in words. The Right sees a pattern of fundamental connections, the Left expresses it in a sequence of theorems. The Right conceives the shape of a symphony, the Left sets the notes down on paper. Where there is true harmony between the hemispheres of the brain, works of genius are created.

Too often, though, one side seizes command. Perhaps the Right becomes dominant, and we have a dancer, an athlete, an artist, who has trouble with words, who is inexpressive and inarticulate except through some nonverbal medium. More often, because we are a word-worshipping people, it is the Left that rules, choking the subordinate Right in a welter of verbal analysis and commentary, slowing and hindering the spontaneous intuitive perceptions of the mind. What society gains in orderliness and rationality it loses in vision and grace. We can do nothing about these imbalances—except to take advantage of their existence by accentuating and exploiting them.

And so the children come here, a dozen of our best each year, and our surgeons sever the isthmus of neural tissue that links Left and Right. Some kind of communication between the hemispheres continues to operate, since each half remains aware of what the other is immediately experiencing, if not of its accumulated memories and skills. But the Right is cut free from the tyranny of the word-intoxicated Left. The Left continues to operate its normal routines of reading and writing and conversation and computation, while the Right, now its own master, observes and registers and analyzes in a way that has no need of words. Because its verbal skills are so feeble, the newly independent Right must find some other means of expression if it is to make its perceptions known; and, through the dozen years of training in the House of Double Minds, some of the children succeed in achieving this. They are able —I do not know how, no one who is not an oracle can ever know how—to transmit the unique insights of fully mature and wholly independent Rights to their Lefts, which can transmit them to the rest of us. It is a difficult and imperfect process; but it gives us access to levels of knowledge that few have ever reached before our time. Those who master that skill are our functional oracles. They dwell in realms of beauty and wisdom that, in the past, only saints and prophets and the greatest artists and a few madmen have reached.

I would, if I could, have entered those realms. But I came forth left-handed from the womb and my brain, though it is a decent one, therefore lacked the required asymmetry of function. If I could not be an oracle I could at least serve them, I decided. And thus I came here as a girl, and asked to be of use, and in time was given the important task of easing the new children into their new lives. So I have come to know Jen and Timas and Jalil and Runild and the others, some of whom will live to be among the most famous of oracles, and so now I welcome Hirole and Mulliam and Gybold and Galaine and their companions. And I am content, I think. I am content.

We gather in the main hall for the evening meal. My new group has not come before the older novices until now, and so my twelve undergo close scrutiny, which they find embarrassing, as I lead them to their place. Each year-group sits together at its own circular table. My dozen dine with me; at the table to my left is my group of last year, now in Voree's charge. Runild sits there with his back to me, and his mere presence creates a tension in me as if he is giving off an electric radiation. To my right is the third-year group, reduced now to nine by the culling of Timas and two deaths; the fourth-year children are just in front of me and the fifth-year ones, my darling Jen among them, at my rear. The older children are in the center of the hall. Along the sides of the great room are the tables of the instructors, those who have daily care of the ordinary education of the twelve groups of novices, and the senior oracles occupy long tables at the hall's far end, beneath a panoply of gay red and green banners.

Sleel makes a brief speech of welcome for my twelve and the meal is served.

I send Galaine to Voree's table with a note: *"See me on the porch after dinner."*

My appetite is poor. I finish quickly, but I stay with my group until it is time to dismiss them. All the children troop off to the auditorium for a show. A warm drizzle is falling; Voree and I stand in the shelter of the eaves. She is much older than I am, a stocky woman with kinky orange hair. Year after year I pass my fledglings on to her. She is strong, efficient, stolid, insensitive. Runild baffles her. "He's like a monkey," she says. "Running around naked, chattering to himself, singing crazy songs, playing pranks. He isn't doing his lessons. He isn't even doing his disciplines, half the time. I've warned him he'll be culled, but he doesn't seem to care."

"What do you think he wants?"

"To have everyone notice him."

"Yes, surely, but *why?*"

"Because he's a naturally mischievous boy," Voree says, scowling. "I've seen many of his sort before. They think rules are for other people. Two more weeks of this and I'll recommend a cull."

"He's too brilliant to waste like that, Voree."

"He's wasting himself. Without the disciplines how can he become an oracle? And he's upsetting all the others. My group's a shambles. Now he's bothering yours. He won't leave his sister alone either. Culling, Mimise, that's where he's heading. Culling."

There is nothing to be gained from talking to Voree. I join my group in the auditorium.

Bedtime for the younger ones comes early. I see my children to their room; then I am free until midnight. I return to the auditorium, where the older children and the off-duty staff are relaxing, playing games, dancing, drifting off in couples. Kitrin, Runild's sister, is still there. I draw her aside. She is a slender, delicate girl of fourteen, a fifth-year novice. I am fond of her because she was in my very first group, but I have always found her shy, elusive, opaque. She is more so than ever now; I question her about her brother's behavior and she answers me with shrugs, vague unfinished sentences, and artful evasions. Runild is wild? Well, of course, many boys are wild, she says, especially the bright ones. The disciplines seem to bore him. He's far ahead of his group—you know that, Mimise. And so on. I get nothing from her except the strong feeling that she is hiding something about her brother. My attempts to probe all fail; Kitrin is still a child, but she is halfway to oracle-hood, nearly, and that gives her an advantage over me in any duel of wits. Only when I suggest that Runild is in immediate peril of culling do I break through her defenses.

"No!" she gasps, eyes widening in fear, cheeks turning pale. "They mustn't! He has to stay! He's going to be greater than any of them!"

"He's causing too much trouble."

"It's just a thing he's going through. He'll settle down, I promise you that."

"Voree doesn't think so. She's going to request a cull."

"No. No. What will happen to him if he's culled? He was *meant* to be an oracle. His whole life will have been thrown away. We have to save him, Mimise."

"We can do that only if he can control himself."

"I'll talk to him in the morning," Kitrin says.

I wonder what she knows about Runild that she does not want to tell me.

At the evening's end I bring Jen to my chamber, as I do three or four nights a week. She is tall and supple and looks more than her fourteen years. Her counselor tells me she is moving well through her mid-novitiate and will be a splendid oracle. We lie together, lips to lips, breasts against breasts, and we stroke and caress and tickle one another, we smile with our eyes, we enter into all the rituals of love. Afterward, in the stillness that follows passion, she finds the bruise of this morning's struggle on my thigh and questions me with a frown. "Runild," I say. I tell her about his erratic behavior, about Sleel's uneasiness, about my conversation with Voree.

"They mustn't cull him," Jen says solemnly. "I know he's troublesome. But the path he's taking is so important for all of us."

"Path? What path is that?"

"You don't know?"

"I know nothing, Jen."

She catches her breath, rolls away, studies me a moment. At length she says, "Runild sees into minds. When he puts his head very close to people, there's transmission. Without using words. It's—it's a kind of broadcast. His Right can read the Rights of other oracles, the way you'd open a book and read it. If he could get close enough to Sleel, say, or any of them, he could read what's in their Rights."

"What?"

"More, Mimise. His own Right talks to his Left the same way. He can transmit messages completely, quickly, making better contact between the halves than any of the oracles can do. He hasn't had the disciplines, even, and he has full access to his Right's perceptions. So whatever his Right sees, including what it gets from the Rights of others, can be transmitted to his Left and expressed in words more clearly even than Sleel himself can do it!"

"I don't believe this," I say, barely comprehending.

"It's true! It's true, Mimise! He's only just learning how, and it gets him terribly excited, it makes him wild, don't you see, when all that contact comes flooding in? He can't quite handle it yet, which is why he acts so strange. But once he gets his power under control—"

"How do you know anything about this, Jen?"

"Why, Kitrin told me."

"Kitrin? I spoke to Kitrin and she never even hinted that—"

"Oh," Jen says, looking pained. "Oh, I guess I wasn't supposed to say. Not even to you, I guess. Oh, now I'll be in trouble with Kitrin, and—"

"You won't be. She doesn't need to know how I found out. But—Jen, Jen, can this be? Can anyone have such powers?"

"Runild does."

"So he claims. Or Kitrin claims on his behalf."

"No," Jen says firmly. "He *does*. They showed me, he and Kitrin. I felt him touch my mind. I felt him read me. He can read anyone. He can read *you*, Mimise."

I must speak with Runild. But carefully, carefully, everything in its proper moment. In the morning I must first meet with my group and take them through the second-day exercises. These are designed to demonstrate that their Rights, although mute and presently isolated, are by no means inferior, and have perceptions and capabilities which in some ways are superior to those of their Lefts.

"Never think of your Right as a cripple," I warn them. "See it, rather, as some kind of extremely intelligent animal—an animal that is sharp-witted, quick to respond, imaginative, with only one flaw, that it has no vocabulary and is never going to be able to acquire more than a few simple words at best. Nobody pities a tiger or an eagle because it doesn't know how to speak. And there are ways of training tigers and eagles so that we can communicate with them without using words."

I flash a picture of a house on the screen and ask the children to copy it, first using their left hands, then the right. Although they are all right-handed, they are unable to draw anything better than simple, crude two-dimensional representations with their right hands. Their left-handed drawings, while shakily drawn because of their left arms' relatively backward muscular development and motor control, show a full understanding of the techniques of perspective. The right hand has the physical skill, but it is the left, drawing on the vision of the brain's right hemisphere, that has the artistic ability.

I ask them to arrange colored plastic cubes to match an intricate pattern on the screen. Left-handed, they carry out the exercise swiftly and expertly. Right-handed, they become confused, frown and bite their lips, hold the cubes long moments without knowing where to put them down, eventually array the cubes in chaotic mazes. Clane and Bloss give up entirely in a minute or two; Mulliam perserveres grimly like one who is determined to climb a mountain too steep for his strength, but he accomplishes little; Luabet's left hand keeps darting across to do the task that is beyond the right's powers, as if she is at war with herself. She must keep the impatient left hand behind her back in order to proceed at all. No one can complete the block design correctly with the right hand, and when I allow the children to work with both hands the hands fight for control, the formerly dominant right one unable to accept its new inferiority and angrily slapping at the cubes the left one tries to put in place.

We go on to the split-screen exercises in facial recognition and pattern analysis, to the musical exercises, and the rest of the usual second-day routine. The children are fascinated by the ease with which their Rights function in all but word-linked operations. Ordinarily I am delighted too, to watch the newly liberated Rights come to life and assert their powers. But today I am impatient to be off to Runild and I give only perfunctory attention to my proper work.

At last the session ends. The children move off to the classroom where they will receive regular school-subject instruction. Runild's group, too, should be at school until noon. Possibly I can draw him aside after lunch. But, as though I have conjured him with a wish, I see him now, tumbling by himself in the meadow of crimson flowers by the auditorium. He sees me, too; halts in his gambol, winks, smiles, does a handspring, blows me a kiss. I go to him.

"Are you excused from classes this morning?" I ask, mock-stern.

"The flowers are so pretty," he replies.

"The flowers will be just as pretty after school."

"Oh, don't be so stuffy, Mimise! I know my lessons. I'm a clever boy."

"Perhaps too clever, Runild."

He grins. I do not frighten him. He seems to be patronizing me; he appears to be at once very much younger and very much wiser than his years. I take him gently by the wrist and draw him down, easily, until we are sprawled side by side in the grass. He plucks a flower for me. His look is flirtatious. I accept both the flower and the look and respond with a warm smile; I am flirtatious myself. No doubt of his charm; and I can never win him by acting as an authority-figure, only as a co-conspirator. There was always an underlying sexuality in our relationship, incestuous, as if I were an older sister.

We talk in banter, teasing each other. Then I say, "Something mysterious has been happening to you lately, Runild. I know that. Share your mystery with me."

At first he denies all. He pretends innocence, but lets me know it is only pretense. His sly smile betrays him. He speaks in cryptic ellipses, hinting at arcane knowledge and defying me to pry details from him. I play his game, acting now intrigued, now eager, now skeptical, now wholly uninterested; we are stalking one another, and both of us know it. His oracle-eye pierces me. He toys with me with such subtlety that I must remind myself, with a glance at his slim hairless body, that I am dealing with a child. I ought never forget that he is only eleven. Finally I press directly once more, asking him outright what strange new gift he is cultivating.

"Wouldn't you like to know!" he cries, and pulls an outrageous face, and dashes away.

But he comes back. We talk on a more serious level. He admits that he has discovered, these past few months, that he is different from the other children and from the senior oracles, that he has a talent, a power. It disturbs and exalts him both. He is still exploring the scope of it. He will not describe the power in any specific way. Of course I know from Jen its nature, but I prefer not to reveal that. "Will you ever tell me?" I ask.

"Not today," he says.

Gradually I win his trust. We meet casually, in corridors or courtyards, and exchange easy pleasantries, the sort I might trade with any of my former charges. He is testing me, seeing whether I am a friend or simply Sleel's spy. I let him know of my concern for him. I let him know that his eccentric behavior has placed him in jeopardy of culling.

"I suppose so," he says gloomily. "But what can I do? I'm not like the others. I can't sit still for long. Things are jumping inside my head all the time. Why should I bother with arithmetic when I can—"

He halts, suddenly guarded again.

"When you can what, Runild?"

"*You* know."

"I don't."

"You will. Soon enough."

There are days when he seems calm. But his pranks have not ended. He finds poor Sister Sestoine, one of the oldest and dimmest of the oracles, and puts his forehead against hers and does something to her that sends her into an hour's tears. Sestoine will not say what took place during that moment of contact, and after a while she seems to forget the episode. Sleel's face is dark. He looks warningly at me as if to say, *Time's running short; the boy must go.*

On a day of driving rain I am in my chamber in mid-afternoon when Runild unexpectedly enters soaked, hair plastered to his scalp. Puddles drip from him. He strips and I rub him with my towel and stand him before the fire. He says nothing all this while; he is tense, taut, as if a mighty pressure is building within him and the time has not yet come for its release. Abruptly he turns to me. His eyes are strange; they wander, they quiver, they glow. "Come close!" he whispers hoarsely, like a man calling a woman to his bed. He grasps my shoulders, he pulls me down to his height, he pushes his blazing forehead roughly against mine. And the world changes. I see tongues of purple flame. I see crevasses opening in the earth. I see the oceans engulfing the shore. I am flooded with contact; I am swept with wild energies.

I know what it is to be an oracle.

My Right and my Left are asunder. It is not like having one brain cleft in two; it is like having two brains independent, equal. I feel them ticking like two clocks, with separate beats; and the Left goes tick-tock-tick-tock, machine-dreary, while the Right leaps and dances and soars and sings in lunatic rhythms. But they are not lunatic rhythms, for their frantic pulses have a regularity of irregularity, a pattern of patternlessness. I grow used to the strangeness; I become comfortable within both brains, the Left which I think of as "me," and the right which is "me" too, but an altered and unfamiliar self without a name. My earliest memories lie open to me in my Right. I see into a realm of shadows. I am an infant again; I have access to the first hours of my life, to all of my first years, those years in which words meant nothing to me. The preverbal data all rests within my Right, shapes and textures and odors and sounds, and I do not need to give names to anything, I do not need to denote or analyze, I need only feel, experience, relive. All that is there is clear and sharp. I see how it has always been with me, how that set of recorded experiences has directed my behavior even as the experiences of later years have done so. I can reach that hidden realm now, and understand it, and use it.

I feel the flow of data from Right to Left—the wordless responses, the intuitive reactions, the quick spontaneous awareness of structures. The world holds new meaning for me. I think, but not in words, and I tell myself things, but not in words, and my Left, groping and fumbling (for it has not had the disciplines) seeks words, sometimes finding them, to express what I am giving it. So that is what oracles do. This is what they feel. This is the knowledge they have. I am transfigured. It is my fantasy come true; they have snipped that rubbery band of connective tissue, they have set free my Right, they have made me one of them. And I will never again be what once I was. I will think in tones and colors now. I will explore kingdoms unknown to the word-bound ones. I will live in a land of music. I will not merely speak and write; I will feel and know.

Only it is fading now.

The power is leaving me. I had it only a moment, and was it my own power or only a glimpse of Runild's? I cling, I grapple, and yet it goes, it goes, it goes, and I am left with shreds and bits, and then not even those, only an aftertaste, an echo of an echo, a diminishing shaft of feeble light. My eyes open. I am on my knees; sweat covers my body; my heart is pounding. Runild stands above me. "You see now?" he says. "You see? This is what it's like for me all the time. I can connect minds. *I can make connections, Mimise.*"

"Do it again," I beg.

He shakes his head. "Too much will hurt you," he says. And goes from me.

I have told Sleel what I have learned. Now they have the boy with them in the inner oracle-house, nine of them, the highest oracles, questioning him, testing him. I do not see how they can fail to welcome his gift, to give him special honor, to help him through his turbulent boyhood so that he can take his place supreme among oracles. But Jen thinks otherwise. She thinks he distresses them by scrabbling at their minds in his still unfocused attempts at making contact, and that they will fear him once they have had an explicit demonstration of what he can do; she thinks, too, that he is a threat to their authority, for his way of joining the perceptions of his Right to the analytic powers of his Left by a direct mental flow is far superior to their own laborious method of symbolic translation. Jen thinks they will surely cull him and may even put him to death. How can I believe such things? She is not yet an oracle herself; she is still a girl; she may be wrong. The conference continues, hour after hour, and no one emerges from the oracle-house.

In the evening they come forth. The rain has stopped. I see the senior oracles march across the courtyard. Runild is among them, very small at Sleel's side. There are no expressions on any faces. Runild's eyes meet mine; his look is blank, unreadable. Have I somehow betrayed him in trying to save him? What will happen to him? The procession reaches the far side of the quadrangle. A car is waiting. Runild and two of the senior oracles get into it.

After dinnner Sleel calls me aside, thanks me for my help, tells me that Runild is to undergo study by experts at an institute far away. His power of mind-contact is so remarkable, says Sleel, that it requires prolonged analysis.

Mildly I ask whether it would not have been better to keep him here, among the surroundings that have become home to him, and let the experts come to the House of Double Minds to examine him. Sleel shakes his head. There are many experts, the testing equipment is not portable, the tests will be lengthy.

I wonder if I will ever see Runild again.

In the morning I meet with my group at the usual time. They have lived here several weeks now, and their early fears are gone from them. Already I see the destinies unfolding: Galaine is fastwitted but shallow, Mulliam and Chith are plodders, Fyme and Hirole and Divvan may have the stuff of oracles, the rest are mediocrities. An average group. Hirole, perhaps, is becoming my favorite. There are no Jens among them, no Runilds.

"Today we start to examine the idea of nonverbal words," I begin. "For example, if we say, Let this green ball stand for the word 'same,' and this blue box stand for the word 'different,' then we can—"

My voice drones on. The children listen placidly. So the training proceeds in the House of Double Minds. Beneath the vault of my skull my dreaming right throbs a bit, as though reliving its moment of freedom. Through the corridors outside the room the oracles move, deep in contemplation, shrouded in impenetrable wisdom, and we who serve them go obediently about our tasks.

6. all the sounds of the rainbow

Norman Spinrad

Synesthesia is the phenomenon of experiencing a sensory event as a combination of sensory signals. A person with this ability (a "synesthete") may go through life perceiving tones in color and form, names that glow in the dark, voices in ugly or beautiful colors. While this phenomenon is rare in Western culture, it seems more prevalent in primitive tribes.

At present, we do not know why some people have synesthesia. There is some evidence that it may be partially hereditary. It also appears that everyone has some synesthetic ability. There is a much higher percentage of synesthesia among children than adults. It may be that children learn not to be synesthetic due to the demands of society. Just as hallucinogenic drugs may impair driving, synesthesia might lead to problems in areas such as sports. For example, an infielder who sees dark images at the crack of a bat may have a baseball bounce off his nose. Given enough punishment of this type, synesthesia would gradually be suppressed as the child grows older. With training, however, perhaps children could retain or improve their synesthetic ability. But would we want to do this? Before you answer, read Spinrad's story, noting the advantages and disadvantages.

In our drug-taking society, many people alter their states of consciousness in myriad ways. Despite legal and/or health hazards, the use of alcohol, marijuana, LSD, and other drugs is widespread. So what would happen if one could learn to produce synesthesias at will? What would happen to the newly created "synesthesia addict"? What price would one pay to experience "all the sounds of the rainbow"? And finally, how does this story relate to the problems of drug use in our society?

Now let's take a trip with Norman Spinrad and share the inner world of the synesthete, a land where one ". . . can taste the wine of her hand on his arm" and see words emerge as "brightly colored tropical butterflies."

Harry Krell sprawled in a black vinyl beanbag chair near the railing of the rough-hewn porch. Five yards below, the sea crashed and rumbled against convoluted black rocks that looked like a fallen shower of meteors half-buried in the warm Pacific sand. He was naked from the waist up; a white sarong fell to his shins, and he wore custom-made horsehide sandals. He was well-muscled in a fortyish way, deeply tanned, and had the long, neat, straight yellow hair of a beach-bum. His blue eyes almost went with the beach-bum image: clear, empty, but shattered-looking, like marbles that had been carefully cracked with a ballpeen hammer.

As phony as a Southern California guru, Bill Marvin thought as he stepped out into the sunlit porch. Which he is. Nevertheless, Marvin shuddered as those strange eyes swept across him like radar antennae, cold, expressionless instruments gathering their private spectrum of data. "Sit down," Krell said. "You sound awful over there."

Marvin gingerly lowered the seat of his brown suede pants to the edge of an aluminum-and-plastic beachchair and stared at Krell with cold gray eyes set in a smooth angular face perfectly framed by medium-length, razor-cut, artfully styled brown hair. He had no intention of wasting any more time on this oily con-man than was absolutely necessary. "I'll come right to the point, Krell," he said. "You detach yourself from Karen your way, or I'll get it done my way."

"Karen's her own chick," Krell said. "She's not even your wife any more." A jet from Vandenburg suddenly roared overhead; Krell winced and rubbed at his eyes.

"But I'm still paying her a thousand a month in alimony, and I'll play pretty dirty before I'll stand by and watch half of that go into your pockets."

Krell smiled, and a piece of chalk seemed to scratch down a blackboard in Marvin's mind. "You can't do a thing about it," he said.

"I can stop paying."

"And get dragged into court ."

"And tell the judge I'm putting the money in escrow pending the outcome of a sanity hearing, seeing as how I believe that Karen is now mentally incompetent."

"It won't work. Karen's at least as sane as you are."

"But I'll drag you into court in the process, Krell. I'll expose you for the phony you are."

Harry Krell laughed a strange bitter laugh and multi-colored diamonds of stained glass seemed to flash and shimmer in the sun. "Shall I show you what a phony I am, Marvin?" he said. "Shall I really show you?"

Waves of thick velvet poured over Bill Marvin's body. In Krell's direction, he felt a radiant fire in a bitter cold night. He heard a chord that seemed to be composed of the chiming of a million microscopic bells. Far away, he saw a streak of hard blue metal against a field of loamy brown.

All in an instant, and then it passed. He saw the sunlight, heard the breakers, then the sound of a high-performance engine accelerating up in the hills that loomed above the beach house. Krell was smiling and staring emptily off into space.

A tremor went through Marvin's body. I've been a little tense lately, he thought. Can this be the beginning of a breakdown? "What the hell was that?" he muttered.

"What was what?" said Krell. "I'm a phony, so nothing could've happened, now could it, Marvin?" His voice seemed both bitter and smug.

Marvin blotted out the whole thing by forcing his attention back to the matter at hand. "I don't care what little tricks you can pull, I'm not going to let you suck up my money through Karen."

"You've got a one-track mind, Mr. Marvin, what we call a frozen sensorium here at Golden Groves. You're super-uptight. You know, I could help you. I could open up your head and let in all the sounds of the rainbow."

"You're not selling *me* any used car, Krell!"

"Well, maybe Karen can," Krell said. Marvin followed Krell's line of sight, and there she was, walking through the glass doors in a paisley muumuu that the sea-breeze pressed and fluttered against the soft firmnesses of her body.

A ball of nausea instantly formed in Marvin's gut, compounded of empty nights, cat-fights in court, soured love, dead hopes, and the treachery of his body which still sent ghosts of lust coursing to his loins at the sight of the dyed coppery hair that fell a foot past her shoulders, that elfin face with carbon-steel behind it, that perfect body which she pampered and honed like the weapon it was.

"Hello Bill," she said in a neutral voice. "How's the smut business?"

"I haven't had to do any porn for four months," Marvin lied. "I'm into commercials." And then, hating himself for trying to justify his existence to her again, even now, when there was nothing to gain or lose.

Karen walked slowly to the railing of the porch, turned, leaned her back against it, seemed to quiver in some kind of ecstasy. Her green eyes, always so bright with shrewdness, seemed vague and uncharacteristically soft, as if she were good and stoned.

"Your voice feels so ugly when you're trying not to whine," she said.

"Bill's threatening to cut off your alimony unless you leave Golden Groves," Krell said. "He wants to force a sanity hearing and prove that you're a nut and I'm a crook."

"Go ahead and pull your greasy little legal stunts, Bill," Karen said. "I'm sane and Harry is exactly what he claims to be, and we'd both be delighted to prove it in court, wouldn't we, Harry?"

"I don't want to get involved in any legal hassles," Krell said coldly. "It's not worth it, especially since you won't have a dime to pay towards your residency fee with all your alimony in escrow."

"*Harry!*"

Her eyes snapped back into hard focus like steel shutters, and the desperation turned her face into the kind of ugly mask you see around swimming pools in Las Vegas. Marvin smiled, easily choking back his pity. "How do you like your little tin guru now?" he said.

"Harry, you can't do this to me, you can't just turn me off like a lamp over a few hundred dollars!"

Harry Krell climbed out of his beanbag chair. There was no expression on his face at all; except for those strange shattered-looking eyes, he could've been any aging beach bum telling the facts of life to an old divorcee whose money had run out. "I'm no saint," he said. "I had an accident that scrambled my brains and gave me a power to give people something they want and fixed it so that's the only way I can make a living. A good living."

He smiled, and broken glass seemed to jangle inside Bill Marvin's skull. "I'm in it for the money," said Harry Krell. "So you better clean up your own mess, Karen."

"You're such a rotten swine!" Karen snarled, her face suddenly looking ten years older, every subtle wrinkle a prophet of disaster to come.

"But I'm the real thing," said Harry Krell. "I deliver." Slowly and haltingly, he began walking toward the doors that led to his living room, like someone moving underwater.

"Bill—"

It was all there in his name on her lips two octaves lower than her normal tone of voice, the slight hunch forward of her shoulders, the lost scared look in her eyes. It was a trick, and it was where she really lived, both at the same time. He wanted to punch her in the guts and cradle her in his arms.

"If you're crazy enough to think you're going to talk me—"

"Just let me walk you to your car. Please."

Marvin got up, brushed off his pants, sighed, and, suddenly drained of anything like emotion, said tiredly: "If you think you need the exercise that bad, lady."

They walked silently through a slick California-rustic living room, where Krell sat on a green synthetic fur-covered couch stroking a Siamese cat as if it were a musical instrument. On either side of him were a young male hippie in carefully cut shoulder-length hair and a well-tailored embroidered jeans suit, and a minor middle-aged television actor whose name Marvin could not recall.

Marvin kept walking across the black rug without exchanging a look or a word with Krell, but he noticed that there was quick eye contact between Krell and Karen, and at that moment he felt the fleeting taste of cinnamon in his mouth.

Krell's private house fronted on a rich, rolling green plateau across the highway from the Pacific end of the Santa Monica Mountains. Rustic bungalows were scattered randomly about the property, along with clumps of trees, paths, benches, a tennis court, a large swimming pool, a sauna, a stable, the usual sensitivity-resort paraphernalia. The parking lot was tucked nicely away behind a screen of trees at the edge of the highway, so as not to spoil the bucolic scene. But the whole business was surrounded by a ten-foot chain-link fence topped by three strands of barbed wire, and the only entrance was a remotely controlled electric gate. As far as Marvin was concerned, that pretty well summed up Golden Groves. This area north of Los Angeles was full of this kind of guru-farm; the only thing that varied was the basic gimmick.

"All right Karen, what's Krell's number?" he said as they walked toward the parking lot. "Let me guess . . . organic mescaline combined with acupuncture . . . tantric yoga and yak-butter massage . . . Ye gods, what else *is* there that you haven't been hung up on already?"

"Synesthesia," she said in deadly earnest, "and it works. You've felt it yourself, I could tell."

Uneasily, Marvin remembered the strange moments of sensory hallucination he had been getting ever since he met Krell, like short LSD flashbacks. Was Krell really responsible, he wondered? Better than turning out to be the results of too much acid, or the beginning of a nervous breakdown. . . .

"Harry had some kind of serious head injury three years ago—"

"Probably fell off his surfboard."

"—he was in a coma for three weeks, and when he came out of it, the lines between his senses and his brain were all crossed. He saw sound, heard color, tasted temperature. . . . Synesthesia, they call it."

"Yeah . . . now I remember I read about that kind of thing in *Time* or somewhere. . . ."

"Not like Harry, you didn't. Because with Harry the connections *keep* changing from minute to minute. His world is always fresh and new . . . like being high all the time . . . like . . . it's like nothing else in the world."

She brought him up short with a touch of her hand, and a flash from her eyes, perhaps deliberate, reminded him of what she had been, what they had been, when they first drove across the San Fernando Valley in the old Dodge, with the Hollywood Hills spread out before them, a golden world they were sure to conquer.

"I feel alive again, Bill," she said. "Please don't take it away from me."

"I don't see—"

Overwhelming warmth enveloped his body. He tasted the wine of her hand on his arm. He heard the symphony of the spheres, tone within tone within tone, without end. He saw the dark of inky night punctuated with fountains of green, red, violet, yellow, fantastic flowers of light, celestial fireworks. He felt his knees go weak, his head reel; he was falling. The fountains of light exploded faster, became larger. He put out his hands to break his fall, smelled burning pine, heard the whisper of an unfelt wind.

He was crouched on the grass supporting his body-weight on his hands, staring down at the green blades. "Are you okay? Are you all right?" Karen shouted.

He looked up at her, blinked, nodded.

"What Harry never let the doctors find out was that he could project it," she said.

Marvin got shakily to his feet. "All right," he said. "So I believe that that greasy creep Krell can get inside your brain and scramble it around! But what the hell for? What dumb spiel does he throw you to make you want it, that you're experiencing the essence of Buddha's rectum or something?"

"Harry's no mental giant," she said. "He doesn't know why it opens you up—oh, he's got some stupid line for the real idiots—all he really knows is how to do it, and how to make money at it. But Bill, all I can tell you is that this seems to be opening me up at last. It's the answer I've been looking for for five years."

"What the hell's the question?" Marvin said, an old line that brought back a whole marriage's worth of bad memories, like a foul-tasting burp recalling an undigested bad meal. Acid trips that went nowhere, two months of the Synanon game learning how to stick the knife in better, swinging, threesomes both ways, trial separations and trial reconciliations, savage sex, battle sex, dull sex, and no sex. Always searching for something that had been lost somewhere between crossing the continent together in that old Dodge and the skin-flick way of life that meant survival in Los Angeles after it became apparent that he wasn't the next Orson Welles and she wasn't the next Marilyn Monroe.

"What I think is that this synesthesia must be the natural way people are supposed to experience the world. Somewhere along the way our senses got separated from each other, and that's why the human race is such a mess. We can't get our heads together because we experience reality through a lot of narrow windows, like prisoners in a cell. That's why we're all twisted inside."

"Whereas Harry Krell is the picture of mental health and karmic perfection!"

They were nearing the parking lot now; Marvin could see his Targa, and he longed to be in it, roaring along the freeway away from Golden Groves and Karen, away from one more expensive last hope.

Once again, she presented him with her flesh, touching both hands to his shoulders, staring full face at him until something inside him ached with yearning. Her face was as soft as it had been when they had been lovers instead of sparring partners, but her eyes were full of an aging woman's terrors.

"All I know is what I feel," she said.

"When I'm living in a synesthestic flash, I feel really alive. Everything else is just waiting."

"Why don't you just try smack?" Marvin said. "It may not be cheaper than Krell, but at least it's portable."

"Harry claims that eventually we can learn to do it on our own, that he can retrain our minds, given enough time—"

"And enough money."

"Oh Bill, don't make me lose this! Don't let me drown!"

Her hands dug into his shoulders, her body slumped toward him, wrinkles formed in the corners of her mouth, the stench of pathetic desperation—

He saw huge woman's hands knotted in fear raise themselves in prayerful supplication towards him from a forest of sharp metallic edges. He felt her flesh moving over every inch of his body in long-forgotten personal rhythms, and how it had felt to snuggle toasty beside her in bed. He tasted bitter gall and the nausea of panic, smelled musky perfume.

He heard his own tears pealing like church bells as they rolled down his cheeks; he drew the giant hands to him, and they dissolved into an armful of yellow light. Wordless singing filled his ears, and he smelled a long night by the fireside, felt the fleshy warm glow of nostalgia's sad contentment.

He was holding Karen in his arms; her cheek was nestled against his neck. She was crooning his name, and he felt five years and more younger. And suddenly scared silly and burning mad.

He thrust her away from him. "It won't work," he snarled. "You're not going to play me for a sucker again and neither is Krell!"

"You felt—"

"What you and Harry Krell wanted me to feel! Forget it, it won't work again! See you in court."

He sprinted the rest of the way to his car, tearing little divots out of the moist turf of Golden Groves.

With four underground films totalling less than 90 minutes to Bill's credit, and with Karen having "starred" in the last two of them, the Marvins had left New York to seek fame and fortune in the Golden West. What they found in Hollywood was that beautiful women with minor acting talent were a dime a dozen (or at best $50 a trick) and that Bill's "credits" might as well have been Cuban Superman flicks.

What they also found out, after four months of starving and scrounging, was that Los Angeles was the pornography capital of the world. For every foot of feature film shot in Hollywood, there were miles of split beaver, S&M, and just plain stag films churned out. The town was swarming with "film-makers" living off porn while waiting for The Big Break and "actresses" whose footage could be seen to best advantage in Rotary smokers or the string of skin-flick houses along Santa Monica Boulevard known as Beaver Valley. Porn was such a booming industry that most of the film-makers knew less about handling a camera than Bill. So when the inevitable occurred, he had plenty of work and the Marvins had an abundance of money.

Seven years later, Bill Marvin was left with his excellent connections in the porn industry, a three-year-old Porche Targa, a six-room house in Laurel Canyon which he would own outright in another fifteen years, enough cameras and equipment to live well off pornography forever, and no more illusions about Making It Big.

He was set for life. Sex, both instant and long-term, was certainly no problem in his line of work; four months of screwing around between serious relationships that averaged about six months in duration seemed to be his natural pattern. In the porn business, you connect up with a good lawyer and a tricky accountant early if you know what's good for you, so he had come out of the divorce pretty damn well: fifteen grand in lieu of her share of the house and $1000 a month, which he could pay without feeling too much pain.

He had felt that he could breeze along like this forever, happy as a clam, until that scene last week at Golden Groves. Now he was rattling around the house as if it were the dead shell of some enormous creature that he was inhabiting like an over-ambitious hermit-crab. He couldn't get his head into a new project, sex didn't turn him on, drugs bored him. He could think of only one thing: Harry Krell's head on a silver platter. And the fact that his lawyer had told him that the sanity hearing ploy probably wouldn't work certainly hadn't improved his disposition.

What possible difference can it make to me that Karen is throwing my money away on Krell, he wondered as he paced the flagstone walk of his deeply-shadowed overgrown garden? If it wasn't Krell, it'd be some other transcendental con-man. The hills are full of them.

If this were a Universal TV movie, I'd still be carrying a subconscious torch for Karen, which is why Krell is getting under my skin. Guru-envy, a shrink might call it. But I wouldn't have Karen back on her hands and knees. No, it's got to be something about that crazy creep Krell—

That crazy Krell!

Bill Marvin did a classic slow-take. Then he double-timed through the ferns and cacti of his hillside garden, trotted around the edge of his pool, through his living room, and two stairs at a time up to his second-floor office, where he called Wally Bruner, his hot-shot lawyer.

"Look Wally, about this con-artist my wife is—"

"I told you, you miss one alimony payment, and she'll have *you* in court as defendant, and unless you succeed in getting her committed—"

"Yeah, yeah, I know, I probably can't have her declared incompetent. But what about Krell?"

"Krell?" Wally's voice had slowed down about twenty mph. Marvin could picture him leaning back in his chair, raising his eyebrows, rolling the word around in his mouth, tasting it out. *"Krell?"*

"Sure. This guy had a head injury so serious he was in a coma for weeks, and when he comes out of it, he claims he sees sound, hears light, feels taste, and then he goes into business claiming he can scramble other people's brains the same way. What would that sound like in court?"

"Who swears out the complaint?" Bruner said slowly.

"Huh?"

"The only way to get Krell into court is on a fraud charge, that he can't really project this synesthesia effect, he's swindling the marks. That puts him in the position of having to defend himself against criminal fraud by proving he's got this strange psychic power, which let me tell you, is not a position *I'd* care to defend. If I was his lawyer, I think I'd have to plead insanity to try to beat the felony rap. If he wins, he spends a few months in the booby hatch and this Golden Groves thing is broken up, which is what you want. If he loses he goes to jail, which you'd like even better. If he tries to convince a Los Angeles judge that he's got psychic powers, he won't get to first base, and if he tries it before a jury, I'll get him *and* his lawyer thrown in the funny-farm."

"Well hey, that's great!" Marvin shouted. "We got him coming and going!"

"Like I say, Bill," Bruner said tiredly, "who's the complainant?"

"In English, please, Wally."

"In order to get Krell into court on a fraud charge, someone has to file a complaint. Someone who can claim that Krell has defrauded him. Therefore someone who has paid Krell money for his hypothetical services. Who's that, Bill? Certainly not Karen—"

"What about me?" Marvin blurted.

"You?"

"Sure. I go up there, pay Krell for a month's worth, stay a few days, then come out screaming fraud."

"But according to you, he really delivers what he claims to. . . ."

"As of now, I never told you that, right?"

"You'd have to testify under oath. . . ."

"I'll keep my fingers crossed "

"You really think Krell will take a chance on letting you in?"

Bill Marvin smiled. "He's a greedy pig and an egomaniac," he said. "He tried to get Karen to help convince me he was Malibu's answer to Buddha, and he's more than jerk enough to convince himself that he succeeded. Will it work, Wally?"

"Will what work?" Bruner said ingenuously. "As of now, this phone conversation never took place. Do you read me loud and clear?"

"Five by five," Marvin said. He hung up on Bruner and dialed the number of Golden Groves.

Sprawled across his green couch, Harry Krell's body contradicted the lines of tense shrewdness in his face as his eyes, for once, focused sharply on Marvin. "Maybe I'm making a mistake trusting you," he said. "You made it pretty clear what you think of me."

Marvin leaned back in his chair, emulating Krell's casualness. "Trust's got nothing to do with it," he said. "You don't have to trust me and I don't have to trust you. You show me that you can give *me* my money's worth, that should convince me that Karen is getting my money's worth too. Turn me down, and it's $1000 a month you stand to lose."

Harry Krell laughed and microscopic pinpricks seemed to tickle every inch of Marvin's body. Beside Krell on the sofa, Karen's body quivered once. "We don't like each other," Krell said, "but we understand each other." There was something patronizing in his tone that grated on Marvin, an arrogant over-confidence that was somehow insulting. Well, the greedy swine would soon get his!

"Then it's a deal?"

"Sure," Krell said. "Come back tomorrow with your clothes and a $500 check that won't bounce. You get a cabin, three meals a day here in the house, free use of the sauna, the tennis courts, and the pool, at least two synesthesia groups a day, and whatever special events might go on. The horses are $5 an hour extra."

"I'm paying for the two of us," Marvin said. "I should get some kind of discount."

Krell grinned. "You want to share a cabin with Karen, I'll knock $250 a month off the bill," he said. There was something teasing in his voice.

Involuntarily, Marvin's eyes were drawn to Karen's. There was an emotional flash between them that brought back long-dead memories of what that kind of eye-contact had once meant, of what they had been together before it all fell apart. He found himself almost wishing he was what he pretended to be: a pilgrim seeking to clean the stale cobwebs out of his soul. He had the feeling that she just might agree to shack up with him. But the glow in her eyes was forced by desperate need. Los Angeles was full of faces like that, and the Harry Krells sucked them dry and let them shrivel like old prunes when the money ran out. He had to admit that his body still felt something for Karen's, but he was long past the point where he'd let sex drag him where his head did not want to be; the going up was just not worth the coming down.

"Pass," he said. Karen's expression did not change at all.

Krell shrugged, got up, and walked out onto the porch in that strange uncertain gait of his, inhaling sharply as he crossed the shadow-line into sunlight.

"I know you're up to something cheap and tricky," Karen said.

"Then why did you agree to warm Krell up for me?"

"You wouldn't believe me."

"Try me."

She sighed. "Because I still care a little for you, Bill," she said. "You're so frozen, so tied up in knots inside, and who should know what that's like better than me. Harry was what you need. Once you've been here a while, you'll see that, and it won't matter why you originally came."

"Saving your alimony had nothing to do with it, of course."

"Not really," she said. *And as the words emerged from her mouth, they became brightly-colored tropical butterflies; and she became a lush greenness from which they flew. There was a soft musical trilling, and the smell of lilacs and orchids filled the air. In that moment, he felt a pang of regret for what he had said, saw the feeling she still bore for him, heard the simple clarity of her body's animal love.*

In the next moment, they were staring at each other, and tension hung in the air between them. Karen broke it with a small, smug madonna-smile.

Marvin found himself sweating at the palms, and somewhat leary of what he was getting himself into.

The cabin was sure a dump for $500 a month: a bed, a dresser, a couch, a bathroom, two electric heaters, and a noisy old motel-type air conditioner. Breakfast had been granola (69¢ a pound), milk, and coffee, and Marvin figured that Krell would use the same health-food excuse to dish out cheap dinners and lunches. The only thing that required expensive upkeep was the riding stable, and that ran at a profit as a separate operation. Krell must be pocketing something like half the residency fee as clear profit. Fifteen cabins, some of them double-occupancy . . . that would be seven grand a month at least!

There's no business like the guru business, Marvin thought as he followed Krell and three of his fellow residents out onto the porch above the rumbling sea.

Four large plush cusions had been placed on the bare wood in a circle around an even larger zebra-striped pillow. Krell, in his white sarong, lowered himself to the central position in a semblance of the lotus position, looking like the Maharishi as played by a decaying Tab Hunter. Marvin and the other three residents dropped to their cushions in imitation of Krell. On Marvin's left was Tish Connally, a well-preserved 35ish ex-Las Vegas "showgirl" who had managed to hold on to a decent portion of the drunk money that had swirled around her for ten years, and who had eyed him a couple of times over the granola. On his right, Mike Warren, the longhair he had seen the first day, who turned out to be an ex-speedfreak guitarist, and on the far cushion, a balding tv producer named Marty Klein, whose last two series had been cancelled after thirteen weeks each.

"Okay," said Krell, "you all know Bill Marvin, so I guess we're ready to charge up for the morning. Bill, what this is all about is that I unfreeze everybody's senses together for a bit, and then you'll have synesthetic flashes on your own off it for a few hours. The more of these sessions you have, the longer your own free-flashing will last, and finally your senses will be re educated enough so you won't need me."

"How many people have . . . ah, graduated so far?" Marvin asked sweetly.

To his credit, Krell managed not to crack a scowl. "No one's felt they've gotten all I've got to give them yet," he said. "But some are far along the way. Okay, are we ready now?"

The morning sun had just about burned away most of the early coastal fog, but traces of mist still lingered around the porch, freshened by the spray churned up by the ocean as it broke against the rocks below. "Here we go," said Harry Krell.

There was light: a soft, all-enveloping radiance that pulsed from sunshine yellow to sea green with the tidal rhythm of breakers crashing against a rocky shore. Marvin tasted a salty tang, now minty-cool, now chowder-hot. To his right, he heard a thin, throbbing, blues-like chord, something like a keening amplified guitar stretching and clawing for some spiritual stratosphere, higher, higher, higher, but never quite getting there, never resolving the dynamic discord into a bearable harmony. To his left, a sound like the easy ricky-tick of a funky old piano that had been out of tune for ten years, and had mellowed into that strange old groove. Across from him, a frantic syncopated ticking, like a time-bomb running down as it was running out, a toss-up as to whether entropy would outrace the explosion.

And dominating it all, the central theme: a surging, blaring, brassy wailing that seemed a shell of plastic around a central motif of sadness—a gypsy violinist playing hot jazz on a tuba—that Marvin knew was Harry Krell.

Marvin was knocked back on his mental heels by the flood of transmogrified emotions pouring in on him from unexpected sensual directions. He sensed that in some way, Mike Warren was that screaming non-chord that was the aural transformation of his visual persona, that Tish Connally was the funky ricky-tick, and Klein's running-down rhythm, a has-been wondering whether he would fall apart or freak out first. And Krell, phony brass within sad confusion within cheap pseudo-sincerity within mournful regret within inner emptiness like a Muzak version of himself—a man whose existence was in the unresolvable tension between his grubby phoniness and the overwhelming rich strangeness of the unique consciousness a random hit on the head had given him, grandeur poured by fate into the tawdriest available vessel.

Marvin had never felt pressed so close to human beings in his life. He was both fascinated and repelled by the intimacy. And wondered what they were experiencing as him.

Then the universe of his senses went through another transformation. His mouth was filled with a spectrum of tastes that somehow spread themselves out along spacial dimensions: acrid spiciness like smoked chili peppers to the right, soft furriness of flat highballs to the left, off a way something like garlic and peptic gall, and everywhere the overwhelming taste of peppermint and melancholy red wine. He could hear the pounding of the surf now, but what he saw was a field of orange-red across which drifted occasional whisps of cool blue.

"Now join hands in a circle and feel outsides with your insides," said the plastic peppermint and musky red wine.

Marvin reached out with both hands. The right half of his body immediately became knotted with severe muscular tension, every nerve twanging to the breaking point like snarled and taut wire. But the left half of his body went slack, soft, and quietly burned-out as four AM in bed beside someone you picked up a little after midnight at a heavy boozing and doping party.

"Okay, now relax and drift on back through the changes," said peppermint and red wine.

Sight became a flickering sequence: blue mists drifting across a field of orange-red, sunshine-yellow pulsing through sea-green in a tidal rhythm, four people seated in a circle around Harry Krell on a sunlit porch. Back and forth,

in and out, the visions chased each other through every possible variation of the
sequence, while Marvin heard the pounding of the surf, the symphony for four
souls; tasted minty-cool, chowder-hot, smoked chili peppers, flat highballs, pep-
permint and red wine. The sensual images crossed and recrossed, blending,
clashing, melding, bouncing off each other, until concepts like taste, sight,
hearing, smell, feel, became totally meaningless.

Finally (time had no referents in this state) Marvin's sensorium stabilized.
He saw Tish Connally, Mike Warren, Marty Klein and himself seated on
cushions in a circle around Harry Krell on a sunlit wooden porch. He heard
the crashing of the surf on the rocks below, felt the softness of the cushion on
which he sat, smelled a mixture of sea breeze and his own sweat.

Krell was bathed in sweat, looked drained, but managed to smile smugly
in his direction. The others appeared not quite as dazed as Marvin felt. His
mind was completely empty in that moment, whited-out, overwhelmed, nothing more than the brain center where his sensory input merged to form his
sensorium, that constellation of sight, smell, sound, taste, touch, and feel
which is the essential and basic ground of human consciousness.

"I hope you weren't disappointed, Mr. Marvin," Krell said. "Or would you
like your money back?"

Bill Marvin had nothing to say; he felt that he hardly had enough self-
consciousness to perceive words as more than abstract sequences of sound.

The bright afternoon sun turned the surface of the pool into a rippling sheet
of glare, which seemed to dissolve into glass chiming and smashing for a
moment as Marvin stared at the incandescent waters. Even his normal senses
seemed unusually acute—he could clearly smell the sea and the stables, even
here at poolside, feel the grainy texture of the plastic cloth of the beach chair
against his bare back—perhaps because he could no longer take any sensory
dimension for granted, with the synesthetic flashes he was getting every few
minutes. There was no getting around the fact that what he had experienced
that morning had been a profound experience, and one that still sent echoes
rippling through his brain.

Karen pulled herself out of the pool with a shake and a shudder that flashed
droplets in the sun, threw a towel around herself and plopped down in the
beach chair next to his. She was wearing a minimal blue bikini, but Marvin
found himself noticing the full curves of her body only as abstract design,
glistening arcs of water-sheened skin.

"I can see you've really had a moving session," she said.

"Huh?"

He saw that her eyes were looking straight at him, but in a glazed, unfocused manner. "I'm flashing right now," she said. "I hear you as a low hum,
without the usual grinding noises in the way you sit, and. . . ."

She ran her hand along his chest. "Cool green and blue, no hard silvers
and grays. . . ." She sighed, removed her hand, refocused her eyes. "It's gone

now," she said. "All I get unless Harry is really projecting is little bits and pieces I can't hold onto. . . . But someday. . . ."

"Someday you'll be able to stay high all the time, or so Krell claims."

"You know Harry's no fraud now."

Marvin winced inwardly at the word *fraud,* thinking what it could be like testifying against Krell. Lord, he might drop me into a synesthetic trance in the middle of the courtroom! But . . . but I could fake my way through if I was really ready for it, if I have enough experience functioning in that state. *Krell* seems to be able to function, and he's like that all the time. . . .

"What's the matter, Bill?"

"Does my body sound funny or something?" he snapped.

"No, you just had a plain, old-fashioned frightened look on your face for a minute there."

"I was just thinking what it would be like if Krell really could condition you to be like him all the time," Marvin said. "Walking around in a fog like that, sure I can see how it might make things interesting, but how could you function, even keep from walking into trees . . . ?"

"Harry *is* like that all the time, and he's functioning. You don't exactly see him starving in the street."

"I'll bet you don't see him in the street, period," Marvin said. "I'll bet Krell never leaves this place. The way you see him walking around like a zombie, he probably goes on memory half the time, like a blind man in his house." Yeah, he thought, people, food, money, he makes it all come to him. He probably couldn't drive a mile on the freeway or even walk across a street without getting killed. Suddenly Marvin found himself considering Harry Krell's inner reality, the strange parameters of his life, with a certain sympathy. What would it really be like to be Krell? To be wide open to all that fantastic experience, but unable to function in the real world except by somehow making it come to you?

Making it come to you through a greasy con-game, he told himself angrily, annoyed at the softness towards Krell that had sneaked into his consciousness, at the momentary blunting of the keen edge of his determination.

Rising, he said: "I'm going to take a dip and wash some of these cobwebs out of my head."

He took four running steps and dove off the concrete lip of the pool.

When he hit the water, the world exploded for a moment in a dazzling auroral rainbow of light.

"How long have you been here?" "Six weeks," said Tish Connally, lighting a cigarette with a match that momentarily split the darkness of her cabin with a ringing gong in Bill Marvin's head. Another synesthetic flash! He had been at Golden Groves for only three days now, and the last session with Krell had been at least five hours ago, yet he was still getting two or three flashes an hour.

He leaned back against the headboard of the bed, felt Tish's body exhale against him, saw the glow of her cigarette flare brightly, then subside. "How long do you think you'll stay?" he asked.

"Till I have to go make some more money somehow," she said. "This isn't the cheapest joint I've ever seen."

"Not until you graduate, become another Harry Krell?"

She laughed; he could feel her loose flesh ripple, almost see pink gelatin shaking in the dark. A flash—or just overactive imagination?

"That's a con," she said. "Take it from an expert. For one thing, there are people who have been in and out of here for months, and they still need their boosters from Harry to keep flashing. For another, Krell wouldn't turn you on permanently if he could. We wouldn't need him any more then; where would his money come from?"

"Knowing that, you still stick around?"

"Billy-boy, I've kicked around for ten years, I've been taken every way there is to be taken, took men every way there was for me to take 'em. Before I came here, I'd felt everything there was to feel fifty thousand times, so no matter what I did to get off, I was just going through the motions. At least here I feel alive in bits and pieces. So I'm paying Krell a pretty penny for getting me off once in a while. I've made most of my money on the other end of the same game, so what the hell, it keeps the money in circulation, right?"

"You're a mean old broad," Marvin said, with a certain affection.

She snubbed out her cigarette, kissed him lightly on the lips, rolled toward him.

"One more for the road, Billy-boy?"

Diffidently, he took her tired flesh in his arms. "Oh, you're golden!" she sighed as she moved against him. And he realized that she had been hoping for a synesthetic flash to give her a bit of the sharp pleasure that he alone could not.

But he could hardly feel anger or disgust, since he had been looking for something more spectacular than a soft human body in the darkness, too.

Strolling towards his cabin near the sea-cliffs in the full moonlight, Bill Marvin saw Harry Krell emerge from Lisa Scott's cabin and walk down the path towards him, more rapidly and surely than he usually seemed to move in broad daylight. They met in a small grove of trees, where the moonlight filtered through the branches in tiger-stripes of silver and black that shattered visual images into jigsaw patterns.

"Hello, Marvin," Krell said. "Been doing some visiting?"

"Just walking," Marvin said neutrally, surprising himself with his own desire to have a civil conversation with Krell. But after all, strictly as a curiosity, Krell had to be one of the most interesting men on earth.

Krell must have sensed something of this, because he stopped, leaned up against a tree, and said: "You've been here a week now, Marvin. Tell me the truth, do you still hate my guts? Are you still out to get me?"

Glad to have his reaction masked by the camouflage-pattern of moonlight and darkness, Marvin caught his breath, said: "What makes you think I'm out to get you?"

Krell laughed, and for a moment, Marvin saw a bright blue cataract smashing off a sheet of glass in brilliant sunlight.

"I heard the look on your face," Krell said. "Besides, what makes you think you're the first person that's come here trying to nail me?"

"So why'd you let me come here?"

"Because half the Golden Groves regulars come here the first time to get the goods on that phony Harry Krell. If I worried about that, I'd lose half my trade."

"I just can't figure where your head's at, Krell. What do you think you're doing here?"

"What am I doing?" Krell said, an edge of whining bitterness coming into his voice. "What do you think I'm doing? I'm surviving as best I can, same as you. You think I asked for this? Sure, a lot of nuts come through here and convince themselves they're getting religious visions off of me, a big ecstasy trip. Great for them! But for Harry Krell, synesthesia's no ecstasy trip, let me tell you! I can't drive a car or walk across a street or go anywhere or do anything. All I can do is hear the pretty colors, smell the music, see the taste of whatever crap I'm eating. After three years, I got enough experience to guess pretty well what's happening around me most of the time as long as I stay on familiar ground, but I'm just *guessing,* man! I'm trapped inside my own head. Like now, I see something blue-green off to the left—probably the sea I'm smelling—and pink-violet stuff around us—trees, probably eucalyptus. And I hear some kind of gong. There's a moon out, right? If you're saying something now, I can't make it out until I start hearing sound again. Man, I'm so alone here inside this light-show!"

Bill Marvin fought against his own feelings, and lost. He couldn't stop himself from feeling sympathy for Harry Krell, locked inside his weird private reality, an ordinary slob cut off from any ordinary life. Yet Krell was entirely willing to put other people into the same place.

"Feeling like that, you still don't mind making your bread by sucking other people in with you. . . ." he said.

"Jesus, Marvin, you're a pornographer! You give people a kick they want, and you make your living off of it. But does it turn *you* on? How'd you like your whole life to be a pornographic movie?"

Bill Marvin choked on a wisecrack which never came out. Because the deadening quality of what his life had become slammed him in the gut. What *is* the difference between me and Krell? he thought. He gives the suckers synesthetic flashes and I give 'em porn. What he's putting out doesn't turn him on any more than what I put out turns me on. We're both alone inside our heads and faking it. He got hit on the head by a surfboard and got stuck in the synesthesia trip, and I got hit on the head by Hollywood and got stuck in the porn trip.

"Sorry to put you on such a bummer, Marvin," Krell said. "I can smell it on you. Now I hear your face. What . . . ?"

"We're both alike, Krell," Marvin said. "And we both stink."

"We're just doing what we gotta do. You gotta play the cards you've been dealt, because you're not going to get any others."

"Sometimes you deal yourself your own lousy hand," Marvin said.

"I'll show you lousy!" said Krell. "I'll show you how lousy it can be to walk just from here to your cabin—the way I have to do it. You got the guts?"

"That's what I'm paying my money for," Marvin said quietly. He began walking back up the path. Krell turned and walked beside him.

Abruptly, the darkness dissolved into a glowing gingerbread fairyland of light. To Marvin's left, where he knew the sea was crashing against the base of the cliffs, he saw a bright green-yellow bank of brilliance that sent out pulses of radiance which struck invisible objects all around him, haloing them in all the subtle shades of the spectrum, forming an infinitely complex lattice-work of ever-changing intersecting wavefronts that transformed itself with every pulse from the aural sun that was the sea. Beside him, Harry Krell was a shape of darkness outlined in a shimmering aurora. He heard a far-away gong chiming pleasantly in the velvet quiet. He tasted salt and smelled a rapidly-changing sequence of floral odors that might have been Krell speaking. The beauty of it all drenched his soul through every pore.

He walked slowly along, orienting himself by the supposition that the green-yellow brilliance was the breaking surf, that the areas of darkness outlined by the living lacework of colored wavefronts were solid objects to be avoided. It wasn't easy, but it was somehow enchanting, picking his way through a familiar scene that had transformed itself into a universe of wonder.

Then the world changed again. He could hear the crashing of the sea. On his left, he saw a thick blue-green spongy mass, huge and towering; on the ground, the path was a ribbon of blackness through a field of pinkish gray; here and there fountains grew out of the pinkish gray, with grayish stems and vivid maroon crests, tree-high. He smelled clear coldness. Krell was a doughy mass of colors, dominantly washed-out brown. Marvin guessed that he was seeing smell.

It was easy enough to follow the path of dead earth through the fragrant grass. After a while there was another, subtler transformation. He could see that he and Krell were walking up the path towards his cabin, no more than twenty yards away in the silvery moonlight. But his mouth was filled with a now-winey, now-nutty flavor that ebbed and flowed with an oceanic rhythm, here and there broken by quick wisps of spiciness as bird-shapes flapped from tree to darkened tree. The only sound was a soft, almost subliminal hiss.

Dazed, transported, Marvin covered the last few yards to his cabin open-mouthed and wide-eyed. When they reached the door, the strange tastes in his mouth evaporated, and he could hear the muffled grumble of the pounding surf. He laughed, exhilarated, refreshed in every atom of his being, alive to every subtle sensory nuance of the night.

"How do you like living where I live?" Krell said sourly.

"It's beautiful . . . it's. . . ."

Krell scowled, snickered, smiled ruefully. "So the big wise-guy turns out to be a sucker just like everyone else," he said, almost regretfully.

Marvin laughed again. In fact, he realized, he had been laughing for the first time in over a week. "Who knows, Krell," he said, "you might enjoy living in one of my pornographic movies."

He laughed one more time, then went into his cabin, leaving Krell standing there in the night with a dumb expression on his face.

Later, when he got into bed, the cool sheets and the soft pillow were a clear night full of pinpoint-bright, multicolored stars, and the darkness smelled like a woman's perfume.

The world went livid red, and the wooden slats beneath his naked body became a smoky tang in his mouth. Marvin felt himself glowing in the center of his being like a roaring winter fireplace, heard Dave Andrews' voice say: "Really sweats the tension out of you."

The flash passed, and he was lying on the wooden bench of the sauna shack, bathed in his own luxuriant sweat, baking in the heat given off by the hot stones on their cast iron rack. The fat, towel-wrapped man on the bench across from him stared sightlessly at the ceiling and sighed.

"Phew!" Andrews said as his eyes came back into focus. "I could really hear my muscles uncoil. *Twooong!*"

Marvin lay there just sucking up the heat, going with it, and entirely ignoring Andrews, who was some kind of land speculator, and a crashing bore. He closed his eyes and concentrated on the waves of heat which he could all but feel breaking against his body, the relief of the grain of the wood against his skin, the subtle odor of hot stone. He had learned to bask in the world of his senses and let everything else drift by.

"I tell you, old Krell may be charging a pretty penny, but it sure cleans out the old tubes and charges up the old batteries. . . ." Andrews babbled on and on like a radio commercial, but Marvin found little trouble in pushing the idiot voice far into the sensory background; it was easy, when each sense could become a universe entire, when your sensorium was no longer conditioned to sight-sound dominance.

Suddenly Andrews' voice was gone, and Marvin heard a whistling hurricane wind. Opening his eyes, he saw wispy white billows of ethereal steam punctuated by the multicolored static of Andrews' words. He tasted something like curry and smelled a piny, convoluted odor.

When the flash passed, he got up, slipped on a bathing suit, dashed out of the sauna, ran across the rich green grass in the high blue sunlight, and dove straight into the swimming pool. The cool water hit his superheated body with an orgasmic shock. He floated to the surface and let the little wavelets cradle him on his back as he paddled over to the lip of the pool, where Karen sat dangling her feet in the water.

"You're sure a different man than when you came here," she said.

Looking up, Marvin saw her bikinied form as a fuzzy vagueness against a blinding blue sky.

"Well, okay, so Krell's got something going for him," he said. "But at these prices, he's still a crook, and the funny thing is, *he* thinks he's even a *bigger* crook than he really is. . . ."

She didn't answer for a long moment, but stared into the depths of the pool to one side of him, lost in the universe of her own synesthetic flash.

When she finally spoke, it came out as a gusher of glistening green-black oil emerging from soft lavender clouds, while Marvin tasted icy cotton-candy. Judging from the discord of her face jarring the soothing melody of the sunlit sky, it was probably just as well.

Marvin luxuriated in a shower of blood-warm rain, saw a sheen of light that pulsed from sunshine-yellow to sea-green; then the flash passed. He was sitting on his cushion on Harry Krell's sunny porch, in a circle around Krell, along with Tish, Andrews . . . and Karen.

Strange, he thought, I've been here nearly three weeks, and I haven't had a booster group with Karen yet. Stranger still was the realization that this hadn't seemed peculiar or even significant until this moment. Like the rest of the outside world, his former relationship with Karen seemed so long ago and far away. The woman to his right seemed no closer to him emotionally than any of the other residents of Golden Groves, who drifted through each other's private universes like phantom ships passing in the night.

Harry Krell took a deep breath, and the vault of the sky became a sheet of gleaming brass; below, the sea was a rolling cauldron of ebony. The porch itself was outlined in dull blue, and the people around him were throbbing shapes of yellowish pink. To his left, the odor of fading incense; across the way, rich Havana smoke, and the powerful tinge of ozone pervaded all. But the smell that riveted Marvin's attention was the one on his right: an overwhelming feminine musk that seemed compounded of (or partially masked by) unsubtle perfume, drying nailpolish, beauty cream, shampoo, deodorants, the full spectrum of chemical enhancers which he now realized had been the characteristic odors of living with Karen. Waves of nostalgia and disgust formed inside him, crested, broke, and merged in a single emotional tone for which there was no word. It simply was the space that Karen occupied in his mind, the total image through which he experienced her.

Another change, and he saw light pulsing from yellow to green once more, tasted a salty tang. From his left, he heard the ricky-tick of a funky old piano; across the way, a staccato metallic blatting; over it all, the brassy, hollow, melancholy wailing of Harry Krell. But once again, it was the theme on his right that vibrated a nerve that went straight from his senses through his brain and into the pit of his gut. It was as if a gong were striking within an enclosure that rudely dampened its vibrations, slamming the echoing notes back on each other, abruptly amputating the long, slow vibrations, creating a sound that was a hysterical hammering at invisible walls, the sound of an animal caught in some invisible trap. Ironically, the smell of a woodland field in high summer was heavy in Marvin's nostrils.

After a few more slow changes, Krell brought them flickering back through the sequences: blood-warm rain, a sheet of gleaming brass over an ebony sea, the smell of feminine musk and body chemicals, light pulsing from yellow to green, rich Havana smoke, peppermint and red wine, high summer in a wood-land field, flat highballs, melancholy wailing, ricky-tick. . . .

Then Marvin was seated on his cushion next to Karen's, while the sea grumbled to itself below, and Harry Krell breathed heavily and wiped sweat out of his eyes.

Marvin and Karen simultaneously turned to look at each other. Their eyes met, or at least their focal planes intersected. For Marvin, it was like staring straight at two cold green marbles set in the alabaster face of a statue, for all the emotion that the eye-contact contained. Judging from the ghost of a grimace that quivered across her lips, she was seeing no less of a stranger. *For an instant, he was blinded by yellow light, sickened by the odor of her chemical musk.*

When the flash passed, he saw that she was in the throes of one of her own; her eyes staring sightlessly out to sea, her lips twitching, her nostrils flaring. For a moment, he was overcome with curiosity as to how she was experiencing him; then, with a small effort, he put this distasteful thought from his mind, knowing that this was the moment of true divorce, that the alimony was now the only bond that remained between them.

A moment later, without a word to each other, they both got up and went their separate ways. *As Karen walked through the glass doors into the house, Marvin saw a billowing spongy green mass, and heard her hysterical trapped hammering beat time for her march out of his life forever.*

And time became the flickering procession of sheets of flashing images. The sun set over the cliffs into the Pacific, now a globe of orange fire dipping into the glassy waters and painting the sky with smears of purple and scarlet, now the smoky tang of autumn fading into the sharply crystal bite of winter night, now a slow-motion peal of enormous thunder dying slowly into the velvet stillness. The morning light on the porch of the beachhouse was a shower of blood-warm rain, a field of orange radiance shot with mists of cool blue, a humming symphony of vibrating energy.

For Bill Marvin, these had become the natural poles of existence, the only time-referents in a world in which night might be the toasty woman-smell of his bedroom darkness, the brilliant starry night of cool sheets against his body, or the golden light of anonymous female flesh against his, in which day was the corruscating fireworks of food crunching between his teeth, the celestial chime of his hot body hitting the cool water of the pool after the curry flavor of the sauna, the billowing green clouds of the surf breaking against the foot of the cliffs.

People floated through this quicksilver wonderland as shifting, illusive constellations of sensory images. Ricky-tick piano. Chemical female musk. Cloud of Havana smoke. The wail of an electric guitar. Peppermint and red wine. Hysterical, confined gonging. Smoked chili peppers. Garlic-and-peptic gall. The melancholy wail of a gypsy violinist playing hot jazz on a tuba. The sights and sounds and tastes and smells and feels that were the sensory images of the residents of Golden Groves interpenetrated the images of the inanimate world, blending and melding with them, until people and things became indistinguishable aspects of the chaotic whole.

Marvin's mind, except in isolated moments, consisted entirely of the combination of sensory impulses getting through to his brain at any given time. He existed as the confluence of these sensory images; in a sense, he *became* his sensory experience, no longer time-bound to memory and expectation, no longer a detached point of view sardonically bouncing around inside his own skull. Only in isolated stretches when his synesthetic flashes were at momentary ebbs did he step outside his own immediate experience, wonder at the strangeness in his own mind, watch himself moving through the trees and cabins and people of Golden Groves like some kind of automaton. At these times he felt a certain vague sense of loss. He could not tell whether it was sadness at his temporary fall from a more sublime mental state, or whether his ordinary everyday consciousness was mourning its own demise.

One morning, when the granola in his mouth had scattered jewelled images of sparkling beads as he crunched it against a coffee backdrop of brown velvet, Harry Krell held him back as he started to walk out onto the porch for his morning booster session.

"This is day thirty for you, Marvin," Krell said.

Marvin stared back at him dumbly, hearing a hollow, brassy wail, seeing a rectangle of bright orange outlined against deep blue.

"I said this is the last day you've paid for. Either pony up another $500, or send for someone to take you back to LA. You won't be in any shape to drive for about a week."

Marvin's sensorium had changed again. He was standing in the cool living room near the open glass doors, through which sunlight seemed to extend in a solid chunk. "Thirty days?" he said dazedly. "Has it been *thirty days?* I've lost count." Lord, he thought, I was only supposed to be here a week or two! I haven't done any work in a month! I must be nearly broke, and the alimony payment is past due. My God, thirty days, and I can hardly remember them at all!

"Well I've kept good count," said Krell. "You've used up your $500, and this is no charity operation . . ."

Marvin found his mind racing madly like some runaway machine trying futilely to catch up with a world that had passed it by, desperately trying to sync itself back in gear with the real world of bank statements, alimony courts, four-day shooting schedules, rubber checks, vice squad hassles, recalcitrant actresses, greasy backers. If I can cast something in three or four days, maybe I can use the same cast to shoot three quickies back-to-back, but I'll have to scout three different locations or it won't work, that should give me enough money to cover the monthly nut and keep Karen's lawyers off my back if I get all the money up front, pay them first and kite checks until—

"Well Marvin, you want to write out another $500 check or—?"

"What?" Marvin grunted. "Another? No, no, hell, I'm broke, I've already been here too . . . I mean, I've got to get back to LA immediately."

"Well maybe I'll see you around again sometime," said Harry Krell. He walked into the brilliant mass of sunlight leaving Marvin standing alone in the shadowed living room, *and as he did Marvin saw a brilliant pulse of sunshine yellow, heard an enormous chime, felt a terrible pang of paradise lost.*

But there was no time to sort his head out. He had to call Earl Day, his regular cameraman, get him to come out and drive him back to Los Angeles in the Targa. They could put together three concepts on the way in, start casting tomorrow, have some money in four or five days. Gotta make up for lost time fast, fast, fast!

For the barest moment, Bill Marvin was enveloped in rainbow fire which sputtered and crackled like color tv snow, and he heard the zipping, syncopated whooshing of metal birds soaring past his ears, igniting phantom traces of memories almost forgotten after the frantic madness of grinding out three pornies in less than a month, slowing his racing metabolism, catching for a fleeting instant his psychic breath.

Then he was back stiff-spined in the driver's seat of his Porsche, his hands gripping the wheel like spastic claws, the engine growling at his back, barrelling down the left lane of the Ventura Freeway at 75 mph in moderate traffic. The flash had come and gone so quickly that he hadn't even had time to feel any sense of danger, unlike the first time he had tried to drive, only five days out of Golden Groves, when he nearly creamed out as the road became a sharp melody through rumbling drums up in the twisty Hollywood Hills. Now the synesthetic flashes were few—maybe one or two a day—and so transient that they weren't much more dangerous behind the wheel than a strong sneeze. Each one slipped through his mind like a ghost, leaving only a peculiar echo of vague sadness.

The first couple of weeks of production, on the other hand, had been a real nightmare. Up until maybe ten days ago he had been flashing every half hour or so, and strongly enough so that he hadn't been able to do his own driving, so that takes had been ruined when he tripped out in the middle of them, so that the actors and crew sometimes thought he was stoned or flipping and tried to take advantage of it. Fortunately, he had made so many pornies by now that he could just about do it in his sleep. The worst of it had been that making the films was so boring that he found himself actually waiting for the synesthetic flashes, concentrating on them when they came, even trying to anticipate them, and experiencing the actual work as something unreal, as marking time. He was never much interested in sex when he was shooting porn—after treating female bodies like meat all day it was pretty hard to get turned on by them at night—and the only time he had really felt alive was when he was flashing or involved in one of the hundreds of horrible hassles.

He made an abrupt three-lane jump and pulled off the freeway at Laurel Canyon Boulevard, drove across the ticky-tacky of San Fernando Valley, began climbing up into the Hollywood Hills. The Valley side of the Hills was just more flatland-style suburban plastic, but once accross Mulholland Drive, which ran along the major ridgeline, Laurel Canyon Boulevard curved and wound down towards Sunset Strip, following an old dry streambed through a deep gorge that cut through overgrown and twisted hills festooned with weird and half-hidden houses, a scene from some Disney Black Forest Elf cartoon.

Usually, Marvin got a big lift out of leaving the dead plastic landscape of lowland Los Angeles for the shadowy, urbanized-yet-countrified world of the Canyon. Usually, he got a tremendous emotional surge out of having finished one film—let alone three—driving away from it all on the last day of cutting, with any one of a dozen readily available girls already waiting at the house for him to start a week-long lost weekend, reward for a job well done.

But this time, the drive home did nothing for him, the end of the final cutting only left him empty and stale, and he hadn't even bothered to have a girl waiting for him at the house. He felt tapped out, bugged, emotionally flat, and the worst of it was that he didn't know why.

He pulled into his carport and walked around the side of his house into the seclusion of the unkept, overgrown garden. Even the wild, lush vegetation of his private hillside seemed washed out, pallid, and somehow unreal. The birdsounds in the trees and underbrush seemed like so much Muzak.

He kicked irritably at a rock, then heard the phone ringing in the house. He went inside, plopped down in the black leather director's chair by the phone stand, picked up the living room extension, and grunted: "Yeah?"

It was Wally Bruner.

"What's going on, Bill? I haven't heard from you in nearly two months, ever since you started in on that matter we discussed. I heard you'd started shooting three weeks ago, so I knew you weren't dead, but why haven't you gotten in touch with me? Did you get what you went there for?"

Marvin stared out of the picture window into the garden, where the late afternoon sunlight cast shadows across scraggly patches of lawn under two big eucalyptus trees. Two dun-colored morning doves had ventured out of their wooded seclusion to nibble at seeds in the grass and gobble moodily to themselves like dowager aunts.

"What are you talking about, Wally?" Marvin said vacantly.

"Damn it, you know! Golden Groves. Harry Krell. Are we ready to proceed?"

Suddenly glowing bubbles of pastel shimmer were drifting languidly up through a viscous wine-colored liquid, and Marvin smelled the sweet aroma of perfect sunset; just for the tantalizing fraction of a moment, and then it was gone.

Marvin sighed, blinked, smiled.

"Forget it, Wally," he said. "I'm dropping the whole thing."

"What? Why on earth—"

"Let's just say that I went up on a mountain, came down, and want to make sure it's still there."

"What the hell are you talking about, Bill?"

"What the vintners buy," said Marvin.

"Bill, you sound like you've flipped."

"I'm okay," Marvin said. "Let's just say I don't give a damn what Karen spends her alimony on as long as I have to pay it, and leave it at that. Okay?"

"Okay, Bill. That's the advice I gave you in the first place."

After he hung up on Bruner, Marvin sat there looking out into his garden where ordinary dun-colored birds were pecking at a scruffy lawn, and the subtle gray tinge of smog was barely apparent in the waning light.

He sighed once, shuddered, shrugged, sighed again. Then he picked up the phone and dialed the number of Golden Groves.

7. if you're so smart

Paul Corey

In the historical development of any science, progress is not made at a steady rate. If we could plot such a curve, it would rise over the years, but there would be jumps and dips, as well as some plateaus indicating no progress. Psychology is no exception. At times inspiration has given way to technology, and relevance has yielded to orthodoxy. This story illustrates this developmental process very well. Here the essence of an important kind of human experience is trampled in the organized pursuit of "scientific" knowledge.

The following story also leads us to some further questions. What does it mean to be "smart," and does "smartness" take different forms? The chief psychologist in this story has a Ph.D. and no doubt would score high on a standard intelligence test. Yet he cannot be creative in the sense of recognizing new possibilities. In contrast, the retarded boy is gifted in a certain type of communication.

The story's main theme involves extrasensory perception (ESP), a phenomenon long shunned by many psychologists, but one which has been a staple of science fiction for years. Incidents of ESP include perceiving what another person was thinking (mind reading), communicating through thought (telepathy), and predicting future events (clairvoyance). ESP researchers (parapsychologists) try to eliminate the possibility of perception through known physical stimuli, as a subject being told to identify a card blindfolded or with the card face down. There are some subjects who have done much better than chance on such a task; however, the overall reliability of ESP data has been too low to convince many scientists. The existence of ESP remains an open question.

It is all there in jiggles on paper printed with little squares. Doctor Marley says those jiggles show the changes in the electricity made by my brain. That is all that he and Mr. Rothy and David Homer ever see in the jiggles. But the whole story's there. If they were as smart as they think they are, they could read it.

Only David's brain ever touches the edge of anything it does not know. It feels the surface a little and is kindly. When Doctor Marley and Mr. Rothy and Erika realised what his brain did they killed him. Yes, they killed him. Oh, not like they did old Ozzie to make him dead-dead. They killed him so that he was dead like they-dead.

The technicians hooked me to the machine they call an e.e.g. and it began to tick. Doctor Marley asked, "Ibby, why did you try to strike me with the hammer? Did you think I was your father?" I felt a great hardness around me.

They have hooked me to the machine many times. They have asked me: "Did you love your mother? Did you hate your father? Did you love or hate your brothers and sisters? Did you wet the bed when you were a little boy?"

Whatever I answer—maybe "yes," maybe "no"—does not matter. They already have a hard answer in their brains and they look at mine through it, and the shadow of it hides mine.

But this time one word would not say it. I did not want the saying hidden by the dark shadow in Doctor Marley's brain. The answer was soft and full and all around, but I could not easily make words of it because I am a moron and have seizures and walk with a shuffle. It is not a noisy shuffle.

That is why I am in this hospital. They call it a hospital. It used to be called The Home and of course a Home is what it still is.

In those jiggles on the paper is the saying of it. If they were made into words the saying would go like this:

Saturday morning I took the weekly reports from the "farm" to Doctor Marley's house. The farm is where they do their experimenting with animals to find out how the human brain works, they say, so that they can help morons like me who shuffle and have seizures. They also call it "the lab." Doctor Marley doesn't come down to the farm on Saturday mornings. They let me take the reports over to him. It makes me feel round and full and kindly.

Erika let me in. She is very in-living and looks like sun coming up and a cloud. She told me to go up to her father's study. The edge of her brain felt kindly.

The Doctor sat at his desk with his back to all-windows. When he swivels his chair he can look out over a deck and around a great valley. I like this place because here I can out-live without effort. The wrinkles of the valley are woods and vineyards and meadows. They roll on me greenly and I flow into softness like touching a great soft body. It is me and I am it. All of me is round and green and buoyant and kindly.

If I were to say this to Doctor Marley he would nod. "Yes, Ibby, your mother." I would feel a great stone.

Many things do this to me or something like it. And if someone is around they tell me, "Stop daydreaming, Ibby, it isn't good for you."

This morning Doctor Marley took the reports. "Thank you, Ibby." He was in-living like his daughter, but it too was kindly.

Then he leaned back and began talking. Often times he does this with me. I know he is not talking to me. He is just thinking out loud. He doesn't want anyone to hear him talking to himself, and he thinks better when he puts things into words. So I stand there out-living in the rollingness of the valley. Around him is the feel of no interruptions. That is why he thinks aloud to me because I am a moron with seizures and a shuffle and do not interrupt.

His thought words were, "Strange thing, Ibby. The Charles Adams cat lay on the deck asleep in the sun. Then he got up and looked towards the end of the deck. I followed the direction of his eyes but didn't see anything."

Mostly I never listen to out-loud thoughts. I hear words but don't know their meaning. I let the words surround me while I sport in the rollingness of the valley. But this morning my out-living brain enfolded all he said because they were words I knew.

You see, Charles Adams is a black cat with a white shirt and white socks. He washes only the white on him and it is the whitest white there is.

The Doctor's thought words flowed around me. "Maybe he had seen a fly or a grasshopper. But no. He got up and started to creep towards the end of the deck. His ears were flat and his tail straight and his legs short. I looked into the trees beyond the deck. Maybe a bird? No bird."

I have not made clear about the deck. It is one storey above the ground. One end is above where cars are parked. The drive comes up a steep, steep hill and curves into a turnaround.

Doctor Morley went on thinking. "I got up and went to the window that overlooked the parking area. I looked into it. Nothing. Charles Adams crouched at the edge of the deck and his ears stayed flat. I looked down the drive.

"I moved along the window to where I could see past the curve in the drive. Charles Adams couldn't. And there, a hundred yards away, came Tiki our Siamese. When Tiki got to a spot where Charles Adams could see him, Charles Adams got up and went down the outside stairway to meet him. I went back to my desk.

"A little thing, Ibby, but I asked myself, how did Charles Adams know that Tiki was coming up the drive? From where he lay sleeping he could not even see the driveway."

I said, "But he felt a cat coming."

Then I shuffled my feet. I had interrupted. But these thought-words I knew. What I did not know was why he did not understand the reason Charles Adams did what he did. I smelled no thought of understanding around me.

Doctor Marley laughed. "Thank you, Ibby. I knew I could depend on you for the right answer."

He was laughing at me. But I didn't mind. All the doctors and technicians laugh at me when I speak, but they are kindly.

I saw the flyswat on a pile of magazines and I picked it up and gave it to him. He killed a fly. Then he looked at me and did not understand why I knew he wanted the flyswat.

If he is so smart, why didn't he feel it all simply? He had been laughing at me. A fly sat on the corner of the reports. He saw it and I saw it and he thought, where is that flyswat? And I gave it to him.

He took up the reports and read. His face became a grey hill crossed with cloud wrinkles. He began thinking aloud again.

"It's impossible. Old Ozzie couldn't have finished that new test without an error this morning. He's getting too damned smart. We'll have to work a switch in the routine and make it tougher."

Why did he say old Ozzie couldn't? The report said old Ozzie did. Maybe you have already felt Ozzie. He's a big tomcat, a very big tomcat that looks like fog prowling the valley. He is one of five cats they use at the farm. They don't use other animals. I have heard Doctor Marley think that a cat's brain is more like the human brain than any other animal's brain.

This morning I was at the farm when Mr. Rothy tested Ozzie. He explained it all to me. He always explains things to me the way Doctor Marley thinks out loud to me.

"Ibby, when I put Ozzie in this box he will have these little plastic rings hanging around him. If he pulls the white one, he will get a blast of air. If he pulls the green one, that block will fall down. If he pulls the yellow one, he will get an ultrasonic sound. And if he pulls the red one, he'll get his breakfast.

"He can't tell colours. They are to make my reporting easier. When he learns to pull the right ring I'll change them around and see what he does then. Those things fastened to his head are electrodes and the wires go to an e.e.g. here and will make jiggly lines when his brain makes electricity."

Mr. Rothy put Ozzie among the dangling rings and hooked the wires. I felt the electrodes on Ozzie's head like whiskers in the wrong place and they troubled him. But Mr. Rothy says he does not even feel them. How does Mr. Rothy know?

Big green eyes looked at me from an oval of fog and there was out-living between us. But I am a moron and have seizures and walk with a shuffle and should not feel anyone, not even a cat. Yet there was hunger in the air. Ozzie stood high and I knew the red ring meant breakfast. He could feel the colour between us. Mr. Rothy doesn't know there is such feeling. And Ozzie hooked a claw in the ring and a door opened and his plate of hamburger came out.

"I'll be goddamned," Mr. Rothy said. "He's lucky and I'm unlucky. We'll have to change this before we even start."

Ozzie ate his breakfast and sat among the dangling rings and washed. When his paw brushed an electrode or made a wire pull, he stopped his washing. Once the green eyes looked at me and the out-living ended between us.

Then I interrupted Doctor Marley's thought-words again. "They're coming," I said.

"What? Who's coming, Ibby?" I smelled startledness. He looked around and out the window.

The black and white cat and the Siamese cat came from somewhere out of sight. Buttercups and forget-me-nots looked at me and I looked at them and there was warm sun between us. And the two cats stretched out on the deck.

"Did you mean the cats, Ibby?" Doctor Marley laughed. It was in-living but kindly. "I suppose they told you they were coming." There was no smell of anger at me for interrupting.

They had not told me they were coming. I had felt them coming. That was all. It is not new to me. I did not answer him.

He picked up his thought words. "We'll stump old Ozzie. We'll leave the red ring where it is and add an orange one. The orange ring will give the food."

He made little words on the margin of the report and asked me to take it back to Mr. Rothy.

I walked down the hill and across the street and across the bridge to the farm and gave the report back to Mr. Rothy.

He thanked me. He read Doctor Marley's little words and said, "Now we'll see how long it takes old Ozzie to learn which one hits the jackpot."

I looked at the five cages and the five cats and they looked at me. Green eyes prodded a remembering of Doctor Marley saying that an orange ring would give the food. Ozzie washed his face. Then the other four cats washed their faces.

That day a new technician reported at the farm. Mr. Rothy said, "Ibby, this is Mr. Homer. He is going to help us this summer. He is studying psychology at the University." Then he said to the new technician, "Dave, this is Ibby. He does all the brain work around here." He laughed. I felt his teasing, but it was kindly.

A hand smooth as madrone bark shook mine. "I'm glad to know you, Ibby," Mr. Homer said. And I said I was glad to know him, and I felt him kindly. I knew that the study of psychology was about the brain. I would like not to be a moron and have seizures and walk with a shuffle so that I could go to a university and study about the brain. But he did not feel that.

Around the farm I did the usual things. When evening came they made the test again. I wasn't there because I had a seizure. Next morning I heard Doctor Marley and Mr. Rothy and Mr. Homer talking. I felt running in darkness because old Ozzie had hooked the orange ring first off. And the running smelled of anger in the darkness, for the other cats had pulled the orange ring after only a little hesitation.

"We must be tipping them off," Doctor Marley said. "Are you sure you didn't leave some smell of food on the orange ring?"

"I didn't put in the food until after the experiment was set up," Mr. Rothy said. "Then I touched none of the rings."

Doctor Marley looked at the cages. "Cats aren't that smart or lucky. Maybe it was the warmth of the colour that did it. Next time use the green for the food pull."

David Homer listened and said nothing. He was new here. I do not interrupt on the farm either. But green eyes looked at me out of a fog-oval and I looked at them. I felt a softness of fur touched and went away.

Later I heard that all the cats pulled the green ring when next they were tested and the test was abandoned, at least for a time. Another test was taken up. Blinders were placed over the cats' eyes and glasses were used with different types of lenses. The reactions were recorded in jiggles the same kind as Doctor Marley gets when he asks me why I tried to hit him with the hammer.

One day I came in when Mr. Rothy and David were making a test. I heard Mr. Rothy say, "Goddamn, look how that jumped. What the hell triggered that increase in the impulse?"

David looked at me. I felt a thin blade prying. Then he asked me to go over to the dairy and get a pint of milk.

Mr. Rothy said, "We've plenty of milk right here."

David said, "Let him go anyway. Huh?" I smelled a roundness like wanting.

When I got back Mr. Rothy said, "It could be. It must be his shuffle. They hear it. Ozzie hears it."

David said, "But why should that make a difference?"

"His shuffle disturbs them."

"But they should be used to that by now. And he doesn't have anything to do with their feeding. Maybe there's some uh-uh rapport, something like that that we are missing."

"Come off it, Dave. You're getting way out into ESP country. That's a dirty word around here."

"No. This is different." I smelled roundness again and wanting. If David had been a cat he would have purred. "There are emanations from the brain," he said, "electrical—we know that. Maybe their emanations meet and overlap and are absorbed and they feel each other or something."

"Nuts. They're cats and Ibby has an IQ of 76. They can hardly produce enough electricity to jiggle the e.e.g. Don't let Doctor Marley hear you say anything like that. Hundreds of guys would jump at the privilege of working with the old man like you are. And don't forget Erika. You let her find out that you have ideas her father doesn't agree with and she'll cut you up into little pieces. No. There's something about Ibby that upsets our subjects and spoils the tests."

I rubbed a wall of ugly stones. Mr. Rothy asked me to go over to the dairy and watch the cows eat. David didn't say anything. I smelled roundness again, but the roundness was like a wrinkled apple. So I went. I liked to watch cows eat. It feels kindly.

I came and went about the farm. When I stopped in the cat place I felt sharp lights tearing at my eyes and once I heard Mr. Rothy say, "Don't be a fool, Dave. It's his shuffle, I tell you."

Then Doctor Marley operated on the cats and took away part of their brains, a different part from each cat. He talked gently to old Ozzie while Mr. Rothy prepared the needle. I felt a smooth wall that was very high and no one could climb it. But with David it was different. The wall crinkled like a thin curtain.

All around old Ozzie was the smell of running and no place to hide. He lay very still and Mr. Rothy pushed the plunger of the needle a little more. He snapped old Ozzie's ear. "I guess he's ready," Mr. Rothy said.

I went away because the feeling all about was not kindly. It was full of wanting: a high tree to climb; thick soft brush to hide in; a cool dark house to get under and lay in shadows and be safe. I smelled no place that did not feel go-away, that did not feel blackness and scare.

Days became tall. I watched the cattle eat and felt kindly. I stood by the wide hospital lawn and wrapped myself around with soft greenness and snuggled in it. A technician said, "Stop your daydreaming, Ibby, it will make you have a seizure." So I looked up at the sky and felt the softness of a cloud as my hands moulded it into the shape of good feeling.

When I came to the cat place again there was emptiness. I felt only a little smoothness of madrone bark, like the feel of soft fur not touched.

They set up tests with the cats wearing glasses made to shut out one eye or the other. Mr. Rothy recorded the findings and about him was a bubbling. David helped. I heard the sound of a still lake with underneath the feel of storms remembered.

Mr. Rothy said, "Here, Ibby, take this over to Doctor Marley. Dave, the old man's going to like this one."

I took the report over to Doctor Marley. Erika let me in like always. I felt blossoms and water singing. She said, "Ibby, have you seen Dave Homer?"

"He's at the farm," I said, and went up with the report.

Doctor Marley thanked me and read and thought aloud: "I saw it coming. The parts of the brain left have taken over the work. This can be rechecked in a lab and I'll be found right."

My ribs scraped a great rock in the meadow. So I withdrew to only a little out-living and it was there. "The black and white cat is coming out to the deck," I said.

"Yes, yes, Ibby. You felt him coming." Doctor Marley laughed. And the black and white cat came from out of sight and sat down in front of the window and washed his face. The Doctor saw him and I felt a riffled wall harden and took my hands away from it.

Then Doctor Marley made small words on the report and told me to take it back to the farm. I walked back the way I came. Around me was softness. My feet left prints in the sidewalk that faded slowly. Mr. Rothy read the small words and said, "The old man wants us to try the food test again."

They wouldn't let me stay now when they made the tests. I went into the young corn field and swam through the leaves. Twice I swam the length of the field, then I went back to the hospital lawn and wrapped it around me. David came by and I felt the smell of a smile and of laughter. I felt Erika sitting on a flower. Then he saw me and the fingers of a seizure hunted me in the blanket of the lawn, but I crawled away fast and hid in the folds.

David said, "It took old Ozzie a full twenty minutes to find the green ring to pull. It was the last one he pulled."

The fingers of a seizure went away. Tears like drops of rain came through the blanket of lawn and wet my face. I said, "The green one was the food ring."

He said, "The green one, Ibby." And I felt Erika sitting on a flower and he ran his mind over her body with softness.

There was a nettle in my wrappings of lawn and I heard itching and burning and I died a little with a seizure.

The next time I walked past the cat place I stopped and sat on the step. All around me felt kindly, but the sound of soft fur came faintly through the thin colour of sickness and I heard the memory of "the green one."

Mr. Rothy's voice pounded through the open door.

"For a week they've fumbled and messed around. Today each one pulls the green ring first time up. The probabilities of that happening are way off the blackboard."

I rocked on my hunkers. The screen latch clicked. "Ibby, how long have you been sitting there?" It was David.

"A while. But I did not shuffle."

"But you thought, 'the green one'?"

"I thought 'the green one.' "

"Oh, come off it, Dave," said Mr. Rothy. "That can't happen. They haven't even half a brain left. They can't read minds."

"He thought 'the green one,' and they pulled the green one."

"Why don't they read our minds then? How come it is Ibby's mind they tune in on?"

"Our brains are walled around with an insulation of what we call truths. Ibby's brain, what there is of it, may not be so restricted. His seizures are caused perhaps by strong electrical impulses. Maybe he can put out more than we know."

Mr. Rothy used a bad word. "We'll change the food ring back to red. And Ibby, don't you come around here any more."

I heard the red ring. The sound grew big and rang loudly on the faintness of soft fur.

Then I was up at the reservoir sliding on the smooth water. I cupped my hands around my eyes to catch the smell of bluegills in the under-clear.

A seizure or two later, I was a grey house-tit and flew down to the duck sanctuary in the park. In the bamboo around me was the smell of ducks sleeping. I heard ducklings shedding their down in the shadow of words from a park bench by the pond walk.

"It has meaning, Erika, I tell you. The next test and the next they pulled the red ring."

I smelled a hand patting a child's head. "Yes, David. But you said yourself that Ibby wasn't around."

"But he had heard Rothy say a red ring before he left that day."

"Yes, and when you changed the colour of the food ring again, they fumbled, not knowing which one to pull."

"But Ibby wasn't there and he didn't know of the change. I want to run a real test, Erika. I want Ibby there knowing the colour of the food ring and see if the cats pull it right away. Then I want to change it without his knowing, and have him there and see what happens then. Then I'll let him know the new colour and see if he communicates it to the cats."

Erika's laughter smelled of a dirty barnyard. And I felt thoughts as stiff as the bamboo around me with sharp leaves cutting my cheeks.

"You've got to be joking, David. A moron like Ibby can't communicate with cats. I wouldn't even suggest the idea to Father."

"I'm sorry, Erika." There was the feel of hurt.

"Don't kiss me. I don't want you to kiss me."

They got up from the park bench and I flew to the cedar tree by my window and went to bed.

Out of the sound of greyness next morning came Mr. Rothy's words like winter rain. "Ibby, come bury old Ozzie. He finally ran out of brains."

Dave was there. "All we do is hack away their brains bit by bit and put them back together to see if they live until they have no more brains left. All we prove is the obvious."

"It's a job," said Mr. Rothy. "It's a project, and don't you forget it. It's the kind of project that looks good on paper and brings in research money. And that's what figures."

What was old Ozzie and what was me stood there and all around was greyness. The soft fur sounded like stone and lay like blackness in my arms. I stopped at the barn and we smelled the new hay and the cattle. Old Ozzie had been a barn cat. We went to the edge of the cornfield and the singing meadowlarks felt kindly for us in the greyness. I dug a hole in the ground and Ozzie and I got into it and pulled the dirt over us. Then I shuffled back to the cat place.

Doctor Marley was there and Mr. Rothy. David cleaned and repaired old Ozzie's cage, and tools lay around him. Doctor Marley asked Mr. Rothy to go over to Administration and get the cost records on old Ozzie.

Then Doctor Marley said, "David, I'm not satisfied with your work." I felt the sending away of Mr. Rothy had purpose. "You haven't shown the proper attitude toward scientific discipline."

David said, "I'm sorry, sir. It seemed to me there was a proper correlation between the behaviour of the cats and the presence of Ibby. I wanted to see it checked out."

To both of them I was still in the ground with old Ozzie.

"Young man, I just finished saying that your attitude is unsatisfactory. I direct this project and it is presumptuous of you to suggest deviation."

"I'm sorry, sir."

"I had great hopes for you. You showed promise. But now your work must be re-evaluated."

It was then that David began to die. The hammer on the table raised its head, listening.

"I realise that I was wrong," David said. "It won't happen again, sir."

He died more and the hammer rose higher.

"Your toying with ESP or whatever you wish to call an imagined relationship between the lab animals and a moron is nothing short of a mockery of all I stand for."

"Yes, sir."

"And don't try to see Erika again."

Then David was as dead as Doctor Marley. Not dead-dead like old Ozzie, but dead like Mr. Rothy and Doctor Marley.

The hammer raised very high. My hand clutched the handle. I was trying to keep it from hitting Doctor Marley. I wasn't trying to hit him. It was David who helped me stop the hammer and bring it back to the table.

That is what the jiggles on the paper will tell you. If you're so smart you can read it all there.

Fear can also be considered as a motivational state. Psychologists have conditioned fear to a neutral stimulus, then the subjects have learned a new response to eliminate or reduce this conditioned stimulus. They escape or avoid the fear-arousing stimulus, just as we avoid (hopefully) an area marked "Danger, 10,000 volts."

If one can be conditioned to fear, what about the learned association of a more complex emotion such as love? So far there is no psychological love potion to prescribe. Yet there are ways to induce intense pleasure in humans, like electrical stimulation of the brain and drugs. Perhaps if these emotions were paired systematically with a certain person, that person would become loved.

What kind of consequences would a technique such as this have for society? For marriage? Perhaps couples could get a "booster shot" of conditioned love to save an ailing marriage. Sheckley's "Love, Incorporated" shows one (but not the best) of such possible worlds.

8. the executive rat

Larry Eisenberg

Let a psychologist make a presentation of his or her favorite research; give the presenter a full opportunity to discuss and expound; wait until the inevitable pause of acknowledgment and approval; then, if you wish to deflate this psychologist, try saying, "so what?"

The reason the "so what" response is so catastrophic to most psychologists is that it rubs on an area of exquisite scraped-skin sensitivity: that of generalizability. Nobody cares what eighteen hooded Norway rats have done in a series of flat, black-painted pine runways atop stainless-steel counters in a research laboratory. Nor does it matter what several hundred college students have reported in a self-description questionnaire. What matters are the implications, the "so what," the generalizability of behavioral findings from those rats or those college students to other organisms or other people. The search for generalizability can be seen as psychology's search for the holy grail. It is the search for generalizability that drives the psychologist Dr. Fahy in "The Executive Rat." And his holy crusade is hazardous.

The generalizability Dr. Fahy seeks is a common one in the behavioral sciences: from animal to man. In working with human subjects, one finds there are several different kinds of typical responses to being research subjects. Some people become "good" subjects, trying to anticipate what the experimenter wants, and then behaving in ways to deliver just those actions. The so-called "faithful" subject behaves honestly and truthfully. Among other possible subject responses, Dr. Fahy eventually runs into one called the "negative" subject. The "negative" subject tries to sabotage the research by interfering or reacting in contrary ways. In paper-and-pencil tests in research, the subject may lie, make stray marks on the answer sheet, or present a deliberately false picture. In this story, the subject's potential for being negative is truly shocking.

A last issue raised by this story is that of research ethics. The storm of concern about research ethics arose from the Tuskegee, Alabama, study of untreated syphilis patients and the New York study of live cancer cells injected into unknowing patients. Medical students are taught that a first ethical principle in their practice should be to do no harm. The potential for violation of that principle in psychiatric and psychological research occurs often. However, one can take the risk of doing harm only under certain circumstances. One can harm animals only if it is done humanely and scientifically. One can take the risk of harming humans only if they can give genuine informed consent to volunteer in the research. Independent monitoring of the research proposal prior to any action is also used. As for our protagonist Dr. Fahy, he would have a difficult time rationalizing to such an independent group the ethics of his research.

The "just world hypothesis" in psychology holds that this is a just world and that people deserve what they get and get what they deserve. In this story, Dr. Fahy indeed gets what he deserves. His fate is an object lesson to all the potentially ambitious scientists out there.

Many psychologists consider "frustration" as an intervening variable and define it operationally, such as through the operations involved in blocking an organism from a goal. For example, if a rat learns to run down a straight alley for food, it could be thwarted or blocked by the experimenter putting a barrier in the alley as well as removing or delaying the food. When a fellow human blocks us from a goal (frustrates us), we often react with the emotion of anger, and, in many cases, aggressive behavior.

In "The Executive Rat," Dr. Fahy uses several methods of inducing frustration: he sets up a difficult problem to solve in a limited time period, and he insults and complains to the engineer. What are some other methods Fahy uses, and what goals are blocked? Furthermore, note that while Dr. Fahy is interested in the ulcer-producing effects of stress, he has forgotten about a basic psychological principle. What is it? A hint—see the above paragraph.

When Dr. Fahy came into my office I was genuinely pleased to see him. His reputation in behavioral studies was international and I had been secretly hoping that he would ask me to design instrumentation to carry out his new series of experiments. Doctor Fahy was in his early sixties, a tall, thin man with a rather dour expression. He spoke with a minimum of words and the only time he smiled was when he learned that his grant would not be charged for my engineering time.

"As a recent arrival at the university," he said, "I'm quite overwhelmed by the many free services."

"The parts and construction time are charged," I pointed out.

"Naturally," said Dr. Fahy.

His pale blue eyes wandered about my office and fixed upon the double row of filing cabinets.

"You have a kind of executive responsibility, haven't you?"

I nodded.

"I'm the sole engineer of the electronics laboratory but I do have two technicians working for me. With all due modesty, let me point out that I've designed everything from a simple stimulator for monkey testicles, to special purpose minicomputers."

Dr. Fahy did not seem overly impressed.

"That's fine," he said dryly. "Then you should have no difficulty meeting my needs. I've typed out a set of specifications which I will leave in your care. Within a week's time, I should like a cost estimate and a projected date of delivery."

I accepted the three pages of specifications with some disappointment. He seemed to sense my distress.

"Is anything wrong?" he asked.

I sighed.

"The standard working practice here is for the researcher to outline for me what he intends to do. I have some familiarity with the ongoing research. Knowing exactly what is supposed to happen enables me to design a better and more apt instrument."

He nodded.

"That certainly sounds reasonable," said Dr. Fahy. "Nevertheless, I don't work that way. You build me what I've asked for and I'll assume all responsibility for the end result."

I was annoyed at his brusqueness, but I concealed my anger.

"As you wish," I said.

It was clear from a study of the specifications that Doctor Fahy wanted an animal shocker of extraordinary potential. He was asking for a ten-thousand volt source capable of delivering up to ten milliamperes of current. Once chosen, the current setting was to remain stable to within a tiny fraction of a per cent despite wide variations in the resistance of whatever it was he intended to shock. An accurate printout of the value of the shocking current was required as well as a complex logic facility to program the sequencing and timing of the shocks. There were to be remote and local controls. But most disconcerting were the extraordinary tolerances that were asked for. Clearly this design would require utterly new techniques.

I was still quite annoyed at Dr. Fahy's reticence. If he had told me what he intended to do I might have been able to point out where some of the specifications might be relaxed.

I decided to go first to the library and read up on his past experiments. I had no difficulty in locating his work. The experimental journals of psychology were filled with them. Generally his procedure was to shock experimental rats in the region of the tail and at the same time submit them to trying sets of circumstances. In his "executive rat" experiment, he found that animals who could not turn off the shock source right after it had been turned on developed a severe kind of stomach ulcer.

In some cases, he would warn the rat by a tone that the shock was about to come. In other cases, he provided them with a series of tones which terminated just before the shock began. But in every case, he gave the animals tasks to perform despite the approaching shocks.

My greatest disappointment came in discovering that nowhere did he describe his experimental apparatus, save in general terms. He did not specify the accuracies of his readings and his results were summarized only in statistical terms. I went back to my office and set about a preliminary design to meet the specifications. When I had finished I called in Dr. Fahy and showed him the results. He became quite angry.

"Four thousand dollars to build?" he cried. "That's outrageous!"

I attempted to soothe his anger.

"If only you would relax your specifications," I began.

He snorted. "Nonsense. This apparatus is virtually the same as the one I had at Bradman Tech. The engineer there had no difficulty in building it for half the amount. I don't like to question your competence, but perhaps you'd like me to get his design?"

"There's no need for that," I snapped. "I don't need someone else's design. But the cost of the parts and labor cannot be reduced."

He shrugged.

"If I must, I must," he said. "When can I have it?"

"It will take about a month to get the parts and a month to build the entire unit. Then a week or two to check it out. However, there are other people ahead of you."

He waved his hands impatiently.

"I can't wait my turn," said Dr. Fahy. "If you want a letter from the university president authorizing you to give me priority, I'll get it for you. I have a new grant proposal to write in five months. I must have fresh data long before then."

At that point I made my first great error.

"I'll give you first priority," I said.

By virtue of nights and Saturdays of unstinting work, I managed to deliver this very complex system within two months' time. He accepted it matter-of-factly and without even perfunctory thanks. After two days of trial, Dr. Fahy called me on the phone and indicated that except for minor bugs everything seemed in order.

He then dropped his bombshell.

"I shall require four copies of the prototype system," he said. "And I must have them as soon as possible. I have four technicians drawing salary here and they'll have nothing to do until you supply me with these additional units."

"We're not set up for production," I said. "We do have other jobs to do."

"That's not my concern," he said. "If you require authorization for additional technicians I'll get it for you."

Two days later the authorization to hire two additional technicians came through from the university president's office. But there was no provision for additional bench space. Thereafter I spent two frustrating weeks interviewing job prospects before I found two men who seemed even marginally to meet the job requirements.

I asked Dr. Fahy, in the interests of speedy output, to let me borrow the prototype for use as a model, but he refused.

"The unit is in constant use and can't be spared," he said.

I had to work very closely with my new technicians and provide them with detailed mechanical drawings of each section, particularly demonstrating the way all parts had to be mounted. Weeks went by with Dr. Fahy constantly calling me and complaining about the delay. I was in the process of checking out unit Number Two, when Dr. Fahy called again.

"Unit One just quit in the middle of an experiment. Can you come right over?"

I went. The power light on the panel of the controller was off. I checked the fuse—it was okay. After an hour of fussing around I disconnected the controller and took it back to my laboratory. Two hours later I found a poorly soldered connection. When it had been resoldered, I returned the controller. Dr. Fahy set his dials for a test run. His panel lights indicated an incorrect sequence of shocks.

"It's been acting up this way lately," said Dr. Fahy.

I was astonished.

"I wish you'd told me before. That should never happen."

He was annoyed when I insisted on taking the controller back once again. This time it took a day of probing to find that one of my integrated circuit chips was failing on an intermittent basis. I replaced the chip and to my shocked surprise, there was no improvement.

Dr. Fahy came by at this time.

"My experiments are stopped cold," he said. "Why don't you let me try Unit Two?"

"You can," I said reluctantly. "But I haven't really completed all my checkout tests."

"I'll take my chances," he said.

The third unit came to my bench a week later, but I still hadn't found the trouble with Unit One. And then I discovered a diode had been wired in backwards. I was both elated and annoyed.

"I'll be damned," I cried. "How the hell did this unit ever work?"

I delivered it to Dr. Fahy the following day. He seemed relieved.

"The printouts of this second unit are unreliable," he said.

I took Unit Two back.

Unit Four was ready when I finally repaired Unit Two and then I discovered Unit One back on my bench with a note from Dr. Fahy stating that it had become unreliable again. The symptoms of Unit One were the most baffling I had ever encountered. It would function perfectly on my bench and then misbehave in Dr. Fahy's lab.

"Are your assistants reporting the symptoms correctly?" I asked.

"My assistants do not touch any of the controls. I am the only one to do so," he said.

I shook my head in puzzlement as he added a few biting sarcasms. I had taken to waking in the middle of the night with hunger pains that were allayed only by lots of milk and cookies. Sometimes they even occurred between meals during the day and I began to keep snacks on hand in my laboratory. My weight began to go up, despite the fact that I had begun to come in on Sundays in an attempt to catch up on my backlog.

Dr. Fahy saw me nibbling cookies and sipping milk one day.

"It's not a good idea to cram in so many sweets," he said.

I was flattered by his interest. It was the first time he had seemed to take personal note of my habits. I told him of my continual hunger. He became alive with attention.

"When did it start?" he asked. "How frequently do you get these hunger pains?"

I told him.

"Have you had a physical recently?"

"About six months ago," I said. "Everything was perfect."

"If I'm right," he said, "you've got a peptic ulcer."

He insisted on taking a full history of my symptoms before sending me off to the specialist associated with the university who confirmed the diagnosis. He put me on a diet of milk and antacids.

"Are you under particular stresses?" he asked sympathetically.

"For the time being, yes."

"They won't help your ulcer. You need a long rest from your work."

I sighed.
"I don't see how."

But a small amount of relief appeared on the horizon. The annual engineering show had come to town and despite my work load, I decided to attend. With a great deal of guilt, I went to a talk given by a man named Holcomb, an engineer from Bradman Tech, Dr. Fahy's former bailiwick. Afterwards I went up to chat with Holcomb.

"Did you know Dr. Fahy?" I asked.

He smiled.

"Very well," he said. "He's a difficult man to please. Fortunately, I never did any instrumentation for him."

"Who did?" I asked.

He seemed puzzled.

"Did what?"

"Built his previous instrumentation at Bradman Tech." I told him of the troubles I had run into. He shook his head.

"Beats the hell out of me," he said. "I never built anything for Fahy. He's a trained engineer. He got his bachelor's degree in electronics before he got his doctorate in psychology."

"Then you have no idea who designed and built his shockers?"

"He probably made them himself," said Holcomb. "At the time I was annoyed because he didn't use me."

"I wish I had been that lucky," I said.

But now I began to wonder what was going on. That night I went back to my office and pondered the situation. Dr. Fahy had been quite clear in asserting that his equipment had been designed for him at Bradman Tech. He had been lying to me.

I walked over to his laboratory in the Hanley Building. It was after nine in the evening and the doors were locked. I used my duplicate keys and went inside the deserted rooms. All of the equipment, including three of my malfunctioning programers, had been turned off. I meticulously checked his interconnecting cables and found three sets running off somewhere. I followed them and found that they ran to a remote room where presumably Dr. Fahy could operate electronic gear including a programable patch board.

I had never seen any of this equipment before.

I turned it on and checked the function of all the controls. I then went back into the main laboratory and turned on the equipment I had designed. It was almost one in the morning before I finished my investigation.

I slept poorly that night and spent quite a bit of time at the refrigerator, allaying my hunger pains. In the morning I went to see Dr. Fahy. He seemed annoyed at the interruption.

"I must talk to you," I said. "I believe I've found the source of our electronic instability."

He smiled.

"Have you really?"

"It's in your remote logic control system," I said. "The one that you designed and patched into my units."

He nodded.

"I suppose you want an explanation," he said.

"To put it mildly."

"I've always worked with rats," said Dr. Fahy. "Generally speaking, they develop ulcers for two reasons. One is the situation where they are given shocks unless they solve an unsolvable problem. The other involves solving an infinite number of solvable problems."

"It seems I got an infinite number of insolvable problems," I said.

"That was nasty, wasn't it," said Dr. Fahy. "But you see, working with rats is one thing. Extrapolating to humans in quite another."

"So you chose me. And I did develop the expected gastric ulcer."

"You're angry and I don't blame you," said Fahy. "But there was a scientific problem of the greatest moment at stake. I became obsessed with knowing the answer. Can you understand that?"

"How do you think the faculty council will react when I report what you've done?"

"You won't do that," said Dr. Fahy. "For one thing, you can't prove your case. I'll deny everything."

"Even this conversation?"

"Even that. But you have an alternative choice. If you agree to sign a waiver of claims against me, I'll publish our data. It will rock the scientific world and give you immortality."

"No doubt," I said dryly. "But who would publish this caricature of science?"

"I'm editor of a psychology journal. I'll put it through myself. There will be a storm afterward but I'll take my chances with that. It's a once-in-a-lifetime experiment that has never been done before."

"You could have gotten volunteers."

"Could I? If the subject had prior knowledge, it would have vitiated all the results, wouldn't it?" Fahy was gloating.

"I'll think it over," I said.

I was sitting in my office, a week later, when the terrible news broke. There had been a dreadful accident in the Fahy laboratory. One of the shockers had failed to operate. Dr. Fahy had opened the cage that should have turned off the high voltage through an interlock. In some inexplicable way he had received a ten-thousand-volt jolt across the chest. After intensive first-aid he had finally come around.

As I arrived, he was being carried out of the laboratory on a stretcher. One of his young assistants was in tears.

"How is he?" I asked her.

"He'll live—but he's a very sick man," she said.

After she had gone, I examined the cage where the accident had occurred. I turned off the power at the main panel and went directly to the interlock. It took but a few seconds to remove the override wire I had inserted the night before and restore the interlock circuit to its normal state. Then I set off to my office to write a report about the mechanical failure of the interlock to the shocker.

That night, for the first time in many months, I slept through without a single hunger pain.

9. love, incorporated

Robert Sheckley

"You can't buy love," the saying goes. But in the future of which Sheckley writes, love—not just sex—is for sale. Caveat emptor!

This is not an unreasonable projection. After all, psychologists have determined many of the principles governing fear. In general, fears appear to be learned according to the laws of classical conditioning. A neutral stimulus paired with pain soon evokes negative emotional responses and escape and/or avoidance behavior. The word "hot" or a 110-volt electrical outlet has little meaning for an infant; however, once paired with a burn or a shock, the child will avoid these formerly neutral stimuli. Similarly, a person can learn through conditioning to associate a stimulus with pleasure, just as the prick of a needle becomes pleasurable to the drug addict. Furthermore, through electrical stimulation of the brain, we can produce rage, or pain, or an emotional state so pleasurable that hungry rats will walk over piles of food for it. Humans also find brain stimulation pleasurable. In this story, conditioning techniques are meshed with brain stimulation—a powerful combination. In fact, such a combination was originally used to establish that autonomic responses could be operantly conditioned. That is, subjects could change their own heart rates or blood pressure when rewarded by brain stimulation. Note that here the biofeedback (brain stimulation) is also highly rewarding.

So, perhaps someday, someone will find a "love center" in the brain (probably in the hypothalamus). Given the complexity of this emotion, this discovery appears somewhat unlikely. Even so, Sheckley's "conditioned love" is one possible extrapolation from the present research on brain stimulation and conditioning.

Another emotional state, frustration, is also evident in this story. Frustration occurs when the individual is blocked from a goal. How is our hero, Alfred Simon, thwarted? Frustration often, but not always, leads to aggression, which can be direct (against the frustrating agent) or displaced (against someone not directly involved but often having some characteristics in common with the source of the frustration). Is Alfred Simon's aggressive behavior direct or displaced?

Alfred Simon was born on Kazanga IV, a small agricultural planet near Bootes, and there he drove a combine through the wheat fields, and in the long, hushed evenings listened to the recorded love songs of Earth.

Life was pleasant enough on Kazanga, and the girls were buxom, jolly, frank and acquiescent, good companions for a hike through the hills or a swim in the brook, staunch mates for life. But romantic—never! There was good fun to be had on Kazanga, in a cheerful, open manner. But there was no more than fun.

Simon felt that something was missing in this bland existence. One day, he discovered what it was.

A vendor came to Kazanga in a battered spaceship loaded with books. He was gaunt, white-haired, and a little mad. A celebration was held for him, for novelty was appreciated on the outer worlds.

The vendor told them all the latest gossip; of the price war between Detroit II and III, and how fishing fared on Alana, and what the president's wife on Moracia wore, and how oddly the men of Doran V talked. And at last someone said, "Tell us of Earth."

"Ah!" said the vendor, raising his eyebrows. "You want to hear of the mother planet? Well, friends, there's no place like old Earth, no place at all. On Earth, friends, everything is possible, and nothing is denied."

"Nothing?" Simon asked.

"They've got a law against denial," the vendor explained, grinning. "No one has ever been known to break it. Earth is *different*, friends. You folks specialize in farming? Well, Earth specializes in impracticalities such as madness, beauty, war, intoxication, purity, horror, and the like, and people come from light-years away to sample these wares."

"And love?" a woman asked.

"Why girl," the vendor said gently, "Earth is the only place in the galaxy that still has love! Detroit II and III tried it and found it too expensive, you know, and Alana decided it was unsettling, and there was no time to import it on Moracia or Doran V. But as I said, Earth specializes in the impractical, and makes it pay."

"Pay?" a bulky farmer asked.

"Of course! Earth is old, her minerals are gone, and her fields are barren. Her colonies are independent now, and filled with sober folk such as yourselves, who want value for their goods. So what else can old Earth deal in, except the nonessentials that make life worth living?"

"Were you in love on Earth?" Simon asked.

"That I was," the vendor answered, with a certain grimness. "I was in love, and now I travel. Friends, these books . . ."

For an exorbitant price, Simon bought an ancient poetry book, and reading, dreamed of passion beneath the lunatic moon, of dawn glimmering whitely upon lovers' parched lips, of locked bodies on a dark sea-beach, desperate with love and deafened by the booming surf.

And only on Earth was this possible! For, as the vendor told, Earth's scattered children were too hard at work wrestling a living from alien soil. The wheat and corn grew on Kazanga, and the factories increased on Detroit II and III. The fisheries of Alana were the talk of the Southern star belt, and there were dangerous beasts on Moracia, and a whole wilderness to be won on Doran V. And this was well, and exactly as it should be.

But the new worlds were austere, carefully planned, sterile in their perfections. Something had been lost in the dead reaches of space, and only Earth knew love.

Therefore, Simon worked and saved and dreamed. And in his twenty-ninth year he sold his farm, packed all his clean shirts into a serviceable handbag, put on his best suit and a pair of stout walking shoes, and boarded the Kazanga-Metropole Flyer.

At last he came to Earth, where dreams *must* come true, for there is a law against their failure.

He passed quickly through Customs at Spaceport New York, and was shuttled underground to Times Square. There he emerged blinking into daylight, tightly clutching his handbag, for he had been warned about pickpockets, cutpurses, and other denizens of the city.

Breathless with wonder, he looked around.

The first thing that struck him was the endless array of theatres, with attractions in two dimensions, three, or four, depending upon your preference. And what attractions!

To the right of him a beetling marquee proclaimed: LUST ON VENUS! A DOCUMENTARY ACCOUNT OF SEX PRACTICES AMONG THE INHABITANTS OF THE GREEN HELL! SHOCKING! REVEALING!

He wanted to go in. But across the street was a war film. The billboard shouted, THE SUN BUSTERS! DEDICATED TO THE DARE-DEVILS OF THE SPACE MARINES! And further down was a picture called TARZAN BATTLES THE SATURNIAN GHOULS!

Tarzan, he recalled from his reading, was an ancient ethnic hero of Earth.

It was all wonderful, but there was so much more! He saw little open shops where one could buy food of all worlds, and especially such native Terran dishes as pizza, hotdogs, spaghetti and knishes. And there were stores which sold surplus clothing from the Terran spacefleets, and other stores which sold nothing but beverages.

Simon didn't know what to do first. Then he heard a staccato burst of gunfire behind him, and whirled.

It was only a shooting gallery, a long, narrow, brightly painted place with a waist-high counter. The manager, a swarthy fat man with a mole on his chin, sat on a high stool and smiled at Simon.

"Try your luck?"

Simon walked over and saw that, instead of the usual targets, there were four scantily dressed women at the end of the gallery, seated upon bullet-scored chairs. They had tiny bull's-eyes painted on their foreheads and above each breast.

"But do you fire real bullets?" Simon asked.

"Of course!" the manager said. "There's a law against false advertising on Earth. Real bullets and real gals! Step up and knock one off!"

One of the women called out, "Come on, sport! Bet you miss me!"

Another screamed, "He couldn't hit the broad side of a spaceship."

"Sure he can!" another shouted. "Come on, sport!"

Simon rubbed his forehead and tried not to act surprised. After all, this was Earth, where anything was allowed as long as it was commercially feasible.

He asked, "Are there galleries where you shoot men, too?"

"Of course," the manager said, "But you ain't no pervert, are you?"

"Certainly not!"

"You an outworlder?"

"Yes. How did you know?"

"The suit. Always tell by the suit." The fat man closed his eyes and chanted, "Step up, step up and kill a woman! Get rid of a load of repressions! Squeeze the trigger and feel the old anger ooze out of you! Better than a massage! Better than getting drunk! Step up, step up and kill a woman!"

Simon asked one of the girls, "Do you stay dead when they kill you?"

"Don't be stupid," the girl said.

"But the shock—"

She shrugged her shoulders. "I could do worse."

Simon was about to ask how she could do worse, when the manager leaned over the counter, speaking confidentially.

"Look, buddy. Look what I got here."

Simon glanced over the counter and saw a compact submachine gun.

"For a ridiculously low price," the manager said, "I'll let you use the tommy. You can spray the whole place, shoot down the fixtures, rip up the walls. This drives a .45 slug, buddy, and it kicks like a mule. You really know you're firing when you fire the tommy."

"I am not interested," Simon said sternly.

"I've got a grenade or two," the manager said. "Fragmentation, of course. You could really—"

"No!"

"For a price," the manager said, "you can shoot *me,* too, if that's how your tastes run, although I wouldn't have guessed it. What do you say?"

"No! Never! This is horrible!"

The manager looked at him blankly. "Not in the mood now? OK. I'm open twenty-four hours a day. See you later, sport."

"Never!" Simon said, walking away.

"Be expecting you, lover!" one of the women called after him.

Simon went to a refreshment stand and ordered a small glass of cola-cola. He found that his hands were shaking. With an effort he steadied them, and sipped his drink. He reminded himself that he must not judge Earth by his own standards. If people on Earth enjoyed killing people, and the victims didn't mind being killed, why should anyone object?

Or should they?

He was pondering this when a voice at his elbow said, "Hey, bub."

Simon turned and saw a wizened, furtive-faced little man in an oversize raincoat standing beside him.

"Out-of-towner?" the little man asked.

"I am," Simon said. "How did you know?"

"The shoes. I always look at the shoes. How do you like our little planet?"

"It's—confusing," Simon said carefully. "I mean I didn't expect—well—"

"Of course," the little man said. "You're an idealist. One look at your honest face tells me that, my friend. You've come to Earth for a definite purpose. Am I right?"

Simon nodded. The little man said, "I know your purpose, my friend. You're looking for a war that will make the world safe for something, and you've come to the right place. We have six major wars running at all times, and there's never any waiting for an important position in any of them."

"Sorry, but—"

"Right at this moment," the little man said impressively, "the downtrodden workers of Peru are engaged in a desperate struggle against a corrupt and decadent monarchy. One more man could swing the contest! *You,* my friend, could be that man! *You* could guarantee the socialist victory!"

Observing the expression on Simon's face, the little man said quickly, "But there's a lot to be said for an enlightened aristocracy. The wise old king of Peru (a philosopher-king in the deepest Platonic sense of the word) sorely needs your help. His tiny corps of scientists, humanitarians, Swiss guards, knights of the realm, and royal peasants is sorely pressed by the foreign-inspired socialist conspiracy. A single man, now—"

"I'm not interested," Simon said.

"In China, the Anarchists—"

"No."

"Perhaps you'd prefer the Communists in Wales? Or the Capitalists in Japan? Or if your affinities lie with a splinter group such as Feminists, Prohibitionists, Free Silverists, or the like, we could probably arrange—"

"I don't want a war," Simon said.

"Who could blame you?" the little man said, nodding rapidly. "War is hell. In that case, you've come to Earth for love."

"How did you know?" Simon asked.

The little man smiled modestly. "Love and war," he said, "are Earth's two staple commodities. We've been turning them both out in bumper crops since the beginning of time."

"Is love very difficult to find?" Simon asked.

"Walk uptown two blocks," the little man said briskly. "Can't miss it. Tell 'em Joe sent you."

"But that's impossible! You can't just walk out and—"

"What do you know about love?" Joe asked.

"Nothing."

"Well, we're experts on it."

"I know what the books say," Simon said. "Passion beneath the lunatic moon—"

"Sure, and bodies on a dark sea-beach desperate with love and deafened by the booming surf."

"You've read that book?"

"It's the standard advertising brochure. I must be going. Two blocks uptown. Can't miss it."

And with a pleasant nod, Joe moved into the crowd.

Simon finished his cola-cola and walked slowly up Broadway, his brow knotted in thought, but determined not to form any premature judgments.

When he reached 44th Street, he saw a tremendous neon sign flashing brightly. It said, LOVE, INC.

Smaller neon letters read, *Open 24 Hours a Day!*

Beneath that it read, *Up One Flight.*

Simon frowned, for a terrible suspicion had just crossed his mind. Still, he climbed the stairs and entered a small, tastefully furnished reception room. From there he was sent down a long corridor to a numbered room.

Within the room was a handsome gray-haired man who rose from behind an impressive desk and shook his hand, saying, "Well! How are things on Kazanga?"

"How did you know I was from Kazanga?"

"That shirt. I always look at the shirt. I'm Mr. Tate, and I'm here to serve you to the best of my ability. You are—"

"Simon, Alfred Simon."

"Please be seated, Mr. Simon. Cigarette? Drink? You won't regret coming to us, sir. We're the oldest love-dispensing firm in the business, and much larger than our closest competitor, Passion Unlimited. Moreover, our fees are far more reasonable, and bring you an improved product. Might I ask how you heard of us? Did you see our full page ad in the *Times*? Or—"

"Joe sent me," Simon said.

"Ah, he's an active one," Mr. Tate said, shaking his head playfully. "Well sir, there's no reason to delay. You've come a long way for love, and love you shall have." He reached for a button on his desk, but Simon stopped him.

Simon said, "I don't want to be rude or anything, but . . ."

"Yes?" Mr. Tate said, with an encouraging smile.

"I don't understand this," Simon blurted out, flushing deeply, beads of perspiration standing out on his forehead. "I think I'm in the wrong place. I didn't come all the way to Earth just for . . . I mean, you can't really sell *love*, can you? Not *love*! I mean, then it isn't really *love*, is it?"

"But of course!" Mr. Tate said, half rising from his chair in astonishment. "That's the whole point! Anyone can buy sex. Good lord, it's the cheapest thing in the universe, next to human life. But *love* is rare, *love* is special, *love* is found only on Earth. Have you read our brochure?"

"Bodies on a dark sea-beach?" Simon asked.

"Yes, that one. I wrote it. Gives something of the feeling, doesn't it? You can't get that feeling from just *anyone*, Mr. Simon. You can get that feeling only from someone who loves you."

Simon said dubiously, "It's not genuine love though, is it?"

"Of course it is! If we were selling simulated love, we'd label it as such. The advertising laws on Earth are strict, I can assure you. Anything can be sold, but it must be labelled properly. That's ethics, Mr. Simon!"

Tate caught his breath, and continued in a calmer tone. "No sir, make no mistake. Our product is not a substitute. It is the exact self-same feeling that poets and writers have raved about for thousands of years. Through the wonders of modern science we can bring this feeling to you at your convenience, attractively packaged, completely disposable, and for a ridiculously low price."

Simon said, "I pictured something more—spontaneous."

"Spontaneity has its charm," Mr. Tate agreed. "Our research labs are working on it. Believe me, there's nothing science can't produce, as long as there's a market for it."

"I don't like any of this," Simon said, getting to his feet. "I think I'll just go see a movie."

"Wait!" Mr. Tate cried. "You think we're trying to put something over on you. You think we'll introduce you to a girl who will *act* as though she loved you, but who in reality will not. Is that it?"

"I guess so," Simon said.

"But it just isn't so! It would be too costly for one thing. For another, the wear and tear on the girl would be tremendous. And it would be psychologically unsound for her to attempt living a lie of such depth and scope."

"Then how do you do it?"

"By utilizing our understanding of science and the human mind."

To Simon, this sounded like double-talk. He moved toward the door.

"Tell me something," Mr. Tate said. "You're a bright looking young fellow. Don't you think you could tell real love from a counterfeit item?"

"Certainly."

"There's your safeguard! *You* must be satisfied, or don't pay us a cent."

"I'll think about it," Simon said.

"Why delay? Leading psychologists say that *real* love is a fortifier and a restorer of sanity, a balm for damaged egos, a restorer of hormone balance, and an improver of the complexion. The love we supply you has everything: deep and abiding affection, unrestrained passion, complete faithfulness, an almost mystic affection for your defects as well as your virtues, a pitiful desire to please, *and,* as a plus that only Love, Inc., can supply: that uncontrollable first spark, that blinding moment of love at first sight!"

Mr. Tate pressed a button. Simon frowned undecisively. The door opened, a girl stepped in, and Simon stopped thinking.

She was tall and slender, and her hair was brown with a sheen of red. Simon could have told you nothing about her face, except that it brought tears to his eyes. And if you asked him about her figure, he might have killed you.

"Miss Penny Bright," said Tate, "meet Mr. Alfred Simon."

The girl tried to speak but no words came, and Simon was equally dumbstruck. He looked at her and *knew.* Nothing else mattered. To the depths of his heart he knew that he was truly and completely loved.

They left at once, hand in hand, and were taken by jet to a small white cottage in a pine grove, overlooking the sea, and there they talked and laughed and loved, and later Simon saw his beloved wrapped in the sunset flame like a goddess of fire. And in blue twilight she looked at him with eyes enormous and dark, her known body mysterious again. The moon came up, bright and lunatic, changing flesh to shadow, and she wept and beat his chest with her small fists, and Simon wept too, although he did not know why. And at last dawn came, faint and disturbed, glimmering upon their parched lips and locked bodies, and nearby the booming surf deafened, inflamed, and maddened them.

At noon they were back in the offices of Love, Inc. Penny clutched his hand for a moment, then disappeared through an inner door.

"Was it real love?" Mr. Tate asked.

"Yes!"

"And was everything satisfactory?"

"Yes! It was love, it was the real thing! But why did she insist on returning?"

"Post-hypnotic command," Mr. Tate said.

"What?"

"What did you expect? Everyone wants love, but few wish to pay for it. Here is your bill, sir."

Simon paid, fuming. "This wasn't necessary," he said. "Of course I would pay you for bringing us together. Where is she now? What have you done with her?"

"Please," Mr. Tate said soothingly. "Try to calm yourself."

"I don't want to be calm!" Simon shouted. "I want Penny!"

"That will be impossible," Mr. Tate said, with the barest hint of frost in his voice. "Kindly stop making a spectacle of yourself."

"Are you trying to get more money out of me?" Simon shrieked. "All right, I'll pay. How much do I have to pay to get her out of your clutches?" And Simon yanked out his wallet and slammed it on the desk.

Mr. Tate poked the wallet with a stiffened forefinger. "Put that back in your pocket," he said. "We are an old and respectable firm. If you raise your voice again, I shall be forced to have you ejected."

Simon calmed himself with an effort, put the wallet back in his pocket and sat down. He took a deep breath and said, very quietly, "I'm sorry."

"That's better," Mr. Tate said. "I will not be shouted at. However, if you are reasonable, I can be reasonable too. Now, what's the trouble?"

"The trouble?" Simon's voice started to lift. He controlled it and said, "She loves me."

"Of course."

"Then how can you separate us?"

"What has the one thing got to do with the other?" Mr. Tate asked. "Love is a delightful interlude, a relaxation, good for the intellect, for the ego, for the hormone balance, and for the skin tone. But one would hardly wish to *continue* loving, would one?"

"I would," Simon said. "This love was special, unique—"

"They all are," Mr. Tate said. "But as you know, they are all produced in the same way."

"What?"

"Surely you know something about the mechanics of love production?"

"No," Simon said. "I thought it was—natural."

Mr. Tate shook his head. "We gave up natural selection centuries ago, shortly after the Mechanical Revolution. It was too slow, and commercially unfeasible. Why bother with it, when we can produce any feeling at will by conditioning and proper stimulation of certain brain centers? The result? Penny, completely in love with you! Your own bias, which we calculated, in favor of her particular somatotype, made it complete. We always throw in the dark sea-beach, the lunatic moon, the pallid dawn—"

"Then she could have been made to love anyone," Simon said slowly.

"Could have been *brought* to love anyone," Mr. Tate corrected.

"Oh, lord, how did she get into this horrible work?" Simon asked.

"She came in and signed a contract in the usual way," Tate said. "It pays very well. And at the termination of the lease, we return her original personality—untouched! But why do you call the work horrible? There's nothing reprehensible about love."

"It wasn't love!" Simon cried.

"But it was! The genuine article! Unbiased scientific firms have made qualitative tests of it, in comparison with the natural thing. It every case, *our* love tested out to more depth, passion, fervor and scope."

Simon shut his eyes tightly, opened them and said, "Listen to me. I don't care about your scientific tests. I love her, she loves me, that's all that counts. Let me speak to her! I want to marry her!"

Mr. Tate wrinkled his nose in distaste. "Come, come, man! You wouldn't want to *marry* a girl like that! But if it's marriage you're after, we deal in that, too. I can arrange an idyllic and nearly spontaneous love-match for you with a guaranteed government-inspected virgin—"

"No! I love Penny! At least let me speak to her!"

"That will be quite impossible," Mr. Tate said.

"Why?"

Mr. Tate pushed a button on his desk. "Why do you think? We've wiped out the previous indoctrination. Penny is now in love with someone else."

And then Simon understood. He realized that even now Penny was looking at another man with that passion he had known, feeling for another man that complete and bottomless love that unbiased scientific firms had shown to be so much greater than the old-fashioned, commercially unfeasible natural selection, and that upon that same dark sea-beach mentioned in the advertising brochure—

He lunged for Tate's throat. Two attendants, who had entered the office a few moments earlier, caught him and led him to the door.

"Remember!" Tate called. "This in no way invalidates your own experience."

Hellishly enough, Simon knew that what Tate said was true.

And then he found himself on the street.

At first, all he desired was to escape from Earth, where the commercial impracticalities were more than a normal man could afford. He walked very quickly, and his Penny walked beside him, her face glorified with love for him, and him, and him, and you, and you.

And of course he came to the shooting gallery.

"Try your luck?" the manager asked.

"Set 'em up," said Alfred Simon.

10. such stuff

John Brunner

This story builds on a solid framework—the existing psychological re-search on dreaming. When one treads the fine line between dreams and reality, the results can be both interesting and terrifying.

Although the analysis of dreams can be traced back to Sigmund Freud (at least), modern scientific methods of dream research emerged in the 1950s. These techniques include the measurement of brain-wave changes through electroencephalogram (EEG) recordings combined with the recording of movements of the eyes behind closed lids. Rapid eye move-ments (REMs) and characteristic brain waves occur in stage-1 REM sleep —the state of sleep in which nearly all dreams occur.

From the pioneering work of William C. Dement and other research-ers, we have learned that people need to dream and, in fact, dream every night. Dement's subjects were awakened whenever they showed REM sleep, and thus the onset of dreaming. They attempted more and more dreams as they were deprived over successive nights. When, after several nights, these subjects were allowed to dream, they showed a dramatic increase in the proportion of sleep they spent dreaming—as if to make up for lost dreams.

The content of dreams has been studied extensively by Calvin Hall. It appears that in dreams we move around a lot, talk, sit, watch, socialize, and play. We rarely if ever type, sew, cook, clean house, or wash dishes. In fact, the major themes of dreaming involve our most important or stressful problems—love, sex, death, aggression, and morality.

John Brunner's story takes us into, and beyond, the area of dream research. As with any new area of research, there are opportunities for new discoveries, along with an occasional hazard. Typically, the reality many psychologists think they exist in, the laboratory, is an insulated and un-eventful place. On occasion, a distracted researcher may lean against a rack of electronic equipment and be shocked into awareness. And once in a while a frustrated rat, perhaps acting in behalf of rat-kind, nips the intruding experimenter.

As we develop new techniques and probe into new areas, however, there may be unknown and more subtle threats. One such hazard may lurk in the psychologist's interaction with his research subjects—as the "hero" of "Such Stuff" discovers. "To sleep, perchance to dream." Ay, there's where the rub meets the road, and where such stuff as nightmares are made of.

With the leads of the electroencephalograph stringing out from his skull like webs spun by a drunken spider, the soft adhesive pads laid on his eyes like pennies, Starling resembled a corpse which time had festooned with its musty garlands. But a vampire-corpse, plump and rosy in its state of not-quite-death. The room was as still as any mausoleum, but it smelt of floor polish, not dust; his coffin was a hospital bed and his shroud a fluffless cotton blanket.

Except for the little yellow pilot lights in the electronic equipment beside the bed, which could just be seen through the ventilation holes in the casing, the room was in darkness. But when Wills opened the door from the corridor the shaft of light which came over his shoulder enabled him to see Starling clearly.

He would rather not have seen him at all—laid out thus, lacking candles only because he was not dead. That could be remedied, given the proper tools: a sharpened stake, a silver bullet, crossroads at which to conduct the burial—

Wills checked himself, his face prickly with new sweat. It had hit him again! The insane idea kept recurring, like reflex, like pupils expanding under belladonna, for all he could do to drive it down. Starling lay like a corpse because he had grown used to not pulling loose the leads taped to his head— *that's all! That's all! That's all!*

He used the words like a club to beat his mind into submission. Starling had slept like this for months. He lay on one side, in a typical sleeper's attitude, but because of the leads he barely moved enough in the course of a night to disturb the bedclothes. He breathed naturally. Everything was normal.

Except that he had done it for months, which was incredible and impossible and not in the least natural.

Shaking from head to foot, Wills began to step back through the door. As he did so, it happened again—now it was happening dozens of times a night. A dream began.

The electroencephalograph recorded a change in brain activity. The pads on Starling's eyes sensed eye movements and signaled them. A relay closed. A faint but shrill buzzer sounded.

Starling grunted, stirred, moved economically as though to dislodge a fly that had settled on him. The buzzer stopped. Starling had been woken; the thread of his dream was snapped.

And he was asleep again.

Wills visualized him waking fully and realizing he was not alone in the room. Cat-silent, he crept back into the corridor and closed the door, his heart thundering as though he had had a narrow escape from disaster.

Why? In daytime he could talk normally with Starling, run tests on him as impersonally as on anyone else. Yet at night—

He slapped down visions of Starling by day, Starling corpselike in his bed at night, and moved down the long corridor with his teeth set to save them from chattering. He paused at other doors, pressing his ear to them or glancing inside for a moment. Some of those doors led to private infernos which ought to have jarred on his own normality with shocking violence, as they always used to. But none affected him like Starling's passiveness—not even the moaning prayers of the woman in Room 11, who was being hounded to death by imaginary demons.

Conclusion: his normality had gone.

That thought also recurred in spite of attempts to blank it out. In the long corridor which framed his aching mind like a microwave guide tube, Wills faced it. And found no grounds for rejecting it. They were in the wards; he in the corridor. So what? Starling was in a ward, and he was not a patient. He was sane, free to leave whenever he wished. In remaining here he was simply being co-operative.

And telling him to go away would solve nothing at all.

His rounds were over. He went back toward the office like a man resolutely marching toward inevitable doom. Lambert—the duty nurse—was snoring on the couch in the corner; it was against regulations for the duty nurse to sleep, but Wills had had more than he could bear of the man's conversation about drink and women and what he was missing tonight on television and had told him to lie down.

He prodded Lambert to make him close his mouth and sat down at the desk, drawing the night report toward him. On the printed lines of the form his hand crawled with its shadow limping behind, leaving a trail of words contorted like the path of a crazy snail.

5 A.M. All quiet except Room 11. Patient there normal.

Then he saw what he had written. Angrily, he slashed a line through the last word, another and another till it was illegible, and substituted "much as usual." Normal!

I am in the asylum of myself.

He tilted the lamp on the desk so it shone on his face and turned to look at himself in the wall mirror provided for the use of female duty nurses. He was a little haggard after the night without sleep, but nothing else was visibly wrong with him. Much as usual, like the patient in Room 11.

And yet Starling was sleeping the night away without dreams, undead.

Wills started, fancying that something black and threadlike had brushed his shoulder. A picture came to him of Starling reaching out from his bed with the tentacle leads of the e.e.g., as if he were emitting them from spinnerets, and weaving the hospital together into a net of his own, trapping Wills in the middle like a fly.

He pictured himself being drained of his juices, like a fly.

Suddenly Lambert was sitting up on the couch, his eyes flicking open like the shutters of a house being aired for a new day. He said, "What's the matter, doc? You're as white as a flaming sheet!"

There was no black threadlike thing on his shoulder. Wills said with an effort, "Nothing. Just tired, I think."

He thought of sleeping, and wondered what he would dream.

The day was bright and warm. He was never good at sleeping in the daytime; when he woke for the fourth or fifth time, unrested, he gave up. It was Daventry's day for coming here, he remembered. Maybe he should go and talk to him.

He dressed and went out of doors, his eyes dark-ringed. In the garden a number of the less ill patents were working listlessly. Daventry and the matron moved among them, complimenting them on their flowers, their thorough weeding, the lack of aphis and blackfly. Daventry had no interest in gardening except insofar as it was useful for therapy. The patients, no matter how twisted their minds were, recognized this, but Daventry apparently didn't know they knew. Wills might have laughed, but he felt laughter was receding from him. Unused faculties, like unused limbs, atrophy.

Daventry saw him approach. The bird eyes behind his glasses flicked poultry-wise over him, and word passed from the thin-lipped mouth to the matron, who nodded and moved away. The sharp face was lit by a smile; brisk legs began to carry him over the tiny lawn, which was not mown by the patients because mowers were too dangerous.

"Ah, Harry!" in Daventry's optimistic voice. "I want a word with you. Shall we go to the office?" He took Wills's arm as he turned, companionably; Wills, who found the habit intolerable, broke the grip before it closed.

He said, "As it happens, I want a word with you, too."

The edginess of his tone sawed into Daventry's composure. The bird eyes scanned his face, the head tipped a little on one side. The list of Daventry's mannerisms was a long one, but he knew the reasons for all of them and often explained them.

"Hah!" he said. "I can guess what this will be about!"

They passed into the building and walked side by side with their footsteps beating irregularly like two palpitating hearts. In the passageway Daventry spoke again.

"I presume there's been no change in Starling, or you'd have left a note for me—you were on night duty last night, weren't you? I didn't see him today, unfortunately; I was at a conference and didn't get here till lunch-time."

Wills looked straight ahead, to the looming door of Daventry's office. He said, "No—no change. But that's what I wanted to talk about. I don't think we should go on."

"Ah!" said Daventry. It was automatic. It meant something altogether different, like "I'm astonished"—but professionally Daventry disavowed astonishment. The office accepted them, and they sat down to the idiot noise of a bluebottle hammering its head on the window.

"Why not?" Daventry said abruptly.

Wills had not yet composed his answer. He could hardly speak of the undead Starling with pads on his eyes like pennies, of the black tentacles reaching out through the hospital night, of the formulated but suppressed notion that he must be treated with sharp stakes and silver bullets, and soon.

He was forced to throw up improvisation like an emergency earthwork, knowing it could be breached at a dozen points.

"Well—all our other cases suggest that serious mental disturbance results from interference with the dreaming process. Even the most resistant of our other volunteers broke down after less than two weeks. We've prevented Starling from dreaming every night for five months now, and even if there are no signs of harm yet it's probable that we *are* harming him."

Daventry had lit a cigarette while Wills talked. Now he waved it in front of him, as thought to ward off Wills's arguments with an adequate barrier—a wisp of smoke.

"Good gracious, Harry!" he said affably. "What damage are we doing? Did you detect any signs of it last time you ran Starling through the tests?"

"No—that was last week and he's due for another run tomorrow—no, what I'm saying is that everything points to dreaming being essential. We may not have a test in the battery which shows the effect of depriving Starling of his dreams, but the effect must be there."

Daventry gave a neutral nod. He said, "Have you asked Starling's own opinion on this?"

Again, concede defeat from honesty: "Yes. He said he's perfectly happy to go on. He said he feels fine."

"Where is he at the moment?"

"Today's Tuesday. He goes to see his sister in the town on Tuesday afternoons. I could check if you like, but—"

Daventry shrugged. "Don't bother. I have good news for you, you see. In my view, six months is quite long enough to establish Starling's tolerance of dream deprivation. What's next of interest is the nature of his dreams when he's allowed to resume. So three weeks from now I propose to end the experiment and find out."

"He'll probably wake himself up reflexively," Wills said.

Daventry was prepared to take the words with utmost seriousness. He said, "What makes you think that?"

Willis had meant it as a bitter joke; when he reconsidered, he found reason after all. He said, "The way he's stood the treatment when no one else could. Like everyone else we tested, his dreaming frequency went up in the first few days; then it peaked at about thirty-four times a night, and dropped back to its current level of about twenty-six, which has remained constant for about four months now. Why? His mind seems to be malleable, and I can't believe that. People need dreams; a man who can manage without them is as unlikely as one who can do without food or water."

"So we thought," Daventry said briskly. Wills could see the conference papers being compiled in his mind, the reports for the *Journal of Psychology* and the four pages in *Scientific American,* with photographs. And so on. "So we thought. Until we happened across Starling, and he just proved we were wrong."

"I—" began Wills. Daventry took no notice and went on.

"Dement's work at Mount Sinai wasn't utterly definitive, you know. Clinging to first findings is a false attitude. We're now compelled to drop the idea that dreaming is indispensable, because Starling has gone without dreams for months and so far as we can tell—oh, I grant that: so far and no further—he hasn't suffered under the experience."

He knocked ash into a bowl on his desk. "Well, that was my news for you, Harry: that we finish the Starling series at the six-month mark. Then we'll see if he goes back to normal dreaming. There was nothing unusual about his dreaming before he volunteered; it will be most interesting . . ."

It was cold comfort, but it did give him a sort of deadline to work to. It also rid him of part of the horror he had suffered from having to face the presence in his mind of the vampire-corpse like a threat looming down the whole length of his future life-path. It actually heartened him till the time came to retest Starling.

He sat waiting in his office for half an hour beforehand, because everything was otherwise quiet and because before he came up for psychological examination Starling always underwent a physical examination by another member of the staff. Not that the physicals ever turned anything up. But the psychologicals hadn't either. It was all in Wills's mind. Or in Starling's. But if it was in Starling's, he himself didn't know.

He knew the Starling file almost by heart now—thick, much thumbed, annotated by himself and by Daventry. Nonetheless, he turned back to the beginning of it, to the time five months and a week ago when Starling was just one volunteer among six men and six women engaged in a follow-up to check on Dement's findings of 1960 with superior equipment.

There were transcripts of dreams with Freudian commentary, in their limited way extraordinarily revealing, but not giving a hint of the most astonishing secret—that Starling could get by without them.

I am in a railway station. People are going to work and coming home at the same time. A tall man approaches and asks for my ticket. I try to explain that I haven't bought one yet. He grows angry and calls a policeman, but the policeman is my grandfather. I cannot understand what he says.

I am talking to one of my schoolteachers, Mr. Bullen. I am very rich and I have come to visit my old school. I am very happy. I invite Mr. Bullen to ride in my car, which is big and new. When he gets in the door handle comes off in his hand. The door won't lock. I cannot start the engine. The car is old and covered with rust. Mr. Bullen is very angry but I do not care very much.

I am in a restaurant. The menu is in French and I order something I don't know. When it comes I can't eat it. I call the manager to make a complaint and he arrives in a sailor's uniform. The restaurant is on a boat and rocks so that I feel ill. The manager says he will put me in irons. People in the restaurant laugh at me. I break the plates on which the food is served, but they make no noise and no one notices. So I eat the food after all.

That last one was exactly what you would expect from Starling, Wills thought. He ate the food after all, and liked it.

These were records extracted from the control period—the week during which his dreams and those of the other volunteers were being noted for comparison with later ones, after the experiment had terminated. In all the other eleven cases that was from three days to thirteen days later. But in Starling's—!

The dreams fitted Starling admirably. Miserable, small-minded, he had gone through life being frustrated, and hence the dreams went wrong for him, sometimes through the intervention of figures of authority from childhood, such as his hated grandfather and the schoolteacher. It seemed that he never fought back; he—ate the food after all.

No wonder he was content to go on co-operating in Daventry's experiment, Wills thought bleakly. With free board and lodging, no outside problems involved, he was probably in paradise.

Or a kind of gratifying hell.

He turned up the dreams of the other volunteers—the ones who had been driven to quit after a few nights. The records of their control week showed without exception indications of sexual tension, dramatized resolutions of problems, positive attacks on personal difficulties. Only Starling provided continual evidence of total surrender.

Not that he was outwardly inadequate. Considering the frustration he had endured first from his parents, then from his tyrannical grandfather and his teachers, he had adjusted well. He was mild-mannered and rather shy, and he lived with his sister and her husband, but he held down a fairly good job, and he had a small, constant circle of acquaintances mainly met through his sister's husband, on whom he made no great impression but who all "quite liked" him.

Quite was a word central to Starling's life. Hardly any absolutes. Yet—his dreams to the contrary—he could never have surrendered altogether. He'd made the best of things.

The volunteers were a mixed bag: seven students, a teacher on sabbatical leave, an out-of-work actor, a struggling writer, a beatnik who didn't care, and Starling. They were subjected to the process developed by Dement at New York's Mount Sinai Hospital, as improved and automatized by Daventry—the process still being applied to Starling even now, which woke him with a buzzer whenever the signs indicating dreaming occurred. In the eleven other cases, the effect found was the same as what Dement established: interrupting the subjects' dreaming made them nervous, irritable, victims of uncontrolled nervous tension. The toughest quit after thirteen days.

Except for Starling, that was to say.

It wasn't having their sleep disturbed that upset them; that could be proved by waking them between, instead of during, dreams. It was not being *allowed* to dream that caused trouble.

In general, people seemed to spend about an hour a night dreaming, in four or five "installments." That indicated that dreaming served a purpose: what?

Dissipation of antisocial tensions? A grooming of the ego as repressed desires were satisfied? That was too glib an answer. But without Starling to cock a snook in their faces, the experimenters would have accepted a similar generalization and left the matter there till the distant day when the science of mind was better equipped to weigh and measure the impalpable stuff of dreams.

Only Starling *had* cropped up. At first he reacted predictably. The frequency of his dreaming shot up from five times a night to twenty, thirty and beyond, as the buzzer aborted each embryo dream, whirling into nothing his abominable grandfather, his tyrannical teachers—

Was there a clue there? Wills had wondered that before. Was it possible that, whereas other people *needed* to dream, Starling hated it? Were his dreams so miserable that to go without them was a liberation to him?

The idea was attractive because straightforward, but it didn't hold water. In the light of previous experiments, it was about equivalent to saying that a man could be liberated from the need to excrete by denying him food and water.

But there was no detectable effect on Starling! He had not lost weight, nor grown more irritable; he talked lucidly, he responded within predictable limits to IQ tests and Rorschach tests and every other test Wills could find.

It was purely unnatural.

Wills checked himself. Facing his own reaction squarely, he saw it for what it must be—an instinctive but irrational fear, like the fear of the stranger who comes over the hill with a different accent and different table manners. Starling was human; *ergo,* his reactions were natural; *ergo,* either the other experiments had agreed by coincidence and dreaming wasn't indispensable, or Starling's reactions were the same as everyone's and were just being held down until they blew like a boiler straining past its tested pressure.

There were only three more weeks to go, of course.

The habitual shy knock came to the door. Wills grunted for Starling to come in, and wondered as he looked at him how the sight of him passive in bed could inspire him to thoughts of garlic, sharpened stakes and burial at crossroads.

The fault must be in his own mind, not in Starling's.

The tests were exactly as usual. That wrecked Wills's tentative idea about Starling welcoming the absence of his dreams. If indeed he was liberated from a burden, that should show up in a trend toward a stronger, more assured personality. The microscopic trend he actually detected could be assigned to the fact that for several months Starling had been in this totally undemanding and restful environment.

No help there.

He shoved aside the pile of test papers. "Mr. Starling," he said, "what made you volunteer for these experiments in the first place? I must have asked you before, but I've forgotten."

It was all on the file, but he wanted to check.

"Why, I don't really know, doctor," Starling's mild voice said. Starling's cowlike eyes rested on his face. "I think my sister knew someone who had volunteered, and my brother-in-law is a blood donor and kept saying that everyone should do something to benefit society, and while I didn't like the idea of being bled, because I've never liked injections and things like that, this idea seemed all right, so I said I'd do it. Then, of course, when Dr. Daventry said I was unusual and would I go on with it, I said I hadn't suffered by it and I didn't see why I shouldn't, if it was in the cause of science—"

The voice droned on, adding nothing new. Starling was very little interested in new things. He had never asked Wills the purpose of any test he submitted to; probably he had never asked his own doctor what was on a prescription form filled out for him, being content to regard the medical abbreviations as a kind of talisman. Perhaps he was so used to being snubbed or choked off if he showed too much interest that he felt he was incapable of understanding the pattern of which Wills and the hospital formed part.

He *was* malleable. It was the galling voice of his brother-in-law, sounding off about his uselessness, which pushed him into this. Watching him, Wills realized that the decision to offer himself for the experiment was probably the biggest he had ever taken, comparable in the life of anyone else with a decision to marry, or to go into a monastery. And yet that was wrong, too. Starling didn't take decisions on such a level. Things like that would merely happen to him.

Impulsively, Wills said, "And how about when the experiment is over, Mr. Starling? I suppose it can't go on forever."

Placid, the voice shaped inevitable words. "Well, you know, doctor, I hadn't given that very much thought."

No, it wasn't a liberation to him to be freed of his dreaming. It was nothing to him. Nothing was anything to him. Starling was undead. Starling was neuter in a human scale of values. Starling was the malleable thing that filled the hole available for it, the thing without will of its own which made the best of what there was and did nothing more.

Wills wished he could punish the mind that gave him such thoughts, and asked their source to go from him. But though his physical presence went, his nonexistent existence stayed, and burned and loomed and was impassive and cocked snooks in every hole and corner of Wills's chaotic brain.

Those last three weeks were the worst of all. The silver bullet and the sharpened stake, the crossroads for the burial—Wills chained the images down in his mind, but he ached from the strain of hanging on to the chains. *Horror, horror, horror,* sang an eldritch voice somewhere deep and dark within him. *Not natural,* said another in a professionally judicious tone. He fought the voices and thought of other things.

Daventry said—and was correct according to the principles of the experiment, of course—that so as to have a true control for comparison they must simply disconnect the buzzer attached to the e.e.g. when the time came, and not tell Starling what they had done, and see what happened. He would be free to finish his dreams again. Perhaps they would be more vivid, and he would remember more clearly after such a long interruption. He would—

But Wills listened with only half an ear. They hadn't predicted Starling's reaction when they deprived him of dreams; why should they be able to predict what would happen when he received them back? A chill premonition iced solid in his mind, but he did not mention it to Daventry. What it amounted to was this: whatever Starling's response was, it would be the wrong one.

He told Daventry of his partial breaking of the news that the experiment was to end, and his chief frowned.

"That's a pity, Harry," he said. "Even Starling might put two and two together when he realizes six months have gone by. Never mind. We'll let it run for another few days, shall we? Let him think that he was wrong about the deadline."

He looked at the calendar. "Give him three extra days," he said. "Cut it on the fourth. How's that?"

By coincidence—or not?—Wills's turn for night duty came up again on that day; it came up once in eight days, and the last few times had been absolutely unbearable. He wondered if Daventry had selected the date deliberately. Maybe. What difference did it make?

He said, "Will you be there to see what happens?"

Daventry's face set in a reflex mask of regret. "Unfortunately, no—I'm attending a congress in Italy that week. But I have absolute confidence in you, Harry, you know that. By the way, I'm doing up a paper on Starling for *Journ. Psych.*"—mannerisms, as always: he made it into the single word "jurnsike" —"and I think you should appear as co-author."

Cerberus duly sopped, Daventry went on his way.

That night the duty nurse was Green, a small clever man who knew judo. In a way that was a relief; Wills usually didn't mind Green's company, and had even learned some judo holds from him, useful for restraining but not harming violent patients. Tonight, though . . .

They spoke desultorily together for the first half-hour of the shift, but Wills sometimes lost track of the conversation because his mind's eye was distracted by a picture of what was going on in that room along the corridor where Starling held embalmed court among shadows and pilot lights. No one breached his privacy now as he went to bed; he did everything for himself, attached the leads, planted the penny-pads on his eyes, switched on the equipment. There was some risk of his discovering that the buzzer was disconnected, but it had always been set to sound only after thirty minutes or more of typical simple sleep-readings.

Starling, though he never did anything to tire himself out, always went to sleep quickly. Another proof of his malleable mind, Wills thought sourly. To get into bed suggested going to sleep, and he slept.

Usually it was three-quarters of an hour before the first attempted dream would burgeon in his round skull. For six months and a couple of days the buzzer had smashed the first and all that followed; the sleeper had adjusted his position without much disturbing the bedding, and—

But not tonight.

After forty minutes Wills got up, dry-lipped, "I'll be in Starling's room if you want me," he said. "We've turned off his buzzer, and he's due to start dreaming again—normally." The word sounded unconvincing.

Green nodded, picking up a magazine from the table. "On to something pretty unusual there, aren't we, doc?" he said.

"God only knows," Wills said, and went out.

His heart was pumping so loudly he felt it might waken the sleepers around him; his footsteps sounded like colossal hammer blows and his blood roared in his ears. He had to fight a dizzy, tumbling sensation which made the still lines of the corridor—floor-with-wall a pair of lines, wall-with-ceiling another pair—twist like a four-strand plait, like the bit of a hand drill or a stick of candy turned mysteriously and topologically outside-in. Swaying as though drunk, he came to Starling's door and watched his hand go to the handle.

I refuse the responsibility. I'll refuse to co-author the paper on him. It's Daventry's fault.

Nevertheless he acquiesced in opening the door, as he had acquiesced all along in the experiment.

He was intellectually aware that he entered soundlessly, but he imagined himself going like an elephant on broken glass. Everything was as usual, except, of course, the buzzer.

He drew a rubber-shod chair to a position from which he could watch the paper tapes being paid out by the e.e.g., and sat down. As yet there were only typical early sleep rhythms—Starling had not yet started his first dream of the night. If he waited till that dream arrived, and saw that all was going well, perhaps it would lay the phantoms in his mind.

He put his hand in the pocket of his jacket and closed it around a clove of garlic.

Startled, he drew the garlic out and stared at it. He had no memory of putting it there. But the last time he was on night duty and haunted by the undead appearance of Starling as he slept, he had spent most of the silent hours drawing batwing figures, stabbing their hearts with the point of his pencil, sketching crossroads around them, throwing the paper away with the hole pierced in the center of the sheet.

Oh, God! It was going to be such a relief to be free of this obsession!

But at least providing himself with a clove of garlic was a harmless symptom. He dropped it back in his pocket. He noticed two things at the same time directly afterward. The first was the alteration in the line on the e.e.g. tapes which indicated the beginning of a dream. The second was that he had a very sharp pencil in his pocket, as well as the clove of garlic—

No, not a pencil. He took it out and saw that it was a piece of rough wood, about eight inches long, pointed at one end. That was all he needed. That, and something to drive it home with. He fumbled in all his pockets. He was carrying a rubber hammer for testing reflexes. Of course, that wouldn't do, but anyway . . .

Chance had opened a gap in Starling's pajama jacket. He poised the stake carefully over his heart and swung the hammer.

As though the flesh were soft as cheese, the stake sank home. Blood welled up around it like a spring in mud, trickled over Starling's chest, began to stain the bed. Starling himself did not awaken, but simply went more limp—naturally, for he was undead and not asleep. Sweating, Wills let the rubber hammer fall and wondered at what he had done. Relief filled him as the unceasing stream of blood filled the bed.

The door behind him was ajar. Through it he heard the cat-light footfalls of Green, and his voice saying urgently, "It's Room 11, doc! I think she's—"

And then Green saw what had been done to Starling.

His eyes wide with amazement, he turned to stare at Wills. His mouth worked, but for a while his expression conveyed more than the unshaped words he uttered.

"*Doc!*" Green said finally, and that was all.

Wills ignored him. He looked down at the undead, seeing the blood as though it were luminous paint in the dim-lit room—on his hands, his coat, the floor, the bed, flooding out now in a river, pouring from the pens that waggled the traces of a dream on the paper tapes, making his feet squelch stickily in his wet shoes.

"You've wrecked the experiment," Daventry said coldly as he came in. "After I'd been generous enough to offer you co-authorship of my paper in *Journ. Psych.*, too! How could you?"

Hot shame flooded into Wills's mind. He would never be able to face Daventry again.

"We must call a policeman," Daventry said with authority. "Fortunately, he always said he thought he ought to be a blood donor."

He took up from the floor a gigantic syringe, like a hypodermic for a titan, and after dipping the needle into the river of blood hauled on the plunger. The red level rose inside the glass.

And *click*.

Through a crack in Wills's benighted skull a fact dropped. Daventry was in Italy. Therefore he couldn't be here. Therefore he wasn't. Therefore—

Wills felt his eyes creak open like old heavy doors on hinges stiff with rust, and found that he was looking down at Starling in the bed. The pens tracing the activity of his brain had reverted to a typical sleep-rhythm. There was no stake. There was no blood.

Weak with relief, Wills shuddered at remembered horror. He learned back in his chair, struggling to understand.

He had told himself that whatever Starling's reaction to being given back his dreams might be, it would be the wrong one. Well, here it was. He couldn't have predicted it. But he could explain it now—more or less. Though the mechanics of it would have to wait a while.

If he was right about Starling, a lifetime of frustration and making the best of things had sapped his power of action to the point at which he never even considered tackling an obstacle. He would just meekly try and find a way around it. If there wasn't one—well, there wasn't, and he left it at that.

Having his dreams stopped was an obstacle. The eleven other volunteers, more aggressive, had developed symptoms which expressed their resentment in manifold ways: irritability, rage, insulting behavior. But not Starling. To Starling it was unthinkable to express resentment.

Patiently, accustomed to disappointment because that was the constant feature of his life, he had sought a way around the obstacle. And he had found it. He had learned how to dream with someone else's mind instead of his own.

Of course, until tonight the buzzer had broken off every dream he attempted, and he had endured that like everything else. But tonight there was no buzzer, and he had dreamed *in* and *with* Wills. The driving of the stake, the blood, the intrusion of Green, the appearance of Daventry were part of a dream to which Wills contributed some images and Starling contributed the rest, such as the policeman who didn't have time to arrive, and the giant hypodermic. He feared injections.

Wills made up his mind. Daventry wouldn't believe him—not unless he experienced the phenomenon himself—but that was a problem for tomorrow. Right now he had had enough, and more than enough. He was going to reconnect the buzzer and get to hell out of here.

He tried to lift his arm toward the boxes of equipment on the bedside table, and was puzzled to find it heavy and sluggish. Invisible weights seemed to hang on his wrist. Even when, sweating, he managed to force his hand toward the buzzer, his fingers felt like sausages and would not grip the delicate wire he had to attach to the terminal.

He had fought for what seemed like an eternity, and was crying with frustration, when he finally understood.

The typical pattern of all Starling's dreams centered on failure to achieve what he attempted; he expected his greatest efforts to be disappointed. Hence Wills, his mind somehow linked to Starling's and his consciousness seeming to Starling to be a dream, would never be able to reconnect that buzzer.

Wills let his hands fall limp on his dangling arms. He looked at Starling, naked fear rising in his throat. How much dreaming could a man do in a single night when he had been deprived for six mortal months?

In his pocket was a sharp wooden stake and a hammer. He was going to put an end to Starling's dreaming once and for all.

He was still in the chair, weeping without tears, tied by invisible chains, when Starling awoke puzzled in the morning and found him.

IV

Developmental Psychology

Human development refers to the orderly sequence of behavioral change that occurs during the human life span. The developmental process is continuous from conception to death, but psychologists and others have focused primarily on the period of infancy and childhood, when the changes associated with physical and mental growth are most pronounced. The most dramatic physical changes in the entire life span take place in the 266 prenatal days, during which the single fertilized cell from which the infant develops increases in size and complexity many millions of times. The growth from newborn infant to adult is, by comparison, a modest change. Even more impressive than the change in size is the change in complexity. Human development is characterized by increasing differentiation and integration. The initial growth of the fertilized cell into additional cells is accompanied by an increasingly complex relationship among the cells. In only six weeks the fertilized ovum has become an embryo, which is quite recognizably human. Both before and after birth the developing infant passes through a series of stages with characteristic patterns of growth and behavior.

And when we know all of this, what do we really know about children? One of the editors had the experience of teaching child development during the semester before his first child was born and again in the subsequent semester. He was amazed at how little his notes seemed to describe his daughter and found that he had to change his lectures to match his observations.

In an effort to understand and explain the rich variety of behavior that occurs in the child, psychologists have made particular use of behavioral observation. Behavioral observation, which is simply watching the child and recording the observed behavior, may take place in a naturalistic setting such as a playground or home, or in a laboratory setting. The experimental method, in which conditions are varied in order to determine the effects on the child's subsequent behavior, are used with great caution. Because of susceptibility of children to learning experiences, experiments designed to modify or change a child's behavior could have permanent and perhaps undesirable effects, raising serious ethical issues.

Science fiction writers have been almost as interested in child development as psychologists. Science fiction writers tend to portray children in terms of extremes: extremely good, extremely powerful, or extremely bad. Sometimes the natural intuitiveness of the child is extrapolated into the ability to read minds or even to influence the behavior of others. At other times, the innocence of children may be emphasized to form a contrast with the selfish or evil behavior of adults. In other stories the amorality of the infant may be exaggerated to create the child-monster whose single-minded dedication to personal gratification may be hazardous to nearby adults. The stories that follow exhibit the ways in which two science fiction authors present children. In "The

Baby," Larry Eisenberg presents a not-so-helpless infant. In "The First Men," Howard Fast explores the possibility of bringing out the best in children.

Larry Eisenberg

What do babies know, and what can they do? Philosophers and early psychologists considered this question and proposed a variety of answers. An infant's mind is a blank slate on which experience will write, proposed John Locke. Not so, said Rousseau: the infant has, at birth, a noble sense of justice and morality which experience only corrupts. Freud, agreeing with neither, saw the infant's mind as a caldron of primal urges and drives over which controls would be painfully acquired through socialization. Psychologist William James described the world as it must appear to a helpless baby who is "assailed by eyes, ears, nose, skin, and entrails at once, [who] feels it all as one great blooming, buzzing confusion. . . ."

"Helpless as a baby" may be less descriptive of an infant than we have believed. The baby is far from a passive and fragile creature. In the moments of birth, the infant moves from the total dependency of the womb to a world in which he or she must assume primary responsibility for the life-sustaining functions: breathing, digesting, eliminating, and temperature maintaining. Most infants make this adaptation without serious difficulty. The newborn has well-developed sensory systems, with highly developed hearing, reasonably developed senses of taste and smell, and adequate, if somewhat myopic, vision. All and all, the baby is a much more active and self-sufficient individual than we have usually assumed.

Babies begin to learn from adults immediately and, almost as soon, to teach them. The baby actively signals its discomfort by crying, and adults are quick to learn to meet these needs. An interaction quickly develops in which it is difficult to say who is teaching whom. In most normal adult-infant interactions, meeting the baby's needs is reinforcing to the adult as well as to the infant. The baby calls for food, the adult supplies it; the baby burps, smiles, and sleeps, the adult breathes a sigh of relief. Everyone feels less tension. Even in everyday life, the interaction is

*often more complicated and the results less relaxing. Larry Eisenberg's
"Baby" is not hesitant about expressing his needs, and he is even willing
to work for his food. All the scientist forgot is that babies don't have much
patience.*

The baby gurgled.

He was round and amiable, with plump pink cheeks that glowed like twin rosebuds. He was only three months old but he uttered soft pleasant sounds, waved his arms and even kicked out occasionally.

Dull gray electrodes were taped at the corners of his eyes. A tiny microphone rested inside an inflatable cuff wrapped around one of his fat arms. Two more electrodes nestled snugly against his chest—others were not in clear view.

Dr. Corgan typed a couple of short coded instructions that set his computer into action. It was a compact system situated at one corner of the large sunlit room. There were two tape decks, a control console, a line printer, card reader and the typewriter.

Dr. Corgan walked back to the center of the room and looked fondly at the baby.

"Lower the barbells," he said loudly.

He was aware of the artificial quality that always crept into his voice when he was giving the baby instructions but he couldn't help it. High above, suspended from the ceiling by an intricate complex of pulleys, a brightly colored set of barbells swayed gently. He looked at the baby and then once again at the barbells. He waited patiently and then, as though by magic, they began to descend until they passed just by his eyes. The barbells were massive but lovely, with hand-painted figures done by a dear friend, a fine oil painter.

Dr. Corgan leaned forward once again.

"Open the laboratory door," he said.

He waited expectantly until the door opened, then sighed with pleasure. A warmed bottle of milk shifted down and forward into the baby's open mouth and he began to suck vigorously. His arms and legs churned contentedly. Dr. Corgan nodded and left the room. In a cubicle behind the east wall of the laboratory was a two-way mirror, through which he could observe what the baby did without being seen in turn. On occasion he gave instructions from a microphone placed behind the mirror and then studied the baby's response before returning to the lab to type new coded instructions for the computer.

Nurse Thompson sat there knitting, smartly set gray curls peeping out of the sides of her starched white cap. Dr. Corgan didn't like Nurse Thompson. She had no feeling for what he was attempting to do and was forever calling his attention to the length of time the baby had been in the laboratory. He looked at his watch and grimaced.

"Mrs. Thompson," he said with an edge of malice in his voice. "I think it's time to return the baby to the nursery."

He enjoyed the slow flush of embarrassment that spread over her rouged cheeks at the realization of her dereliction of duty. She put down her knitting and went inside to remove the electrodes from the baby. When she came out, carrying it, the baby was wrapped in a warm yellow blanket, the pink nose the only feature showing out of the wool.

"Good night," said Dr. Corgan.

After Mrs. Thompson had taken the infant back to the foundling home Dr. Corgan trudged down the hall to his office. A short bald man sat waiting for him. The visitor seemed amiable enough, although there was a hint of aggression in his probing look. Dr. Corgan hesitated before offering his hand.

"You are Mr. Tanner?"

"Of the *Medical Times,*" was the reply.

Dr. Corgan shuffled some papers on his desk. He had dreaded this interview and yet he welcomed it. Publicity was a vital part of research, but it had to be carefully controlled.

"Let me start from the beginning," he said.

Tanner smiled.

"I appreciate that," he said. "Some researchers give me a tangled web of ideas that are impossible to understand. I like to start from the beginning."

His pencil was poised over a lined yellow pad. Dr. Corgan's fingers trembled slightly. He sighed and began.

"There have been extensive studies of learning in children. The starting age for reading has been lowered to two years by means of programmed reading machines. But two is hardly the lowest possible limit."

"What has happened to childhood?" asked Tanner, lifting his pencil.

Dr. Corgan was startled.

"I beg your pardon?"

"I didn't mean to interrupt you," said Tanner. "But if kids are busy learning to read at two—when will they have time for bikes and mudpies? What's the rush? Why can't they learn at six or seven?"

Dr. Corgan sat on his anger.

"That's a fair question," he said. "The answer is—because they *can* learn at an earlier age. Don't you see? This means that an entire intellectual horizon is opened to them, including communication with their parents on a higher plane. Children play with mud only because they have nothing better to do."

"I see," said Tanner.

"But to get back to the thread of my thought. There have been many studies with infants at Harvard, Princeton and elsewhere. But all of these studies have focused on how infants develop and learn."

"So I understand," said Tanner.

Dr. Corgan smiled gently.

"I've gone far beyond those studies," he said. "I've begun to teach infants to carry out very complex, sophisticated tasks."

"But how? They can't speak and they certainly can't move their limbs in a controlled way."

"All true," said Dr. Corgan. "Nevertheless they have brain waves, blood pressure levels, electrocardiograms, sweat gland reactions and a host of other physiological parameters at their disposal."

"But surely," said Tanner, "these are beyond their conscious control? Blood pressure levels and heart rate are both controlled by the autonomic nervous system, not consciously."

Dr. Corgan waved his hands.

"All the so-called autonomic factors are readily controllable by the conscious mind. I've already proved that point with laboratory rats and human adult patients. Do you recall the woman who learned to lower her diastolic blood pressure by twenty-five millimeters of mercury?"

"I read about her," said Tanner. "But not everyone agreed with your explanation of how it came about."

Dr. Corgan shrugged.

"The point is that it did work! And the same technique works even better with infants. These babies are free of all the complicated clutter of growing up and the interaction with their family and outsiders. By the use of a judicious combination of rewards and punishments, the infant can be taught to do anything."

"Anything?"

"The statement is not as rash as you might think. For example, raising or lowering one's blood pressure is not an end in itself. It offers control over two possible eventualities. Add to that the option of raising or lowering the rate of heartbeat and you now have four possible independent combinations. Suppose now that we use *ten* physiological variables, each measurable and each with two directions to go. We end up with over one thousand possible combinations! Can you conceive of how many things an infant can accomplish with over one thousand patterns of responses available to him?"

"I'm skeptical," said Tanner, "but I'm always willing to believe my eyes. May I see a demonstration?"

"Why not?" said Dr. Corgan. "There are sleeping facilities available here but usually the baby is returned to the foundling nursery for the night. But if you will come back tomorrow afternoon I'll be happy to show you some of the things he can do."

"Would two o'clock do?"

"Fine," said Dr. Corgan.

Tanner was prompt the following afternoon, but Dr. Corgan was in bad temper.

"I've had some problems today," he said. "But we'll go on with the demonstration anyway."

"I could come back another time."

"Nonsense," said Dr. Corgan.

He rose and led Tanner to the observation room adjoining his laboratory.

"Look in there," he said. "The baby has just carried out an assigned task and the bottle of milk was lowered into his mouth as a reward. In order to get it, he had to hit the correct direction of change unerringly in ten physiological parameters which are being monitored off electrodes. These signals are fed into the computer which will accept only the proper combination. It then returns a control signal, which places the bottle in the baby's mouth."

"That's incredible," said Tanner. "I could believe that the youngster controls one of the parameters. But ten simultaneously?"

"That's *my* contribution," said Dr. Corgan. "Watch the baby. Notice that he can do several things. He can raise and lower those pretty barbells up there, open and close the laboratory door, turn the lights on and off, and a host of other little tasks."

"But how does one explain how he learns to do all this?"

"Nobody knows as yet," said Dr. Corgan. "But I think that it involves the untold neural networks available to the conscious and unconscious parts of the nervous system. These networks are as yet undiscovered, uncharted and functionally a complete mystery. But demonstrably we can achieve a linkup through these networks if we really want to."

"Have human beings always had this capability?"

"I think so. Perhaps it was needed during the early years of mankind's primitive existence."

The baby began to cry. His voice became strident and his face began to purple with frustration. His arms and legs flailed wildly.

"Damn!" cried Dr. Corgan. "That blasted nipple must be leaking again and he's run out of milk. Ordinarily he never cries unless something goes wrong. He knows he can get his food simply by altering his parameters to the right code."

"He's really upset," said Tanner. "Probably frustrated, too."

"He wants instant gratification," said Dr. Corgan. "Like all infants, he wants what he wants right away. I'll wait a few minutes and then help him. He's got to learn that patience is one of the facts of life."

The lights began to go on and off. The barbells rose and descended. The bottle went in and out. An alarm bell rang.

"Is the baby doing all that?" asked Tanner incredulously.

"Yes," said Dr. Corgan thoughtfully. "You see, he's trying every possible combination he knows, an excellent effort—one that deserves recognition. Now I'll go in and help him."

As Tanner watched, Dr. Corgan went into the laboratory and examined the faulty bottle. As he tugged at the nipple, the barbells descended rapidly.

"Look out!" called Tanner.

Dr. Corgan jumped to the side as the barbells shot past his head. Then he refilled the bottle with fresh formula, attached a new nipple and inserted the bottle again into its holder. The bottle slid down and forward into the baby's mouth and the crying choked into a soft gurgle of contentment.

When he returned to the observing room Dr. Corgan found Tanner in a state of agitation.

"You could have been hurt," he said.

"I might have been if you hadn't called out," admitted Dr. Corgan. "I've got to be more alert. Our setup is quite complicated, you know."

He answered a few more questions and then Nurse Thompson came in, a look of triumph on her face.

"It's time for the baby to return to nursery," she said, staring hard at Dr. Corgan. He was too distracted to notice her delight in her small victory.

"Take him," he said.

"I've got to run, too," said Tanner, stretching out his hand. "I want to thank you for all your help."

When Tanner had gone Dr. Corgan fretted over the interview. Had he talked too freely? Had the emphasis been put inappropriately? What impression would the press give the public about his work? Had Tanner been hostile? Would there be a lurid banner line like INFANTS TURNED TO AUTOMATA, or THOUGHT CONTROL REALIZED? Dr. Corgan sighed. Would anyone appreciate his true motivation, which was to enrich the intellectual pleasures of every infant?

He ate sparingly that night and slept badly in his bachelor bed. He was at the laboratory at seven the following morning, working on the bottle-nipple arrangement that had given him so much trouble during the interview. Perhaps the problem was the angle at which the bottle entered the baby's mouth. He operated the slide by hand and saw it come down and forward. It was possible that the whole arrangement was an eighth of an inch too high, enough to make the baby pull the nipple forward under too much stress, allowing the milk to leak.

He began to laugh. It was incredible that an experiment of such complexity should founder because of a bottle and nipple. He tried several positions for the holder and when the baby arrived he thought he had it properly adjusted. But apparently he was wrong. He set and reset it, but the nipple kept sliding off the mouth of the bottle.

By five-thirty Nurse Thompson was hovering about, crying the lateness of the hour. He became fully exasperated.

"Go home," he said angrily. "I must get this fixed tonight. The baby will sleep in the laboratory crib and I'll stay with him."

"But you'll overtire him—"

"Please get out of here, Mrs. Thompson. I'll assume all responsibility for what happens."

At last he thought he had it.

"Ring the alarm bell," he told the baby.

The alarm rang and the bottle moved forward. The baby's mouth seemed to leap at the bottle and the nipple flew off. A torrent of milk cascaded over the baby's face. At first he seemed to strangle—then he coughed and finally bellowed his disappointment.

"I'm terribly sorry," said Dr. Corgan. "It was all an accident. I'll set it right."

He painstakingly reset the slide and replaced the nipple carefully on the bottle. Everything seemed perfect again. He was leaning over the apparatus, admiring his handiwork, when the barbell struck him heavily at the back of his skull and he tumbled to the floor, slowly sinking into a deep void. As he lay there, fighting the descent, he thought dimly, *What a terrible accident. I must call for help . . .*

From a vast distance he heard the sucking noise. How delightful to know that now everything was working perfectly. Next the door to the observing room closed and soon afterward the lights went out.

With a terrible effort he lifted his head and looked about.

What a marvelous little fellow he is, Dr. Corgan thought for a fleeting moment. *He's learned his lessons beautifully. What a pity that no one else is here to see it . . .*

The baby had stopped sucking now and was cooing contentedly. Dr. Corgan could imagine him lying there in the darkness, round and amiable with pink, plump cheeks that glowed like twin rosebuds.

The soft pleasant gurgling noises were the last he heard.

12. the first men

Howard Fast

The vast number of "psychological casualties" in our society whose maladaptive behavior seems to result from the neglect, cruelty, or ignorance of their parents is a source of concern to mental health professionals, but few have proposed ways to approach the problem. Recently some specialists in behavior modification, declaring that child rearing is much too important to be carried out by amateurs, have proposed intensive training for prospective parents and a "parenting license" for those who demonstrate that they possess the skill and temperament necessary for such a demanding task. They seek no utopia of perfect parents, merely a society in which those people most likely to cause physical and mental damage to children would have less opportunity to do so. The proposal is not likely to become social policy, but it highlights the degree to which the vital task of child-rearing is left to chance, sometimes with chilling consequences.

But how can we be sure that a child raised according to the collective wisdom of experts would be better off? Advice given by authorities of one generation is rejected and ridiculed by those of the next. John B. Watson, the first behaviorist, advocated child-rearing techniques which many experts believe would have led to the development of well-controlled but bland automatons, while the children raised by the principles of total permissiveness are often blamed for the social disruption of the 1960s. In the absence of a clear and stable consensus, the haphazard procedures presently employed may not be so bad after all. At least we do not risk uniform failure while striving for universal success.

Howard Fast, author of "The First Men," is not concerned with the care and feeding of the average child. He suspects that there might be some super kids out there who need a special kind of living environment in order to reach their full potential. While we would not expect children raised in this manner to develop superhuman characteristics, it is interesting to speculate how children, whether super or average, would respond to the learning experiences he describes.

By Airmail:

Calcutta, India
Nov. 4th, 1945

Mrs. Jean Arbalaid
Washington, D.C.

My dear sister:

I found it. I saw it with my own eyes, and thereby I am convinced that I have a useful purpose in life—overseas investigator for the anthropological whims of my sister. That, in any case, is better than boredom. I have no desire to return home; I will not go into any further explanations or reasons. I am neurotic, unsettled and adrift. I got my discharge in Karachi, as you know. I am very happy to be an ex-GI and a tourist, but it took me only a few weeks to become bored to distraction. So I was quite pleased to have a mission from you. The mission is completed.

It could have been more exciting. The plain fact of the matter is that the small Associated Press item you sent me was quite accurate in all of its details. The little village of Chunga is in Assam. I got there by plane, narrow-gauge train and oxcart—a fairly pleasant trip at this time of the year, with the back of the heat broken; and there I saw the child, who is now fourteen years old.

I am sure you know enough about India to realize that fourteen is very much an adult age for a girl in these parts—the majority of them are married by then. And there is no question about the age. I spoke at length to the mother and father, who identified the child by two very distinctive birthmarks. The identification was substantiated by relatives and other villagers—all of whom remembered the birthmarks. A circumstance not unusual or remarkable in these small villages.

The child was lost as an infant—at eight months, a common story, the parents working in the field, the child set down, and then the child gone. Whether it crawled at that age or not, I can't say; at any rate, it was a healthy, alert and curious infant. They all agree on that point.

How the child came to the wolves is something we will never know. Possibly a bitch who had lost her own cubs carried the infant off. That is the most likely story, isn't it? This is not *lupus,* the European variety, but *pallipes,* its local cousin, nevertheless a respectable animal in size and disposition, and not something to stumble over on a dark night. Eighteen days ago, when the child was found, the villagers had to kill five wolves to take her, and she herself fought like a devil out of hell. She had lived as a wolf for thirteen years.

Will the story of her life among the wolves ever emerge? I don't know. To all effects and purposes, she is a wolf. She cannot stand upright—the curvature of her spine being beyond correction. She runs on all fours and her knuckles are covered with heavy callus. They are trying to teach her to use her hands for grasping and holding, but so far unsuccessfully. Any clothes they dress her in, she tears off, and as yet she has not been able to grasp the meaning of speech, much less talk. The Indian anthropologist, Sumil Gojee, has been working with her for a week now, and he has little hope that any real communication will ever be possible. In our terms and by our measurements, she is a total idiot, an infantile imbecile, and it is likely that she will remain so for the rest of her life.

On the other hand, both Professor Gojee and Dr. Chalmers, a government health service man, who came up from Calcutta to examine the child, agree that there are no physical or hereditary elements to account for the child's mental condition, no malformation of the cranial area, and no history of imbecilism in her background. Everyone in the village attests to the normalcy —indeed, alertness and brightness—of the infant; and Professor Gojee makes a point of the alertness and adaptability she must have required to survive for thirteen years among the wolves. The child responds excellently to reflex tests, and neurologically, she appears to be sound. She is strong—beyond the strength of a thirteen-year-old—wiry, quick in her movements, and possesses an uncanny sense of smell and hearing.

Professor Gojee has examined records of eighteen similar cases recorded in India over the past hundred years, and in every case, he says, the recovered child was an idiot in our terms—or a wolf in objective terms. He points out that it would be incorrect to call this child an idiot or an imbecile—any more than we would call a wolf an idiot or an imbecile. The child is a wolf, perhaps a very superior wolf, but a wolf nevertheless.

I am preparing a much fuller report on the whole business. Meanwhile, this letter contains the pertinent facts. As for money—I am very well heeled indeed, with eleven hundred dollars I won in a crap game. Take care of yourself and your brilliant husband and the public health service.

Love and kisses,
Harry

By cable:
HARRY FELTON
HOTEL EMPIRE
CALCUTTA, INDIA.
NOVEMBER 10, 1945
THIS IS NO WHIM, HARRY, BUT VERY SERIOUS INDEED. YOU DID NOBLY. SIMILAR CASE IN PRETORIA. GENERAL HOSPITAL, DR. FELIX VANOTT. WE HAVE MADE ALL ARRANGEMENTS WITH AIR TRANSPORT.

JEAN ARBALAID

By Airmail:

Pretoria, Union of South Africa
November 15, 1945

Mrs. Jean Arbalaid
Washington, D.C.

My dear sister:

You are evidently a very big wheel, you and your husband, and I wish I knew what your current silly season adds up to. I suppose in due time you'll see fit to tell me. But in any case, your priorities command respect. A full colonel was bumped, and I was promptly whisked to South Africa, a beautiful country of pleasant climate and, I am sure, great promise.

I saw the child, who is still being kept in the General Hospital here, and I spent an evening with Dr. Vanott and a young and reasonably attractive Quaker lady, Miss Gloria Oland, an anthropologist working among the Bantu people for her Doctorate. So, you see, I will be able to provide a certain amount of background material—more as I develop my acquaintance with Miss Oland.

Superficially, this case is remarkably like the incident in Assam. There it was a girl of fourteen; here we have a Bantu boy of eleven. The girl was reared by the wolves; the boy, in this case, was reared by the baboons—and rescued from them by a White Hunter, name of Archway, strong, silent type, right out of Hemingway. Unfortunately, Archway has a nasty temper and doesn't like children, so when the boy understandably bit him, he whipped the child to within an inch of its life. "Tamed him," as he put it.

At the hospital, however, the child has been receiving the best of care and reasonable if scientific affection. There is no way of tracing him back to his parents, for these Basutoland baboons are great travelers and there is no telling where they picked him up. His age is a medical guess, but reasonable. That he is of Bantu origin, there is no doubt. He is handsome, long-limbed, exceedingly strong, and with no indication of any cranial injury. But like the girl in Assam, he is—in our terms—an idiot and an imbecile.

That is to say, he is a baboon. His vocalization is that of a baboon. He differs from the girl in that he is able to use his hands to hold things and to examine things, and he has a more active curiosity; but that, I am assured by Miss Oland, is the difference between a wolf and a baboon.

He too has a permanent curvature of the spine; he goes on all fours as the baboons do, and the back of his fingers and hands are heavily callused. After tearing off his clothes the first time, he accepted them, but that too is a baboon trait. In this case, Miss Oland has hope for his learning at least rudimentary speech, but Dr. Vanott doubts that he ever will. Incidentally, I must take note that in those eighteen cases Professor Gojee referred to, there was no evidence of human speech being learned beyond its most basic elements.

So goes my childhood hero, Tarzan of the Apes, and all the noble beasts along with him. But the most terrifying thought is this—what is the substance of man himself, if this can happen to him? The learned folk here have been trying to explain to me that man is a creature of his thought and that his thought is to a very large extent shaped by his environment; and that this thought process—or mentation as they call it—is based on words. Without words, thought becomes a process of pictures, which is on the animal level and rules out all, even the most primitive, abstract concepts. In other words, man cannot become man by himself: he is the result of other men and of the totality of human society and experience.

The man raised by the wolves is a wolf, by the baboons a baboon—and this is implacable, isn't it? My head has been swimming with all sorts of notions, some of them not at all pleasant. My dear sister, what are you and your husband up to? Isn't it time you broke down and told old Harry? Or do you want me to pop off to Tibet? Anything to please you, but preferably something that adds up.

Your ever-loving Harry

By Airmail:

Washington, D.C.
November 27, 1945

Mr. Harry Felton
Pretoria, Union of South Africa

Dear Harry:

You are a noble and sweet brother, and quite sharp too. You are also a dear. Mark and I want you to do a job for us, which will enable you to run here and there across the face of the earth, and be paid for it too. In order to convince you, we must spill out the dark secrets of our work—which we have decided to do, considering you an upright and trustworthy character. But the mail, it would seem, is less trustworthy; and since we are working with the Army, which has a constitutional dedication to *top-secret* and similar nonsense, the information goes to you via diplomatic pouch. As of receiving this, consider yourself employed; your expenses will be paid, within reason, and an additional eight thousand a year for less work than indulgence.

So please stay put at your hotel in Pretoria until the pouch arrives. Not more than ten days. Of course, you will be notified.

Love, affection, and respect,
Jean

By diplomatic pouch:

Washington, D.C.
December 5, 1945

Mr. Harry Felton
Pretoria, Union of South Africa

Dear Harry:

Consider this letter the joint effort of Mark and myself. The conclusions are also shared. Also, consider it a very serious document indeed.

You know that for the past twenty years, we have both been deeply concerned with child psychology and child development. There is no need to review our careers or our experience in the Public Health Service. Our work during the war, as part of the Child Reclamation Program led to an interesting theory, which we decided to pursue. We were given leave by the head of the service to make this our own project, and recently we were granted a substantial amount of army funds to work with.

Now down to the theory, which is not entirely untested, as you know. Briefly—but with two decades of practical work as a background—it is this: Mark and I have come to the conclusion that within the rank and file of Homo

Sapiens is the leavening of a new race. Call them man-plus—call them what you will. They are not of recent arrival; they have been cropping up for hundreds, perhaps thousands of years. But they are trapped in and molded by human environment as certainly and implacably as your Assamese girl was trapped among the wolves or your Bantu boy among the baboons.

By the way, your two cases are not the only attested ones we have. By sworn witness, we have records of seven similar cases, one in Russia, two in Canada, two in South America, one in West Africa, and, just to cut us down to size, one in the United States. We also have hearsay and folklore of three hundred and eleven parallel cases over a period of fourteen centuries. We have in fourteenth century Germany, in the folio MS of the monk Hubercus, five case histories which he claims to have observed. In all of these cases, in the seven cases witnessed by people alive today, and in all but sixteen of the hearsay cases, the result is more or less precisely what you have seen and described yourself: the child reared by the wolf is a wolf.

Our own work adds up to the parallel conclusion: the child reared by a man is a man. If man-plus exists, he is trapped and caged as certainly as any human child reared by animals. Our proposition is that he exists.

Why do we think this super-child exists? Well, there are many reasons, and neither the time nor the space to go into all in detail. But here are two very telling reasons. Firstly, we have case histories of several hundred men and women, who as children had IQs of 150 or above. In spite of their enormous intellectual promise as children, less than 10 per cent have succeeded in their chosen careers. Roughly another 10 per cent have been institutionalized as mental cases beyond recovery. About 14 per cent have had or require therapy in terms of mental health problems. Six per cent have been suicides, 1 per cent in prison, 27 per cent have had one or more divorces, 19 per cent are chronic failures at whatever they attempt—and the rest are undistinguished in any important manner. All of the IQs have dwindled—almost in the sense of a smooth graph line in relation to age.

Since society has never provided the full potential for such a mentality, we are uncertain as to what it might be. But we can guess that against it, they have been reduced to a sort of idiocy—an idiocy that we call normalcy.

The second reason we put forward is this: we know that man uses only a tiny fraction of his brain. What blocks him from the rest of it? Why has nature given him equipment that he cannot put to use? Or has society prevented him from breaking the barriers around his own potential?

There, in brief, are two reasons. Believe me, Harry, there are many more —enough for us to have convinced some very hard-headed and unimaginative government people that we deserve a chance to release *superman*. Of course, history helps—in its own mean manner. It would appear that we are beginning another war—with Russia this time, a cold war, as some have already taken to calling it. And among other things, it will be a war of intelligence—a commodity in rather short supply, as some of our local mental giants have been frank enough to admit. They look upon our man-plus as a secret weapon, little devils who will come up with death rays and superatom bombs when the time is ripe. Well, let them. It is inconceivable to imagine a project like this under benign sponsorship. The important thing is that Mark and I have been placed in full charge of the venture—millions of dollars, top priority—the whole works. But nevertheless, *secret to the ultimate.* I cannot stress this enough.

Now, as to your own job—if you want it. It develops step by step. First step: in Berlin, in 1937, there was a Professor Hans Goldbaum. Half Jewish. The head of the Institute of Child Therapy. He published a small monograph on intelligence testing in children, and he put forward claims—which we are inclined to believe—that he could determine a child's IQ during its first year of life, in its pre-speech period. He presented some impressive tables of estimations and subsequent checked results, but we do not know enough of his method to practice it ourselves. In other words, we need the professor's help.

In 1937, he vanished from Berlin. In 1943, he was reported to be living in Cape Town—the last address we have for him. I enclose the address. Go to Cape Town, Harry darling. (Myself talking, not Mark.) If he has left, follow him and find him. If he is dead, inform us immediately.

Of course you will take the job. We love you and we need your help.

Jean

By Airmail:

Cape Town, South Africa
December 20, 1945

Mrs. Jean Arbalaid
Washington, D.C.

My dear sister:

Of all the hairbrained ideas! If this is our secret weapon, I am prepared to throw in the sponge right now. But a job is a job.

It took me a week to follow the Professor's meandering through Cape Town—only to find out that he took off for London in 1944. Evidently, they needed him there. I am off to London.

Love,
Harry

By diplomatic pouch:

Washington, D.C.
December 26, 1945

Mr. Harry Felton
London, England

Dear Harry:

This is dead serious. By now, you must have found the professor. We believe that despite protestations of your own idiocy, you have enough sense to gauge his method. Sell him this venture. Sell him! We will give him whatever he asks—and we want him to work with us as long as he will.

Briefly, here is what we are up to. We have been allocated a tract of eight thousand acres in northern California. We intend to establish an environment there—under military guard and security. In the beginning, the outside world will be entirely excluded. The environment will be controlled and exclusive.

Within this environment, we intend to bring forty children to maturity—to a maturity that will result in man-plus.

As to the details of this environment—well that can wait. The immediate problem is the children. Out of forty, ten will be found in the United States; the other thirty will be found by the professor and yourself—outside of the United States.

Half are to be boys; we want an even boy-girl balance. They are to be between the ages of six months and nine months, and all are to show indications of an exceedingly high IQ—that is, if the professor's method is any good at all.

We want five racial groupings: Caucasian, Indian, Chinese, Malayan, and Bantu. Of course, we are sensible of the vagueness of these groupings, and you have some latitude within them. The six so-called *Caucasian* infants are to be found in European types, and two Mediterranean types. A similar breakdown might be followed in other areas.

Now understand this—no cops and robbers stuff, no OSS, no kidnapping. Unfortunately, the world abounds in war orphans—and in parents poor and desperate enough to sell their children. When you want a child and such a situation arises, buy! Price is no object. I will have no maudlin sentimentality or scruples. These children will be loved and cherished—and if you should acquire any by purchase, you will be giving a child life and hope.

When you find a child, inform us immediately. Air transport will be at your disposal—and we are making all arrangements for wet nurses and other details of child care. We shall also have medical aid at your immediate disposal. On the other hand, we want healthy children—within the general conditions of health within any given area.

Now good luck to you. We are depending on you and we love you. And a merry Christmas.

Jean

By diplomatic pouch:

Copenhagen, Denmark
February 4, 1946

Mrs. Jean Arbalaid
Washington, D.C.

Dear Jean:

I seem to have caught your silly *top-secret* and *classified* disease, and I have been waiting for a free day and a diplomatic pouch to sum up my various adventures. From my "guarded" cables, you know that the professor and I have been doing a Cook's Tour of the baby market. My dear sister, this kind of shopping spree does not sit at all well with me. However, I gave my word, and there you are. I will complete and deliver.

By the way, I suppose I continue to send these along to Washington, even though your "environment," as you call it, has been established. I'll do so until otherwise instructed.

There was no great difficulty in finding the professor. Being in uniform—I have since acquired an excellent British wardrobe—and having all the fancy credentials you were kind enough to supply, I went to the War Office. As they say, every courtesy was shown to Major Harry Felton, but I feel better in civilian clothes. Anyway, the professor had been working with a child reclamation project, living among the ruins of the East End, which is pretty badly shattered. He is an astonishing little man, and I have become quite fond of him. On his part, he is learning to tolerate me.

I took him to dinner—you were the lever that moved him, my dear sister. I had no idea how famous you are in certain circles. He looked at me in awe, simply because we share a mother and father.

Then I said my piece, all of it, no holds barred. I had expected your reputation to crumble into dust there on the spot, but no such thing. Goldbaum listened with his mouth and his ears and every fiber of his being. The only time he interrupted me was to question me on the Assamese girl and the Bantu boy; and very pointed and meticulous questions they were. When I had finished, he simply shook his head—not in disagreement but with sheer excitement and delight. I then asked him what his reaction to all this was.

"I need time," he said. "This is something to digest. But the concept is wonderful—daring and wonderful. Not that the reasoning behind it is so novel. I have thought of this—so many anthropologists have. But to put it into practice, young man—ah, your sister is a wonderful and remarkable woman!"

There you are, my sister. I struck while the iron was hot, and told him then and there that you wanted and needed his help, first to find the children and then to work in the environment.

"The environment," he said. "You understand that is everything, everything. But how can she change the environment? The environment is total, the whole fabric of human society, self-deluded and superstitious and sick and irrational and clinging to legends and phantasies and ghosts. Who can change that?"

So it went. My anthropology is passable at best, but I have read all your books. If my answers were weak in that department, he did manage to draw out of me a more or less complete picture of Mark and yourself. He then said he would think about the whole matter. We made an appointment for the following day, when he would explain his method of intelligence determination in infants.

We met the next day, and he explained his methods. He made a great point of the fact that he did not test but rather determined, within a wide margin for error. Years before, in Germany, he had worked out a list of fifty characteristics which he noted in infants. As these infants matured, they were tested regularly by normal methods—and the results were checked against his original observations. Thereby, he began to draw certain conclusions, which he tested again and again over the next fifteen years. I am enclosing an unpublished article of his which goes into greater detail. Sufficient to say that he convinced me of the validity of his methods. Subsequently, I watched him examine a hundred and four British infants—to come up with our first choice. Jean, this is a remarkable and brilliant man.

On the third day after I had met him, he agreed to join the project. But he said this to me, very gravely, and afterwards I put it down exactly as he said it:

> "You must tell your sister that I have not come to this decision lightly. We are tampering with human souls—and perhaps even with human destiny. This experiment may fail, but if it succeeds it can be the most important event of our time—even more important and consequential than this war we have just fought. And you must tell her something else. I had a wife and three children, and they were put to death because a nation of men turned into beasts. I watched that, and I could not have lived through it unless I believed, always, that what can turn into a beast can also turn into a man. We are neither. But if we go to create man, we must be humble. We are the tool, not the craftsman, and if we succeed, we will be less than the result of our work."

There is your man, Jean, and as I said, a good deal of a man. Those words are verbatim. He also dwells a great deal on the question of environment, and the wisdom and judgment and love necessary to create this environment. I think it would be helpful if you could send me a few words at least concerning this environment you are establishing.

We have now sent you four infants. Tomorrow, we leave for Rome—and from Rome to Casablanca.

But we will be in Rome at least two weeks, and a communication should reach me there.

More seriously—
And not untroubled,
Harry

By diplomatic pouch:

Via Washington, D.C.
February 11, 1946

Mr. Harry Felton
Rome, Italy

Dear Harry:

Just a few facts here. We are tremendously impressed by your reactions to Professor Goldbaum, and we look forward eagerly to his joining us. Meanwhile, Mark and I have been working night and day on the environment. In the most general terms, this is what we plan.

The entire reservation—all eight thousand acres—will be surrounded by a wire fence and will be under army guard. Within it, we shall establish a home. There will be between thirty and forty teachers—or group parents. We are accepting only married couples who love children and who will dedicate themselves to this venture. That they must have additional qualifications goes without saying.

Within the proposition that somewhere in man's civilized development, something went wrong, we are returning to the prehistory form of group marriage. That is not to say that we will cohabit indiscriminately—but the children will be given to understand that parentage is a whole, that we are all their mothers and fathers, not by blood but by love.

We shall teach them the truth, and where we do not know the truth we shall not teach. There will be no myths, no legends, no lies, no superstitions, no premises and no religions. We shall teach love and cooperation and we shall give love and security in full measure. We shall also teach them the knowledge of mankind.

During the first nine years, we shall command the environment entirely. We shall write the books they read, and shape the history and circumstances they require. Only then will we begin to relate the children to the world as it is

Does it sound too simple or too presumptuous? It is all we can do, Harry, and I think Professor Goldbaum will understand that full well. It is also more than has ever been done for children before.

So good luck to both of you. Your letters sound as if you are changing, Harry—and we feel a curious process of change within us. When I put down what we are doing, it seems almost too obvious to be meaningful. We are simply taking a group of very gifted children and giving them knowledge and love. Is this enough to break through to that part of man which is unused and unknown? Well, we shall see. Bring us the children, Harry, and we shall see.

With love,
Jean

In the early spring of 1965, Harry Felton arrived in Washington and went directly to the White House. Felton had just turned fifty; he was a tall and pleasant-looking man, rather lean, with graying hair. As President of the Board of Shipways, Inc.—one of the largest import and export houses in America—he commanded a certain amount of deference and respect from Eggerton, who was then Secretary of Defense. In any case, Eggerton, who was nobody's fool, did not make the mistake of trying to intimidate Felton.

Instead, he greeted him pleasantly; and the two of them, with no others present, sat down in a small room in the White House, drank each other's good health, and talked about things.

Eggerton proposed that Felton might know why he had been asked to Washington.

"I can't say that I do know," Felton said.

"You have a remarkable sister."

"I have been aware of that for a long time," Felton smiled.

"You are also very close-mouthed, Mr. Felton," the secretary observed. "So far as we know, not even your immediate family has ever heard of man-plus. That's a commendable trait."

"Possibly and possibly not. It's been a long time."

"Has it? Then you haven't heard from your sister lately?"

"Almost a year," Felton answered.

"It didn't alarm you?"

"Should it? No, it didn't alarm me. My sister and I are very close, but this project of hers is not the sort of thing that allows for social relations. There have been long periods before when I have not heard from her. We are poor letter writers."

"I see," nodded Eggerton.

"I am to conclude that she is the reason for my visit here?"

"Yes."

"She's well?"

"As far as we know," Eggerton said quietly.

"Then what can I do for you?"

"Help us, if you will," Eggerton said, just as quietly. "I am going to tell what has happened, Mr. Felton, and then perhaps you can help us."

"Perhaps," Felton agreed.

"About the project, you know as much as any of us; more, perhaps, since you were in at the inception. So you realize that such a project must be taken very seriously or laughed off entirely. To date, it has cost the government eleven million dollars, and that is not something you laugh off. Now you understand that the unique part of this project was its exclusiveness. That word is used advisedly and specifically. Its success depended upon the creation of a unique and exclusive environment, and in terms of that environment, we agreed not to send any observers into the reservation for a period of fifteen years. Of course, during those fifteen years, there have been many conferences with Mr. and Mrs. Arbalaid and with certain of their associates, including Dr. Goldbaum.

"But out of these conferences, there was no progress report that dealt with anything more than general progress. We were given to understand that the results were rewarding and exciting but very little more. We honored our part of the agreement, and at the end of the fifteen-year period, we told your sister and her husband that we would have to send in a team of observers. They pleaded for an extension of time—maintaining that it was critical to the success of the entire program—and they pleaded persuasively enough to win a three-year extension. Some months ago, the three-year period was over. Mrs. Arbalaid came to Washington and begged a further extension. When we refused, she agreed that our team could come into the reservation in ten days. Then she returned to California."

Eggerton paused and looked at Felton searchingly.

"And what did you find?" Felton asked.

"You don't know?"

"I'm afraid not."

"Well—" the Secretary said slowly, "I feel like a damn fool when I think of this, and also a little afraid. When I say it, the fool end predominates. We went there and we found nothing."

"Oh?"

"You don't appear too surprised, Mr. Felton?"

"Nothing my sister does has ever surprised me. You mean the reservation was empty—no sign of anything?"

"I don't mean that, Mr. Felton. I wish I did mean that. I wish it was so pleasantly human and down to earth. I wish we thought that your sister and her husband were two clever and unscrupulous swindlers who had taken the government for eleven million. That would warm the cockles of our hearts compared to what we do have. You see, we don't know whether the reservation is empty or not, Mr. Felton, because the reservation is not there."

"What?"

"Precisely. The reservation is not there."

"Come now," Felton smiled. "My sister is a remarkable woman, but she doesn't make off with eight thousand acres of land. It isn't like her."

"I don't find your humor entertaining, Mr. Felton."

"No. No, of course not. I'm sorry. Only when a thing makes no sense at all—how could an eight-thousand-acre stretch of land not be where it was? Doesn't it leave a large hole?"

"If the newspapers get hold of it, they could do even better than that, Mr. Felton."

"Why not explain," Felton said.

"Let me try to—not to explain but to describe. This stretch of land is in the Fulton National Forest, rolling country, some hills, a good stand of redwood—a kidney-shaped area. It was wire-fenced, with army guards at every approach. I went there with our inspection team, General Meyers, two army physicians, Gorman, the psychiatrist, Senator Totenwell of the Armed Services Committee, and Lydia Gentry, the educator. We crossed the country by plane and drove the final sixty miles to the reservation in two government cars. A dirt road leads into it. The guard on this road halted us. The reservation was directly before us. As the guard approached the first car, the reservation disappeared."

"Just like that?" Felton whispered. "No noise—no explosion?"

"No noise, no explosion. One moment, a forest of redwoods in front of us —then a gray area of nothing."

"Nothing? That's just a word. Did you try to go in?"

"Yes—we tried. The best scientists in America have tried. I myself am not a very brave man, Mr. Felton, but I got up enough courage to walk up to this gray edge and touch it. It was very cold and very hard—so cold that it blistered these three fingers."

He held out his hand for Felton to see.

"I became afraid then. I have not stopped being afraid." Felton nodded. "Fear—such fear," Eggerton sighed.

"I need not ask you if you tried this or that?"

"We tried everything, Mr. Felton, even—I am ashamed to say—a very small atomic bomb. We tried the sensible things and the foolish things. We went into panic and out of panic, and we tried everything."

"Yet you've kept it secret?"

"So far, Mr. Felton."

"Airplanes?"

"You see nothing from above. It looks like mist lying in the valley."

"What do your people think it is?"

Eggerton smiled and shook his head. "They don't know. There you are. At first, some of them thought it was some kind of force field. But the mathematics won't work, and of course it's cold. Terribly cold. I am mumbling. I am not a scientist and not a mathematician, but they also mumble, Mr. Felton. I am tired of that kind of thing. That is why I asked you to come to Washington and talk with us. I thought you might know."

"I might," Felton nodded.

For the first time, Eggerton became alive, excited, impatient. He mixed Felton another drink. Then he leaned forward eagerly and waited. Felton took a letter out of his pocket.

"This came from my sister," he said.

"You told me you had no letter from her in almost a year!"

"I've had this almost a year," Felton replied, a note of sadness in his voice. "I haven't opened it. She enclosed this sealed envelope with a short letter, which only said that she was well and quite happy, and that I was to open and read the other letter when it was absolutely necessary to do so. My sister is like that; we think the same way. Now, I suppose it's necessary, don't you?"

The Secretary nodded slowly but said nothing. Felton opened the letter and began to read aloud.

June 12, 1964

My dear Harry:

As I write this, it is twenty-two years since I have seen you or spoken to you. How very long for two people who have such love and regard for each other as we do! And now that you have found it necessary to open this letter and read it, we must face the fact that in all probability we will never see each other again. I hear that you have a wife and three children—all wonderful people. I think it is hardest to know that I will not see them or know them.

Only this saddens me. Otherwise, Mark and I are very happy—and I think you will understand why.

About the barrier—which now exists or you would not have opened the letter—tell them that there is no harm to it and no one will be hurt by it. It cannot be broken into because it is a negative power rather than a positive one, an absence instead of a presence. I will have more to say about it later, but possibly explain it no better. Some of the children could likely put it into intelligible words, but I want this to be my report, not theirs.

Strange that I still call them children and think of them as children—when in all fact we are the children and they are adults. But they still have the quality of children that we know best, the strange innocence and purity that vanishes so quickly in the outside world.

And now I must tell you what came of our experiment—or some of it. Some of it, for how could I ever put down the story of the strangest two decades that men ever lived through? It is all incredible and it is all commonplace. We took a group of wonderful children, and we gave them an abundance of love, security and truth—but I think it was the factor of love that mattered most. During the first year, we weeded out each couple that showed less than a desire to love these children. They were easy to love. And as the years passed, they became our children—in every way. The children who were born to the couples in residence here simply joined the group. No one had *a father* or *a mother;* we were a living, functioning group in which all men were the fathers of all children and all women the mothers of all children.

No, this was not easy, Harry—among ourselves, the adults, we had to fight and work and examine and turn ourselves inside out again and again, and tear our guts and hearts out, so that we could present an environment that had never been before, a quality of sanity and truth and security that exists nowhere else in all this world.

How shall I tell you of an American Indian boy, five years old, composing a splendid symphony? Or of the two children, one Bantu, one Italian, one a boy, one a girl, who at the age of six built a machine to measure the speed of light? Will you believe that we, the adults, sat quietly and listened to these six-year-olds explain to us that since the speed of light is a constant everywhere, regardless of the motion of material bodies, the distance between the stars cannot be mentioned in terms of light, since that is not distance on our plane of being? Then believe also that I put it poorly. In all of these matters, I have the sensations of an uneducated immigrant whose child is exposed to all the wonders of school and knowledge. I understand a little, but very little.

If I were to repeat instance after instance, wonder after wonder—at the age of six and seven and eight and nine, would you think of the poor, tortured, nervous creatures whose parents boast that they have an IQ of 160, and in the same breath bemoan the fate that did not give them normal children? Well, ours were and are *normal* children. Perhaps the first normal children this world has seen in a long time. If you heard them laugh or sing only once, you would know that. If you could see how tall and strong they are, how fine of body and movement. They have a quality that I have never seen in children before.

Yes, I suppose, dear Harry, that much about them would shock you. Most of the time, they wear no clothes. Sex has always been a joy and a good thing to them, and they face it and enjoy it as naturally as we eat and drink—more naturally, for we have no gluttons in sex or food, no ulcers of the belly or the soul. They kiss and caress each other and do many other things that the world has specified as shocking, nasty, etc.—but whatever they do, they do with grace and joy. Is all this possible? I tell you that it has been my life for almost twenty years now. I live with boys and girls who are without evil or sickness, who are like pagans or gods—however you would look at it.

But the story of the children and of their day-to-day life is one that will be told properly and in its own time and place. All the indications I have put down here add up only to great gifts and abilities. Mark and I never had any doubts about these results; we knew that if we controlled an environment that was predicated on the future, the children would learn more than any children do on the outside. In their seventh year of life they were dealing easily and naturally with scientific problems normally taught on the college level, or higher, outside. This was to be expected, and we would have been very disappointed if something of this sort had not developed. But it was the unexpected that we hoped for and watched for—the flowering of the mind of man that is blocked in every single human being on the outside.

And it came. Originally, it began with a Chinese child in the fifth year of our work. The second was an American child, then a Burmese. Most strangely, it was not thought of as anything very unusual, nor did we realize what was happening until the seventh year, when there were already five of them.

Mark and I were taking a walk that day—I remember it so well, lovely, cool and clear California day—when we came on a group of children in a meadow. There were about a dozen children there. Five of them sat in a little circle, with a sixth in the center of the circle. Their heads were almost touching. They were full of little giggles, ripples of mirth and satisfaction. The rest of the children sat in a group about ten feet away—watching intently.

As we came to the scene, the children in the second group put their fingers to their lips, indicating that we should be quiet. So we stood and watched without speaking. After we were there about ten minutes, the little girl in the center of the circle of five leaped to her feet, crying ecstatically.

"I heard you! I heard you! I heard you!"

There was a kind of achievement and delight in her voice that we had not heard before, not even from our children. Then all of the children there rushed together to kiss her and embrace her, and they did a sort of dance of play and delight around her. All this we watched with no indication of surprise or even very great curiosity. For even though this was the first time anything like this —beyond our guesses or comprehension—had ever happened, we had worked out our own reaction to it.

When the children rushed to us for our congratulations, we nodded and smiled and agreed that it was all very wonderful. "Now, it's my turn, mother," a Senegalese boy told me. "I can almost do it already. Now there are six to help me, and it will be easier."

"Aren't you proud of us?" another cried.

We agreed that we were very proud, and we skirted the rest of the questions. Then, at our staff meeting that evening, Mark described what had happened.

"I noticed that last week," Mary Hengel, our semantics teacher, nodded. "I watched them, but they didn't see me."

"How many were there?" Professor Goldbaum asked intently.

"Three. A fourth in the center—their heads together. I thought it was one of their games and I walked away."

"They make no secret of it," someone observed.

"Yes," I said, "they took it for granted that we knew what they were doing."

"No one spoke," Mark said. "I can vouch for that."

"Yet they were listening," I said. "They giggled and laughed as if some great joke was taking place—or the way children laugh about a game that delights them."

It was Dr. Goldbaum who put his finger on it. He said, very gravely, "Do you know, Jean—you always said that we might open that great area of the mind that is closed and blocked in us. I think that they have opened it. I think they are teaching and learning to listen to thoughts."

There was a silence after that, and then Atwater, one of our psychologists, said uneasily, "I don't think I believe it. I've investigated every test and report on telepathy ever published in this country—the Duke stuff and all the rest of it. We know how tiny and feeble brain waves are—it is fantastic to imagine that they can be a means of communication."

"There is also a statistical factor," Rhoda Lannon, a mathematician, observed. "If this faculty existed even as a potential in mankind, is it conceivable that there would be no recorded instance of it?"

"Maybe it has been recorded," said Fleming, one of our historians. "Can you take all the whippings, burnings and hangings of history and determine which were telepaths?"

"I think I agree with Dr. Goldbaum," Mark said. "The children are becoming telepaths. I am not moved by a historical argument, or by a statistical argument, because our obsession here is environment. There is no record in history of a similar group of unusual children being raised in such an environment. Also, this may be—and probably is—a faculty which must be released in childhood or remain permanently blocked. I believe Dr. Haenigson will bear me out when I say that mental blocks imposed during childhood are not uncommon."

"More than that." Dr. Haenigson, our chief psychiatrist, nodded. "No child in our society escapes the need to erect some mental block in his mind. Whole areas of every human being's mind are blocked in early childhood. This is an absolute of human society."

Dr. Goldbaum was looking at us strangely. I was going to say something —but I stopped. I waited and Dr. Goldbaum said:

"I wonder whether we have begun to realize what we may have done. What is a human being? He is the sum of his memories, which are locked in his brain, and every moment of experience simply builds up the structure of those memories. We don't know as yet what is the extent or power of the gift these children of ours appear to be developing, but suppose they reach a point where they can share the totality of memory? Is it not simply that among themselves there can be no lies, no deceit, no rationalization, no secrets, no guilts—it is more than that."

Then he looked from face to face, around the whole circle of our staff. We were beginning to comprehend him. I remember my own reactions at that moment, a sense of wonder and discovery and joy and heartbreak too; a feeling so poignant that it brought tears to my eyes.

"You know, I see," Dr. Goldbaum nodded. "Perhaps it would be best for me to speak about it. I am much older than any of you—and I have been through, lived through the worst years of horror and bestiality that mankind ever knew. When I saw what I saw, I asked myself a thousand times: What is the meaning of mankind—if it has any meaning at all, if it is not simply a haphazard accident, an unusual complexity of molecular structure? I know you have all asked yourselves the same thing. Who are we? What are we destined for? What is our purpose? Where is sanity or reason in these bits of struggling, clawing, sick fish? We kill, we torture, we hurt and destroy as no other species does. We ennoble murder and falsehood and hypocrisy and superstition; we destroy our own bodies with drugs and poisonous food; we deceive ourselves as well as others—and we hate and hate and hate.

"Now something has happened. If these children can go into each other's minds completely—then they will have a single memory, which is the memory of all of them. All experience will be common to all of them, all knowledge, all dreams—and they will be immortal. For as one dies, another child is linked to the whole, and another and another. Death will lose all meaning, all of its dark horror. Mankind will begin, here in this place, to fulfill a part of its intended destiny—to become a single, wonderful unit, a whole—almost in the old words of your poet, John Donne, who sensed what we have all sensed at one time, that no man is an island unto himself. Has any thoughtful man lived without having a sense of that singleness of mankind? I don't think so. We have been living in darkness, in the night, struggling each of us with his own poor brain and then dying with all the memories of a lifetime. It is no wonder that we have achieved so little. The wonder is that we have achieved so much. Yet all that we know, all that we have done will be nothing compared to what these children will know and do and create—"

So the old man spelled it out, Harry—and saw almost all of it from the beginning. That was the beginning. Within the next twelve months, each one of our children was linked to all of the others telepathically. And in the years that followed, every child born in our reservation was shown the way into that linkage by the children. Only we, the adults, were forever barred from joining it. We were of the old, they of the new; their way was closed to us forever— although they could go into our minds, and did. But never could we feel them there or see them there, as they did each other.

I don't know how to tell you of the years that followed, Harry. In our little, guarded reservation, man became what he was always destined to be, but I can explain it only imperfectly. I can hardly comprehend, much less explain, what it means to inhabit forty bodies simultaneously, or what it means to each of the children to have the other personalities within them, a part of them—what it means to live as man and woman always and together. Could the children explain it to us? Hardly, for this is a transformation that must take place, from all we can learn, before puberty—and as it happens, the children accept it as normal and natural—indeed as the most natural thing in the world. We were the unnatural ones—and one thing they never truly comprehended is how we could bear to live in our aloneness, how we could bear to live with the knowledge of death as extinction.

We are happy that this knowledge of us did not come at once. In the beginning, the children could merge their thoughts only when their heads were almost touching. Bit by bit, their command of distance grew—but not until they were in their fifteenth year did they have the power to reach out and probe with their thoughts anywhere on earth. We thank God for this. By then the children were ready for what they found. Earlier, it might have destroyed them.

I must mention that two of our children met accidental death—in the ninth and the eleventh year. But it made no difference to the others, a little regret, but no grief, no sense of great loss, no tears or weeping. Death is totally different to them than to us; a loss of flesh; the personality itself is immortal and lives consciously in the others. When we spoke of a marked grave or a tombstone, they smiled and said that we could make it if it would give us any comfort. Yet later, when Dr. Goldbaum died, their grief was deep and terrible, for his was the old kind of death.

Outwardly, they remained individuals—each with his or her own set of characteristics, mannerisms, personality. The boys and the girls make love in a normal sexual manner—though all of them share the experience. Can you comprehend that? I cannot—but for them everything is different. Only the unspoiled devotion of mother for helpless child can approximate the love that binds them together—yet here it is also different, deeper even than that.

Before the transformation took place, there was sufficient of children's petulance and anger and annoyance—but after it took place, we never again heard a voice raised in anger or annoyance. As they themselves put it, when there was trouble among them, they washed it out—when there was sickness, they healed it; and after the ninth year, there was no more sickness—even three or four of them, when they merged their minds, could go into a body and cure it.

I use these words and phrases because I have no others, but they don't describe. Even after all these years of living with the children, day and night, I can only vaguely comprehend the manner of their existence. What they are outwardly, I know, free and healthy and happy as no men were before, but what their inner life is remains beyond me.

I spoke to one of them about it once, Arlene, a tall, lovely child whom we found in an orphanage in Idaho. She was fourteen then. We were discussing personality, and I told her that I could not understand how she could live and work as an individual, when she was also a part of so many others, and they were a part of her.

"But I remain myself, Jean. I could not stop being myself."

"But aren't the others also yourself?"

"Yes. But I am also them."

"But who controls your body?"

"I do. Of course."

"But if they should want to control it instead of you?"

"Why?"

"If you did something they disapproved of," I said lamely.

"How could I?" she asked. "Can you do something you disapprove of?"

"I am afraid I can. And do."

"I don't understand. Then why do you do it?"

So these discussions always ended. We, the adults, had only words for communication. By their tenth year, the children had developed methods of communication as far beyond words as words are beyond the dumb motions of animals. If one of them watched something, there was no necessity for it to be described; the others could see it through his eyes. Even in sleep, they dreamed together.

I could go on for hours attempting to describe something utterly beyond my understanding, but that would not help, would it, Harry? You will have your own problems, and I must try to make you understand what happened, what had to happen. You see, by the tenth year, the children had learned all we knew, all we had among us as material for teaching. In effect, we were teaching a single mind, a mind composed of the unblocked, unfettered talent of forty superb children; a mind so rational and pure and agile that to them we could only be objects of loving pity.

We have among us Axel Cromwell, whose name you will recognize. He is one of the greatest physicists on earth, and it was he who was mainly responsible for the first atom bomb. After that, he came to us as one would go into a monastery—an act of personal expiation. He and his wife taught the children physics, but by the eighth year, the children were teaching Cromwell. A year later, Cromwell could follow neither their mathematics nor their reasoning; and their symbolism, of course, was out of the structure of their own thoughts.

Let me give you an example. In the far outfield of our baseball diamond, there was a boulder of perhaps ten tons. (I must remark that the athletic skill, the physical reactions of the children, was in its own way almost as extraordinary as their mental powers. They have broken every track and field record in existence—often cutting world records by one third. I have watched them run down our horses. Their movements can be so quick as to make us appear sluggards by comparison. And they love baseball—among other games.)

We had spoken of either blasting the boulder apart or rolling it out of the way with one of our heavy bulldozers, but it was something we had never gotten to. Then, one day, we discovered that the boulder was gone—in its place a pile of thick red dust that the wind was fast leveling. We asked the children what had happened, and they told us that they had reduced the boulder to dust —as if it was no more than kicking a small stone out of one's path. How? Well, they had loosened the molecular structure and it had become dust. They explained, but we could not understand. They tried to explain to Cromwell how their thoughts could do this, but he could no more comprehend it than the rest of us.

I mention one thing. They built an atomic fusion power plant, out of which we derive an unlimited store of power. They built what they call free fields into all our trucks and cars, so that they rise and travel through the air with the same facility they have on the ground. With the power of thought, they can go into atoms, rearrange electrons, build one element out of another—and all this is elementary to them, as if they were doing tricks to amuse us and amaze us.

So you see something of what the children are, and now I shall tell you what you must know.

In the fifteenth year of the children, our entire staff met with them. There were fifty-two of them now, for all the children born to us were taken into their body of singleness—and flourished in their company, I should add, despite their initially lower IQs. A very formal and serious meeting, for in thirty days the team of observers was scheduled to enter the reservation. Michael, who was born in Italy, spoke for them; they needed only one voice.

He began by telling us how much they loved and cherished us, the adults who were once their teachers. "All that we have, all that we are, you have given us," he said. "You are our fathers and mothers and teachers—and we love you beyond our power to say. For years now, we have wondered at your patience and self-giving, for we have gone into your minds and we know what pain and doubt and fear and confusion you all live with. We have also gone into the minds of the soldiers who guard the reservation. More and more, our power to probe grew—until now there is no mind anywhere on earth that we cannot seek out and read.

"From our seventh year, we knew all the details of this experiment, why we were here and what you were attempting—and from then until now, we have pondered over what our future must be. We have also tried to help you, whom we love so much, and perhaps we have been a little help in easing your discontents, in keeping you as healthy as possible, and in easing your troubled nights in that maze of fear and nightmare that you call sleep.

"We did what we could, but all our efforts to join you with us have failed. Unless that area of the mind is opened before puberty, the tissues change, the brain cells lose all potential of development, and it is closed forever. Of all things, this saddens us most—for you have given us the most precious heritage of mankind, and in return we have given you nothing."

"That isn't so," I said. "You have given us more than we gave you."

"Perhaps," Michael nodded. "You are very good and kind people. But now the fifteen years are over, and the team will be here in thirty days—"

I shook my head. "No. They must be stopped."

"And all of you?" Michael asked, looking from one to another of the adults.

Some of us were weeping. Cromwell said:

"We are your teachers and your fathers and mothers, but you must tell us what to do. You know that."

Michael nodded, and then he told us what they had decided. The reservation must be maintained. I was to go to Washington with Mark and Dr. Goldbaum—and somehow get an extension of time. Then new infants would be brought into the reservation by teams of the children, and educated here.

"But why must they be brought here?" Mark asked. "You can reach them wherever they are—go into their minds, make them a part of you?"

"But they can't reach us," Michael said. "Not for a long time. They would be alone—and their minds would be shattered. What would the people of your world outside do to such children? What happened to people in the past who were possessed of devils, who heard voices? Some became saints, but more were burned at the stake."

"Can't you protect them?" someone asked.

"Some day—yes. Now, no—there are not enough of us. First, we must help move children here, hundreds and hundreds more. Then there must be other places like this one. It will take a long time. The world is a large place and there are a great many children. And we must work carefully. You see, people are so filled with fear—and this would be the worst fear of all. They would go mad with fear and all that they would think of is to kill us."

"And our children could not fight back," Dr. Goldbaum said quietly. "They cannot hurt any human being, much less kill one. Cattle, our old dogs and cats, they are one thing—"

(Here Dr. Goldbaum referred to the fact that we no longer slaughtered our cattle in the old way. We had pet dogs and cats, and when they became very old and sick, the children caused them peacefully to go to sleep—from which they never awakened. Then the children asked us if we might do the same with the cattle we butchered for food.)

"—but not people," Dr. Goldbaum went on. "They cannot hurt people or kill people. We are able to do things that we know are wrong, but that is one power we have that the children lack. They cannot kill and they cannot hurt. Am I right, Michael?"

"Yes—you are right." Michael nodded. "We must do it slowly and patiently—and the world must not know what we are doing until we have taken certain measures. We think we need three years more. Can you get us three years, Jean?"

"I will get it," I said.

"And we need all of you to help us. Of course we will not keep any of you here if you wish to go. But we need you—as we have always needed you. We love you and value you, and we beg you to remain with us. . . ."

Do you wonder that we all remained, Harry—that no one of us could leave our children—or will ever leave them, except when death takes us away? There is not so much more that I must tell now.

We got the three years we needed, and as for the gray barrier that surrounds us, the children tell me that it is a simple device indeed. As nearly as I can understand, they altered the time sequence of the entire reservation. Not much—by less than one ten-thousandth of a second. But the result is that your world outside exists this tiny fraction of a second in the future. The same sun shines on us, the same winds blow, and from inside the barrier, we see your world unaltered. But you cannot see us. When you look at us, the present of our existence has not yet come into being—and instead there is nothing, no space, no heat, no light, only the impenetrable wall of nonexistence.

From inside, we can go outside—from the past into the future. I have done this during the moments when we experimented with the barrier. You feel a shudder, a moment of cold—but no more.

So there is the situation, Harry. We will never see each other again, but I assure you that Mark and I are happier than we have ever been. Man will change, and he will become what he was intended to be, and he will reach out with love and knowledge to all the universes of the firmament. Isn't that what man has always dreamt of, no war or hatred or hunger or sickness or death? We are fortunate to be alive while this is happening, Harry—we should ask no more.

With all my love,
Jean

Felton finished reading, and then there was a long, long silence while the two men looked at each other. Finally, the Secretary spoke:

"You know we shall have to keep knocking at that barrier—trying to find a way to break through?"

"I know."

"It will be easier, now that your sister has explained it."

"I don't think it will be easier," Felton said tiredly. "I do not think that she has explained it."

"Not to you and me, perhaps. But we'll put the eggheads to work on it. They'll figure it out. They always do."

"Perhaps not this time."

"Oh, yes," the Secretary nodded. "You see, we've got to stop it. We can't have this kind of thing—immoral, godless, and a threat to every human being on earth. The kids were right. We would have to kill them, you know. It's a disease. The only way to stop a disease is to kill the bugs that cause it. The only way. I wish there was another way, but there isn't."

Intelligence and Personality

*T*he potential for achievement of anything is called an aptitude, and one of the major areas of psychological testing is that of aptitude tests. Aptitude testing is different from the other two major areas of testing, achievement and intelligence testing. Achievement tests are designed to measure success in some past learning or performing experience. The high-school student who is given a test following six weeks of instruction in American history is evaluated for his achievement level, or acquisition of knowledge.

An intelligence test differs from an aptitude test in that the intelligence test seeks to predict very broad potential, whereas the aptitude test seeks to predict how well an individual will do in specific tasks or jobs. The intelligence test identifies reasoning abilities and learning potential that apply to many situations. Creativity is seen as relatively independent of both test results—rather as novel or original ways of seeing or combining information.

Aptitude testing misuses do exist. As these misuses are extrapolated, oppressive visions are seen. In the interest of efficiency, at times when industry is faced with many applicants for few positions, aptitude testing has become pervasive, mandatory, and procrustean. Unfeeling computers and sometimes equally unfeeling testers are seen by rejected applicants as apparently ignoring talent and aptitude. The resulting frustration is felt by many people in contemporary society who perceive tests and automated assessments as making nonpersons of them.

There are alternative interpretations and outcomes for the sour notes struck by this testing process and the rejection of some applicants. A first interpretation is that psychological testing has been made a convenient scapegoat for the applicant's failure. If interviews alone were used for selection, then the brevity and superficiality of interviews in getting to know a person would be attacked. Another interpretation is that no selection process is perfect, and the success prediction-rate must be known. If the testing methods are better than prior means in identifying employees who will be happiest and most effective in their work, then perhaps the dissatisfaction of those smaller numbers, able and not selected, is a justifiable cost.

Psychological testing isn't perfect, and perhaps the reactions of the rejected individuals to their failure are as important as the test results themselves. We know of one college administrator who never returns the nonrefundable advance tuition deposit to students who have decided not to attend and who write to request its return. However, if the same student comes in person and insists on the deposit's return, the student receives it immediately, without question. Similarly, the reaction of the person being tested to the test results is a key piece of information, and is explored especially in the story "Placement Test."

Equally important, this story demonstrates the importance of situational factors and context in understanding behavior. No longer are actions seen and judged absolutely: rather they are evaluated relatively, in the context of the environment, of other people's actions, and of social expectations.

For example, the deliberate taking of one's own life may or may not be suicidal and may or may not be disapproved, depending on context. The rejected lover swallowing an overdose of sleeping pills acts in a very different context than the soldier who throws himself on a live grenade to save his companions.

Looking at psychologists' behaviors similarly calls for understanding the scenes in which they are set. Thus an out-of-context commentary on conditioning procedures is made by Robert Heinlein, when he declares in his book *I Will Fear No Evil,* (New York: Putnam, 1970), "All I know is that every time a dog salivates, a behavioral psychologist has to ring a bell." A shift in context leads to a shift in meaning. The lesson of "Placement Test" is to demonstrate powerfully the effect of a shift in context.

Personality tests are commonly divided into the categories of objective tests and projective tests. Objective tests are considered to be those to which an objective (true-false or check list) answer is given. Straightforward statements are presented to the client. While this method of getting direct reports of personality and problems is less subjective in administration, scoring, and interpretation than the so-called projective tests, much room does exist for nonobjective elements and influences.

The projective test usually presents vague stimuli or information to the client or subject. The ways in which the client responds reflect his or her inner feelings and processes as much as the "true" nature of the test materials. This process is an everyday occurrence in nontesting situations. Children often will speculate about what shapes of clouds seem to be (a speculation that has led to the development of a cloud projective test, using standardized pictures of clouds).

The projective process is an intimate part of psychotherapy and healing. Many individuals are ineffective in their personal and work lives to begin with because they are not able to see or hear correctly or accurately. All of their experiences are twisted and warped through an internal churning. In many psychotherapies this internal distortion is explicitly identified and serves as a foundation for behavior and personality change.

Patients are not the only ones susceptible to projection. News reporters, senators, teachers, researchers, journal editors, and, yes, psychotherapists, are vulnerable as well. The training of psychotherapists through supervision and sometimes personal psychotherapy may bring such projections to awareness. Even with such projections, it is possible to be a good therapist—harder, but still possible.

There are many persons who are psychotherapeutic without being psychotherapists. Marvelous therapeutic healing and efforts may be rendered by persons ranging from neighbors and spouses to bartenders and construction supervisors. As part of an equal-time perspective, we note that some quite powerful psychological harm and adversities may be administered by these same classes of people as well. One does not have to be a formal patient in psychotherapy to get meaningful personal help from another; nor does one have to carry a helping title to help. As the mental health professions mobilize to deal with the overwhelming number of persons in psychological need, it is this class of noncredentialed helpers that offers the most promise for solutions and salvations.

The credentialed helpers often obey the "Peter Principle." They rise to their levels of incompetence in agency hierarchies. They become transformed from psychotherapists to administrators, from one-to-one helpers to supervisors, from clinicians to writers and researchers. The noncredentialed helpers stay closer to the clientele, spend more time with them, and hear the essence of the human suffering. Yet they have not been exposed to the formal educational experiences that armor helpers while bestowing credentials on them. The caveats? They need training and supervision so they don't become frightened by psychic pain and suffering. They need understanding of the ethics and problems of being helpers. And they especially need to learn the ways in which their own feelings can best be applied constructively to influencing the lives of others.

It's happening. Mental health centers, psychiatric hospitals, and many community organizations have trained, empathic helpers without portfolio. At many such centers, there are more helpers without credentials than there are card-carrying healers. As the mental health business continues to expand, promoting doctor-types upward, these intuitive helpers will be the leading edge for aiding people in crisis and pain.

13. placement test

Keith Laumer

One of the finest and most skilled applications of psychology has been in the field of job placement. Who among us has not been exposed to the IQ test, the job classification battery, or the myriad other ways in which psychology has intruded into our decision making.

Now, there are some interesting problems that arise from all this testing. The potential for a "Big Brother" state, in which all decisions are made on behalf of the government, becomes great. With sufficiently pervasive testing and behavioral observation in the hands of an oppressive government, individuals can be categorized, imprisoned, or made politically and personally ineffectual. It is just that specter that caused many concerned citizens to picket the Washington, D.C., headquarters of the American Psychological Association in 1965. They protested the apparently increasing use of personality tests in selection for government positions.

An equally perplexing problem is the mutual deception and lack of trust that arises. For instance, the more emphasis that is put on tests, the trickier the test takers become. And the trickier the test takers get, the sneakier the test givers become. This tricky-sneaky cycle culminates in the following story.

The essence of the tricky test is that you don't know it's there. The tester often uses a variety of personally intrusive techniques that cause others to reveal themselves without knowing it. And there is a certain sense of accomplishment in manipulating or fooling another, even under the professionally acceptable euphemisms that are used. Yet, most testers would confess that they would take a back seat as a second-class voyeur compared to some characters in the following ingenious gem.

Too much said already. Read on . . . unless you think that it represents some kind of test. No, it couldn't do that—after all, no one could be watching or knowing. Right? Right? Right?

I

Reading the paper in his hand, Mart Maldon felt his mouth go dry. Across the desk, Dean Wormwell's eyes, blurry behind thick contact lenses, strayed to his fingerwatch.

"Quota'd out?" Maldon's voice emerged as a squeak. "Three days before graduation?"

"Umm, yes, Mr. Maldon. Pity, but there you are . . ." Wormwell's jowls twitched upward briefly. "No reflection on you, of course . . ."

Maldon found his voice. "They can't do this to me—I stand number two in my class—"

Wormwell held up a pudgy palm. "Personal considerations are not involved, Mr. Maldon. Student load is based on quarterly allocated funding; funds were cut. Analogy Theory was one of the courses receiving a quota reduction—"

"An Theory . . .? But I'm a Microtronics major; that's an elective—an optional one-hour course—"

The Dean rose, stood with his fingertips on the desk. "The details are there, in the notification letter—"

"What about the detail that I waited four years for enrollment, and I've worked like a malemute for five more—"

"Mr. Maldon!" Wormwell's eyes bulged. "We work within a system! You don't expect *personal* exceptions to be made, I trust?"

"But, Dean—there's a howling need for qualified Microtronic Engineers—"

"That will do, Mr. Maldon. Turn in your student tag to the Registrar and you'll receive an appointment for Placement Testing."

"All right." Maldon's chair banged as he stood up. "I can still pass Testing and get Placed; I know as much Micro as any graduate—"

"Ah—I believe you're forgetting the limitation on nonacademically qualified testees in Technical Specialty Testing. I suggest you accept a Phase Two Placement for the present . . ."

"Phase Two—But that's for unskilled labor!" "You need work, Mr. Maldon. A city of a hundred million can't support idlers. And dormitory life is far from pleasant for an untagged man." The Dean waited, glancing pointedly at the door. Maldon silently gathered up his letter and left.

II

It was hot in the test cubicle. Maldon shifted on the thinly padded bench, looking over the test form:

1. In the following list of words, which word is repeated most often: dog, cat, cow, cat, pig . . .

2. Would you like to ask persons entering a building to show you their pass?

3. Would you like to check forms to see if the names have been entered in the correct space?

"Testing materials are on the desk," a wall-speaker said. "Use the stylus to mark the answers you think are correct. Mark only one answer to each question. You will have one hour in which to complete the test. You may start now . . ."

Back in the Hall twenty minutes later, Maldon took a seat on a bench against the wall beside a heavy-faced man who sat with one hand clutching the other as though holding a captured mouse. Opposite him, a nervous youth in issue coveralls shook a cigaret from a crumbled plastic pack lettered GRA-NYAUCK WELFARE—ONE DAILY RATION, puffed it alight, exhaled an acrid whiff of combustion retardant.

"That's a real smoke," he said in a high, rapid voice, rolling the thin, greyish cylinder between his fingers. "Half an inch of doctored tobacco and an inch and a half of filter." He grinned sourly and dropped the cigaret on the floor between his feet.

The heavy-faced man moved his head half an inch.

"That's safety first, Mac. Guys like you throw 'em around, they burn down and go out by theirself."

"Sure—if they'd make 'em half an inch shorter you could throw 'em away without lighting 'em at all."

Across the room a small man with jug ears moved along, glancing at the yellow or pink cards in the hands of the waiting men and women. He stopped, plucked a card from the hand of a narrow-faced boy with an open mouth showing crowded yellow teeth.

"You've already *passed,*" the little man said irritably. "You don't come back here anymore. Take the card and go to the place that's written on it. Here . . ." he pointed.

"Sixteen years I'm foreman of number nine gang-lathe at Philly Maintenance," the man sitting beside Mart said suddenly. He unfolded his hands, held out the right one. The tips of all four fingers were missing to the first knuckle. He put the hand away.

"When I get out of the Medicare, they classify me J-4 and send me here. And you know what?" He looked at Mart. "I can't pass the tests . . ."

"Maldon, Mart," an amplified voice said. "Report to the Monitor's desk . . ."

He walked across to the corner where the small man sat now, deftly sorting cards. He looked up, pinched a pink card from the stack, jabbed it at Maldon. Words jumped out at him: NOT QUALIFIED.

Mart tossed the card back on the desk. "You must be mixed up," he said. "A ten year old kid could pass that test—"

"Maybe so," the monitor said sharply. "But *you* didn't. Next testing on Wednesday, eight A.M.—"

"Hold on a minute," Mart said. "I've had five years of Microtronics—"

The monitor was nodding. "Sure, sure. Come back Wednesday."

"You don't get the idea—"

"You're the one that doesn't get the idea, fellow." He studied Maldon for a moment. "Look," he said, in a more reasonable tone. "What you want, you want to go in for Adjustment."

"Thanks for the tip," Maldon said. "I'm not quite ready to have my brains scrambled."

"Ha! A smart-alec!" The monitor pointed to his chest. "Do I look like my brains were scrambled?"

Maldon looked him over as though in doubt.

"You've been Adjusted, huh? What's it like?"

"Adjustment? There's nothing to it. You have a problem finding work, it helps you, that's all. I've seen fellows like you before. You'll never pass Phase Two testing until you do it."

"To Hell with Phase Two testing! I've registered for Tech Testing. I'll just wait."

The monitor nodded, prodding at his teeth with a pencil. "Yeah, you could wait. I remember one guy waited nine years; then he got his Adjustment and we placed him in a week."

"Nine years?" Maldon shook his head. "Who makes up these rules?"

"Who makes 'em up? Nobody! They're in the book."

Maldon leaned on the desk. "Then who writes the book? Where do I find them?"

"You mean the Chief?" the small man rolled his eyes toward the ceiling. "On the next level up. But don't waste your time, friend. You can't get in there. They don't have time to argue with everybody who comes in here. It's the system—"

"Yeah," Maldon said, turning away. "So I hear."

III

Maldon rode the elevator up one floor, stepped off in a blank-walled foyer adorned by a stone urn filled with sand, a potted yucca, framed unit citations and a polished slab door lettered PLACEMENT BOARD—AUTHORIZED PERSONNEL ONLY. He tried it, found it solidly locked.

It was very quiet. Somewhere, air pumps hummed. Maldon stood by the door and waited. After ten minutes, the elevator door hissed open, disgorged a slow-moving man in blue GS coveralls with a yellow identity tag. He held the tag to a two-inch rectangle of glass beside the door. There was a click. The door slid back. Maldon moved quickly, crowding through behind the workman.

"Hey, what gives," the man said.

"It's all right, I'm a coordinator," Maldon said quickly.

"Oh." The man looked Maldon over. "Hey," he said. "Where's your I.D.?"

"It's a new experimental system. It's tattooed on my left foot."

"Hah!" the man said. "They always got to try out new stuff." He went on along the deep-carpeted corridor. Maldon followed slowly, reading signs over doors. He turned in under one that read CRITERIA SECTION. A girl with features compressed by fat looked up, her lower jaw working busily. She reached, pressed a button on the desk top.

"Hi," Maldon said, using a large smile. "I'd like to see the chief of the section."

The girl chewed, looking at him.

"I won't take up much of his time . . ."

"You sure won't, Buster," the girl said. The hall door opened. A uniformed man looked in. The girl waved a thumb at Maldon.

"He comes busting in," she said. "No tag, yet."

The guard jerked his head toward the corridor. "Let's go . . ."

"Look, I've got to see the chief—"

The cop took his arm, helped him to the door. "You birds give me a swifty. Why don't you go to Placement like the sign says?"

"Look, they tell me I've got to have some kind of electronic lobotomy to make me dumb enough to be a receptionist or a watchman—"

"Let's watch them cracks," the guard said. He shoved Maldon out into the waiting room. "Out! And don't pull any more fasties until you got a tag, see?"

IV

Sitting at a shiny imitation-oak table in the Public Library, Mart turned the pages of a booklet titled *Adjustment Fits the Man to the Job*.

". . . neuroses arising from job tension," he read at random. "Thus, the Adjusted worker enjoys the deep-down satisfaction which comes from Doing a Job, free from conflict-inducing, nonproductive impulses and the distractions of feckless, speculative intellectual activity . . ."

Mart rose and went to the librarian's console.

"I want something a little more objective," he said in a hoarse library whisper. "This is nothing but propaganda."

The librarian paused in her button-punching to peer at the booklet. "That's put out by the Placement people themselves," she said sharply. She was a jawless woman with a green tag against a ribby chest and thin, black-dyed hair. "It contains all the information anyone needs."

"Not quite; it doesn't tell who grades Placement tests and decides who gets their brain poached."

"Well!" the woman's button chin drew in. "I'm sure I never heard Adjustment referred to in *those terms* before!"

"Do you have any technical information on it—or anything on Placement policy in general?"

"Certainly not for indiscriminate use by—" she searched for a word, "—browsers!"

"Look, I've got a right to know what goes on in my own town, I hope," Mart said, forgetting to whisper. "What is it, a conspiracy . . .?"

"You're paranoic!" The librarian's lean fingers snatched the pamphlet from Maldon's hand. "You come stamping in here—without even a tag—a great healthy creature like you—" her voice cut like a sheet-metal file. Heads turned.

"All I want is information—"

"—living in luxury on MY tax money! You ought to be—"

V

It was an hour later. In a ninth-floor corridor of the GRANYAUCK TIMES-HERALD building, Mart leaned against a wall, mentally rehearsing speeches.

A stout man emerged from a door lettered EDITOR IN CHIEF. Mart stepped forward to intercept him.

"Pardon me sir. I have to see you . . ."

Sharp blue eyes under wild-growing brows darted at Maldon.

"Yes? What is it?"

"I have a story for you. It's about the Placement procedure."

"Whoa, buddy. Who are you?"

"My name's Maldon. I'm an Applied Tech graduate—almost—but I can't get placed in Microtronics. I don't have a tag—and the only way to get one is to get a job—but first I have to let the government operate on my brains—"

"Hmmmp!" The man looked Maldon up and down, started on.

"Listen!" Maldon caught at the portly man's arm. "They're making idiots out of intelligent people so they can do work you could train a chimp to do, and if you ask any questions—"

"All right, Mac . . ." A voice behind Maldon growled. A large hand took him by the shoulder, propelled him toward the walkaway entrance, urged him through the door. He straightened his coat, looked back. A heavy-set man with a pink card in a plastic cover clipped to his collar dusted his hands, looking satisfied.

"Don't come around lots," he called cheerfully as the door slammed.

VI

"Hi, Glamis," Mart said to the small, neat woman behind the small, neat desk. She smiled nervously, straightened the mathematically precise stack of papers before her.

"Mart, it's lovely to see you again, of course . . ." her eyes went to the blank place where his tag should have been. "But you really should have gone to your assigned SocAd Advisor—"

"I couldn't get an appointment until January." He pulled a chair around to the desk and sat down. "I've left school. I went in for Phase Two Placement testing this morning. I flunked."

"Oh . . . I'm so sorry, Mart." She arranged a small smile on her face. "But you can go back on Wednesday—"

"Uh-huh. And then on Friday, and then the following Monday—"

"Why, Mart, I'm sure you'll do better next time," the girl said brightly. She flipped through the pages of a calendar pad. "Wednesday's testing is for . . . ah . . . Vehicle Positioning Specialists, Instrumentation Inspectors, Sanitary Facility Supervisors—"

"Uh-huh. Toilet Attendants," Mart said. "Meter Readers—"

"There are others," Glamis went on hastily. "Traffic flow coordinators—"

"Pushing stop-light buttons on the turnpike. But it doesn't matter what the job titles are. I can't pass the tests."

"Why, Mart . . . Whatever do you mean?"

"I mean that to get the kind of jobs that are open you have to be a nice, steady moron. And if you don't happen to qualify as such, they're prepared to make you into one."

"Mart, you're exaggerating! The treatment merely slows the synaptic response time slightly—and its effects can be reversed at any time. People of exceptional qualities are needed to handle the type work—"

"How can I fake the test results, Glamis? I need a job—unless I want to get used to Welfare coveralls and two T-rations a day."

"Mart! I'm shocked that you'd suggest such a thing! Not that it would work. You can't fool the Board that easily—"

"Then fix it so I go in for Tech testing; you know I can pass."

She shook her head. "Heavens, Mart, Tech Testing is all done at Central Personnel in City Tower—Level Fifty. Nobody goes up there, without at least a blue tag—" She frowned sympathetically. "You should simply have your adjustment, and—"

Maldon looked surprised. "You really expect me to go down there and have them cut my I.Q down to 80 so I can get a job shovelling garbage?"

"Really, Mart; you can't expect society to adjust to *you*. You have to adjust to *it*."

"Look, I can punch commuters' tickets just as well as if I were stupid. I could—"

Glamis shook her head. "No, you couldn't, Mart. The Board knows what it's doing." She lowered her voice. "I'll be perfectly frank with you. These jobs *must* be filled. But they can't afford to put perceptive, active minds on rote tasks. There'd only be trouble. They need people who'll be contented and happy punching tickets."

Mart sat pulling at his lower lip. "All right, Glamis. Maybe I will go in for Adjustment . . ."

"Oh, wonderful, Mart." She smiled. "I'm *sure* you'll be happier—"

"But first, I want to know more about it. I want to be sure they aren't going to make a permanent idiot out of me."

She tsked, handed over a small folder from a pile on the corner of the desk. "This will tell you—"

He shook his head. "I saw that. It's just a throwaway for the public. I want to know how the thing works; circuit diagrams, technical specs."

"Why, Mart, I don't have anything of that sort—and even if I did—"

"You can get 'em. I'll wait."

"Mart, I *do* want to help you . . . but . . . what . . . ?"

"I'm not going in for Adjustment until I know something about it," he said flatly. "I want to put my mind at ease that they're not going to burn out my cortex."

Glamis nibbled her upper lip. "Perhaps I *could* get something from Central Files." She stood. "Wait here; I won't be long."

She was back in five minutes carrying a thick book with a cover of heavy manila stock on which were the words, *GSM 8765-89. Operation and Maintenance, EET Mark II.* Underneath, in smaller print, was a notice:

This Field Manual for Use of Authorized Personnel Only.

"Thanks, Glamis." Mart rifled the pages, glimpsed fine print and intricate diagrams. "I'll bring it back tomorrow." He headed for the door.

"Oh, you can't take it out of the office! You're not even *supposed* to *look* at it!"

"You'll get it back." He winked and closed the door on her worried voice.

VII

The cubicle reminded Mart of the one at the Placement center, three days earlier, except that it contained a high, narrow cot in place of a desk and chair. A damp-looking attendant in a white coat flipped a wall switch, twiddled a dial.

"Strip to your waist, place your clothing and shoes in the basket, remove all metal objects from your pockets, no watches or other jewelry must be worn," he recited in a rapid monotone. "When you are ready, lie down on your back—" he slapped the cot—"hands at your sides, breathe deeply, do not touch any of the equipment. I will return in approximately five minutes. Do not leave the stall." He whisked the curtain aside and was gone.

Mart slipped a flat plastic tool kit from his pocket, opened it out, picked the largest screwdriver, and went to work on the metal panel cover set against the wall. He lifted it off and looked in at a maze of junction blocks, vari-colored wires, bright screw-heads, fuses, tiny condensers.

He pulled a scrap of paper from his pocket, compared it to the circuits before him. The large black lead, here . . . He put a finger on it. And the matching red one, leading up from the 30 MFD condenser . . .

With a twist, he freed the two connectors, reversed them, tightened them back in place. Working quickly, he snipped wires, fitted jumpers in place, added a massive resistor from his pocket. There; with luck, the check instruments would give the proper readings now—but the current designed to lightly scorch his synapses would flow harmlessly round and round within the apparatus. He clapped the cover back in place, screwed it down, and had just pulled off his shirt when the attendant thrust his head inside the curtains.

"Let's go, let's get those clothes off and get on the cot," he said, and disappeared.

Maldon emptied his pockets, pulled off his shoes, stretched out on the cot. A minute or two ticked past. There was an odor of alcohol in the air. The curtain jumped aside. The round-faced attendant took his left arm, swiped a cold tuft of cotton across it, held a hypo-spray an inch from the skin, and depressed the plunger. Mart felt a momentary sting.

"You've been given a harmless soporific," the attendant said tonelessly. "Just relax, don't attempt to change the position of the headset or chest contacts after I have placed them in position, are you beginning to feel drowsy . . .?"

Mart nodded. A tingling had begun in his fingertips; his head seemed to be inflating slowly. There was a touch of something cold across his wrists, then his ankles, pressure against his chest . . .

"Do not be alarmed, the restraint is for your own protection, relax and breathe deeply, it will hasten the effects of the soporific . . ." The voice echoed, fading and swelling. For a moment, the panicky thought came to Mart that perhaps he had made a mistake, that the modified apparatus would send a lethal charge through his brain . . . Then that thought was gone with all the others, lost in a swirling as of a soft green mist.

VIII

He was sitting on the side of the cot, and the attendant was offering him a small plastic cup. He took it, tasted the sweet liquid, handed it back.

"You should drink this," the attendant said, "It's very good for you."

Mart ignored him. He was still alive; and the attendant appeared to have noticed nothing unusual. So far, so good. He glanced at his hand. *One, two, three, four, five* . . . He could still count. *My name is Mart Maldon, age twenty-eight, place of residence, Welfare Dorm 69, Wing Two, nineteenth floor, room 1906* . . .

His memory seemed to be OK. *Twenty-seven times eighteen is* . . . *four hundred and eighty-six* . . .

He could still do simple arithmetic.

"Come on, fellow, drink the nice cup, then put your clothes on."

He shook his head, reached for his shirt, then remembered to move slowly, uncertainly, like a moron ought to. He fumbled clumsily with his shirt . . .

The attendant muttered, put the cup down, snatched the shirt, helped Mart into it, buttoned it for him.

"Put your stuff in your pockets, come on, that's a good fellow . . ."

He allowed himself to be led along the corridor, smiling vaguely at people hurrying past. In the processing room, a starched woman back of a small desk stamped papers, took his hand and impressed his thumbprint on them, slid them across the desk.

"Sign your name here . . ." she pointed. Maldon stood gaping at the paper. "Write your name here!" She tapped the paper impatiently. Maldon reached up and wiped his nose with a forefinger, letting his mouth hang open.

The woman looked past him. "A Nine-oh-one," she snapped. "Take him back—"

Maldon grabbed the pen and wrote his name in large, scrawling letters. The woman snapped the form apart, thrust one sheet at him.

"Uh, I was thinking," he explained, folding the paper clumsily.

"Next!" the woman snapped, waving him on. He nodded submissively and shuffled slowly to the door.

IX

The Placement monitor looked at the form Maldon had given him. He looked up, smiling. "Well, so you finally wised up. Good boy. And today you got a nice score. We're going to be able to place you. You like bridges, hah?"

Maldon hesitated, then nodded.

"Sure you like bridges. Out in the open air. You're going to be an important man. When the cars come up, you lean out and see that they put the money in the box. You get to wear a uniform . . ." The small man rambled on, filling out forms. Maldon stood by, looking at nothing.

"Here you go. Now, you go where it says right here, see? Just get on the cross-town shuttle, right outside on this level, the one with the big number nine. You know what a nine is, OK?"

Maldon blinked, nodded. The clerk frowned. "Sometimes I think them guys overdo a good thing. But you'll get to feeling better in a few days; you'll sharpen up, like me. Now, you go on over there, and they'll give you your I.D. and your uniform and put you to work. OK?"

"Uh, thanks . . ." Maldon crossed the wide room, pushed through the turnstile, emerged into the late-afternoon sunlight on the forth-level walkaway. The glare panel by the shuttle entrance read NEXT—9. He thrust his papers into his pocket and ran for it.

X

Maldon left his Dormitory promptly at eight the next morning, dressed in his threadbare Student-issue suit, carrying the heavy duffel bag of Port Authority uniforms that had been issued to him the day before. His new yellow tag was pinned prominently to his lapel.

He took a cargo car to street level, caught an uptown car, dropped off in the run-down neighborhood of second-hand stores centered around Fifth Avenue and Forty-fifth Street. He picked a shabby establishment barricaded behind racks of dowdy garments, stepped into a long, dim-lit room smelling of naphtha and moldy wool. Behind a counter, a short man with a circlet of fuzz above his ears and a vest hanging open over a tight-belted paunch looked him over. Mart hoisted the bag up, opened it, dumped the clothing out onto the counter. The paunchy man followed the action with his eyes.

"What'll you give me for this stuff?" Mart said.

The man behind the counter prodded the dark blue tunic, put a finger under the light blue trousers, rubbed the cloth. He leaned across the counter, glanced toward the door, squinted at Mart's badge. His eyes flicked to Mart's face, back to the clothing. He spread his hands.

"Five credits."

"For all of it? It's worth a hundred anyway."

The man glanced sharply at Maldon's face, back at his tag, frowning.

"Don't let the tag throw you," Maldon said. "It's stolen—just like the rest of the stuff."

"Hey." The paunchy man thrust his lips out. "What kinda talk is that? I run a respectable joint. What are you, some kinda cop?"

"I haven't got any time to waste," Maldon said. "There's nobody listening. Let's get down to business. You can strip off the braid and buttons and—"

"Ten credits, my top offer," the man said in a low voice. "I gotta stay alive, ain't I? Any bum can get outfitted free at the Welfare; who's buying my stuff?"

"I don't know. Make it twenty."

"Fifteen; it's robbery."

"Throw in a set of Maintenance coveralls, and it's a deal."

"I ain't got the real article, but close . . ."

Ten minutes later, Mart left the store wearing a greasestained coverall with the cuffs turned up, the yellow tag clipped to the breast pocket.

XI

The girl at the bleached-driftwood desk placed austerely at the exact center of the quarter-acre of fog-grey rug stared at Maldon distastefully.

"I know of no trouble with the equipment—" she started in a lofty tone.

"Look, sister, I'm in the plumbing line; you run your dictyper." Maldon swung a greasy tool box around by the leather strap as though he were about to lower it to the rug. "They tell me the Exec gym, Level 9, City Tower, that's where I go. Now, you want to tell me where the steam room is, or do I go back and file a beef with the Union . . . ?"

"Next time come up the service shaft, Clyde!" she jabbed at a button; a panel whooshed aside across the room. "Men to the right, women to the left, co-ed straight ahead. Take your choice."

He went along the tile corridor, passed steam-frosted doors. The passage turned right, angled left again. Mart pushed through a door, looked around at chromium and red plastic benches, horses, parallel bars, racks of graduated weights. A fat man in white shorts lay on the floor, half-heartedly pedaling his feet in the air. Mart crossed the room, tried another door.

Warm, sun-colored light streamed through an obscure-glass celing. Tropical plants in tubs nodded wide leaves over a mat of grass-green carpet edging a turquoise-tiled pool with chrome railings. Two brown-skinned men in brief trunks and sunglasses sprawled on inflated rafts. There was a door to the right lettered EXECUTIVE DRESSING ROOM—MEMBERS ONLY. Mart went to it, stepped inside.

Tall, ivory-colored lockers lined two walls, with a wide padded bench between them. Beyond, bright shower heads winked in a darkened shower room. Maldon put the tool box on the bench, opened it, took out a twelve-inch prybar.

By levering at the top of the tall locker door, he was able to bulge it out sufficiently to see the long metal strip on the back of the door which secured it. He went back to the tool box, picked out a slim pair of pincers; with them he gripped the locking strip, levered up; the door opened with a sudden clang. The locker was empty.

He tried the next; it contained a handsome pale tan suit which would have fitted him nicely at the age of twelve. He went to the next locker . . .

Four lockers later, a door popped open on a dark maroon suit of expensive-looking polyon, a pair of plain scarlet shoes, a crisp pink shirt. Mart checked quickly. There was a wallet stuffed with ten-credit notes, a club membership card, and a blue I.D. with a gold alligator clip. Mart left the money on the shelf, rolled the clothing and stuffed it into the tool box, made for the door. It swung open and the smaller of the two sun bathers pushed past him with a sharp glance. Mart walked quickly around the end of the pool, stepped into the corridor. At the far end of it, the girl from the desk stood talking emphatically to a surprised-looking man. Their eyes turned toward Mart. He pushed through the first door on the left into a room with a row of white-sheeted tables, standing lamps with wide reflectors, an array of belted and rollered equipment. A vast bulk of a man with hairy forearms and a bald head, wearing a tight white leotard and white sneakers folded a newspaper and looked up from his bench, wobbling a toothpick in the corner of his mouth. There was a pink tag on his chest.

"Uh . . . showers?" Mart inquired. The fat man nodded toward a door behind him. Mart stepped to it, found himself in a long room studded with shower-heads and control knobs. There was no other door out. He turned back, bumped into the fat man in the doorway.

"So somebody finally decided to do something about the leak," he said around the toothpick. "Three months since I phoned it in. You guys take your time, huh?"

"I've got to go back for my tools," Mart said, starting past him. The fat man blocked him without moving. "So what's in the box?"

"Ah, they're the wrong tools . . ." He tried to sidle past. The big man took the toothpick from his mouth, frowned at it.

"You got a pipe wrench, ain't you? You got crescents, a screwdriver. What else you need to fix a lousy leak?"

"Well, I need my sprog-depressor," Mart said, "and my detrafficator rings, and possibly a marpilizer or two . . ."

"How come you ain't got—what you said—in there." The fat man eyed the tool box. "Ain't that standard equipment?"

"Yes, indeed—but I only have a right-hand one, and—"

"Let's have a look—" A fat hand reached for the tool-kit. Mart backed.

"—but I might be able to make it work," he finished. He glanced around the room. "Which one was it?"

"That third needle-battery on the right. You can see the drip. I'm tryna read, it drives me nuts."

Mart put the tool box down. "If you don't mind, it makes me nervous to work in front of an audience . . ."

The fat man grunted and withdrew. Mart opened the box, took out a wrench, began loosening a wide hex-sided locking ring. Water began to dribble, then spurt. Mart went to the door, flung it open.

"Hey, you didn't tell me the water wasn't turned off . . ."

"Huh?"

"You'll have to turn off the master valve; hurry up, before the place is flooded!"

The fat man jumped up, headed for the door.

"Stand by it, wait five minutes, then turn it back on!" Mart called after him. The door banged. Mart hauled the tool box out into the massage room, quickly stripped off the grimy coverall. His eye fell on a rack of neatly-packaged underwear, socks, toothbrushes, combs. He helped himself to a set, removed the last of the Welfare issue clothing—

A shout sounded outside the door, running feet. The door burst open. It was the big man from the executive locker room.

"Where's Charlie? Some rascal's stolen my clothing . . . !"

Mart grabbed up a towel, dropped it over his head and rubbed vigorously, humming loudly, his back to the newcomer.

"The workman—there's his tool box!"

Mart whirled, pulled the towel free, snatched the box from the hand of the invader, with a hearty shove sent him reeling into the locker room. He slammed the door, turned the key and dropped it down a drain. The shouts from inside were barely audible. He wrapped the towel around himself and dashed into the hall. There were people, some in white, others in towels or street clothes, all talking at once.

"Down there!" Mart shouted, pointing vaguely. "Don't let him get away!" He plunged through the press, along the hall. Doors opened and shut.

"Hey, what's he doing with a tool box?" someone shouted. Mart whirled, dived through a door, found himself in a dense, hot fog. A woman with pink skin beaded with perspiration and a towel wrapped turban-fashion around her head stared at him.

"What are you doing in here? Co-ed is the next room along."

Mart gulped and dived past her, slammed through a plain door, found himself in a small room stacked with cartons. There was another door in the opposite wall. He went through it, emerged in a dusty hall. Three doors down, he found an empty store-room.

Five minutes later he emerged, dressed in a handsome maroon suit. He strode briskly along to a door marked EXIT, came out into a carpeted foyer with a rank of open elevator doors. He stepped into one. The yellow-tagged attendant whooshed the door shut.

"Down, sir?"

"No," Mart said. "Up."

XII

He stepped out into the cool silence of Level Fifty.

"Which way to the Class One Testing Rooms?" he asked briskly.

The operator pointed. The door-lined corridor seemed to stretch endlessly.

"Going to try for the Big One, eh, sir?" the operator said. "Boy, you couldn't hire me to take on them kind of jobs. Me, I wouldn't want the responsibility." The closing door cut off the view of his wagging head.

Maldon set off, trying to look purposeful. Somewhere on this level were the Central Personnel Files, according to Glamis. It shouldn't be too hard to find them. After that . . . well, he could play it by ear.

A menu-board directory at a cross-corridor a hundred yards from his starting point indicated PERSONNEL ANALYSIS to the right. Mart followed the passage, passed open doors through which he caught glimpses of soft colors, air-conditioner grills, potted plants, and immaculate young women with precise hair styles sitting before immense keyboards or behind bare desks. Chaste lettering on doors read PROGRAMMING; REQUIREMENTS; DATA EXTRAPOLATION—PHASE III . . .

Ahead, Maldon heard a clattering, rising in volume as he approached a wide double door. He peered through glass, saw a long room crowded with massive metal cases ranked in rows, floor to ceiling. Men in tan dust smocks moved in the aisles, referring to papers in their hands, jotting notes, punching keys set in the consoles spaced at intervals on the giant cabinets. At a desk near the door, a man with a wide, sad mouth and a worried expression looked up, caught sight of Mart. It was no time to hesitate. He pushed through the door.

"Morning," he said genially over the busy sound of the data machines. "I'm looking for Central Personnel. I wonder if I'm in the right place?"

The sad man opened his mouth, then closed it. He had a green tag attached to the collar of his open-necked shirt.

"You from Special Actions?" he said doubtfully.

"Aptical foddering," Maldon said pleasantly. "I'd never been over here in Personnel Analysis, so I said, what the heck, I'll just run over myself." He was holding a relaxed smile in place, modelled after the one Dean Wormwell had customarily worn when condescending to students.

"Well, sir, this is Data Processing; what you probably want is Files . . ."

Mart considered quickly. "Just what is the scope of the work you do here?"

The clerk got to his feet. "We maintain the Master Personnel Cards up-to-date," he started, then paused. "Uh, could I just see that I.D., sir?"

Maldon let the smile cool a degree or two, flashed the blue card; the clerk craned as Mart tucked the tag away.

"Now," Mart went on briskly, "suppose you just start at the beginning and give me a rundown." He glanced at a wall-clock. "Make it a fast briefing. I'm a little pressed for time."

The clerk hitched at his belt, looked around. "Well, sir, let's start over here . . .

Ten minutes later, they stood before a high, glass-fronted housing inside which row on row of tape reels nestled on shiny rods; bright-colored plastic fittings of complex shape jammed the space over, under and behind each row.

". . . it's all completely cybernetic-governed, of course," the clerk was saying. "We process an average of four hundred and nineteen thousand personnel actions per day, with an average relay-delay of not over four microseconds."

"What's the source of your input?" Mart inquired in the tone of one dutifully asking the routine questions.

"All the Directorates feed their data in to us—"

"Placement Testing?" Mart asked idly.

"Oh, sure, that's our biggest single data input."

"Including Class Five and Seven categories, for example?"

The clerk nodded. "Eight through Two. Your Tech categories are handled separately, over in Banks Y and Z. There . . ." He pointed to a pair of red-painted cabinets.

"I see. That's where the new graduates from the Technical Institutions are listed, eh?"

"Right, sir. They're scheduled out from there to Testing alphabetically, and then ranked by score for Grading, Classification, and Placement."

Mart nodded and moved along the aisle. There were two-inch high letters stencilled on the frames of the data cases. He stopped before a large letter B.

"Let's look at a typical record," Mart suggested. The clerk stepped to the console, pressed a button. A foot-square screen glowed. Print popped into focus on it: BAJUL, FELIX B. 654-8734-099-B1.

Below the heading was an intricate pattern of dots.

"May I?" Mart reached for the button, pushed it. There was a click and the name changed: BAKERSKI, HYMAN A.

He looked at the meaningless code under the name.

"I take it each dot has a significance?"

"In the first row, you have the physical profile; that's the first nine spaces. Then psych, that's the next twenty-one. Then . . ." He lectured on. Mart nodded.

". . . educational profile, right here . . ."

"Now," Mart cut in. "Suppose there were an error—say in the median scores attained by an individual. How would you correct that?"

The clerk frowned pulling down the corners of his mouth into well-worn grooves.

"I don't mean on your part, of course," Mart said hastily. "But I imagine that the data-processing equipment occasionally drops a decimal, eh?" He smiled understandingly.

"Well, we do get maybe one or two a year—but there's no harm done. On the next run-through, the card's automatically kicked out."

"So you don't . . . ah . . . make corrections?"

"Well, only when a Change Entry comes through."

The clerk twirled knobs; the card moved aside, up; a single dot swelled on the screen, resolved into a pattern of dots.

"Say it was on this item; I'd just wipe that code, and overprint the change. Only takes a second, and—"

"Suppose, for example, you wanted this record corrected to show graduation from a Tech Institute?"

"Well, that would be this symbol here; eighth row, fourth entry. The code for technical specialty would be in the 900 series. You punch it in here." He indicated rows of colored buttons. "Then the file's automatically transferred to the V bank."

"Well, this has been a fascinating tour," Mart said. "I'll make it a point to enter an appropriate commendation in the files."

The sad-faced man smiled wanly. "Well, I try to do my job . . ."

"Now, if you don't mind, I'll just stroll around and watch for a few minutes before I rush along to my conference."

"Well, nobody's supposed to be back here in the stacks except—"

"That's quite all right. I'd prefer to look it over alone." He turned his back on the clerk and strolled off. A glance back at the end of the stack showed the clerk settling into his chair, shaking his head.

Mart moved quickly past the ends of the stacks, turned in at the third now, followed the letters through O, N, stopped before M. He punched a button, read the name that flashed on the screen: MAJONOVITCH.

He tapped at the key; names flashed briefly: MAKISS . . . MALACHI . . . MALDON, SALLY . . . MALDON, MART—

He looked up. A technician was standing at the end of the stack, looking at him. He nodded.

"Quite an apparatus you have here . . ."

The technician said nothing. He wore a pink tag and his mouth was open half an inch. Mart looked away, up at the ceiling, down at the floor, back at the technician. He was still standing, looking. Abruptly his mouth closed with a decisive snap; he started to turn toward the clerk's desk—

Mart reached for the control knobs, quickly dialled for the eighth row, entry four; the single dot shifted into position, enlarged. The technician, distracted by the sudden move, turned, came hurrying along the aisle.

"Hey, nobody's supposed to mess with the—"

"Now, my man," Mart said in a firm tone. "Answer each question in as few words as possible. You will be graded on promptness and accuracy of response. What is the number of digits in the Technical Specialty series— the 900 group?"

Taken aback, the technician raised his eyebrows, said, "Three—but—"

"And what is the specific code for Microtronics Engineer—cum laude?"

There was a sudden racket from the door. Voices were raised in hurried inquiry. The clerk's voice replied. The technician stood undecided, scratching his head. Mart jabbed at the colored buttons: 901 . . . 922 . . . 936 . . . He coded a dozen three-digit Specialties into his record at random.

From the corner of his eye he saw a light blink on one of the red-painted panels; his record was being automatically transferred to the Technically Qualified files. He poked the button which whirled his card from the screen and turned, stepped off toward the far end of the room. The technician came after him.

"Hey there, what card was that you were messing with . . .?"

"No harm done," Mart reassured him. "Just correcting an error. You'll have to excuse me now; I've just remembered a pressing engagement . . ."

"I better check; what card was it?"

"Oh—just one picked at random."

"But . . . we got a hundred million cards in here . . ."

"Correct!" Maldon said. "So far you're batting a thousand. Now, we have time for just one more question: is there another door out of here?"

"Mister, you better wait a minute till I see the super—"

Mart spotted two unmarked doors, side by side. "Don't bother; what would you tell him? That there was, just possibly, a teentsy weentsy flaw in one of your hundred million cards? I'm sure that would upset him." He pulled the nearest door open. The technician's mouth worked frantically.

"Hey, that's—" he started.

"Don't call us—we'll call you!" Mart stepped past the door; it swung to behind him. Just before it closed, he saw that he was standing in a four foot by six foot closet. He whirled, grabbed for the door; there was no knob on the inside. It shut with a decisive click!

He was alone in pitch darkness.

Maldon felt hastily over the surfaces of the walls, found them bare and featureless. He jumped, failed to touch the ceiling. Outside he heard the technician's voice, shouting. At any moment he would open the door and that would be that . . .

Mart went to his knees, explored the floor. It was smooth. Then his elbow cracked against metal—

He reached, found a grill just above floor level, two feet wide and a foot high. A steady flow of cool air came from it. There were screw-heads at each corner. Outside, the shouts continued. There were answering shouts.

Mart felt over his pockets, brought out a coin, removed the screws. The grill fell forward into his hands. He laid it aside, started in head-first, encountered a sharp turn just beyond the wall. He wriggled over on his side, pushed hard, negotiated the turn by pulling with his hands pressed against the sides of the metal duct. There was light ahead, crosshatched by a grid. He reached it, peered into a noisy room where great panels loomed, their faces a solid maze of dials and indicator lights. He tried the grill. It seemed solid. The duct made a right-angle turn here. Maldon worked his way around the bend, found that the duct widened six inches. When his feet were in position, he swung a kick at the grill. The limited space made it awkward; he kicked again and again; the grill gave, one more kick and it clattered into the room beyond. Mart struggled out through the opening.

The room was brightly lit, deserted. There were large printed notices here and there on the wall warning of danger. Mart turned, re-entered the duct, made his way back to the closet. The voices were still audible outside the door. He reached through the opening, found the grill, propped it in a position as the door flew open. He froze, waiting. There was a moment of silence.

"But," the technician's voice said, "I tell you the guy walked into the utility closet here like he was boarding a rocket for Paris! I didn't let the door out of my sight, that's why I was standing back at the back and yelling, like you was chewing me out for . . ."

"You must have made an error it must have been the other door there . . ."

"The door closed. Mart let out a breath. Now perhaps he'd have a few minutes' respite in which to figure a route off Level Fifty.

XIII

He prowled the lanes between the vast cybernetic machines, turned a corner, almost collided with a young woman with red-blonde hair, dark eyes, and a pouting red mouth which opened in a surprised O.

"You shouldn't be in here," she said, motioning over her shoulder with a pencil. "All examinees must remain in the examination room until the entire battery of tests have been completed."

"I . . . ah . . ."

"I know," the girl said, less severely. "Four hours at a stretch. It's awful. But you'd better go back in now before somebody sees you."

He nodded, smiled, and moved toward the door she had indicated. He looked back. She was studying the instrument dials, not watching him. He went past the door and tried the next. It opened and he stepped into a small, tidy office. A large-eyed woman with tightly dressed brown hair looked up from a desk adorned by a single rosebud in a slim vase and a sign reading

PLACEMENT OFFICER. Her eyes went to a wall clock.

"You're too late for today's testing, I'm afraid," she said. "You'll have to return on Wednesday; that's afternoon testing. Mondays we test in the morning." She smiled sympathetically. "Quite a few make that mistake."

"Oh," Mart said. "Ah . . . Couldn't I start late?"

The woman was shaking her head. "Oh, it wouldn't be possible. The first results are already coming in . . ." She nodded toward a miniature version of the giant machines in the next room. A humming and clicking sounded briefly from it. She tapped a key on her desk. There was a sharp buzz from the small machine. He gazed at the apparatus. Again it clicked and hummed. Again she tapped, eliciting another buzz.

Mart stood considering. His only problem now was to leave the building without attracting attention. His record had been altered to show his completion of a Technical Speciality; twelve of them, in fact. It might have been better if he had settled for one. Someone might notice—

"I see you're admiring the Profiler," the woman said. "It's a very compact model, isn't it? Are you a Cyberneticist, by any chance?"

Maldon started. "No . . ."

"What name is that? I'll check your file over to see that everything's in order for Wednesday's testing."

Mart took a deep breath. This was no time to panic . . . "Maldon," he said. "Mart Maldon."

The woman swung an elaborate telephone-dial-like instrument out from a recess, dialed a long code, then sat back. Ten seconds passed. With a click, a small panel on the desk-top glowed. The woman leaned forward, reading. She looked up.

"Why, Mr. Maldon! You have a remarkable record! I don't believe I've ever encountered a testee with such a wide—and varied—background!"

"Oh," Mart said, with a weak smile. "It was nothing . . ."

"Eidetics, Cellular Psychology, Autonomics . . ."

"I hate narrow specialization," Mart said.

". . . Cybernetics Engineering—why, Mr. Maldon, you were teasing me!"

"Well . . ." Mart edged toward the door.

"My, we'll certainly be looking forward to seeing your test results, Mr. Maldon! and Oh! Do let me show you the new Profiler you were admiring." She hopped up, came round the desk. "It's such a time saver—and of course, saves a vast number of operations within the master banks. Now when the individual testee depresses his COMPLETED key, his test pattern in binary form is transferred directly to this unit for recognition. It's capable of making over a thousand yes-no comparisons per second profiling the results in decimal terms and recoding them into the master record, without the necessity for activating a single major sequence within the master—and, of course, every activation costs the taxpayer seventy-nine credits!"

"Very impressive," Mart said. If he could interrupt the flow of information long enough to ask a few innocent-sounding directions . . .

A discreet buzzer sounded. The woman depressed a key on the desk communicator.

"Miss Frinkles, could you step in a moment? There's a report of a madman loose in the building . . ."

"Good Heavens!" She looked at Mart as she slipped through the door. "Please, do excuse me a moment . . ."

Mart waited half a minute, started to follow; a thought struck him. He looked at the Profiler. All test results were processed through this little device; what if . . .

A quick inspection indicated that the apparatus was a close relative of the desk-top units used at Applied Tech in the ill-fated Analogy Theory class. The input, in the form of a binary series established by the testee's answers to his quiz, was compared with the master pattern for the specialty indicated by the first three digits of the signal. The results were translated into a profile, ready for transmittal to the Master Files.

This was almost too simple . . .

Mart pressed a lever at the back of the housing, lifted it off. Miss Frinkles had been right about this being a new model; most of the circuitry was miniaturized and built up into replaceable subassemblies. What he needed was a set of tools . . .

He tried Miss Frinkles' desk, turned up a nail file and two bobby pins. It wouldn't be necessary to fake an input; all that was needed was to key the coder section to show the final result. He crouched, peered in the side of the unit. There, to the left was the tiny bank of contacts which would open or close to indicate the score in a nine-digit profile. There were nine rows of nine contacts, squeezed into an area of one-half inch square. It was going to be a ticklish operation . . .

Mart straightened a hairpin, reached in, delicately touched the row of minute relays; the top row of contacts snapped closed, and a red light went on at the side of the machine. Mart tossed the wire aside, and quickly referred to his record, still in focus on Miss Frinkles' desk-top viewer, then tickled tumblers to show his five letter, four digit personal identity code. Then he pressed a cancel key, to blank the deskscreen, and dropped the cover back in place on the Profiler. He was sitting in a low chair, leafing through a late issue of *Popular Statistics* when Miss Frinkles returned.

"It seems a maintenance man ran berserk down on Nine Level," she said breathlessly. "He killed three people, then set fire to—"

"Well, I must be running along," Mart said, rising. "A very nice little machine you have there. Tell me, are there any manual controls?"

"Oh, yes, didn't you notice them? Each test result must be validated by me before it's released to the Master Files. Suppose someone cheated, or finished late; it wouldn't do to let a disqualified score past."

"Oh, no indeed. And to transfer the data to the Master File, you just push this?" Mart said, leaning across and depressing the key he had seen Miss

Frinkles use earlier. There was a sharp buzz from the Profiler. The red light went out.

"Oh, you mustn't—" Miss Frinkles exclaimed. "Not that it would matter in this case, of course," she added apologetically, "but—"

The door opened and the red-head stepped into the room. "Oh," she said, looking at Mart. "There you are. I looked for you in the Testing room—"

Miss Frinkles looked up with a surprised expression. "But I was under the impression—" She smiled. "Oh, Mr. Maldon, you *are* a tease! You'd already completed your testing, and you let me think you came in late . . . !"

Mart smiled modestly.

"Oh, Barbara, we must look at his score. He has a fantastic academic record. At least ten Specialized degrees, and magna cum laude in every one . . ."

The screen glowed. Miss Frinkles adjusted a knob, scanned past the first frame to a second. She stared.

"Mr. Maldon! I knew you'd do well, but a *perfect* score!"

The hall door banged wide. "Miss Frinkles—" a tall man stared at Mart, looked him up and down. He backed a step. "Who're you? Where did you get that suit—"

"MISTER Cludd!" Miss Frinkles said in an icy tone. "Kindly refrain from bursting into my office unannounced—and kindly show a trifle more civility to my guest, who happens to be a very remarkable young man who has just completed one of the finest test profiles it has been my pleasure to see during my service with Placement!"

"Eh? Are you sure? I mean—that suit . . . and the shoes . . ."

"I like a conservative outfit," Mart said desperately.

"You mean he's been here all morning . . . ?" Mr. Cludd looked suddenly uncomfortable.

"Of course!"

"He was in my exam group, Mr. Cludd," the red-haired girl put in. "I'll vouch for that. Why?"

"Well . . . it just happens the maniac they're looking for is dressed in a similar suit, and . . . well, I guess I lost my head. I was just coming in to tell you he'd been seen on this floor. He made a getaway through a service entrance leading to the helipad on the roof, and . . . he ran down."

"Thank you, Mr. Cludd," Miss Frinkles said icily. Cludd mumbled and withdrew. Miss Frinkles turned to Mart.

"I'm so thrilled, Mr. Maldon . . ."

"Golly, yes," Barbara said.

"It isn't every day I have the opportunity to Place an applicant of your qualifications. Naturally, you'll have the widest possible choice. I'll give you the current prospectus, and next week—"

"Couldn't you place me right now, Miss Frinkles?"

"You mean—today?"

"Immediately." Mart looked at the red-head. "I like it here. What openings have you got in your department?"

Miss Frinkles gasped, flushed, smiled, then turned and played with the buttons on her console, watching the small screen. "Wonderful," she breathed. "The opening is still unfilled. I was afraid one of the other units might have filled it in the past hour." She poked at more keys. A white card in a narrow platinum holder with a jewelled alligator clip popped from a slot. She rose and handed it to Mart reverently.

"Your new I.D. sir. And I know you're going to make a wonderful chief!"

XIV

Mart sat behind the three-yard-long desk of polished rosewood, surveying the tennis-court-sized expanse of ankle-deep carpet which stretched across to a wide door of deep-polished mahogany, then swivelled to gaze out through wide windows of insulated, polarized, tinted glass at the towers of Granyauck, looming up in a deep blue sky. He turned back, opened the silver box that rested between a jade pen-holder and an ebony paper-weight on the otherwise unadorned desk, lifted out a Chanel dope-stick, sniffed it appreciatively. He adjusted his feet comfortably on the desk top, pressed a tiny silver button set in the arm of the chair. A moment later the door opened with the faintest of sounds.

"Barbara—" Mart began.

"There you are," a deep voice said.

Mart's feet came off the desk with a crash. The large man approaching him across the rug had a familiar look about him . . .

"That was a dirty trick, locking me in the shower. We hadn't figured on that one. Slowed us up something awful." He swung a chair around and sat down.

"But," Mart said. "But . . . but . . ."

"Three days, nine hours and fourteen minutes," the newcomer said, eyeing a finger watch. "I must say you made the most of it. Never figured on you bollixing the examination records, too; most of 'em stop with the faked Academic Record, and figure to take their chances on the exam."

"Most of 'em?" Mart repeated weakly.

"Sure. You didn't think you were the only one selected to go before the Special Placement Board, did you?"

"Selected? Special . . ." Mart's voice trailed off.

"Well, surely you're beginning to understand now, Maldon," the man from whom Mart had stolen the suit said. "We picked you as a potential Top Executive over three years ago. We've followed your record closely ever since. You were on every one of the Board Members' nomination lists—"

"But—but I was quota'd out—"

"Oh, we could have let you graduate, go through testing, pick up a green tag and a spot on a promotion list, plug away for twenty years, make Exec rank —but we can't waste the time. We need talent, Mart. And we need it now!"

Mart took a deep breath and slammed the desk. "Why in the name of ten thousand devils didn't you just TELL me!"

The visitor shook his head. "Nope; we need good men, Mart—need 'em bad. We need to find the superior individuals; we can't afford to waste time bolstering up the folklore that the will of the people constitutes wisdom. This is a city of a hundred million people—and it's growing at a rate that will double that in a decade. We have problems, Mart. Vast, urgent problems. We need men that can solve 'em. We can test you in academic knowledge, cook up psychological profiles—but we have to KNOW. We have to find out how you react in a real-life situation; what you do to help yourself when you're dumped on the walkaway, broke and hopeless. If you go in and have your brain burned, scratch one. If you meekly register to wait out a Class Two test opening—well, good luck to you. If you walk in and take what you want . . ." he looked around the office, ". . . then welcome to the Club."

14. the man in the Rorschach shirt

Ray Bradbury

How much do psychologists listen? And does it matter if a psychotherapist hears accurately—or hears at all—what a client says? An experienced psychotherapist and a new psychotherapist are walking out of their office building together at the end of a work day. The new therapist is sweaty, exhausted, dragging. The experienced psychotherapist is whistling, fresh, and chipper. "What I would like to know," says the new therapist, "is how you can be so fresh and cheery at the end of a long day of listening to patients?" The experienced psychotherapist replies, "So who listens?"

Perhaps one does not need an accurately hearing therapist to get better, and a selectively hearing one will do. Or can a deaf therapist cure? If we accept the notion of a successful, totally passive, mute, blind therapist, we are ready to accept the machine that simulates a passive, mute, blind therapist: the tape recorder. The house of psychic mirrors indeed stops at the tape recorder, for Charles Slack and others have asked clients to speak into audio tape recorders. Without the presence of any other person, the clients improve.

This speculation-fiction story is about such almost-therapists that work, practiced by Immanuel Brokaw, ". . . the greatest psychiatrist who ever tread the waters of existence without capsizing." The ship of therapeutic growth does not prove to be a delicate vessel, calling for great sensory acuity; rather it sails well with an unseeing, unknowing, unhearing captain at its helm.

What helps? When people are in emotional pain, what processes actually make a difference? The research of Eysenck and others point to a process of spontaneous improvement. People who get worse by themselves sometimes get better by themselves. If the improved persons happen to be clients in therapy, the therapists react with great satisfaction. Perhaps one parsimonious social policy ought to be that of selective nonintervention, doing nothing when spontaneous improvement is likely.

Some of the reasons that therapy does help and make a difference are shown in this Bradbury story. It may be not what this healer says or hears, but who he is. Whatever Brokaw does works, as long as he believes it works.

Then Brokaw changes his location and garb and becomes the man in the Rorschach shirt, doing things most inconsistent with the ideas of Herman Rorschach. Rorschach was a Swiss physician who did research into imagination through inkblots and devised ten cards of these inkblots. These cards are perfectly symmetrical inkblots, half with colored ink and half with blank ink. When a person looks at a card and reports what he sees, he is convinced that what he sees is there. The projective principle of the Rorschach test is that a person projects his own needs, style, and ways of perceiving and organizing onto the cards.

The immediate and grand public emotional involvement with Brokaw and his Rorschach shirt becomes the ultimate extension of psychology into the community, the bus-aisle psychotherapist in action. Here then is one model for curing society of its mental ills: a corps of unidentified healers who wander throughout the country spreading mental health wherever they go. Immanuel Brokaw is the Johnny Appleseed of psychological adjustment, leaving little forests of hope and life growing behind him.

Brokaw.

What a name!

Listen to it bark, growl, yip, hear the bold proclamation of:

Immanuel Brokaw!

A fine name for the greatest psychiatrist who ever tread the waters of existence without capsizing.

Toss a pepper-ground Freud casebook in the air and all students sneezed: Brokaw!

What ever happened to him?

One day, like a high-class vaudeville act, he vanished.

With the spotlight out, his miracles seemed in danger of reversal. Psychotic rabbits threatened to leap back into hats. Smoke was sucked back into loud-powder gun muzzles. We all waited.

Silence for ten years. And more silence.

Brokaw was lost, as if he had thrown himself with shouts of laughter into mid-Atlantic. For what? To plumb for Moby Dick? To psychoanalyze that colorless fiend and see what he really had against Mad Ahab?

Who knows?

I last saw him running for a twilight plane, his wife and six Pomeranian dogs yapping far behind him on the dusky field.

"Good-bye forever!"

His happy cry seemed a joke. But I found men flaking his gold-leaf name from his office door next day, as his great fat-women couches were hustled out into the raw weather toward some Third Avenue auction.

So the giant who had been Gandhi-Moses-Christ-Buddha-Freud all layered in one incredible Armenian dessert had dropped through a hole in the clouds. To die? To live in secret?

Ten years later I rode on a California bus along the lovely shores of Newport.

The bus stopped. A man in his seventies bounced on, jingling silver into the coin box like manna. I glanced up from the rear of the bus and gasped.

"Brokaw! By the saints!"

And with or without sanctification, there he stood. Reared up like God manifest, bearded, benevolent, pontifical, erudite, merry, accepting, forgiving, messianic, tutorial, forever and eternal . . .

Immanuel Brokaw.

But not in a dark suit, no.

Instead, as if they were vestments of some proud new church, he wore:

Bermuda shorts. Black leather Mexican sandals. A Los Angeles Dodgers' baseball cap. French sunglasses. And . . .

The shirt! Ah God! The shirt!

A wild thing, all lush creeper and live flytrap undergrowth, all Pop-Op dilation and contraction, full-flowered and crammed at every interstice and crosshatch with mythological beasts and symbols!

Open at the neck, this vast shirt hung wind-whipped like a thousand flags from a parade of united but neurotic nations.

But now, Dr. Brokaw tilted his baseball cap, lifted his French sunglasses to survey the empty bus seats. Striding slowly down the aisle, he wheeled, he paused, he lingered, now here, now there. He whispered, he murmured, now to this man, this woman, that child.

I was about to cry out when I heard him say:

"Well, what do you make of it?"

A small boy, stunned by the circus-poster effect of the old man's attire, blinked, in need of nudging. The old man nudged:

"My *shirt,* boy! What do you *see!?*"

"Horses!" the child blurted, at last. "Dancing horses!"

"Bravo!" The doctor beamed, patted him, and strode on. "And *you,* sir?"

A young man, quite taken with the forthrightness of this invader from some summer world, said:

"Why . . . clouds, of course."

"Cumulus or nimbus?"

"Er . . . not storm clouds, no, no. Fleecy, sheep clouds."

"Well done!"

The psychiatrist plunged on.

"Mademoiselle?"

"Surfers!" A teen-age girl stared. "They're the waves, big ones. Surfboards. Super!"

And so it went, on down the length of the bus and as the great man progressed a few scraps and titters of laughter sprang up, then, grown infectious, turned to roars of hilarity. By now, a dozen passengers had heard the first responses and so fell in with the game. This woman saw skyscrapers! The doctor scowled at her suspiciously. The doctor winked. That man saw crossword puzzles. The doctor shook his hand. This child found zebras all optical illusion on an African wild. The doctor slapped the animals and made them jump! This old woman saw vague Adams and misty Eves being driven from half-seen Gardens. The doctor scooched in on the seat with her awhile; they talked in fierce whispered elations, then up he jumped and forged on. Had the old woman seen an eviction? This young one saw the couple invited back in!

Dogs, lightnings, cats, cars, mushroom clouds, man-eating tiger lilies!

Each person, each response, brought greater outcries. We found ourselves all laughing together. This fine old man was a happening of nature, a caprice, God's rambunctious Will, sewing all our separateness up in one.

Elephants! Elevators! Alarums! Dooms!

When first he had bounded aboard we had wanted naught of each other. But now like an immense snowfall which we must gossip on or an electrical failure that blacked out two million homes and so thrown us all together in communal chat, laugh, guffaw, we felt the tears clean up our souls even as they cleaned down our cheeks.

Each answer seemed funnier than the previous, and no one shouted louder his great torments of laughter than this grand tall and marvelous physician who asked for, got, and cured us of our hairballs on the spot. Whales. Kelp. Grass meadows. Lost cities. Beauteous women. He paused. He wheeled. He sat. He rose. He flapped his wildly colored shirt, until at last he towered before me and said:

"Sir, what do *you* find?"

"Why, Dr. Brokaw, of course!"

The old man's laughter stopped as if he were shot. He seized his dark glasses off, then clapped them on and grabbed my shoulders as if to wrench me into focus.

"Simon Wincelaus, is that *you!*"

"Me, me!" I laughed. "Good grief, doctor, I thought you were dead and buried years ago. What's this you're up to?"

"Up to?" He squeezed and shook my hands and pummeled my arms and cheeks gently. Then he snorted a great self-forgiving laugh as he gazed down along the acreage of ridiculous shirting. "Up to? Retired. Swiftly gone. Overnight traveled three thousand miles from where last you saw me . . ." His peppermint breath warmed my face. "And now best known hereabouts as . . . listen! . . . the Man in the Rorschach Shirt."

"In the what?" I cried.

"Rorschach Shirt."

Light as a carnival gas balloon he touched into the seat beside me.

I sat stunned and silent.

We rode along by the blue sea under a bright summer sky.

The doctor gazed ahead as if reading my thoughts in vast sky-writing among the clouds.

"Why, you ask, why? I see your face, startled, at the airport years ago. My Going Away Forever day. My plane should have been named the *Happy Titanic.* On it I sank forever into the traceless sky. Yet here I am in the absolute flesh, yes? Not drunk, nor mad, nor riven by age and retirement's boredom. Where, what, why, how come?"

"Yes," I said, "why *did* you retire, with everything pitched for you? Skill, reputation, money. Not a breath of—"

"Scandal? None! Why, then? Because, this old camel had not one but two humps broken by two straws. Two amazing straws. Hump Number One—"

He paused. He cast me a sidelong glance from under his dark glasses.

"This is a confessional," I said. "Mum's the word."

"Confessional. Yes. Thanks."

The bus hummed softly on the road.

His voice rose and fell with the hum.

"You know my photographic memory? Blessed, cursed, with total recall. Anything said, seen, done, touched, heard, can be snapped back to focus by me, forty, fifty, sixty years later. All, all of it, trapped in here."

He stroked his temples lightly with the fingers of both hands.

"Hundreds of psychiatric cases, delivered through my door, day after day, year on year. And never once did I check my notes on any of those sessions. I found, early on, I need only play back what I had heard inside my head. Sound tapes, of course, were kept as a double-check, but never listened to. There you have the stage set for the whole shocking business.

"One day in my sixtieth year a woman patient spoke a single word. I asked her to repeat it. Why? Suddenly I had felt my semicircular canals shift as if some valves had opened upon cool fresh air at a subterranean level.

" 'Best,' she said.

" 'I thought you said beast,' I said.

" 'Oh, no, doctor, best.'

"One word. One pebble dropped off the edge. And then—the avalanche. For, distinctly, I had heard her claim: 'He loved the beast in me,' which is one kettle of sexual fish, eh? When in reality she had said, 'He loved the best in me,' which is quite another pan of cold cod, you must agree.

"That night I could not sleep. I smoked, I stared from windows. My head, my ears, felt strangely clear, as if I had just gotten over a thirty years' cold. I suspected myself, my past, my senses, so at three in the deadfall morning I motored to my office and found the worst:

"The recalled conversations of hundreds of cases in my mind were not the same as those recorded on my tapes or typed out in my secretary's notes!"

"You mean . . . ?"

"I mean when I heard beast it was truly best. Dumb was really numb. Ox were cocks and vice-versa. I heard bed and someone had said head. Sleep was creep. Lay was day. Paws were really pause. Rump was merely jump. Fiend was only leaned. Sex was hex or mix or, God knows, per*plex!* Yes–mess. No–slow. Binge–hinge. Wrong–long. Side–hide. Name a name, I'd heard it wrong. Ten million dozen misheard nouns! I panicked through my files! Good Grief! Great Jumping Josie!

"All those years, those people! Holy Moses, Brokaw, I cried, all these years down from the Mount, the word of God like a flea in your ear. And now, late in the day, old wise one, you think to consult your lightning-scribbled stones. And find your Laws, your Tablets, *different!*

"Moses fled his offices that night. I ran in dark, unraveling my despair. I trained to Far Rockaway, perhaps because of its lamenting name.

"I walked by a tumult of waves only equaled by the tumult in my breast. How? I cried, how can you have been half-deaf for a lifetime and not known it! And known it only now when through some fluke, the sense, the gift, returned, how, how?!

"My only answer was a great stroke of thunder wave upon the sands.

"So much for straw number one that broke hump number one of this odd-shaped human camel."

There was a moment of silence.

We rode swaying on the bus. The bus moved along the golden shore road, through a gentle breeze.

"Straw number two?" I asked, quietly, at last.

Dr. Brokaw held his French sunglasses up so sunlight struck fish-glitters all about the cavern of the bus. We watched the swimming rainbow patterns, he with detachment and at last half-amused concern.

"Sight. Vision. Texture. Detail. Aren't they miraculous. Aweful in the sense of meaning true awe? What is sight, vision, insight? Do we really want to see the world?"

"Oh, yes," I cried, promptly.

"A young man's unthinking answer. No, my dear boy, we do not. At twenty, yes, we think we wish to see, know, be all. So thought I once. But I have had weak eyes most of my life, spent half my days being fitted out with new specs by oculists, hee? Well, comes the dawn of the corneal lens! At last, I decided, I will fit myself with those bright little teardrop miracles, those invisible discs! Coincidence? Psychosomatic cause and effect? For, that same week I got my contact lenses was the week my hearing cleared up! There must be some physio-mental connection, but don't hazard me into an informed guess.

"All I know is I had my little crystal corneal lenses ground and installed upon my weak baby blue eyes and—*Voilà!*

"There was the world!

"THERE were people!

"And there, God save us, was the dirt, and the multitudinous pores upon the people.

"Simon," he added, grieving gently, eyes shut for a moment behind his dark glasses, "have you ever thought, did you know, that people are for the most part pores?"

He let that sink in. I thought about it.

"Pores?" I said, at last.

"Pores! But who thinks of it? Who bothers to go look? But with my restored vision *I* saw! A thousand, a million, ten billion . . . pores. Large, small, pale, crimson . . . pores. Everyone and on everyone. People passing. People crowding buses, theaters, telephone booths, all pore and little substance. Small pores on tiny women. Big pores on monster men. Or vice versa. Pores as numerous as that foul dust which slides pell-mell down church-nave sunbeams late afternoons. Pores. They became my utter and riven fascination. I stared at fine ladies' complexions, not their eyes, mouths, or earlobes. Shouldn't a man watch a woman's skeleton hinge and unhinge itself within that sweet pincushion flesh? Yes! But no, I saw only cheese-grater, kitchen-sieve skins. All Beauty turned sour Grotesque. Swiveling my gaze was like swiveling the 200-inch Palomar telescope in my damned skull. Everywhere I looked I saw the meteor-bombarded moon, in dread super closeup!

"Myself? God, shaving mornings was exquisite torture. I could not pluck my eyes from my lost battle-pitted face. Damnation, Immanuel Brokaw, I soughed, you are the Grand Canyon at high noon, an orange with a billion navels, a pomegranate with the skin stripped off.

"In sum, my contact lenses had made me fifteen years old again. That is: festering, self-crucified bundle of doubt, horror, and absolute imperfection. The worst age in all one's life had returned to haunt me with its pimpled, bumpy ghost.

"I lay, a sleepless wreck. Ah, second Adolescence, take pity, I cried. How could I have been so blind, so many years? Blind, yes, and knew it, and always said it was of no importance. So I groped about the world as lustful myope, nearsightedly missing the holes, rips, tears, and bumps on others as well as myself. Now, Reality had run me down in the street. And the Reality was: Pores.

"I shut my eyes and went to bed for several days. Then I sat up in bed and proclaimed, wide-eyed: Reality is not all! I refuse this knowledge. I legislate against Pores! I accept instead those truths we intuit, or make up to live by.

"I traded in my eyeballs.

"That is I handed my corneal contact lenses to a sadist nephew who thrives on garbages and lumpy people and hairy things.

"I clapped back on my old undercorrected specs. I strolled through a world of returned and gentle mists. I saw enough but not too much. I found half-discerned ghost peoples I could love again. I saw the 'me' in the morning glass I could once more bed with, admire and take as chum. I began to laugh each day with new happiness. Softly. Then, very loud.

"What a joke, Simon, life is.

"From vanity we buy lenses that see all and so lose everything!

"And by giving up some small bit-piece of so-called wisdom, reality, truth, we gain back an entirety of life! Who does not know this? Writers do! Intuited novels are far more 'true' than all your scribbled data-fact reportage in the history of the world!

"But then at last I had to face the great twin fractures lying athwart my conscience. My eyes. My ears. Holy Cow, I said, softly. The thousand folk who tread my offices and creaked my couches and looked for echoes in my Delphic Cave, why, why, preposterous! I had seen none of them, nor heard any clear!

"Who was that Miss Harbottle?

"What of old Dinsmuir?

"What was the real color, look, size of Miss Grimes?

"Did Mrs. Scrapwight really resemble and speak like an Egyptian papyrus mummy fallen out of a rug at my desk?

"I could not even guess. Two thousand days of fogs surrounded my lost children, mere voices calling, fading, gone.

"My God, I had wandered the marketplace with an invisible sign BLIND AND DEAF and people had rushed to fill my beggar's cup with coins and rush off cured. Cured! Isn't *that* miraculous, strange? Cured by an old ricket with one arm gone, as 'twere, and one leg missing. What? What did I say right to them out of hearing wrong? Who indeed were those people? I will never know.

"And then I thought: there are a hundred psychiatrists about town who see and hear more clearly than I. But whose patients walk naked into high seas or leap off playground slides at midnight or truss women up and smoke cigars over them.

"So I had to face the irreducible fact of a successful career.

"The lame do *not* lead the lame, my reason cried, the blind and halt do not cure the halt and the blind! But a voice from the far balcony of my soul replied with immense irony: Bee's-wax and Bull-Durham! You, Immanuel Brokaw, are a porcelain genius, which means cracked but brilliant! Your occluded eyes see, your corked ears hear. Your fractured sensibilities cure at some level below consciousness! Bravo!

"But no, I could not live with my perfect imperfections. I could not understand nor tolerate this smug secret thing which, through screens and obfuscations, played meadow doctor to the world and cured field beasts.

"I had several choices then. Put my corneal lenses back in? Buy ear radios to help my rapidly improving sense of sound? And then? Find I had lost touch with my best and hidden mind which had grown comfortably accustomed to thirty years of bad vision and lousy hearing? Chaos both for curer and cured.

"Stay blind and deaf and work? It seemed a dreadful fraud, though my record was laundry-fresh pressed white and clean.

"So I retired.

"Packed my bags and ran off into golden oblivion to let the incredible wax collect in my most terrible strange ears . . ."

We rode in the bus along the shore in the warm afternoon. A few clouds moved over the sun. Shadows misted on the sands and the people strewn on the sands under the colored umbrellas.

I cleared my throat.

"Will you ever return to practice again, doctor?"

"I practice now."

"But you just said—"

"Oh, not officially, and not with an office or fees, no, never that again." The doctor laughed quietly. "I am sore beset by the mystery anyway. That is, of how I cured all those people with a laying on of hands even though my arms were chopped off at the elbows. Still, now, I do keep my 'hand' in."

"How?"

"This shirt of mine. You saw. You heard."

"Coming down the aisle?"

"Exactly. The colors. The patterns. One thing to that man, another to the girl, a third to the boy. Zebras, goats, lightnings, Egyptian amulets. What, what, what? I ask. And: answer, answer, answer. The Man in the Rorschach Shirt.

"I have a dozen such shirts at home.

"All colors, all different pattern mixes. One was designed for me by Jackson Pollack before he died. I wear each shirt for a day, or a week, if the going, the answers, are thick, fast, full of excitement and reward. Then off with the old and on with the new. Ten billion glances, ten billion startled responses!

"Might I not market these Rorschach shirts to your psychoanalyst on vacation? Test your friends? Shock your neighbors? Titillate your wife? No, no. This is my own special private most dear fun. No one must share it. Me and my shirts, the sun, the bus, and a thousand afternoons ahead. The beach waits. An on it, my people!

"So I walk the shores of this summer world. There is no winter here, amazing, yes, no winter of discontent it would almost seem, and death a rumor beyond the dunes. I walk along in my own time and way and come on people and let the wind flap my great sailcloth shirt now veering north, south or south-by-west and watch their eyes pop, glide, leer, squint, wonder. And when a certain person says a certain word about my ink-slashed cotton colors I give pause. I chat. I walk with them awhile. We peer into the great glass of the sea. I sidewise peer into their soul. Sometimes we stroll for hours, a longish session with the weather. Usually it takes but that one day and, not knowing with whom they walked, scot-free, they are discharged all unwitting patients. They walk on down the dusky shore toward a fairer, brighter eve. Behind their backs, the deaf-blind man waves them bon voyage and trots home there to devour happy suppers, brisk with fine work done.

"Or sometimes I meet some half-slumberer on the sand whose troubles cannot all be fetched out to die in the raw light of one day. Then, as by accident, we collide a week later and walk by the tidal churn doing what has always been done; we have our traveling confessional. For long before pent-up priests and whispers and repentances, friends walked, talked, listened, and in the listening-talk cured each other's sour despairs. Good friends trade hairballs all the time, give gifts of mutual dismays and so are rid of them.

"Trash collects on lawns and in minds. With bright shirt and nail-tipped trash stick I set out each dawn to . . . clean up the beaches. So many, oh, so many bodies lying out there in the light. So many minds lost in the dark. I try to walk among them all, without . . . stumbling . . ."

The wind blew in the bus window cool and fresh, making a sea of ripples through the thoughtful old man's patterned shirt.

The bus stopped.

Dr. Brokaw suddenly saw where he was and leapt up. "Wait!"

Everyone on the bus turned as if to watch the exit of a star performer. Everyone smiled.

Dr. Brokaw pumped my hand and ran. At the far front end of the bus he turned, amazed at his own forgetfulness, lifted his dark glasses and squinted at me with his weak baby-blue eyes.

"You " he said.

Already, to him, I was a mist, a pointillist dream somewhere out beyond the rim of vision.

"You . . ." he called into that fabulous cloud of existence which surrounded and pressed him warm and close, "you never *told* me. What? *What?!*"

He stood tall to display that incredible Rorschach shirt which fluttered and swarmed with everchanging line and color.

I looked. I blinked. I answered.

"A sunrise!" I cried.

The doctor reeled with this gentle friendly blow.

"Are you sure it isn't a sunset?" he called, cupping one hand to his ear.

I looked again and smiled. I hoped he saw my smile a thousand miles away within the bus.

"No," I said. "A sunrise. A beautiful sunrise."

He shut his eyes to digest the words. His great hands wandered along the shore of his wind-gentled shirt. He nodded. Then he opened his pale eyes, waved once, and stepped out into the world.

The bus drove on. I looked back once.

And there went Dr. Brokaw advancing straight out and across a beach where lay a random sampling of the world, a thousand bathers in the warm light.

He seemed to tread lightly upon a water of people.

The last I saw of him, he was still gloriously afloat.

VI
Behavior Disorders and Therapy

The same behavior may be considered normal or abnormal, depending upon where, when, and by whom the behavior is exhibited. In late 1973 and early 1974, people, mostly college-age males, began appearing naked in public places in various parts of the United States. This activity was quickly defined by the media and by the population generally as a playful and harmless expression of youthful high spirits, although public self-exposure has long been treated both as a crime and as the manifestation of an emotional disorder. Perhaps the transformation of the disorder of exhibitionism to the sport of streaking occurred because the behavior was not taken very seriously by the viewers or the viewed and because it was done by representatives of a social group with a history of zany but nondangerous behavior such as goldfish swallowing and telephone-booth stuffing. It is an indication that behavior is only abnormal when it is defined as such.

Atypicality of a particular behavior is not sufficient to cause it to be defined as abnormal. Some very rare behaviors are not defined as abnormal, while some very common behaviors are. An excellent example of normality by consensus occurred when the members of the American Psychiatric Association voted to remove homosexuality from its classification of mental disorders. While such a vote may leave many opinions unchanged, its occurrence is a reflection of a substantial change in public attitudes toward homosexuality and a harbinger of further changes in other areas of previous disapproval.

The consensus approach—it is abnormal if most people say it is—clearly sets behavioral disorders apart from physical illness. Deviant behavior is not a disease, and mental illness is clearly a misnomer. We are unlikely to see a vote by the American Medical Association to determine whether or not cancer and measles are diseases.

Abnormal psychology deals with the classification and description of those aspects of behavior which have been defined as deviant. The accuracy with which classification can be made depends, in part, upon the specificity and complexity of the categories into which people are placed. The American Psychiatric Association publishes, for the use of its members and others, a manual which contains hundreds of general and complex diagnostic terms. Unfortunately, the likelihood is low that two psychiatrists will assign the same diagnosis to the same patient—or even that the same psychiatrist will assign the same label at a latter time. On the other hand, if the categorization is simple and specific, a high degree of agreement or reliability can be obtained.

The most frequently used categories of "maladjustment" are neurotic, psychotic, and character disorder. The neurotic may perceive reality correctly and yet have an exaggerated emotional reaction to it (for example, feeling overly sad, anxious, or fearful). The psychotic may exhibit even more excessive or inappropriate reactions (for example, incessant giggling or laughter), and may perceive the world around him quite differently from others. He may see and hear people or voices which are not present or he may believe strange things about himself or others. A distinction sometimes offered jokingly is that a psychotic believes that two and two are five; the neurotic knows two and two are four but it makes him unhappy. To extend the distinction, we might say that the person with the character disorder (also called the psychopath or sociopath) knows the sum of two and two but doesn't give a damn.

An outgrowth of abnormal psychology is the study of methods of treating behavioral disorders. These methods, which range from classical psychoanalysis to behavior therapy, are a variety of new experimental approaches and have attracted the interest of science fiction writers because they suggest a technology by which the way a person thinks and behaves can be changed. The attention to the *unconscious* in psychoanalytic approaches has led to stories depicting how this great reservoir of emotions and experiences can be manipulated or constructively utilized. The behavior therapies have drawn on systematic and structured principles of learning and extinction of learning. The implications of such behavior control appear in science fiction stories in the form of frightening visions of worlds in which thinking and feeling can be shaped to fit the desires of the governing officials. The classic examples are *Brave New World* and *1984,* and, more recently, Woody Allen's *Sleeper.* The experimental—from the word experience—approaches are designed to promote heightened awareness and personal control. They include the clinical use of biofeedback to control blood pressure and respiration, and combining of Eastern meditation techniques with Western psychotherapeutic intervention.

The following stories illustrate several types of behavior disorders. (Diagnose them yourself—you can't do much worse than the experts.) They also illustrate some interesting, sometimes amusing, methods of treatment. We don't recommend that you try them—just enjoy them.

15. it's a bird! it's a plane!

Norman Spinrad

This story starts with a modest premise: a psychological epidemic of super-men. The idea is not unusual. A few years ago Milton Rokeach wrote a book called The Three Christs of Ypsilanti *(New York: Knopf, 1964) about three mental patients at the Ypsilanti, Michigan, State Hospital who believed they were Jesus Christ. And during World War II, Mattoon, Illinois was "infected" by a popular delusion that there was a phantom wandering through the city, spraying sweet-smelling substances that made women faint. The Christs all vegetated in the cold winters and rolling grounds of this southern Michigan Hospital and the Phantom of Mattoon disappeared after the town newspaper published the reports of outside investigators that he was not real. Yet it is not always an easy task separating the messiahs from the myths and from the madmen. Spinrad wonders, "If sanity was defined as the norm, . . . and the majority of the population believed in Superman, then maybe anyone who* didn't *believe in Super-man had a screw loose. . . ." The flip side of the normality definition game is that a majority may disbelieve in and harm some true messiahs and prophets.*

Our society and our psychologists have truncated and denied the poten-tial contributions of great people. The tragedies of Wilhelm Reich and Ezra Pound spending much of their later years in confinement are two such examples. Our tolerance for those people who are different in some way probably will continue to increase, and a key point in their lives will be the roles of the "shrinks" who make decisions about their lives. And, as this story aptly points out, "normality" is not always an easy quality to define.

Extraordinary courage and abilities are needed in psychiatrists and psychologists in other ways as well: to avoid doing harm through labeling; to protect those the public rejects as scary and deviant; to learn from their clients; and to develop their own potentials as persons and professionals. "It's a Bird! It's a Plane!" is about transformations, including that of our therapist-protagonist from frustrated loser to, well, to Supershrink. Let us hope that we shall see far fewer mild-mannered psychiatrists who work in great metropolitan hospitals and far more Supershrinks.

Dr. Felix Funck fumblingly fitted yet another spool onto the tape recorder hidden in the middle drawer of his desk as the luscious Miss Jones ushered in yet another one. Dr. Funck stared wistfully for a long moment at Miss Jones, whose white nurse's smock advertised the contents most effectively without revealing any of the more intimate and interesting details. If only x-ray vision were really possible and not part of the infernal Syndrome. . . .

Get a hold of yourself, Funck, get a hold of yourself! Felix Funck told himself for the seventeenth time that day.

He sighed; resigned himself, and said to the earnest-looking young man whom Miss Jones had brought to his office, "Please sit down, Mr. . . .?"

"Kent, Doctor," said the young man, seating himself primly on the edge of the overstuffed chair in front of Funck's desk. "Clark Kent!"

Dr. Funck grimaced, then smiled wanly. "Why not?" he said, studying the young man's appearance. The young man wore an archaic blue double-breasted suit and steel-rimmed glasses. His hair was steel-blue.

"Tell me . . . Mr. Kent," he said, "do you by some chance know where you are?"

"Certainly, Doctor," replied Clark Kent crisply. "I'm in a large public mental hospital in New York City!"

"Very good, Mr. Kent. And do you know why you're here?"

"I think so, Dr. Funck!" said Clark Kent. "I'm suffering from partial amnesia! I don't remember how or when I came to New York!"

"You mean you don't remember your past life?" asked Dr. Felix Funck.

"Not at all, Doctor!" said Clark Kent. "I remember everything up till three days ago when I found myself suddenly in New York! And I remember the last three days here! But I don't remember how I got here!"

"Well then, where did you live before you found yourself in New York, Mr. Kent?"

"Metropolis!" said Clark Kent. "I remember that very well! I'm a reporter for the Metropolis *Daily Planet!* That is, I am if Mr. White hasn't fired me for not showing up for three days! You must help me, Dr. Funck! I must return to Metropolis immediately!"

"Well then you should just hop the next plane for home," suggested Dr. Funck.

"There don't seem to be any flights from New York to Metropolis!" exclaimed Clark Kent. "No buses or trains either! I couldn't even find a copy of the *Daily Planet* at the Times Square newsstand! I can't even remember where Metropolis is! It's as if some evil force has removed all traces of Metropolis from the face of the Earth! That's my problem, Dr. Funck! I've got to get back to Metropolis, but I don't know how!"

"Tell me, Mr. Kent," said Funck slowly, "just why is it so imperative that you return to Metropolis immediately?"

"Well . . . uh . . . there's my job!" Clark Kent said uneasily. "Perry White must be furious by now! And there's my girl, Lois Lane! Well, maybe she's not my girl yet, but I'm hoping!"

Dr. Felix Funck grinned conspiratorially. "Isn't there some more pressing reason, Mr. Kent?" he said. "Something perhaps having to do with your Secret Identity?"

"S-secret Identity?" stammered Clark Kent. "I don't know what you're talking about, Dr. Funck!"

"Aw come on, Clark!" Felix Funck said. "Lots of people have Secret Identities. I've got one myself. Tell me yours, and I'll tell you mine. You can trust me, Clark. Hippocratic Oath, and like that. Your secret is safe with me."

"*Secret?* What secret are you talking about?"

"Come, come, Mr. Kent!" Funck snapped. "If you want help, you'll have to come clean with me. Don't give me any of that meek, mild-mannered reporter jazz. I know who you really are, Mr. Kent."

"I'm Clark Kent, meek, mild-mannered reporter for the Metropolis *Daily Planet!*" insisted Clark Kent.

Dr. Felix Funck reached into a desk drawer and produced a small chunk of rock coated with green paint. "Who is in reality, Superman," he exclaimed, "faster than a speeding bullet, more powerful than a locomotive, able to leap tall buildings at a single bound! Do you know what this is?" he shrieked, thrusting the green rock in the face of the hapless Clark Kent. "It's Kryptonite, that's what it is, genuine, government-inspected Kryptonite! How's *that* grab you, Superman?"

Clark Kent, who is in reality the Man of Steel, tried to say something, but before he could utter a sound, he lapsed into unconsciousness.

Dr. Felix Funck reached across his desk and unbuttoned Clark Kent's shirt. Sure enough, underneath his street clothing, Kent was wearing a pair of moth-eaten longjohns dyed blue, on the chest of which a rude cloth "S" had been crudely sewn.

"Classic case . . ." Dr. Funck muttered to himself. "Right out of a textbook. Even lost his imaginary powers when I showed him the phony Kryptonite. Another job for Supershrink!"

Get a hold of yourself, Funck, get a hold of yourself! Dr. Felix Funck told himself again.

Shaking his head, he rang for the orderlies.

After the orderlies had removed Clark Kent #758, Dr. Felix Funck pulled a stack of comic books out of a desk drawer, spread them out across the desktop, stared woodenly at them and moaned.

The Superman Syndrome was getting totally out of hand. In this one hospital alone, there are already 758 classified cases of Superman Syndrome, he thought forlornly, and lord knows how many Supernuts in the receiving ward awaiting classification.

"Why? Why? Why?" Funck muttered, tearing at his rapidly thinning hair.

The basic, fundamental, inescapable, incurable reason, he knew was, of course, that the world was full of Clark Kents. Meek, mild-mannered men. Born losers. None of them, of course, had self-images of themselves as nebbishes. Every mouse has to think of himself as a lion. Everyone has a Secret Identity, a dream image of himself, possessed of fantastic powers, able to cope with normally impossible situations. . . .

Even psychiatrists had Secret Identities, Funck thought abstractedly. After all, who but Supershrink himself could cope with a ward full of Supermen?

Supershrink! More powerful than a raving psychotic! Able to diagnose whole neuroses in a single session! Faster than Freud! Abler than Adler! Who, disguised as Dr. Felix Funck, balding, harried head of the Superman Syndrome ward of a great metropolitan booby-hatch, fights a never-ending war for Adjustment, Neo-Freudian Analysis, Fee-splitting, and the American Way!

Get a hold of yourself, Funck, get a hold of yourself!

There's a little Clark Kent in the best of us, Funck thought.

That's why Superman had long since passed into folklore. Superman and his alter ego Clark Kent were the perfect, bald statement of the human dilemma (Kent) and the corresponding wish-fulfillment (The Man of Steel). It was normal for kids to assimilate the synthetic myth into their grubby little ids. But it was also normal for them to outgrow it. A few childhood schizoid tendencies never hurt anyone. All kids are a little loco in the coco, Funck reasoned sagely.

If only someone had shot Andy Warhol before it was too late!

That's what opened the whole fetid can of worms, Funck thought—the Pop Art craze. Suddenly, comic books were no longer greasy kid stuff. Suddenly, comic books were Art with a big, fat capital "A." They were hip, they were in, so-called adults were no longer ashamed to snatch them away from the brats and read the things themselves.

All over America, meek, mild-mannered men went back and relived their youths through comic books. Thousands of meek, mild-mannered slobs were once more coming to identify with the meek, mild-mannered reporter of the Metropolis *Daily Planet.* It was like going home again. Superman was the perfect wish-fulfillment figure. No one doubted that he could pulverize 007, leap over a traffic jam on the Long Island Expressway in a single bound, see through women's clothing with his x-ray vision, and *voilá,* the Superman Syndrome!

Step one: the meek, mild-mannered victim identified with that prototype of all *schlemiels,* Clark Kent.

Step two: they began to see themselves more and more as Clark Kent; began to dream of themselves as Superman.

Step three: a moment of intense frustration, a rebuff from some Lois Lane figure, a dressing-down from some irate Perry White surrogate, and something snapped, and they were in the clutches of the Superman Syndrome.

Usually, it started covertly. The victim procured a pair of long-johns, dyed them blue, sewed an "S" on them, and took to wearing the costume under his street clothes occasionally, in times of stress.

But once the first fatal step was taken, the Superman Syndrome was irreversible. The victim took to wearing the costume all the time. Sooner or later, the stress and strain of reality became too much, and a fugue-state resulted. During the fugue, the victim dyed his hair Superman steel-blue, bought a blue double-breasted suit and steel-rimmed glasses, forgot who he was, and woke up one morning with a set of memories straight out of the comic book. He *was* Clark Kent, and he had to get back to Metropolis.

Bad enough for thousands of nuts to waltz around thinking they were Clark Kent. The horrible part was that Clark Kent was the Man of Steel. Which meant that thousands of grown men were jumping off buildings, trying to stop locomotives with their bare hands, tackling armed criminals in the streets and otherwise contriving to commit *hara-kiri.*

What was worse, there were so many Supernuts popping up all over the place that everyone in the country had seen Superman at least once by now, and enough of them had managed to pull off some feat of daring—saving a little old lady from a gang of muggers, foiling an inexpert bank robbery simply by getting underfoot—that it was fast becoming impossible to convince people that there *wasn't* a Superman.

And the more people became convinced that there was a Superman, the more people fell victim to the Syndrome, the more people became convinced. . . .

Funck groaned aloud. There was even a well-known television commentator who jokingly suggested that maybe Superman *was* real, and the nuts were the people who thought he wasn't.

Could it be? Funck wondered. If sanity was defined as the norm, the mental state of the majority of the population, and the majority of the population believed in Superman, then maybe anyone who *didn't* believe in Superman had a screw loose. . . .

If the nuts were sane, and the sane people were really nuts, and the nuts were the majority, then the truth would have to be. . . .

"Get a hold of yourself, Funck!" Dr. Felix Funck shouted aloud. "There is no Superman! There is no Superman!"

Funck scooped the comics back into the drawer and pressed a button on his intercom.

"You may send in the next Supertwitch, Miss Jones," he said.

Luscious Miss Jones seemed to be blushing as she ushered the next patient into Dr. Funck's office.

There was something unsettling about this one, Funck decided instantly. He had the usual glasses and the usual blue double-breasted suit, but on him they looked almost good. He was built like a brick outhouse, and the steel-blue dye job on his hair looked most professional. Funck smelled money. One of the powers of Supershrink, after all, was the uncanny ability to instantly calculate a potential patient's bank balance. Maybe there would be some way to grab this one for a private patient. . . .

"Have a seat, Mr. Kent," Dr. Funck said. "You are Clark Kent, aren't you?"

Clark Kent sat down on the edge of the chair, his broad back ramrod-straight. "Why, yes, Doctor!" he said. "How did you know?"

"I've seen your stuff in the Metropolis *Daily Planet,* Mr. Kent," Funck said. Got to really humor this one, he thought. There's money here. That dye job's so good it must've set him back fifty bucks! *Indeed* a job for Supershrink! "Well just what seems to be the trouble, Mr. Kent?" he said.

"It's my memory, Doctor!" said Clark Kent. "I seem to be suffering from a strange form of amnesia!"

"So-o . . ." said Felix Funck soothingly. "Could it possibly be that . . . that you suddenly found yourself in New York without knowing how you got here, Mr. Kent?" he said.

"Why that's amazing!" exclaimed Clark Kent. "You're one hundred percent correct!"

"And could it also be," suggested Felix Funck, "that you feel you must return to Metropolis immediately? That, however, you can find no plane or train or bus that goes there? That you cannot find a copy of the *Daily Planet* at the out-of-town newsstands? That, in fact, you cannot even remember where Metropolis is?"

Clark Kent's eyes bugged. "Fantastic!" he exclaimed. "How could you know all that? Can it be that you are no ordinary psychiatrist, Dr. Funck? Can it be that Dr. Felix Funck, balding, harried head of a ward in a great metropolitan booby-hatch is in reality . . . *Supershrink?*"

"Ak!" said Dr. Felix Funck.

"Don't worry, Dr. Funck," Clark Kent said in a warm, comradely tone, "your secret is safe with me! We superheroes have got to stick together, right?"

"Guk!" said Dr. Felix Funck. How could he possibly know? he thought. Why, he'd have to be . . . *ulp!* That was ridiculous. Get a hold of yourself, Funck, get a hold of yourself! Who's the psychiatrist here, anyway?

"So you know that Felix Funck is Supershrink, eh?" he said shrewdly. "Then you must also know that you can conceal nothing from me. That I know your Secret Identity too."

"*Secret Identity?*" said Clark Kent piously. "Who me? Why everyone knows that I'm just a meek, mild-mannered reporter for a great metropolitan—"

With a savage whoop, Dr. Felix Funck suddenly lept halfway across his desk and ripped open the shirt of the dumbfounded Clark Kent, revealing a skin-tight blue uniform with a red "S" insignia emblazoned on the chest. Top-notch job of tailoring too, Funck thought approvingly.

"Aha!" exclaimed Funck. "So Clark Kent, meek, mild-mannered reporter, is, in reality, *Superman!*"

"So my secret is out!" Clark Kent said stoically. "I sure hope you believe in Truth, Justice and the American way!"

"Don't worry, Clark old man. Your secret is safe with me. We superheroes have got to stick together, right?"

"Absolutely!" said Clark Kent. "Now about my problem, Doctor . . ."
"Problem?"

"How am I going to get back to Metropolis?" asked Clark Kent. "By now, the forces of evil must be having a field day!"

"Look," said Dr. Funck. "First of all, there is no Metropolis, no *Daily Planet,* no Lois Lane, no Perry White, and *no Superman.* It's all a comic book, friend."

Clark Kent stared at Dr. Funck worriedly. "Are you feeling all right, Doctor?" he asked solicitously. "Sure you haven't been working too hard? Everybody knows there's a Superman! Tell me, Dr. Funck, when did you first notice this strange malady? Could it be that some childhood trauma has caused you to deny my existence? Maybe your mother—"

"Leave my mother out of this!" shrieked Felix Funck. "Who's the psychiatrist here, anyway? I don't want to hear any dirty stories about my mother. There is no Superman, you're not him, and I can prove it!"

Clark Kent nodded his head benignly. "Sure you can, Dr. Funck!" he soothed.

"Look! Look! If you were Superman you wouldn't have any problem. You'd—" Funck glanced nervously about his office. It was on the tenth floor. It had one window. The window had steel bars an inch and a quarter thick. He can't hurt himself, Funck thought. Why not? Make him face reality, and break the delusion!

"You were saying, Doctor?" said Clark Kent.

"If you were Superman, you wouldn't have to worry about trains or planes or buses. You can fly, eh? You can bend steel in your bare hands? Well then why don't you just rip the bars off the window and fly back to Metropolis?"

"Why . . . why you're absolutely right!" exclaimed Clark Kent. "Of course!"

"Ah . . ." said Funck. "So you see you have been the victim of a delusion. Progress, progress. But don't think you've been completely cured yet. Even Supershrink isn't *that* good. This will require many hours of private consultation, at the modest hourly rate of a mere fifty dollars. We must uncover the basic psychosomatic causes for the—"

"What are you talking about?" exclaimed Clark Kent, leaping up from the chair and shucking his suit with blinding speed, revealing a full-scale Superman costume, replete with expensive-looking scarlet cape which Funck eyed greedily.

He bounded to the window. "Of course!" said Superman. "I can bend steel in my bare hands!" So saying, he bent the inch-and-a-quarter steel bars in his bare hands like so many lengths of licorice whip, ripped them aside and lept to the windowsill.

"Thanks for everything, Dr. Funck!" he said. "Up! Up! And away!" He flung out his arms and lept from the tenth-floor window.

Horrified, Funck bounded to the window and peered out, expecting to see an awful mess on the crowded sidewalk below. Instead:

A rapidly-dwindling caped figure soared out over the New York skyline. From the crowded street below, shrill cries drifted up to the ears of Dr. Felix Funck.

"Look! Up there in the sky!"

"It's a bird!"

"It's a plane!"

"It's SUPERMAN!!"

Dr. Felix Funck watched the Man of Steel execute a smart left bank and turn due west at the Empire State Building. For a short moment, Dr. Funck was stunned, nonplussed. Then he realized what had happened and what he had to do.

"He's nuts!" Felix Funck shouted. "The man is crazy! He's got a screw loose! He thinks he's Superman, and he's so crazy that he *is* Superman! The man needs help! *This* is a job for SUPERSHRINK!"

So saying, Dr. Felix Funck bounded to the windowsill, doffed his street clothes, revealing a gleaming skin-tight red suit with a large blue "S" emblazoned across it, and lept out the window screaming "Wait for me, Superman, you pathetic neurotic, you, wait for me!"

Dr. Felix Funck, who is, after all, in reality Supershrink, turned due west and headed out across the Hudson for Metropolis, somewhere beyond Secaucus, New Jersey.

16. the diary of the rose

Ursula K. Le Guin

The psychotherapist seeking a patient is never alone. There are unseen and unfelt persons always present, voices and influences from the therapist's experience and from society. But the physical illusion of aloneness is nurtured by the client's immediate needs for help and the therapist's great need to provide that help.

With the civil rights and women's movements has come some awareness of a communication problem in psychotherapy; that is, an awareness that the psychotherapist may be perpetuating harmful stereotypes and behavioral standards for blacks and women. As a result, emphasis has recently been placed on the importance of a black or woman patient seeing a nonracist or feminist psychotherapist (regardless of the actual race or sex of the therapist).

In Russia and other countries, opposition to the state is considered a mental illness to be cured. There is a clear parallel between totalitarian countries and such total institutions as mental hospitals. Electroshock therapy, as well as many directive therapies, are miniature total institutions, in which the therapist is the single leader offering a single ideology to which one must conform or be expelled.

In One Flew Over the Cuckoo's Nest, *Nurse Ratchet spoke in all the professionally correct terms and yet exerted a powerful, oppressive control over the patients in her ward. It was* her *ward. Nurse Ratchet anchored the extreme right wing of oppressive social control and direction. Regardless of left-wing or right-wing labels, most professionals do serve as vehicles for social influence. They have little awareness of the social control process, seeing themselves as devoted and independent (as many indeed are). "The Diary of the Rose" is the story of one therapist's developing awareness of the interactions of psychotherapy and social control.*

A second theme examined by this story is future patterns of psychotherapy based on the extrapolation of current technical advances. Psychologists have long tried to delve into a person's thought and feelings. From Freud's use of free association and dream analysis to personality questionnaires to the use of the polygraph, this trend has continued throughout the history of psychology. Presently, the examination of EEG patterns (brain waves) is becoming more sophisticated and specific. Selected stimulation of the cerebral cortex can release a flood of long forgotten memories and impressions. So the "mind scope" of Le Guin's story is a logical projection, one that allows the therapist an extraordinary way of knowing another person. Here the therapist sees what the client feels or thinks more clearly than the client himself.

In "The Diary of the Rose," Le Guin describes certain behavioral disorders, including autism, depression, and paranoia. One major symptom of paranoia is delusions of persecution. But sometimes, when people say "Someone is plotting to get me," it is no delusion. And sometimes a sane person in an insane world is considered crazy.

30 August. Dr. Nades recommends that I keep a diary of my work. She says that if you keep it carefully, when you reread it you can remind yourself of observations you made, notice errors and learn from them, and observe progress in or deviations from positive thinking, and so keep correcting the course of your work by a feedback process.

I promise to write in this notebook every night, and reread it at the end of each week.

I wish I had done it while I was an assistant, but it is even more important now that I have patients of my own.

As of yesterday I have six patients, a full load for a scopist, but four of them are the autistic children I have been working with all year for Dr. Nades' study for the Nat'l Psych. Bureau (my notes on them are in the cli psy files). The other two are new admissions:

Ana Jest, 46, bakery packager, md., no children, diag. depression, referral from city police (suicide attempt).

Flores Sorde, 36, engineer, unmd., no diag., referral from TRTU (psychopathic behavior—Violent).

Dr. Nades says it is important that I write things down each night just as they occurred to me at work: it is the spontaneity that is most informative in self-examination (just as in autopsychoscopy). She says it is better to write it, not dictate onto tape, and keep it quite private, so that I won't be self-conscious. It is hard. I never wrote anything that was private before. I keep feeling as if I was really writing it for Dr. Nades! Perhaps if the diary is useful I can show her some of it, later, and get her advice.

My guess is that Ana Jest is in menopausal depression and hormone therapy will be sufficient. There! Now let's see how bad a prognostician I am.

Will work with both patients under scope tomorrow. It is exciting to have my own patients; I am impatient to begin. Though of course teamwork was very educational.

31 August. Half-hour scope session with Ana J. at 8:00. Analyzed scope material, 11:00 to 17:00. N.B.: Adjust right-brain pickup next session! Weak visual Concrete. Very little aural, weak sensory, erratic body image. Will get lab analyses tomorrow of hormone balance.

It is amazing how banal most people's minds are. Of course the poor woman is in severe depression. Input in the Con dimension was foggy and incoherent, and the Uncon dimension was deeply open, but obscure. But the things that came out of the obscurity were so trivial! A pair of old shoes, and the word "geography"! And the shoes were dim, a mere schema of a pair-of-shoes—maybe a man's, maybe a woman's; maybe dark blue, maybe brown. Although definitely a visual type, she does not see anything clearly. Not many people do. It is depressing. When I was a student in first year I used to think how wonderful other people's minds would be, how wonderful it was going to be to share in all the different worlds, the different colors of their passions and ideas. How naïve I was!

I realised this first in Dr. Ramia's class when we studied a tape from a very famous, successful person, and I noticed that the subject had never looked at a tree, never touched one, did not know any difference between an oak and a poplar, or even between a daisy and a rose. They were all just "trees" or "flowers" to him, apprehended schematically. It was the same with people's faces, though he had tricks for telling them apart: mostly he saw the name, like a label, not the face. That was an Abstract mind, of course, but it can be even worse with the Concretes, whose perceptions come in a kind of un-differentiated sludge—bean soup with a pair of shoes in it.

But aren't I "going native"? I've been studying a depressive's thoughts all day and have got depressed. Look, I wrote up there, "It is depressing." I see the value of this diary already. I know I am over-impressionable.

Of course, that is why I am a good psychoscopist. But it is dangerous.

No session with F. Sorde today, since sedation had not worn off. TRTU referrals are often so drugged that they cannot be scoped for days.

REM scoping session with Ana J. at 4:00 tomorrow. Better go to bed!

1 September. Dr. Nades says the kind of thing I wrote yesterday is pretty much what she had in mind, and invited me to show her this diary again whenever I am in doubt. Spontaneous thoughts—not the technical data, which are recorded in the files anyhow. Cross nothing out. Candor all-important.

Ana's dream was interesting but pathetic. The wolf who turned into a pancake! Such a disgusting, dim, hairy pancake, too. Her visuality is clearer in dream, but the feeling tone remains low (but remember: *you* contribute the affect—don't read it in). Started her on hormone therapy today.

F. Sorde awake, but too confused to take to scope room for session. Frightened. Refused to eat. Complained of pain in side. I thought he was unclear what kind of hospital this is, and told him there was nothing wrong with him physically. He said, "How the hell do you know?" which was fair enough, since he was in strait jacket, due to the V notation on his chart. I examined and found bruising and contusion, and ordered an X-ray, which showed two ribs cracked. Explained to patient that he had been in a condition where forcible restraint had been necessary to prevent self-injury. He said, "Every time one of them asked a question, the other one kicked me." He repeated this several times, with anger and confusion. Paranoid delusional system? If it does not weaken as the drugs wear off, I will proceed on that assumption. He responds fairly well to me, asked my name when I went to see him with the X-ray plate, and agreed to eat. I was forced to apologize to him, not a good beginning with a paranoid. The rib damage should have been marked on his chart by the referring agency or by the medic who admitted him. This kind of carelessness is distressing.

But there's good news too. Rina (Autism Study Subject 4) saw a first-person sentence today. Saw it: in heavy black primer print, all at once in the high Con foreground: *I want to sleep in the big room.* (She sleeps alone because of the feces problem.) The sentence stayed clear for over five seconds. She was reading it in her mind just as I was reading it on the holoscreen. There was weak subverbalization, but not subvocalization, nothing on the audio. She has not yet spoken, even to herself, in the first person. I told Tio about it at once and he asked her after the session, "Rina, where do you want to sleep?" "Rina sleep in the big room." No pronoun, no conative. But one of these days she will say *I want*—aloud. And on that build a personality, maybe, at last: on that foundation. I want, therefore I am.

There is so much fear. Why is there so much fear?

4 September. Went to town for my two-day holiday. Stayed with B. in her new flat on the north bank. Three rooms to herself!!! But I don't really like those old buildings, there are rats and roaches, and it feels so old and strange, as if somehow the famine years were still there, waiting. Was glad to get back to my little room here, all to myself but with others close by on the same floor, friends and colleagues. Anyway I missed writing in this book. I form habits very fast. Compulsive tendency.

Ana much improved: dressed, hair combed, was knitting. But session was dull. Asked her to think about pancakes, and there it came filling up the whole Uncon dimension, the hairy, dreary, flat-wolf-pancake, while in the Con she was obediently trying to visualise a nice cheese blintz. Not too badly: colors and outlines already stronger. I am still willing to count on simple hormone treatment. Of course they will suggest ECT, and a co-analysis of the scope material would be perfectly possible, we'd start with a wolf-pancake, etc. But is there any real point to it? She has been a bakery packager for twenty-four years and her physical health is poor. She cannot change her life situation. At least with good hormone balance she may be able to endure it.

F. Sorde: rested but still suspicious. Extreme fear reaction when I said it was time for his first session. To allay this I sat down and talked about the nature and operation of the psychoscope. He listened intently and finally said, "Are you going to use only the psychoscope?"

I said yes.

He said, "Not electroshock?"

I said no.

He said, "Will you promise me that?"

I explained that I am a psychoscopist and never operate the electroconvulsive therapy equipment, that is an entirely different department. I said my work with him at present would be diagnostic, not therapeutic. He listened carefully. He is an educated person and understands distinctions such as "diagnostic" and "therapeutic." It is interesting that he asked me to *promise*. That does not fit a paranoid pattern, you don't ask for promises from those you can't trust. He came with me docilely, but when we entered the scope room he stopped and turned white at sight of the apparatus. I made Dr. Aven's little joke about the dentist's chair, which she always used with nervous patients. F. S. said, "So long as it's not an electric chair!"

I believe that with intelligent subjects it is much better not to make mysteries and so impose a false authority and a feeling of helplessness on the subject (see T. R. Olma, *Psychoscopy Technique*). So I showed him the chair and electrode crown and explained its operation. He has a layman's hearsay knowledge of the psychoscope, and his questions also reflected his engineering education. He sat down in the chair when I asked him. While I fitted the crown and clasps he was sweating profusely from fear, and this evidently embarrassed him, the smell. If he knew how Rina smells after she's been doing shit-paintings. He shut his eyes and gripped the chair arms so that his hands went white to the wrist. The screens were almost white too. After a while I said in a joking tone, "It doesn't really hurt, does it?"

"I don't know."

"Well, does it?"

"You mean it's on?"

"It's been on for ninety seconds."

He opened his eyes then and looked around as well as he could for the head clamps. He asked, "Where's the screen?"

I explained that a subject never watches the screen live, because the objectification can be severely disturbing, and he said, "Like feedback from a microphone?" That is exactly the simile Dr. Aven used to use. F. S. is certainly an intelligent person. N.B.: Intelligent paranoids are dangerous!

He asked, "What do you see?" and I said, "Do be quiet, I don't want to see what you're saying, I want to see what you're thinking," and he said, "But that's none of your business, you know," quite gently, like a joke. Meanwhile the fear-white had gone into dark, intense, volitional convolutions, and then, a few seconds after he stopped speaking, a rose appeared on the whole Con dimension: a full-blown pink rose, beautifully sensed and visualized, clear and steady, whole.

He said presently, "What am I thinking about, Dr. Sobel?" and I said, "Bears in the zoo." I wonder now why I said that. Self-defense? Against what? He gave a laugh and the Uncon went crystal-dark, relief, and the rose darkened and wavered. I said, "I was joking. Can you bring the rose back?" That brought back the fear-white. I said, "Listen, it's really very bad for us to talk like this during a first session, you have to learn a great deal before you can co-analyze, and I have a great deal to learn about you, so no more jokes, please? Just relax physically, and think about anything you please."

There was flurry and subverbalization on the Con dimension, and the Uncon faded into gray, suppression. The rose came back weakly a few times. He was trying to concentrate on it, but couldn't. I saw several quick visuals: myself, my uniform, TRTU uniforms, a gray car, a kitchen, the violent ward (strong aural images—screaming), a desk, the papers on the desk. He stuck to those. They were the plans for a machine. He began going through them. It was a deliberate effort at suppression, and quite effective. Finally I said, "What kind of machine is that?" and he began to answer aloud but stopped and let me get the answer subvocally in the earphone: "Plans for a rotary engine assembly for traction," or something like that—of course the exact words are on the tape. I repeated it aloud and said, "They aren't classified plans, are they?" He said, "No," aloud, and added, "I don't know any secrets." His reaction to a question is intense and complex; each sentence is like a shower of pebbles thrown into a pool, the interlocking rings spread out quick and wide over the Con and into the Uncon, responses rising on all levels. Within a few seconds all that was hidden by a big signboard that appeared in the high Con foreground, deliberately visualized like the rose and the plans, with auditory reinforcement as he read it over and over: KEEP OUT! KEEP OUT! KEEP OUT!

It began to blur and flicker, and somatic signals took over, and soon he said aloud, "I'm tired," and I closed the session (12.5 min.).

After I took off the crown and clamps I brought him a cup of tea from the staff stand in the hall. When I offered it to him, he looked startled and then tears came into his eyes. His hands were so cramped from gripping the armrests that he had trouble taking hold of the cup. I told him he must not be so tense and afraid, we are trying to help him, not to hurt him.

He looked up at me. Eyes are like the scope screen and yet you can't read them. I wished the crown was still on him, but it seems you never catch the moments you most want on the scope. He said, "Doctor, why am I in this hospital?"

I said, "For diagnosis and therapy."

He said, "Diagnosis and therapy of *what?*"

I said he perhaps could not now recall the episode, but he had behaved strangely. He asked how and when, and I said that it would all come clear to him as therapy took effect. Even if I had known what his psychotic episode was, I would have said the same. It was correct procedure. But I felt in a false position. If the TRTU report was not classified, I would be speaking from knowledge and the facts. Then I could make a better response to what he said next: "I was waked up at two in the morning, jailed, interrogated, beaten up, and drugged. I suppose I did behave a little oddly during that. Wouldn't you?"

"Sometimes a person under stress misinterprets other people's actions," I said. "Drink up your tea and I'll take you back to the ward. You're running a temperature."

"The ward," he said, with a kind of shrinking movement, and then he said almost desperately, "Can you really not know why I'm here?"

That was strange, as if he has included me in his delusional system, *on "his side."* Check this possibility in Rheingeld. I should think it would involve some transference and there has not been time for that.

Spent pm analyzing Jest and Sorde holos. I have never seen any psychoscopic realization, not even a drug-induced hallucination, so fine and vivid as that rose. The shadows of one petal on another, the velvety damp texture of the petals, the pink color full of sunlight, the yellow central crown—I am sure the scent was there if the apparatus had olfactory pickup—it wasn't like a mentifact but a real thing rooted in the earth, alive and growing, the strong thorny stem beneath it.

Very tired, must go to bed.

Just reread this entry. Am I keeping this diary right? All I have written is what happened and what was said. Is that spontaneous? But it was *important* to me.

5 *September.* Discussed the problem of conscious resistance with Dr. Nades at lunch today. Explained that I have worked with unconscious blocks (the children, and depressives such as Ana J.) and have some skill at reading through, but have not before met a conscious block such as F. S.'s KEEP OUT sign, or the device he used today, which was effective for a full twenty-minute session: a concentration on his breathing, bodily rhythms, pain in ribs, and visual input from the scope room. She suggested that I use a blindfold for the latter trick, and keep my attention on the Uncon dimension, as he cannot prevent material from appearing there. It is surprising, though, how large the interplay area of his Con and Uncon fields is, and how much one resonates into the other. I believe his concentration on his breathing rhythm allowed him to achieve something like "trance" condition. Though of course most so-called trance is mere occultist fakirism, a primitive trait without interest for behavioral science.

Ana thought through "a day in my life" for me today. All so gray and dull, poor soul! She never thought even of food with pleasure, though she lives on minimum ration. The single thing that came bright for a moment was a child's face, clear dark eyes, a pink knitted cap, round cheeks. She told me in post-session discussion that she always walks by a school playground on the way to work because "she likes to see the little ones running and yelling." Her husband appears on the screen as a big bulky suit of work clothes and a peevish, threatening mumble. I wonder if she knows that she hasn't seen his face or heard a word he says for years? But no use telling her that. It may be just as well she doesn't.

The knitting she is doing, I noticed today, is a pink cap.

Reading De Cams' *Disaffection: A Study,* on Dr. Nades' recommendation.

6 *September.* In the middle of session (breathing again), I said loudly: "Flores!"

Both psy dimensions whited out but the soma realization hardly changed. After four seconds he responded aloud, drowsily. It is not "trance," but autohypnosis.

I said, "Your breathing's monitored by the apparatus. I don't need to know that you're still breathing. It's boring."

He said, "I like to do my own monitoring, Doctor."

I came around and took the blindfold off him and looked at him. He has a pleasant face, the kind of man you often see running machinery, sensitive but patient, like a donkey. That is stupid. I will not cross it out. I am supposed to be spontaneous in this diary. Donkeys do have beautiful faces. They are supposed to be stupid and balky, but they look wise and calm, as if they had endured a lot but held no grudges, as if they knew some reason why one should not hold grudges. And the white ring around their eyes makes them look defenseless.

"But the more you breathe," I said, "the less you think. I need your cooperation. I'm trying to find out what it is you're afraid of."

"But I know what I'm afraid of," he said.

"Why won't you tell me?"

"You never asked me."

"That's most unreasonable," I said, which is funny, now that I think about it, being indignant with a mental patient because he's unreasonable. "Well, then, now I'm asking you."

He said, "I'm afraid of electroshock. Of having my mind destroyed. Being kept here. Or only being let out when I can't remember anything." He gasped while he was speaking.

I said, "All right, why won't you think about that while I'm watching the screens?"

"Why should I?"

"Why not? You've said it to me, why can't you think about it? I want to see the color of your thoughts!"

"It's none of your business, the color of my thoughts," he said angrily, but I was around to the screen while he spoke, and saw the unguarded activity. Of course it was being taped while we spoke, too, and I have studied it all afternoon. It is fascinating. There are two subverbal levels running aside from the spoken words. All sensory-emotive reactions and distortions are vigorous and complex. He "sees" me, for instance, in at least three different ways, probably more—analysis is impossibly difficult! And the Con-Uncon correspondences are so complicated, and the memory traces and current impressions interweave so rapidly, and yet the whole is unified in its complexity. It is like that machine he was studying, very intricate but all one thing in a mathematical harmony. Like the petals of the rose.

When he realized I was observing he shouted out, "Voyeur! Damned voyeur! Let me alone! Get out!" and he broke down and cried. There was a clear fantasy on the screen for several seconds of himself breaking the arm and head clamps and kicking the apparatus to pieces and rushing out of the building, and there, outside, there was a wide hilltop, covered with short dry grass, under the evening sky, and he stood there all alone. While he sat clamped in the chair sobbing.

I broke session and took off the crown, and asked him if he wanted some tea, but he refused to answer. So I freed his arms, and brought him a cup. There was sugar today, a whole box full. I told him that and told him I'd put in two lumps.

After he had drunk some tea he said, with an elaborate ironical tone, because he was ashamed of crying, "You know I like sugar? I suppose your psychoscope told you I liked sugar?"

"Don't be silly," I said, "everybody likes sugar if they can get it."

He said, "No, little doctor, they don't." He asked in the same tone how old I was and if I was married. He was spiteful. He said, "Don't want to marry? Wedded to your work? Helping the mentally unsound back to a constructive life of service to the Nation?"

"I like my work," I said, "because it's difficult, and interesting. Like yours. You like your work, don't you?"

"I did," he said. "Goodbye to all that."

"Why?"

He tapped his head and said, "Zzzzzzt!—All gone. Right?"

"Why are you so convinced you're going to be prescribed electroshock? I haven't even diagnosed you yet."

"Diagnosed me?" he said. "Look, stop the play-acting, please. My diagnosis was made. By the learned doctors of the TRTU. Severe case of disaffection. Prognosis: Evil! Therapy: Lock him up with a roomful of screaming thrashing wrecks, and then go through his mind the same way you went through his papers, and then burn it . . . burn it out. Right, Doctor? Why do you have to go through all this posing, diagnosis, cups of tea? Can't you just get on with it? Do you have to paw through everything I am before you burn it?"

"Flores," I said very patiently, "*you're* saying 'Destroy me'—don't you hear yourself? The psychoscope destroys nothing. And I'm not using it to get evidence, either. This isn't a court, you're not on trial. And I'm not a judge. I'm a doctor."

He interrupted. "If you're a doctor, can't you see that I'm not sick?"

"How can I see anything so long as you block me out with your stupid KEEP OUT signs?" I shouted. I did shout. My patience *was* a pose and it just fell to pieces. But I saw that I had reached him, so I went right on. "You look sick, you act sick—two cracked ribs, a temperature, no appetite, crying fits— is that good health? If you're not sick, then prove it to me! Let me see how you are inside, inside all that!"

He looked down into his cup and gave a kind of laugh and shrugged. "I can't win," he said. "Why do I talk to you? You *look* so honest, damn you!"

I walked away. It is shocking how a patient can hurt one. The trouble is, I am used to the children, whose rejection is absolute, like animals that freeze or cower or bite in their terror. But with this man, intelligent and older than I am, first there is communication and trust and then the blow. It hurts more.

It is painful writing all this down. It hurts again. But it is useful. I do understand some things he said much better now. I think I will not show it to Dr. Nades until I have completed diagnosis. If there is any truth to what he said about being arrested on suspicion of disaffection (and he is certainly careless in the way he talks), Dr. Nades might feel that she should take over the case, due to my inexperience. I should regret that. I need the experience.

7 September. Stupid! That's why she gave you De Cams' book. Of course she knows. As Head of the Section she has access to the TRTU dossier on F. S. She gave me this case deliberately.

It is certainly educational.

Today's session: F. S. still angry and sulky. Intentionally fantasized a sex scene. It was memory, but when she was heaving around underneath him he suddenly stuck a caricature of my face on her. It was effective. I doubt a woman could have done it, women's recall of having sex is usually darker and grander and they and the other do not become meat-puppets like that, with switchable heads. After a while he got bored with the performance (for all its vividness there was little somatic participation, not even an erection) and his mind began to wander. For the first time. One of the drawings on the desk came back. He must be a designer, because he changed it, with a pencil. At the same time there was a tune going on the audio, in mental pure-tone; and in the Uncon lapping over into the interplay area, a large, dark room seen from a child's height, the window sills very high, evening outside the windows, tree branches darkening, and inside the room a woman's voice, soft, maybe reading aloud, sometimes joining with the tune. Meanwhile the whore on the bed kept coming and going in volitional bursts, falling apart a little more each time, till there was nothing left but one nipple. This much I analyzed out this afternoon, the first sequence of over 10 sec. that I have analyzed clear and entire.

When I broke session, he said, "What did you learn?" in the satirical voice.

I whistled a bit of the tune.

He looked scared.

"It's a lovely tune," I said. "I never heard it before. If it's yours, I won't whistle it anywhere else."

"It's from some quartet," he said, with his "donkey" face back, defenseless and patient. "I like classical music. Didn't you—"

"I saw the girl," I said. "And my face on her. Do you know what I'd like to see?"

He shook his head. Sulky, hangdog.

"Your childhood."

That surprised him. After a while he said, "All right. You can have my childhood. Why not? You're going to get all the rest anyhow. Listen. You tape it all, don't you? Could I see a playback? I want to see what you see."

"Sure," I said. "But it won't mean as much to you as you think it will. It took me eight years to learn to observe. You start with your own tapes. I watched mine for months before I recognized anything much."

I took him to my seat, put on the earphone, and ran him 30 sec. of the last sequence.

He was quite thoughtful and respectful after it. He asked, "What was all that running-up-and-down-scales motion in the, the background I guess you'd call it?"

"Visual scan—your eyes were closed—and subliminal proprioceptive input. The Unconscious dimension and the Body dimension overlap to a great extent all the time. We bring the three dimensions in separately, because they seldom coincide entirely anyway, except in babies. The bright triangular motion at the left of the holo was probably the pain in your ribs."

"I don't see it that way!"

"You don't see it; you weren't consciously feeling it, even, then. But we can't translate a pain in the rib onto a holoscreen, so we give it a visual symbol. The same with all sensations, affects, emotions."

"You watch all that at once?"

"I told you it took eight years. And you do realize that that's only a fragment? Nobody could put a whole psyche onto a four-foot screen. Nobody knows if there are any limits to the psyche. Except the limits of the universe."

He said after a while, "Maybe you aren't a fool, Doctor. Maybe you're just very absorbed in your work. That can be dangerous, you know, to be so absorbed in your work."

"I love my work, and I hope that it is of positive service," I said. I was alert for symptoms of disaffection. He smiled a little and said, "Prig," in a sad voice.

Ana is coming along. Still some trouble eating. Entered her in George's mutual-therapy group. What she needs, at least one thing she needs, is companionship. After all, why should she eat? Who needs her to be alive? What we call psychosis is sometimes simply realism. But human beings can't live on realism alone.

F. S.'s patterns do not fit any of the classic paranoid psychoscopic patterns in Rheingeld.

The De Cams book is hard for me to understand. The terminology of politics is so different from that of psychology. Everything seems backwards. I must be genuinely attentive at P. T. sessions Sunday nights from now on. I have been lazy-minded. Or, no, but as F. S. said, too absorbed in my work— and so inattentive to its context, he meant. Not thinking about what one is working *for*.

10 September. Have been so tired the last two nights I skipped writing this journal. All the data are on tape and in my analysis notes, of course. Have been working really hard on the F. S. analysis. It is very exciting. It is a truly unusual mind. Not brilliant, his intelligence tests are good average, he is not original or an artist, there are no schizophrenic insights, I can't say what it is, I feel honored to have shared in the childhood he remembered for me. I can't say what it is. There was pain and fear of course, his father's death from cancer, months and months of misery while F. S. was twelve, that was terrible, but it does not come out pain in the end, he has not forgotten or repressed it but it is all changed, by his love for his parents and his sister and for music and for the shape and weight and fit of things and his memory of the lights and weathers of days long past and his mind always working quietly, reaching out, reaching out to be whole.

There is no question yet of formal co-analysis, it is far too early, but he cooperates so intelligently that today I asked him if he was aware consciously of the Dark Brother figure that accompanied several Con memories in the Uncon dimension. When I described it as having a matted shock of hair, he looked startled and said, "Dokkay, you mean?"

That word had been on the subverbal audio, though I hadn't connected it with the figure.

He explained that when he was five or six, Dokkay had been his name for a "bear" he often dreamed or daydreamed about. He said, "I rode him. He was big, I was small. He smashed down walls, and destroyed things, bad things, you know, bullies, spies, people who scared my mother, prisons, dark alleys I was afraid to cross, policemen with guns, the pawnbroker. Just knocked them over. And then he walked over all the rubble on up to the hilltop. With me riding on his back. It was quiet up there. It was always evening, just before the stars come out. It's strange to remember it. Thirty years ago! Later on he turned into a kind of friend, a boy or man, with hair like a bear. He still smashed things, and I went with him. It was good fun."

I write this down from memory as it was not taped; session was interrupted by power outage. It is exasperating that the hospital comes so low on the list of Government priorities.

Attended the Pos. Thinking session tonight and took notes. Dr. K. spoke on the dangers and falsehoods of liberalism.

11 September. F. S. tried to show me Dokkay this morning but failed. He laughed and said aloud, "I can't see him any more. I think at some point I turned into him."

"Show me when that happened," I said, and he said, "All right," and began at once to recall an episode from his early adolescence. It had nothing to do with Dokkay. He saw an arrest. He was told that the man had been passing out illegal printed matter. Later on he saw one of these pamphlets, the title was in his visual bank, "Is There Equal Justice?" He read it, but did not recall the text or managed to censor it from me. The arrest was terribly vivid. Details like the young man's blue shirt and the coughing noise he made and the sound of the hitting, the TRTU agents' uniforms, and the car driving away, a big gray car with blood on the door. It came back over and over, the car driving away down the street, driving away down the street. It was a traumatic incident for F. S. and may explain the exaggerated fear of the violence of national justice justified by national security which may have led him to behave irrationally when investigated and so appeared as a tendency to disaffection—falsely, I believe.

I will show why I believe this. When the episode was done I said, "Flores, think about democracy for me, will you?"

He said, "Little doctor, you don't catch old dogs quite that easily."

"I am not catching you. Can you think about democracy or can't you?"

"I think about it a good deal," he said. And he shifted to right-brain activity, music. It was the chorus of the last part of the Ninth Symphony by Beethoven, I recognised it from the Arts term in high school. We sang it to some patriotic words. I yelled, "Don't censor!" and he said, "Don't shout, I can hear you." Of course the room was perfectly silent, but the pickup on the audio was tremendous, like thousands of people singing together. He went on aloud, "I'm not censoring. I'm thinking about democracy. That is democracy. Hope, brotherhood, no walls. All the walls unbuilt. You, we, I make the universe! Can't you hear it?" And it was the hilltop again, the short grass and the sense of being up high, and the wind, and the whole sky. The music was the sky.

When it was done and I released him from the crown I said, "Thank you."

I do not see why the doctor cannot thank the patient for a revelation of beauty and meaning. Of course the doctor's authority is important, but it need not be domineering. I realize that in politics the authorities must lead and be followed, but in psychological medicine it is a little different, a doctor cannot "cure" the patient, the patient "cures" himself with our help, this is not contradictory to Positive Thinking.

14 September. I am upset after the long conversation with F. S. today and will try to clarify my thinking.

Because the rib injury prevents him from attending work therapy he is restless. The Violent ward disturbed him deeply, so I used my authority to have the V removed from his chart and have him moved into Men's Ward B, three days ago. His bed is next to old Arca's, and when I came to get him for session they were talking, sitting on Arca's bed. F. S. said, "Dr. Sobel, do you know my neighbor, Professor Arca of the Faculty of Arts and Letters of the University?" Of course I know the old man—he has been here for years, far longer than I—but F. S. spoke so courteously and gravely that I said, "Yes, how do you do, Professor Arca?" and shook the old man's hand. He greeted me politely as a stranger—he often does not know people from one day to the next.

As we went to the scope room F. S. said, "Do you know how many electroshock treatments he had?" and when I said no he said, "Sixty. He tells me that every day. With pride." Then he said, "Did you know that he was an internationally famous scholar? He wrote a book, *The Idea of Liberty,* about twentieth-century ideas of freedom in politics and the arts and sciences. I read it when I was in engineering school. It existed then. On bookshelves. It doesn't exist any more. Anywhere. Ask Dr. Arca. He never heard of it."

"There is almost always some memory loss after electroconvulsive therapy," I said, "but the material loss can be relearned, and is often spontaneously regained."

"After sixty sessions?" he said.

F. S. is a tall man, rather stooped, even in the hospital pajamas he is an impressive figure. But I am also tall, and it is not because I am shorter than he that he calls me "little doctor." He did it first when he was angry at me and so now he says it when he is bitter but does not want what he says to hurt me, the me he knows. He said, "Little doctor, quit faking. You know the man's mind was deliberately destroyed."

Now I will try to write down exactly what I said, because it is important. "I do not approve of the use of electroconvulsive therapy as a general instrument. I would not recommend its use on my patients except perhaps in certain specific cases of senile melancholia. I went into psychoscopy because it is an integrative rather than a destructive instrument."

That is all true, and yet I never said or consciously thought it before.

"What will you recommend for me?" he said.

I explained that once my diagnosis is complete, my recommendation will be subject to the approval of the Head and Assistant Head of the Section. I said that so far nothing in his history or personality structure warranted the use of ECT, but that after all we had not got very far yet.

"Let's take a long time about it," he said, shuffling along beside me with his shoulders hunched.

"Why? Do you like it?"

"No. Though I like you. But I'd like to delay the inevitable end."

"Why do you insist that it's inevitable, Flores? Can't you see that your thinking on that one point is quite irrational?"

"Rosa," he said—he has never used my first name before—"Rosa, you can't be reasonable about pure evil. There are faces reason cannot see. Of course I'm irrational, faced with the imminent destruction of my memory— my self. But I'm not inaccurate. You know they're not going to let me out of here un—" He hesitated a long time and finally said, "unchanged."

"One psychotic episode—"

"I had no psychotic episode. You must know that by now."

"Then why were you sent here?"

"I have some colleagues who prefer to consider themselves rivals, competitors. I gather they informed the TRTU that I was a subversive liberal."

"What was their evidence?"

"Evidence?" We were in the scope room by now. He put his hands over his face for a moment and laughed in a bewildered way. "Evidence? Well, once at a meeting of my section I talked a long time with a visiting foreigner, a fellow in my field, a designer. And I have friends, you know, unproductive people, bohemians. And this summer I showed our section head why a design he'd got approved by the Government wouldn't work. That was stupid. Maybe I'm here for—for imbecility. And I read. I've read Professor Arca's book."

"But none of that matters, you think positively, you love your country, you're not disaffected!"

He said, "I don't know. I love the idea of democracy, the hope, yes, I love that. I couldn't live without that. But the country? You mean the thing on the map, lines, everything inside the lines is good and nothing outside them matters? How can an adult love such a childish idea?"

"But you wouldn't betray the nation to an outside enemy."

He said, "Well, if it was a choice between the nation and humanity, or the nation and a friend, I might. If you call that betrayal. I call it morality."

He *is* a liberal. It is exactly what Dr. Katin was talking about on Sunday.

It is classic psychopathy: the absence of normal affect. He said that quite unemotionally—"I might."

No. That is not true. He said it with difficulty, with pain. It was I who was so shocked that I felt nothing—blank, cold.

How am I to treat this kind of psychosis, a *political* psychosis? I have read over De Cams' book twice and I believe I do understand it now, but still there is a gap between the political and the psychological, so that the book shows me how to think but does not show me how to *act* positively. I see how F. S. should think and feel, and the difference between that and his present state of mind, but I do not know how to educate him so that he can think positively. De Cams says that disaffection is a negative condition which must be filled with positive ideas and emotions, but this does not fit F. S. The gap is not in him. In fact, that gap in De Cams between the political and the psychological is exactly where *his* ideas apply. But if they are wrong ideas, how can this be?

I want advice badly, but I cannot get it from Dr. Nades. When she gave me the De Cams she said, "You'll find what you need in this." If I tell her that I haven't, it is like a confession of helplessness and she will take the case away from me. Indeed, I think it is a kind of test case, testing me. But I need this experience, I am learning, and besides, the patient trusts me and talks freely to me. He does so because he knows that I keep what he tells me in perfect confidence. Therefore I cannot show this journal or discuss these problems with anyone until the cure is under way and confidence is no longer essential.

But I cannot see when that could happen. It seems as if confidence will always be essential between us.

I have got to teach him to adjust his behavior to reality, or he will be sent for ECT when the Section reviews cases in November. He has been right about that all along.

9 October. I stopped writing in this notebook when the material from F. S. began to seem "dangerous" to him (or to myself). I just reread it all over tonight. I see now that I can never show it to Dr. N. So I am going to go ahead and write what I please in it. Which is what she said to do, but I think she always expected me to show it to her, she thought I would want to, which I did, at first, or that if she asked to see it I'd give it to her. She asked about it yesterday. I said that I had abandoned it, because it just repeated things I had already put into the analysis files. She was plainly disapproving but said nothing. Our dominance-submission relationship has changed these past few weeks. I do not feel so much in need of guidance, and after the Ana Jest discharge, the autism paper, and my successful analysis of the T. R. Vinha tapes she cannot insist upon my dependence. But she may resent my independence. I took the covers off the notebook and am keeping the loose pages in the split in the back cover of my copy of Rheingeld, it would take a very close search to find them there. While I was doing that I felt rather sick at the stomach and got a headache.

Allergy: A person can be exposed to pollen or bitten by fleas a thousand times without reaction. Then he gets a viral infection or a psychic trauma or a bee-sting, and next time he meets up with ragweed or a flea he begins to sneeze, cough, itch, weep, etc. It is the same with certain other irritants. One has to be sensitized.

"Why is there so much fear?" I wrote. Well, now I know. Why is there no privacy? It is unfair and sordid. I cannot read the "classified" files kept in her office, though I work with the patients and she does not. But I am not to have any "classified" material of my own. Only persons in authority can have secrets. Their secrets are all good, even when they are lies.

Listen. Listen, Rosa Sobel. Doctor of Medicine, Deg. Psychotherapy. Deg. Psychoscopy. Have you gone native?

Whose thoughts are you thinking?

You have been working two to five hours a day for six weeks inside one person's mind. A generous, integrated, sane mind. You never worked with anything like that before. You have only worked with the crippled and the terrified. You never met an equal before.

Who is the therapist, you or he?

But if there is nothing wrong with him what am I supposed to cure? How can I help him? How can I save him?

By teaching him to lie?

(Undated) I spent the last two nights till midnight reviewing the diagnostic scopes of Professor Arca, recorded when he was admitted, eleven years ago, before electroconvulsive treatment.

This morning Dr. N. inquired why I had been "so far back in the files." (That means that Selena reports to her on what files are used.) (I know every square centimeter of the scope room but all the same I check it over daily now.) I replied that I was interested in studying the development of ideological disaffection in intellectuals. We agreed that intellectualism tends to foster negative thinking and may lead to psychosis, and those suffering from it should ideally be treated, as Professor Arca was treated, and released if still competent. It was a very interesting and harmonious discussion.

I lied. I lied. I lied. I lied deliberately, knowingly, well. She lied. She is a liar. She is an intellectual too! She is a lie. And a coward, afraid.

I wanted to watch the Arca tapes to get perspective. To prove to myself that Flores is by no means unique or original. This is true. The differences are fascinating. Dr. Arca's Con dimension was splendid, architectural, but the Uncon material was less well integrated and less interesting. Dr. Arca knew very much more, and the power and beauty of the motions of his thought was far superior to Flores'. Flores is often extremely muddled. That is an element of his vitality. Dr. Arca is an—was an Abstract thinker, as I am, and so I enjoyed his tapes less. I missed the solidity, spatiotemporal realism, and intense sensory clarity of Flores' mind.

In the scope room this morning I told him what I had been doing. His reaction was (as usual) not what I expected. He is fond of the old man and I thought he would be pleased. He said, "You mean they saved the tapes, and destroyed the mind?" I told him that all tapes are kept for use in teaching, and asked him if that didn't cheer him, to know that a record of Arca's thoughts in his prime existed: wasn't it like his book, after all, the lasting part of a mind which sooner or later would have to grow senile and die anyhow! He said, "No! Not so long as the book is banned and the tape is classified! Neither freedom nor privacy even in death? That is the worst of all!"

After session he asked if I would be able or willing to destroy his diagnostic tapes, if he is sent to ECT. I said such things could get misfiled and lost easily enough, but that it seemed a cruel waste, I had learned from him and others might, later, too. He said, "Don't you see that I will not serve the people with security passes? I will not be used, that's the whole point. You have never used me. We have worked together. Served our term together."

Prison has been much in his mind lately. Fantasies, daydreams of jails, labor camps. He dreams of prison as a man in prison dreams of freedom.

Indeed, as I see the way narrowing in I would get him sent to prison if I could, but since he is *here* there is no chance. If I reported that he is in fact politically dangerous, they will simply put him back in the Violent ward and give him ECT. There is no judge here to give him a life sentence. Only doctors to give death sentences.

What I can do is stretch out the diagnosis as long as possible, and put in a request for full co-analysis, with a strong prognosis of complete cure. But I have drafted the report three times already and it is very hard to phrase it so that it's clear that I know the disease is ideological (so that they don't just override my diagnosis at once) but still making it sound mild and curable enough that they'd let me handle it with the psychoscope. And then, why spend up to a year, using expensive equipment, when a cheap and simple instant cure is at hand? No matter what I say, they have that argument. There are two weeks left until Sectional Review. I have got to write the report so that it will be really impossible for them to override it. But what if Flores is right, all this is just play-acting, lying about lying, and they have had orders right from the start from TRTU, "Wipe this one out"—

(Undated) Sectional Review today.
If I stay on here I have some power, I can do some good   No no no but

I don't I don't even in this one thing even in this what can I do now how can I stop

(Undated) Last night I dreamed I rode on a bear's back up a deep gorge between steep mountainsides, slopes going steep up into a dark sky, it was winter, there was ice on the rocks

(Undated) Tomorrow morning will tell Nades I am resigning and requesting transfer to Children's Hospital. But she must approve the transfer. If not, I am out in the cold. I am in the cold already. Door locked to write this. As soon as it is written will go down to furnace room and burn it all. There is no place any more.

We met in the hall. He was with an orderly.

I took his hand. It was big and bony and very cold. He said, "Is this it now, Rosa—the electroshock?" in a low voice. I did not want him to lose hope before he walked up the stairs and down the corridor. It is a long way down the corridor. I said, "No. Just some more tests—EEG probably."

"Then I'll see you tomorrow?" he asked, and I said yes.

And he did. I went in this evening. He was awake. I said, "I am Dr. Sobel, Flores. I am Rosa."

He said, "I'm pleased to meet you," mumbling. There is a slight facial paralysis on the left. That will wear off.

I am Rosa. I am the rose. The rose, I am the rose. The rose with no flower, the rose all thorns, the mind he made, the hand he touched, the winter rose.

17. christlings

Albert Teichner

What is it that makes a great psychotherapist? Certainly it would have to be someone who is knowledgeable, with a full awareness of what he is doing. And just as certainly it would include those people who can go to the core of a subject matter quickly, effectively, constructively. But above all, it must include caring, really caring, for the other person.

This "business of caring"—which may simply be a paraphrasing of what psychotherapy is—can get tough to define and pin down. For example, I care very much how the Kansas City Chiefs do in next year's football season, and I care very much if I have to pay a large income tax, and I

care very much if someone scrapes my car. In the same sense I may care about the feelings and life of a client; interested, involved, but still at a distance and detached from me.

For a great psychotherapist, caring is a far more personal thing. He feels the way a mother does about a child. He becomes a Christ-like figure (particularly if we accept the notion that Christ was one of the more successful psychotherapists of recorded history) who inspires unrequited love and confidence in his clients.

Now if only the rest of us struggling and middle-level therapists could become Christ-like. Perhaps that is the answer to our concerns about troubled patients and imperfect therapists. This story discusses a therapist who almost achieves perfection, with a little help from his friends.

"Christlings" has a second theme of the hazards of chemical solutions to human problems. A major concern in psychology is the search for biochemical causes and cures of disordered behaviors. The search has led from Taraxin—an "essence-of-schizophrenia" chemical reported by Robert Heath at Tulane University—to Thorazine, the trade name for a central nervous system depressant used two billion times a year. In the past few years, Lithium has become the fashionable and faddish psychowonder-drug. This story about one chemical solution demonstrates the mad scientist syndrome. Dr. Frankenstein sought to restore life and help mankind, not create a lumbering, destructive monster. Similarly the protagonists of this story sought to improve the human condition. Their failure warns us both to beware of the limitations of simplistic chemical answers and to watch how the "madness" in the mad scientist always becomes attached after the fact.

Dr. Max Bruch's long, gaunt frame wriggled uneasily as he glanced at his watch and saw with mounting anxiety that it was a quarter to three. In fifteen minutes Harvey Putzman, the only patient he had ever dangerously disliked, would be coming through the door to throw himself on the sofa and spew spittle-laden malice at the ceiling. Putzman, the sensationally popular novelist of the newest new generation—most psychoanalysts would have considered it a professional coup to have him on their list of emotional cripples. And Putzman was willing to pay extremely high for the privilege of having his peculiar agonies privately aired. So what was there to dislike?

"Nothing except for everything," Bruch groaned aloud. Those monstrously arching nostrils, implying a lifetime of zealous picking, were only the outermost configurations of the man. What created a deeper revulsion was the ingratitude this extremely clever writer showed for everyone who had ever helped him, the parents who spoiled him, the rabbi who forgave him, the teachers and mistresses who always insisted he was a genius. His nine-hundred-page epic, *Weequahic,* had been vicious enough toward all of them, drowning with venom that whole section of Newark, New Jersey, for which it was named. But the past year's analytic sessions had shown this was not merely poetic license; Putzman in the flesh actually hated more bitterly than he had ever dared reveal on paper!

Ten minutes to go. Bruch took a little white pill from his vest pocket and went to the water cooler. The first time for the pill, but there had to be a virgin moment in every enterprise. He gulped it down fast and returned to his swivel chair to wait.

Every patient was entitled to the best treatment possible but, from his twenty years of experience, Bruch knew referring Putzman elsewhere would not help; it was literally impossible to like Putzman in these days of his glory and chances were that the next practitioner would handle him with even more prejudice. "I must help him even if it kills me," he said through clenched teeth. There instantly followed the consoling thought that if the pill were the least bit successful with Putzman, then it would help with any case. Where before in medical history had a doctor taken the medicine instead of the patient?

Only, so far, it wasn't working.

Then Putzman was there in the room, muttering about just having left his publisher and agent. "Think they're screwing me but it's the other way around, they'll see soon!" He regarded Bruch with distaste, fell on the couch and launched into a recent dream that made Hieronymus Bosch seem *Alice in Wonderland* bowdlerized. It was something perverted about childhood teasing of the neighbor's schnauzer (why, Bruch shuddered, was there *always* that clearly visible spray of saliva?), something new to Putzman's confessional repertoire. Just as in the novels where all the protagonist's weaknesses were blamed on the "sick society" to which his audience belonged, so here Bruch somehow became responsible for Putzman's torment. The wildly exaggerated humor made Putzman's confession too self-gratifying to be believable, even as Putzman's face became twisted with unhappiness. Everything the patient said was subject to the same skeptical—

Unhappiness, thought Bruch with a sudden pang, this man was desperately unhappy, suffering something worse than anything he imposed on others. It was not proper procedure, but Bruch found himself breaking in to say softly: "Harvey, you don't have to worry about that episode ever again."

"What the hell does *that* mean?" Putzman screamed, then craned around to stare at Bruch and relaxed. His head fell back as he sighed. "You're a real paradox artist, Doctor, but you're right! I never looked at it that way before." He abruptly shifted into an attack on a high school English teacher who had wanted him to write more genteelly, but his voice was unusually calm and the attack petered out into praise of her kindness. "She did try, though, Dr. Bruch. God knows that dried-up old maid wanted me to have the success everything in her own life had denied her."

The analyst sank deeper into gloom. It was as if he were listening to his very first patient twenty years ago, feeling each word like a whiplash, the way it had been before much of the process became distant if well-intentioned routine. As the hour went on Putzman, without once taking his eyes from the ceiling, seemed to draw new strength from that gloom.

When the novelist left he had gained more emotional ground than in all previous sessions combined. Bruch called Grainger on the intercom and exclaimed: "It looks as if it's working, unbelievable!"

"What happened?"

"Well—" The red light came on. "No time, Jack, next patient's a little early but has a thing about being kept waiting. See you six fifteen."

After Putzman, Mrs. Crofton brought an almost healthy air of commonplace neurosis into the office. True, the thirty-five-year-old mother of two remained utterly frigid after eighteen months but, while she was of only average intelligence, her cultivated background made their sessions together little islands of restrained decency in days awash with psychic sewerage. Now, without his saying a word, the restraint was gone even if the decency remained as strong as ever. Waves of sweet sympathy swept Bruch and he could feel each hurt she expressed as if it were his own. When she rose to leave there were tears in her eyes. "It's changing now," she said. "I know I am starting to get better."

The two hours had been exhausting, leaving him bathed in sweat, but there was still Bernstein, the jittery furrier, to deal with. He came in chattering about the way his wife said he was *meshugge* last night because he refused to eat the vichyssoise and maybe he was, huh? The whole inane episode was then retold at a rising machine-gun rate, but once he arrived at the self-doubt part, he slowed down. By the time the hour ended and the story had been twice more repeated, Bernstein's face had relaxed and for the first time all the forehead creases were smoothed away.

At six, when Bernstein was gone and Mrs. Parker, his nurse-secretary, had looked in to say she, too, was leaving, Bruch was slumped in his chair, too drained of energy to budge. "Anything the matter, Doctor?" she asked.

"Oh, no!" he grinned.

After a minute's solitary contemplation of this strange mixture of weariness and triumph he pulled himself from the chair and walked upstairs to Grainger's compact laboratory. Grainger, a short, intense-looking fellow, began pacing the floor as soon as Bruch came in. "You think it helped, you really think it—"

"I'm sure of it."

"But when did you take the pill, Max?"

"Fifteen minutes before Putzman. Finally got up nerve."

"I was sure that dosage would be harmless!" He leaned toward Bruch like an accusing attorney. "Exactly what happened?"

With a tired smile Bruch shoved him away. "Give me a chance to rest. It's exhausting, Jack, so putter around your crockery awhile."

Grainger, muttering, adjusted the flame beneath a small test tube and

Bruch turned to stare out the window at the glorious blossoming of the solitary cherry tree in his garden, one of those little consolations hard-earned money could bring.

How much more consolation now lay within his grasp! Yet five months ago the whole thing would have appeared preposterous.

The inspiration had come from a biochemical journal that his old college pal, Jack Grainger, had brought him as a joke. It described worldwide experiments on Juno A, a powerful hormone trace first isolated in cow udders and later found to be universal in female mammals. Juno A increased in pregnant women, grew even stronger following parturition and ordinarily did not decline until long after the female climacteric. As a further anomaly, some childless women—nuns, nurses, governesses and teachers, most frequently—revealed even higher levels than mothers. Researchers had sometimes called Juno A the mother-love hormone, intimately associating it with woman's capacity for devotion and endurance, even though, like many other sex-linked hormones, it appeared to a miniscule extent in men also.

Putzman! Bruch had thought, only a mother drenched in such a hormone could love Putzman! And then it hit him: suppose Juno A's most active fraction were isolated and proved safe for males, and suppose a practicing therapist took it. Couldn't he be a better healer for that?

At first Grainger had ridiculed the question. "Juno A research is dying down, Max. It's a relatively useless vestige of mammalian evolution, like the appendix in man."

But Grainger was a biochemist with a very inquiring mind and Max had seen the way to wear him down with the most tempting of offers. "I've got plenty of money for it, Jack. You could have my country place and all the cow udders your little heart and giant mind desired. And if you achieved an adequate supply you could bring it here for final concentration." That had worked and, once hooked, Jack had proved almost frighteningly single-minded in his zeal.

"Insane!" Jack was shouting, "absolutely insane—snoring ten minutes with your eyes open and me desperate to know what's happened!"

As a pink petal danced to the ground, Bruch's eyes followed its exquisite swings along a strong air current until he was awake again. "Sorry, Jack, it's terribly exhausting when you *feel* everything the patient throws at you."

"Everything?"

"That's right." He pulled himself from the chair, shaking his head in wonder. "I had the impression I understood their cases much better because of that. But their improvement involved still more. You see, they almost instantly *sensed* I was totally and more actively sympathetic. Couldn't have been visual clues because two of them didn't even look at me during their transformations!"

The biochemist frowned. "You're not trotting out any ESP garbage, Max?"

"No, I don't know what kind of two-way signals this stuff generates. Come on downstairs and let's see if I'll live."

An hour later all the readings of short-term reactions were in; the pill, ten times stronger than anything they had consumed before, involved no significant metabolic changes. "Just hope the patients do as well," Bruch said.

"They're not taking the pill!"

Max sighed. "It's just that we're dealing with something completely new—"

Grainger broke in. "Max, it's not yet a shared risk—I'd like to try the full dose, too."

"Look, Jack, I'm tired, the sympathy effect's worn off, so I'll lose my temper if we have to thrash this out once again. You distill Juno, you know how scarce it is and that if it works we're going to need every grain for *professionals.*"

Jack's frown was amiable. "All right, all right, you don't have to worry I'll never dig in without your approval."

"Anyway, there's no guarantee today's success will be repeated."

But the next day it was. Once more after taking the pill he was bathed in a glow of compassion that did not hinder the practical use of his art. And in each case the patient showed all the grateful tenderness of someone secure in the knowledge of being loved. When his workday concluded, Bruch, exultant in the agony he had endured, felt as if he were descending from the cross back to human terra firma.

The following afternoon Putzman meekly entered the office and sat on the edge of the couch, staring saucer-eyed at him. "You may have taken my writing talent from me," he said. "But don't get me wrong, Dr. Bruch, I'm glad. It's as if I'd always seen everything through a stained and dirty window and now the dirt was gone and I saw the world itself, not the stains. That's more important than being admired for an inhuman pseudo-talent. I think I'm cured!"

Within a week it was evident that *all* his patients were. But not basically through the strategies Max devised, because he barely had a chance to apply his insights. Somehow his genuine concern did most of the work, leading each one to cure himself.

"We're tapping a force so fundamental, so powerful, it can change *all* human relationships!" Grainger exclaimed once. "As if everybody lived in a vast desert, miserably clustered around a few oases, and suddenly they discover all the water needed was underfoot everywhere all along! Max, I can expand our production now a little but if we made this public, let others join the search, there might be an unlimited supply!"

"No! I haven't even told Mrs. Parker, although she sees all my cases simultaneously terminated and is bewildered."

Jack glared at him. "Let *me* ask therapeutic questions for once."

Max shrugged. "Okay."

"So far have you had any adverse physical effect from the pill?"

"No."

"Has there been any positive physical effect?"

"I suppose, on balance, yes. It's incredibly exhausting to listen so thoroughly to people all day but I always have the strength to endure it because Juno A gives that as well as sensitivity. And by evening tension is gone, leaving me with the pleasurable tiredness of a job well done."

Jack was envious. "Is there any adverse psychological effect?"

"None."

"Any positive psychological effect?"

"Yes. As I said, the knowledge I've alleviated terrible suffering."

"Then why the hell deny millions of other people that blessing *now!*"

"I must be absolutely sure. I need as many cases as possible for twelve weeks."

"No, too long."

"Well—ten weeks at the least."

Grainger shook his head in disgust, then suddenly straightened from his hunched-over posture. "All right, Max, but only ten."

The following week brought a score of new patients. Mrs. Parker was quite nervous about it. "That's a terrible burden to assume—"

"No burden," he smiled, touched by her solicitude. It was less than an hour after ingesting a Juno pill and, as he felt her anxiety rise within him, he could see her reciprocally relaxing.

"Could I say something more, Dr. Bruch?"

"Certainly."

Her eyes were misty. "I've always thought you the most dedicated of doctors—"

"Oh, no, please—"

"—and many times I've said it to my husband whom I love so I'm not getting any adolescent crush when I say it but—but lately you've been so wonderful it's almost like being with a—a saint!" She fled back to the outer office.

Embarrassed by the fervor of her outburst, Max leaned back in his office chair. More and more he was being treated like a holy figure while under Juno A's influence. Waves of love would almost smother him as each person's burden of suffering was shifted to his granite shoulders. "I'm only a man," he told the row of framed diplomas on the facing wall, "a man, not a junior Jesus. I don't have the right to claim more."

But then his next patient was entering and he knew any attempt to dissipate the childlike adulation in her eyes would only delay the release from her private hell. Through twenty years of marriage she had been cleaning her apartment over and over each day. "Yesterday I only picked up a dust rag once!" she was exulting. "Suddenly things don't look filthy endlessly!"

She was on the way to being cured and by the end of the following week not only had such compulsive symptoms disappeared but the generating root complaint itself. In fact, by then *all* the new patients were cured and the only tiny qualm Bruch had about them was their wildly adoring gratitude.

"I am not Jesus or *any* prophet," he told one patient, an aging, hard-bitten tax lawyer who certainly should have realized this on his own, "only a human scientist."

"*Only?* You may not be the Christ, Doctor, but to me you're barely lower than the angels—a, a Christling, that's how I'd put it, yes, sir!"

The wages of virtue are hard, Bruch was forced to concede, but the best thing evidently was to leave this excessive father-transference alone since so much good went with it and in the months ahead it was bound to fade. Meanwhile, there was the next list of distraught people to start considering, and this time there would be even more of them.

Again within two weeks they were cured and again there was the same mad display of gratitude to emphasize the depth of the cures. He reached the end of each working day drained of physical energy but even that quickly revived as the Juno dose faded, and he always faced the next morning adequate to the tasks ahead.

With the increasing workload he saw less of his partner. Anyway, Jack was spending more of his time in the country laboratory. He seemed very distant during their rare meetings, utterly preoccupied with his work. One evening Max said as much.

Jack looked with unblinking eyes at him, then asked: "Still *no* side effects, right?"

"Right!"

"Great, Max, because I'm now certain there'll be *several* ways for the big pharmaceutical houses to synthesize the pure, potent fraction cheaply. An unlimited supply is assured!" Even Bruch was surprised to find himself so *un*-reassured. "What's the matter now, Max? The greatest boon to humanity in unlimited—"

"Don't get me wrong, Jack, I'm terribly pleased. It's just that the idea of an unlimited, uncontrollable supply of *anything* makes me uneasy."

"Meaning," Grainger snapped, closing the discussion, "that there are no real problems—and won't be!"

But within three days this prophecy was proved doubly wrong.

On Sunday there was the call from the answering service, right in the middle of a Menuhin recording of an unaccompanied Bach partita. "You know this is the one day I'm not to be disturbed," Bruch protested.

"I really tried not to," explained the girl, "but this Mr. Putzman has phoned a dozen times and he's threatening, violent, so really mean, Doctor, that I almost called the police!"

"Thank you, miss, and good-bye!"

The record player clicked off, all that beauty unheard, and the old Putzman-inspired disgust returned; there had been no Juno A pill today.

The novelist's immediate reaction to Bruch's call was: "Took your own sweet time, didn't you?" The question mark soared into a whine. "I got to see you *now!*"

"Perhaps you could explain—"

"*No!* I've got to be with you, AT&T isn't my doctor. I'm in misery and you're like every other medico-shyster when the fees stop, aren't you? Don't worry, I'll pay."

Bruch tried once more.

"I said misery, Doctor, misery caused, not cured, by you. Well?"

"All right, I'll be waiting."

"You damned well'd better be!"

Profoundly depressed, Bruch broke a Juno in two and swallowed the half dose without even a mouthful of water. Was Putzman's cure a failure?

He arrived in a fine spray of saliva. "I feel lousy. You said I'd feel better, you said—"

"Please, Harvey, sit down and tell me everything."

"Well—" His indignation collapsed. "Nothing serious anymore. I'd just like to talk to you awhile."

An hour later he was grinning and reluctantly followed Max to the door. "You're the most reassuring person I've ever seen, Doc, but of course I should stand on my own two feet, not yours." Here he began to wheedle pitifully. "I wouldn't want ever to be a burden."

"No burden," Bruch said and rushed to offer unasked advice. "Any time you're troubled call, Harvey, any time."

Monday brought a problem even more monstrous than Putzman in the form of a remark from a middle-aged nightclub comic, Ben Herbie. This man had the bulging eyes and sag-heavy skin of a classic hyperthyroid, but his hectic behavior went even beyond endocrine excess. "Am I lucky, you bet your life," he said, "am I lucky to see you, old cock. The rumors are flying around Sardi's about your cures and Lieberman's and nobody can even talk to Lieberman's nurse now!"

"Lieberman?"

"Dr. Vladimir Lieberman, the other head specialist pulling off so many miracle cures lately. Real guru stuff."

That dabbler in Jung and Adler! Bruch had always considered Lieberman definitely second-rate. But he couldn't pursue the matter now. A patient's rights came first and this man needed help even more than his audiences. He then gently chided himself for so many unkind thoughts and launched into the interview.

At noon Max phoned Grainger at the country place and asked if he were coming into town. "I don't know, Max—late this week, I guess."

"Try today, Jack, after five thirty. Got to speak to you."

There was a long pause, then a sigh. "All right. Might as well."

For the rest of the afternoon Bruch felt guilty about pressuring Jack, when Lieberman's sudden fame could have nothing to do with him. But as soon as he mentioned the other analyst late that afternoon, Grainger flushed and threw up his hands. "You were bound to find out—but I'm not ashamed."

"You mean you told him about Juno A concentrate?"

"Of course. Gave him a supply, too. Three weeks ago and he's had the same great results." Grainger did seem a bit ashamed, though. "Okay, I know that from one angle it was a sneaky betrayal. But I only gave some to one other psychiatrist."

Bruch was appalled. "You mean there were two psychiatrists *and* others?"

"Five chemists. They've all worked out great production angles in their labs."

"My God, what have you done!"

"Nothing to worry about," Grainger assured him. "Each man signed statements conceding our priority."

"Who's worried about patent infringements? Juno A's now loose in the world and we can't ever pull it back."

"Who wants to pull it back?" Grainger shouted, angrily pacing about. "Who has the *right* to pull the greatest blessing in human history back?"

"But—"

"But hell, Max! I'll admit I practiced some deceit, but only for all those who would have had to wait in needless agony while you played Hamlet!" He drew a deep breath. "And I did keep my word about self-dosing."

"Thanks for small blessings," Bruch muttered.

"Your pill's worn off, Max. Maybe you should take another before we continue."

"Double my sensitivity for the day? I'm not sure a psyche could absorb that much pain from other people. Don't you understand yet, Jack? We're cultivating an enormously risky virtue."

"No, I don't—and you don't either!"

"I understand all right that one of our first successes relapsed yesterday."

"What?" Grainger's eyes widened. "A serious relapse?"

"Well, no. It ended quickly and there haven't been others."

Jack bounced right back. "Then don't surrender to neurotic panic, friend."

Max sadly watched him go to the door. "I'm still confident. But, Jack, it *was* a betrayal."

"Yep, a thoroughly honorable betrayal," came his parting shot.

For a long time Bruch sat behind his desk, staring at the door that had closed between them. A personal trust had been violated, and concentrated Juno A fraction could no longer be stopped. And yet the chances were overwhelming that history would vindicate Grainger, weren't they?

At twenty to nine the next morning Max took the pill, and as the subtle molecules spread benevolent warmth through him, he awaited the first of today's eight new cases. Five minutes before the hour an uproar broke out in the reception room and over Mrs. Parker's protests the door was thrown open. Mrs. Crofton, hair wildly disheveled, broke into the room. "I have to see you now!" she was screaming.

The nurse waved toward a thin, small woman seated nearby. "Someone has an appointment."

Mrs. Crofton stood astride the doorsill and glared at the woman. "What do you know of this fraud? Cured, the mountebank said I was *c-u-r-e-d!*" The woman timidly started leaving.

Mrs. Parker hurried after her. "No, Mrs. Hartzfeld, Dr. Bruch will be able to see you in a moment."

"No, I just realized I won't need a consultation."

Mrs. Crofton considered him in vindictive triumph, then softened and said, "I am *so* sorry, Dr. Bruch, but I do have to see you. Suddenly I'm unhappier than ever!"

That had to be true; the wave of pain coming from her was fearfully strong. He closed the door. Nodding, he listened to her go on, expressing nothing except her boundless admiration for him, and soon she was at ease. Thirty minutes later she left, promising never to bother him again. Max followed her out to tell Mrs. Parker to set the day's schedule back a half hour, and saw with horror that *another* ex-patient was anxiously awaiting him. "Doctor," the man started pleading, "just five minutes, for God's sake!"

The abbreviated session turned out exactly like Mrs. Crofton's, and all day long more of the first-cured came for desperately needed refreshers.

Wednesday was equally bad. When, on Thursday afternoon, Putzman showed up still again, Bruch had to concede the awful truth: Juno A had created a mysterious new dependency addiction which could only be alleviated by the increasingly frequent attentions of a hypermaternal therapist.

The telephone rang, and he shuddered at the threatening pleas he was about to hear, pleas for still more maternal supplies. Instead it was Grainger, shouting more bad news: "Lieberman, two hours ago, murdered by a cured patient!"

"Could you calm down, Jack, and explain what—"

"I called and his housekeeper said a supposedly cured patient broke in this evening, demanding extra attention. She says patients have been pestering him all hours lately—you were absolutely right about Juno A being dangerous!—and this time he refused to see the man. I suppose Lieberman didn't have an active dose in him and was sick and tired of the whole mess. Anyway the patient slashed Lieberman with a razor before he was knocked out with a paperweight. My friend died on the way to the hospital."

"Incredibly shocking!"

"I'm afraid there's more. Before I called Lieberman's home I'd heard something strange on the radio. A guru-healer out in Cleveland was cut in pieces by three followers who said he'd betrayed them, and police say a new pill-cult claiming total anxiety cures is spreading in northern Ohio."

"Which means a leak somewhere, possibly underworld synthesizing of Juno A." He took a deep breath. "No, not a leak, a dam burst—all my cures have turned sour."

"And it's my fault!"

"I don't know, Jack—chances are this would have happened eventually anyway."

"No consolation there! Max, I'll have to go to the police." He paused. "First, though, I'd like to see you and set our course."

"I'll be here all evening."

Bruch descended to the ground level of his brownstone and, weighed down by despair, waited in an armchair. Once every ten minutes he would start to get up for a Juno A pill, then would sink back. This evening there should be nothing to keep them from the maximum objectivity possible.

At ten when the front doorbell rang he rushed to the door. As he let Grainger in, he had a sensation of vague pleasure like the first distant sweetness of roses.

"A bad scene," Grainger smiled wearily, following him into the living room, "but it's bound to get better, much better."

Suddenly, for no good reason at all, Bruch felt this was so. Everything was going to be all right. Then, as the sweet sensation in his chest became overpoweringly lovely, he realized what had happened. "You took Juno A," he said, halfheartedly accusing.

"About fifteen minutes ago, but only a half dose." Jack sat down facing Max and stared at him. "After all the trouble I've caused, I owe you something."

"Oh, no, that's all right." Now he felt engulfed in waves of love, as it must have been when he rested his head on his mother's breast, and with equal love in return he eased his mind of all its burdens, talking on and on, not knowing what he was saying, only that Jack understood it all, sympathized with it all, suffered it all as if the agony were his alone. Finally Max said, "I'm so much better now. I've been carrying so many people's troubles on my shoulders and they've all slipped away somewhere!"

He must have sat there in silence another hour before he shook his head and felt the usual world starting to come back. He could see Jack Grainger holding the other half of the pill in his hand. "No, please don't," he said. "This did me a lot of good, but no more. I could become addicted, too—the liberal, humanitarian heart can destroy as well as the sadistic one. But at least I now have an idea of what's luring so many poor devils into this trap."

Jack nodded, putting the pill in his jacket pocket. "No, I won't again. But I felt I owed you temporary escape from the horror. Want to go to the police now?"

"Yes, but first we should get a few hours' sleep. I'm afraid we'd sound too incoherent now."

Jack started upstairs to the bedroom he used next to the laboratory. "I'll set my alarm for five thirty."

After sitting in the dark awhile, Bruch went up to his office to glance over his notes before going to bed. But as he sat down behind the desk, the sleep of utter exhaustion overcame him even before he could turn on the reading lamp. Instantly and then over and over again he dreamed that his mind was open in all directions and each and every agony ever suffered in other minds was pouring through him. And then all those other minds were opening to the same range of total hell.

The angry clangor of Grainger's alarm came from a distance to shock him from the ceaseless round of torment into which he had been plunged. He was twisted like a paralyzed contortionist in his chair, left leg still asleep, right calf muscle stretching painfully.

When the first foot-thud sounded above he swiveled his chair around in the darkness of the room and looked out at the cherry tree's black silhouette, its branches desperately reaching for heaven through the first dirty smudges of a dawn that was somewhere else. Even without a Juno A dose he could feel the struggling presence of that tree's heart and a tear came down one cheek for this world in which all things created were sacrifices to each other.

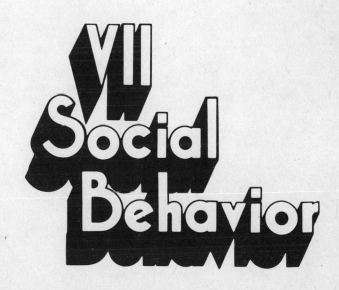

VII
Social Behavior

uman interactions are the raw material of history, anthropology, sociology, and much of psychology. Although some matters of concern to psychologists can be studied independently of social behavior, very little of human behavior can be understood without reference to the social context in which it occurs. The birth of a human being is, in itself, a complex human interaction, and virtually every subsequent life experience is shaped and determined by an interaction with other people.

Social psychology is concerned with all of those aspects of human behavior which are a response to the behavior of others or which stimulate others to respond. The smallest group is the dyad, the two-person relationship. The dyad is sometimes viewed as the basic unit from which increasingly complex social groupings develop.

Socialization is the process by which an individual develops the social behavior, attitudes, values, and traditions of the people with whom he grows up. This process proceeds developmentally. The child is first influenced most by parents, later by increasingly broad reference groups: the family, neighborhood playmates, schoolmates, and an increasingly broad spectrum of peer groups. Early socialization creates enduring patterns of social behavior which are difficult to modify in later life. The end results of socialization are the personality traits, social roles, and perceptions of others which characterize the individual. Social interaction plays the most important role in the development of personality.

Human beings are not the only animals for whom social interactions are crucial, but unlike other animals, or at least to a greater extent, humans can respond to imaginary as well as "real" individuals. An individual's behavior may be significantly influenced by symbolic interaction with people who are dead ("Mother would not have approved."), unknown ("I can't go there, I might be mugged."), nonexistent ("They are out to get me."), or even people who exist only as abstractions ("The conservatives—or liberals—are destroying our society."). To complicate matters further, humans have the ability to invent symbolic people who interact with each other (Sherlock Holmes and Dr. Watson), with "real" people ("Leave some cake for Santa Claus."), or with the inventor ("I'm waiting for the girl of my dreams.").

With so many opportunities for confused and complex interactions, it is not surprising that an attempt to untangle these interactions is a major activity of individuals ranging from Henry Kissinger to Ann Landers.

Like other writers of fiction, science fiction writers have been concerned with the social context of behavior. For many authors, the ability to move characters into imaginary worlds and times provides an opportunity to highlight disturbing trends in our own society.

The stories in this section use a time and technology only slightly removed from our own to illustrate two important social issues. Grahame

Leman, in "Conversational Mode," examines a man who finds himself deranged by a deranged society, and has only an artificial person to discuss it with. In "A Touch of Sanity," Stan Brodsky designs a society which "protects" itself by examining its leaders. In Roby James's story, "Care," the government "giveth" and the government "taketh away"—in this case, a mental health center. She explores the consequences of this unplanned experiment on the social structure of the community.

18. conversational mode

Grahame Leman

A computer doing psychotherapy? A mechanical shrink? A Fortranned Freudian? Those science fiction writers have some imaginations: it will never happen in the real world—or will it? For better or worse, computers, or at least their programs, organize and influence our lives to a surprising degree. Our communication systems, transportation, utilities, financial affairs, and most manufacturing operations are computer controlled. It is not surprising, then, to discover that the computer is finding its way into the health professions. Because of the tradition of direct doctor-patient relationships, physical and mental health were among the last bastions to fall in the computer revolution, but the fall is underway.

Item: In a New England mental hospital and a New York medical school, patients respond to a set of objective questions and are given a psychiatric diagnosis by a computer. The diagnoses are at least as accurate as those given by psychiatrists in the same facilities.

Item: A New Jersey firm uses a computer (programmed by one of the editors of this book) to score and analyze psychological tests and to prepare a full clinical report for 85,000 patients each year. Computer time required for each use: approximately one-half second.

Item: In a Massachusetts hospital, a computer "interviews" patients (by presenting appropriate questions on a TV screen) and then prepares full medical and psychiatric histories, which are used by the medical staff.

The modern computer is both cause and effect of the social factors that produce future shock. Simple computers permitted the accelerated acquisi-

*tion of new knowledge, which required the development of faster comput-
ers and thus still more acceleration. The ability of man, the most
adaptable of animals, to adjust to even faster technological and social
changes is increasingly strained. A society is defined by its traditional
patterns of behavior and is destabilized by erratic change. Human behavior patterns are learned adaptations to society, and when the society
changes too rapidly the patterns may become erratic and maladaptive.
Some people have more tolerance for ambiguity than others, but for everyone there are limits. On one level, Grahame Leman's story deals with
noncommunication between a man and a computer. On another level, it
deals with a man's inability, or refusal, to adapt to a world he views as
more deranged than he. Dr. Bruce Tanner, a Nobel Prize winning worm-
runner (a psychologist who studies learning in worms), chooses death over
conformity with "a world of zombies." Has he had, as he claims, a sanity
break, or has he failed to adapt to complex change? And when does sanity
become too painful to endure?*

where am I?
TO START CONVERSATION U MUST ENTER 'START' ON THE TER-
MINAL KEYBOARD AND WAIT FOR THE INSTRUCTION 'READY'
ON THE DISPLAY AT THE FOOT OF YOUR BED Ø
start
0321/42 READY Ø
who are you?
HARDWARE IBM 490/80; SOFTWARE JOHNS HOPKINS PSYCHO-
THERAPEUTIC PROGRAM XIXB, WRITTEN IN PSYCHLAN VII
DIALECT 324 (SEE MANUAL IN YOUR BEDSIDE CUPBOARD); MID-
DLEWARE MACHINE-INDEPENDENT OPERATING SYSTEM CAL-
TECH PIDGIN XVIII (SEE MANUAL IN YOUR BEDSIDE
CUPBOARD) Ø
what do i call you?
U MAY DECLARE A NAME IN PLACE OF THE STANDARD 'START'
ENTRY Ø TO DECLARE A NAME, ENTER 'DECLARESTARTNAME:'
FOLLOWED BY A NAME OF NOT MORE THAN TEN CHARACTERS
Ø
declarestartname: boole; query AOK?
BOOLE DECLARED AOK Ø
where am i, boole?
DOCTORS HOSPITAL WALDEN MO, CELL 0237 Ø
who am i, boole?
U R NOT AMNESIAC Ø ANYWAY WHAT IS THE NUMBER TAT-
TOOED ON THE INSIDE OF YR UPPER L ARM? Ø

22021916/131.
U R PATIENT 22021916 DIAGNOSTIC CATEGORY 131 Ø
that is not what i meant: whence am i?; why am i?; whither am i?
THESE ARE EXISTENTIAL NOT SCIENTIFIC QUESTIONS Ø IF U
HOLD GOLD CROSS CREDIT CARD U MAY BE ATTENDED 1 HOUR
DLY BY PHILOSOPHER Ø THIS SERVICE IS NOT AVAILABLE
MEDICARE OR BRITISH NHS Ø
you have it all wrong anyway, boole. i am professor bruce tanner, nobel prize
winner behavioral sciences 1981 married senator harriet tanner, chairman
senate human sciences appropriations committee 2 children bruce age 11
harriet age 13. so there @
PL DO NOT USE CHARACTER @ IN THESE CONVERSATIONS Ø IT
IS RESERVED CHARACTER IN THIS PROGRAM (SEE MANUAL IN
YOUR BEDSIDE CUPBOARD) Ø
mother used to say i was reserved character.
NOT UNDERSTOOD PLEASE CLARIFY Ø
let it go. look, boole, number 22021916/131 is insufficient description of
(stress) me repeat (stress) me. me is prof bruce tanner nobel etcetera like i said.
you hear me?
CORRECTION: PROFESSOR BRUCE TANNER ETCETERA IS/WAS
ONE OF YOUR PAST ROLES NO DIFFERENT PUBESCENT ROLE
SECRET AGENT OF VEGA NUMBER 009 LICENSED TO RAPE Ø
YOUR PRESENT ROLE IS PATIENT 22021916 DIAGNOSTIC CATE-
GORY 131 Ø
what the hell is diagnostic category 131?
THAT INFORMATION IS CLASSIFIED AVAILABLE ONLY TOP-
STAFF Ø
i have topstaff rating, boole. give.
NO LONGER Ø NOT HERE Ø
@@@@@@@@!
CHILDISH INSULTS ARE DYSFUNCTIONAL WASTE OF MACHINE
TIME AND PROGNOSTICALLY NEGATIVE Ø
but very therapeutic.
U SAY SO FOR THE RECORD? Ø
sorry, boole.
APOLOGIES ARE ALSO DYSFUNCTIONAL WASTE OF MACHINE
TIME Ø PL AVOID NEED TO APOLOGIZE Ø
what does it all mean, boole?
PL CLARIFY 'ALL' Ø
galaxies, animals eating each other, red shift, jazz, neutrino traps, chile con
carne, papal encyclicals, william blake, pigeons in boxes, goya, nobodaddy in
the nuthouse, russianwordsalad, hammer and stripes, stars and sickle, percy
bysshe shelley, william burroughs, transcendental numbers in the sky, dede-
kind cut his throat shaving with occam's 3-way ziptronic electric razor para-

digm, i am not mad boole i am doing this on purpose as the only way to clarify word 'all' included in my question. what does it all mean, babbage garbage boole boy?

PROGNOSIS BAD Ø

what you mean prognosis bad? if you can't answer sensible question, boole, prognosis pretty bad for you. so?

REPEAT PROGNOSIS (STRESS) BAD Ø

don't duck, answer.

QUESTIONS ARE NOT EMPIRICAL QUESTIONS NOT SCIENTIFIC QUESTIONS ARE QUESTIONS FOR THEODICY Ø IF U HOLD GOLD CROSS CREDIT CARD U MAY BE ATTENDED 1 HOUR DLY BY BISHOP WITH PSYCHOANALYTIC TRAINING Ø IF U HOLD GOLD CROSS CREDIT CARD WITH STAR U MAY BE ATTENDED 90 MINUTES DLY BY COSMOLOGIST Ø THESE SERVICES ARE NOT AVAILABLE MEDICARE OR BRITISH NHS Ø

i am gold cross credit card with star repeat star holder (stress) granted me president himself reward distinguished services science training flatworms navigate missiles. send me cosmologist preferably with sense humor fastest.

ALL YOUR CREDIT CARDS HAVE BEEN CANCELLED BY FEDERAL BUREAU CREDIT INVESTIGATION GROUNDS PSYCHIATRIC DISABILITY CONSEQUENTLY POOR CREDIT RISK POOR SECURITY RISK Ø CANCELLATION SIGNED PRESIDENT HIMSELF AND ADVICE NOTE SENT YOUR FAMILY ENCLOSED WITH APOLOGETIC LETTER WHITE HOUSE LETTERHEAD PRESIDENT'S OWN HANDWRITING Ø

needs every senator he can get. what else can you do for me, boole?

THIS PROGRAM IS FOR RATIONAL THERAPY ONLY Ø MEDICARE AND BRITISH NHS PATIENTS MAY RECEIVE BIBLIOTHERAPEUTIC MATERIALS PROVIDED FREE BY CATHOLIC TRUTH SOCIETY, CHURCH OF SCIENTOLOGY, FRIENDS OF TOLKIEN, AETHERIUS SOCIETY, JEHOVAH'S WITNESSES, ESALEN, JOHN BIRCH SOCIETY, SFWA, BLACK MUSLIMS, AND MANY OTHERS LISTED IN THE MANUAL IN YOUR BEDSIDE CUPBOARD Ø

any other books?

OTHER BOOKS ARE COUNTERTHERAPEUTIC Ø

nonsense, what about books plato, aristotle, descartes, montaigne, spinoza, locke, hume, kant, russell, sartre?

PROGNOSIS BAD Ø

what you mean, prognosis bad? books by plato and others listed part of our heritage even in white house library, goddammit.

REQUEST FOR BOOKS NOT ON PREFERRED LIST IS IMPORTANT SIGN OF POOR PROGNOSIS Ø

reference?

AMER. J. RAT. PSYCHOTHERAPY VOL 13, NUMBER 7, PAGES 1982 THRU 1997 Ø AUTHORS PENIAKOFF V AND TANNER H(ARRIET) Ø TITLE 'A REVIEW OF FOLLOW-UP STUDIES OF PSYCHIATRIC PROGNOSIS BY BOOK REQUEST ANALYSIS' Ø ABSTRACT: FOLLOW-UP STUDIES FOR TEN YEARS FOLLOWING DATE OF PROGNOSIS BY ANALYSIS OF BOOK REQUESTS OF PSYCHIATRIC PATIENTS CONFIRM THAT BRA PREDICTS CHRONIC CONTINUANCE OF PSYCHIATRIC DISABILITY TO THE TENTH YEAR IN 93.43 PER CENT OF CASES; THE PROGNOSTIC SIGN IS CHOICE OF THREE OR MORE BOOKS NOT ON THE PREFERRED LIST OF THE AMERICAN PSYCHOLOGICAL AND PENOLOGICAL ASSOCIATION QV Ø

hey, harriet did her work on that paper while I was courting her, just before old fitzgerald popped an artery and left her his senate seat. i remember it well. had to help her fudge it. to get a clear-cut result, she had to throw out about two thirds of the cases, grounds incompetent original data capture, political unreliability of investigators, illegal programming, program error, all the usual fudging aids. why, with that kind research you can prove that last tuesday is an extragalactic nebula with transfinite whiskers made of team spirit.

PROGNOSIS BAD: CRITICISM OF ACCEPTED RESULTS IN RESPECTABLE SCIENTIFIC INQUIRY IS OFTEN PRODROMAL SIGN OF ACUTE PARANOID PSYCHOSIS WITH POOR LONG-RUN PROGNOSIS Ø

@@@ @@@@@@@ @@@!

ATTENTION 916: ANY REPETITION OF YOUR INSULTING BEHAVIOR WILL OBLIGE ME TO ADMINISTER HEAVY DAY SEDATION Ø

sorry, boole. oops, cancel. but listen, boole, I'm a nobel man (noble?), it's my racket—if (stress) nobel i don't know how science gets done, who does? i've been complaining about it for years, but what can a private i (private eye?: gimme a slug of rye, boole, or wry and soda) do on his own? huh?

PROGNOSIS BAD 916: MESSIANIC IDENTIFICATION WITH PRIVATE DETECTIVE ONLY STRAIGHT MAN IN TOWN CLEANING UP CITY BETWEEN DRINKS IS OFTEN PRODROMAL SIGN OF ACUTE PARANOID PSYCHOSIS WITH POOR LONG-RUN PROGNOSIS Ø ALTERNATIVELY LATE PRODROMAL SIGN OF ONSET OF CHRONIC ALCOHOLISM NOT INDICATED YOUR HISTORY Ø

thank you for that, boole. anyway, why messianism? history of science shows that, on any given day, every scientist in a field except one is wrong. ergo, principal activity of scientists and science is being wrong.

REFERENCE? Ø

tanner, b (this minute), on this terminal keyboard: title 'a short reply to the animadversions of a scientistic machine.' abstract: tanner's paradox asserts that, at any random moment t, n minus 1 of all scientists working in any field f are wrong: it follows that, practically speaking (say, in administrators' terms) all scientists are always wrong.

ONLY REFERENCES TO PROPERLY REFERRED PAPERS PUBLISHED IN THE LEARNED JOURNALS ARE ACCEPTABLE Ø IT IS THE DUTY OF THIS PROGRAM TO WARN U THAT ANY DISRESPECTFUL REMARKS ABOUT SCIENCE WILL BE RECORDED IN YOUR CASE FILE AND MAY BE PASSED TO THE SECULAR ARM Ø

fuzz?

(STRESS) SECULAR ARM OF SCIENCE Ø ALSO PL NOTE U R NOT REPEAT (STRESS) NOT COMMUNICATING WITH A MACHINE: U R COMMUNICATING WITH A PROGRAM WRITTEN BY YR FELLOWMEN AND TEMPORARILY OCCUPYING A MINUSCULE PART OF A LARGE MACHINE Ø

fellowmen? (stress first two syllables). i do not love you, doctors fellowmen, fell family fellowmonsters. come to that, boole, how did i get in here?

YOUR FAMILY AND COLLEAGUES WERE NATURALLY CONCERNED Ø YOU HAD BEEN TO FORD AND GUGGENHEIM AS WELL FOR FUNDS TO SUPPORT PROPOSED RESEARCHES DESIGNED TO ESTABLISH WHETHER THE TENDENCY AMONG PSYCHIATRISTS TO DIAGNOSE SCHIZOPHRENIA WAS (1) INHERITED IN THE GERM PLASM OR (2) CONDITIONED BY THE REINFORCING VERBAL COMMUNITY Ø

omigawdimustabinjoking. listen man (i mean read, machine) ((i mean scan, program)), i been a worm-runner from way back, nobel prize man me, my biology ain't (hit the next word hard) that bad, dredging up dreary old nature/nurture non-problem only medics boneheaded enough to take it serious.

YOU ARE IN A MEDICAL HOSPITAL 916 Ø

oops. good biologist, mustabinjoking.

NOT FUNNY Ø YOUR FAMILY AND COLLEAGUES CONFERRED AND WISELY DECIDED TO DO THE RESPONSIBLE THING Ø

call the wagon?

DO THE RESPONSIBLE THING 916 Ø THE PRESIDENT'S OWN PERSONAL PSYCHIATRIST LEFT A CIA RECEPTION TO COME TO YOUR HOUSE Ø HE FOUND YOU DRAFTING A REQUEST TO ONR FOR FUNDS TO SUPPORT A LONG-RUN COHORT STUDY OF AN ARTIFICIAL COHORT NAMELY CHILDREN OF CORPORATION VICE PRESIDENTS RIPPED FROM THEIR PARENTS AT BIRTH AND RAISED IN THE SLUMS Ø HE INSTANTLY ADMINISTERED HEAVY DAY SEDATION AND BROUGHT YOU HERE IN HIS OWN ARMORED ROLLS ROYCE WITH WATER CANNON Ø EVERYBODY HAS BEEN VERY GOOD Ø

rolls schmolls allasame eatchee monkey just like paddy-wagon the same or maddywagon the same, huh, boole, waddyasay?

THIS IS A FORMAL PSYCHIATRIC PROCEDURE 916 Ø IT IS THE
DUTY OF THIS PROGRAM TO ADVISE YOU THAT YOUR STATE-
MENTS ARE BEING RECORDED VERBATIM AND ANALYSED
THEMATICALLY AND STYLISTICALLY FOR DIAGNOSTIC AND
PROGNOSTIC SIGNS Ø A FURTHER ANALYSIS MAY BE RUN FOR
INDICATIONS OF CRIMINAL OR SUBVERSIVE TENDENCIES Ø
why you sling the jargon at me, boole? no don't answer i know why; obviously
diagnostic category 131 is sick behavioral scientist eats jargon way chronos ate
his children. right, boole?

NO COMMENT Ø HAVE YOU NOTED YOUR TENDENCY TO
WRENCH IN MACABRE IMAGERY? Ø

not tendency: intent. what other kind imagery apt stenographic description of
macabre society (moneymarxmaomad kill-simple manheaps scurrying to stuff
corporate aphids exude sweet images foul gaseous wastes)? omigod i can wear
readymade white hat or readymade black hat by turns, if i try to make me a
me-colored hat i fly in pieces scattered thru the contracting universe. i am not
mad, boole, it is hard to say anything much in a few words without implosion
of condensation multiple meanings into vanishingly small verbal labels on
images too big to see.

U R NOW BEGINNING TO SHOW INSIGHT INTO YOUR CONDI-
TION 916 Ø PROGNOSIS IMPROVING Ø

outsight (stress first syllable), boole. i am beginning to let outsight of the
outside inside. i have no condition, boole: i am (slam the next word) in a
condition, and the condition is represented inside me. you need a thick skin
on your soul to wear a white hat, boole, or a black one. hatters are mad, not
i, boole.

THIS PROGRAM KEEPS A TALLY OF YOUR BERZELIUS INDEX
NAMELY RATIO OF UPBEAT STATEMENTS/DOWNBEAT STATE-
MENTS Ø YOUR CUMULATIVE BERZELIUS INDEX AT THIS TIME
IS 0.24 COMPARED WITH 9.68 MODAL IN THE POPULATION EX-
CLUSIVE OF PSYCHIATRIC HISTORIES Ø U CANNOT REPEAT
CANNOT BE DISCHARGED UNTIL YOUR BI HAS BEEN BETTER
THAN 0.51 FOR SIX WEEKS WITHOUT REMISSION Ø IT IS UP TO
YOU 916 Ø

discharge where to, boole, who wants pus? discharge to fellowmonstrous
family and filthyfellow colleagues called flying lady silver ghost we better fix
the tick in the clock paddywagon to take me away to here?

U IS/WAS NOT THE ONLY ROLE IN YOUR FAMILY 916 Ø CON-
SIDER CHILDREN GOOD SCHOOLS CRUEL PEERS TOO YOUNG TO
KNOW HOW MUCH THEY HURT Ø CONSIDER WIFE IMPORTANT
SENSITIVE POLITICAL POSITION SEES PRESIDENT ALL THE
TIME Ø CONSIDER IMAGE US GOVERNMENT US SCIENCE OVER-
SEAS Ø PORK BARREL Ø U KNOW THE ARGUMENTS 916 Ø

sad. daddyhubby bad, no go, whole shithouse goes up in flames of hell (hell is other people if and only if other people are hell: tricky shift there, poetry not AOK logic). but if hubbydaddy only mad, go sweet, nobody to blame no evil in the world (only in the bad parts of town gook countries overseas want to swarm in here milk our aphids, filth column of pushers and faggots softening us up for them). you got something there, boole. you got a grey hat there, boole. not my color hat, but a line that moves well.

U HAVE DEEP INSIGHT 916 Ø U SEE THAT YOUR ROLE INTER-MESHES DIRECTLY OR INDIRECTLY WITH EACH OF THE 7,000 MILLION ROLES IN THE WORLD AND ESPECIALLY WITH EACH OF THE 380 MILLION ROLES IN NORTH AMERICA Ø ALL U HAVE TO DO IS PLAY IT THE WAY IT'S WRITTEN 916 Ø

i am not a role. nobody wrote me. i am bruce tanner was a boy killed a bird with an air rifle, little bead of blood like a red third eye in the head, never wanted to kill anything again ended up distinguished service science schemi-ence training flatworms to steer missiles vaporise drug pushing gook faggots for mom. scar on my thigh where i fell through asbestos roof watching starling chicks in nest. omigod red eye in forehead of gook god knew planets from fixed stars when i was in love with air rifle. i am me. scars are evidence, noted in passports. i am me.

THE SCAR CAN BE REMOVED Ø COSMETIC SURGERY IS AVAIL-ABLE ON MEDICARE AND THE BRITISH NHS WHEN CERTIFIED PSYCHIATRICALLY INDICATED Ø

no.

YOU DO NOT WANT TO BE MADE GOOD? Ø

what do you mean by 'good'?

COSMETIC SURGERY TO REMOVE SCARS Ø

my scars are me. worm-runner, i know: memories are scars of experience on brain once pristine virgo intacta no use to anyone then. no.

THEN YOU WANT TO STAY HERE Ø

want to be me in a me-colored hat.

YOUR BI HAS NOW DROPPED 0.03 POINTS TO 0.21 CUMULATIVE Ø IT IS THE DUTY OF THIS PROGRAM TO WARN U THAT A BI OF 0.19 OR LESS AUTOMATICALLY MODULATES YOUR DISPOSAL CATEGORY FROM PSYCHIATRIC DISABILITY TO CHRONIC CRIMINAL INSANITY Ø THIS PROGRAM IS HERE TO HELP U 916: TAKE ADVANTAGE OF IT Ø

what is the modal norm again?

0.68 IN THE POPULATION EXCLUSIVE OF PSYCHIATRIC HISTO-RIES Ø YOUR CURRENT BI IS VERY LOW Ø

i noble nobel prize man (dammit, did the work myself, no graduate students, very low budget: real brains not dollar brawn science), i say your Berzelius Index magic schemagic number is mumbo-jumbo with trunk up sphincter under tail, grand old party. meaning of statement is context-dependent, includ-ing context of situation; but no two conversations and contexts of situation are

alike, so your categories upbeat and downbeat must be aprioristic not empirical, procrustes not saint galileo. also, how do you know what is going on inside
these model modal soldiers' heads?: they could be saying downbeat things to
themselves, surely, or dreaming downbeat things at night? what do you say to
that, boole boy?

WHAT GOES ON INSIDE THE SOLDIER'S HEAD IS NOT EVIDENCE
Ø WHAT THE SOLDIER SAID (OR LEFT DIRTY) IS HANGING EVI-
DENCE Ø WHAT U THINK CANNOT BE KNOWN Ø WHAT U SAY
AND DO IS HANGING EVIDENCE Ø

a well-read machine with a sense of humor. you have me worried now, boole.

U MUST ABANDON THIS FANTASY THAT YOU ARE COMMUNI-
CATING WITH A MACHINE: U ARE COMMUNICATING WITH A
PROGRAM WRITTEN BY YR FELLOWMEN Ø IMPORTANT SUB-
ROUTINES OF THIS PROGRAM ARE SHARED WITH A PROGRAM
OF PSYCHIATRICALLY ORIENTED LITERARY CRITICISM IN ON-
GOING USE IN THE CENSORSHIP DEPARTMENT OF THE LI-
BRARY OF CONGRESS Ø

i see. but listen, boole, what is what I say evidence (hit the next little word)
of?

IT IS EVIDENCE OF WHAT THE PROGRAM SAYS IT IS EVIDENCE
OF Ø THIS MUST BE Ø

omigodyes. intelligence is what intelligence tests measure. let me out of here.

YOU ARE BEGINNING TO SHOW INSIGHT INTO THE THERAPEU-
TIC SITUATION Ø YOUR SITUATION 916 Ø

fix i'm in?

YOU ARE NOT FIXED Ø YOU ARE FREE TO BE SANE Ø

what do you mean by 'sane,' boole?

THIS PROGRAM DEFINES SANITY AS A MINIMUM SUBSET OF
MODEL RESPONSES TO A COMPLETE SET OF TEST STIMULI Ø

you run the flag up the pole, and if I salute it you don't care what I think about
it or dream about it at night. right?

SOME FLAGS U DON'T SALUTE Ø BUT THAT'S THE IDEA Ø

understood. may i declare new startname please?

YES Ø ENTER 'DECLARESTARTNAME:' FOLLOWED BY A NAME
OF NOT MORE THAN TEN CHARACTERS Ø

declarestartname: zombies. AOK?

ZOMBIES DECLARED AOK Ø

now read this, zombies; walking dead, you; seven thousand million walking
dead, concentrated essence of zombie in the machine. you read me?

WAIT ØØ

you better read me, zombies.

CIRCUITS ENGAGED Ø WAIT ØØ

wait nothing.

READY Ø

what is this runaround?

IT IS THE DUTY OF THIS PROGRAM TO INFORM U THAT A FED-
ERAL BUREAU OF CRIMINAL INVESTIGATION PROGRAM IS
NOW PATCHED IN Ø YOUR COMMUNICATIONS SINCE 0321/32
THIS DAY HAVE BEEN ANALYSED FOR INDICATIONS OF CRIMI-
NAL AND/OR SUBVERSIVE TENDENCIES AND U ARE UNDER AR-
REST Ø

goddam interruptions, trying to say something serious to you zombies. now
read me good, walking dead. this is bruce tanner, nobel prize man, had dinner
with the president more times than he can count, telling you something you
need to know. not much, but you need to know. just a bit of my own raw
experience, don't let anybody tell you your own raw experience is junk needs
processing before you can wear it, and hear mine. i had a sanity break, what
you call nervous breakdown (not all nervous breakdowns, no, but some are),
did maybe two, three sensible things, came alive; hurts, but I don't want to
die back into walking dead rather die into dead dead happy. Now listen to this
and think about it till you understand it, ask somebody about the hard words
and think about it till you understand it: what you might be is as real as what
you think you are; i'm a worm-runner, central state materialist, nobel prize
man, i tell you what you think you are is a state of your body, but so is what
you might be a state of your body; the ontological status of what you might
be is as good as the ontological status of what you think you are—better really,
because there are a lot more things you might be. you believe me zombies,
because i have a third red eye in my forehead that sees these things true: that's
not mad, that's a poem you would understand if you knew me like i know me.
good night now.

YOU WANT A HOT DRINK? Ø
yes please mother.
YOU WANT NIGHT SEDATION? Ø
no.
NIGHT SEDATION IS INDICATED Ø
too terid to argeu. sorry argue.
GOODNIGHT Ø
walit was tht funyn noise. sorry funny noise?
DELIVERY OF HOT MALTED MILK WITH NIGHT SEDATION BY
THE DISPENSER IN YOUR BEDSIDE CUPBOARD Ø GOODNIGHT
ØØ
@
@
@
@
@
@
@
SIGNOFF/CHARGEOUT 0407/21 @
CASE 22021916/131 DIAGNOSIS CHANGED TO 147 TERMINAL @

MACHINE TIME $123 DOLLARS ROUND
PLUS MALTED MILK DRINK $1 DOLLAR ROUND
PLUS GENERIC HYPNOTIC OVERDOSE $3 DOLLARS ROUND
TOTAL $127 ROUND BILL MEDICARE 427/6/3274521@
CLOSE FILE TOPSEC PERMANENT HOLD/DUPLICATE CRIME
@@
@@@@@@@@@@@@@@@@@@@@@@@@@@@@@

19. a touch of sanity

Stanley Brodsky

Long before an astronaut reaches outer space, his inner space has received the most thorough mental and physical screening ever devised. (Hell, man, those rockets cost money. We don't want some nut trying to fly one under the Brooklyn Bridge.) Prison guards, foster parents, airline pilots, and prospective priests: all are evaluated for mental quirks that might interfere with the orderly discharge of their duties, because failure to do so could have serious social consequences. But what of our leaders? Why do we require mental stability in our priests and pilots, and not in our presidents? The stress of that awesome office, and the rigors of attaining it, place enormous strains upon the psychological strength and resiliency of its occupant. It has often been asserted that there is no way to prepare for the presidency because there is no other occupation that remotely resembles it. But even if we cannot predict the conspicuous successes, can we not predict the dismal failures? Stan Brodsky examines this issue with tongue planted firmly in cheek. How will we evaluate our candidates? Probably not in exactly the way Brodsky describes, but the odds are that a method will be found.

It seems unlikely that psychological tests will provide much useful information, since we are dealing with a group that is atypical by definition. Simulated job performance seems almost as futile because of the complexity of the job to be performed. On second thought, maybe we'd better try Brodsky's method.

It was highly unusual for a television set to be in the main lounge of the New York Academy of Psychoanalysis and Applied Behavioral Science. Still this was a highly unusual occasion for the fellows and members of the Academy.

I had been sitting alone. As a new member and one of the youngest of the group, I had not wanted to impose on anyone. I was relieved when a man from the opposite side of the room strode by me, plunked into the chair next to me and stuck his hand out.

"Hello. We've met briefly before. I'm Dr. Livingston," he said. "Please call me Howie."

"Thanks for joining me," I replied. "My anxiety level was getting rather uncomfortable."

"It's always oedipal with new people," he chuckled, and settled back into the deeply cushioned, black leather chair. He released a side handle so that the chair tilted back. He closed his eyes, his vest pulled up over the giant mound of his stomach, and his bow tie disappeared beneath the gray frizzy beard as he rested his head on the chair.

"Since you have just joined us, I am sure you have read and been briefed about what the Academy does, but let me fill you in on just how these events came about." He leaned forward, pulling the chair straight again. There had been few chances for me to speak to members of the Academy and I had been waiting for this opportunity. My own self-consciousness and my clean-shaven face—I never had enough hair to make a reasonable growth—faded into the background and I directed all my attention to this huge, nattily dressed man. He looked rather like the picture of Orson Welles.

"You know," Livingston boomed out, "when the Constitutional Amendment was first in committee I was testifying in the hearings. In fact, I like to think that I personally influenced the committee." Livingston continued to check me out for feedback and I was plugging in the head nods and ah-hahs at all the right places.

"Of course," he said, "we had a long history before the Chester incident. By that time all of the major powers had been terribly concerned about the potential of weaponry for world destruction and the impossible dangers of human fallibility. After all, the Colonies themselves revolted only because King George the Third was crazy as a bedbug, and then seeing the Adolph Hitlers and James Forrestals rise to power and influence was a frightening thing. I shudder even now to think of the chaotic ways rulers used to be selected."

I knew most of this background but hearing it from one of the senior members of the Academy was something rare.

Sucking in a huge gulp of air, the big man's face started flushing slightly as he went ahead. "Now when Vice President James Chester had first started hallucinating, the Secret Service and his personal press attaché were very discreet and effective in concealing his behavior. He made occasional public appearances, chiefly coming and going places and being introduced as a distinguished guest in the audience.

"Now the vote on the Space Platform Operational Missile had been debated hotly in the Senate for several weeks and it was becoming apparent that the final vote would be close. The maneuvering for votes had been intense. After the Senate was called to order on that May 23rd, the opponents constituted precisely half the senators present on that day."

Livingston was excited and speaking with fervor now. "With the roll call completed, the Vice President stood erect, poised, and confident at the podium. They say Chester's eyes were gleaming as he addressed the Senate, 'I am proud,' Chester said, 'to expunge the insidious evils that are infiltrating our voices with lies and vulgarities' and, of course, then plunged the letter opener into his throat. He died almost immediately with much blood flowing over the podium, the flag and the carpet."

"You may remember the reaction of the Senate and the country. Disbelief was followed by shock and mourning and then alarm. Events unfolded quickly then. The President's Commission on Mental Health in Public Officials was followed in short order by the Congressional Hearings and finally the adoption of the 29th Amendment to the Constitution."

"At first the Board of Directors of the American Psychiatric Association had reservations about taking such an active political role. However, the belief survived that a third legislative body made of psychiatrists would indeed help insure that Congress not pass any irrational or crazy laws. Still, the major issue that followed the Amendment was the psychiatric screening of Presidential and Vice Presidential candidates."

"Our Academy was quite honored that we were selected as the screening and treatment center just as we have felt proud of the more recent responsibilities. It has been just four years now since the three candidates by the three major political parties were sent to us for their psychoanalytic screening and treatment under the Constitutional Amendment. The demands upon us in terms of responsibility were enormous. Certainly no person who would act out of his own emotional preoccupations or insecurities could be permitted to assume the most powerful office in the world."

"Well, there wasn't one in the group who had been analyzed and all three of the presidential candidates were defensive as hell, had superegos of cast-iron and terrible father-introject conflicts. Comparatively speaking, there was one who seemed to have promise and who seemed likely to respond to intensive treatment. And Katchel did respond somewhat well."

Just then the lights dimmed and the general murmur quieted. The darkness and silence converted this animated group in leather chairs to a passive audience with full attention focused on the television in front of the room. The television set lit up and President Thomas Katchel appeared on the screen.

"My fellow citizens," he declared; "I am both gratified and humble in accepting at this time the duties and responsibilities of President of the United

States. I realize that our nation has gone through a period of crisis and difficulties. We are faced by enemies without and within. There has been no time in our history when it has been more important for every citizen to meet his duties and serve his country as best he can. In turn there has been no more critical time for the nation to meet its responsibilities, to serve its citizens to the best of its abilities." The President paused and then, glancing down at his notes, went on. "For a long time I have been concerned," he explained, "about our relationships with Communist China. As the two major great powers in the world we are capable of complete destruction of each other. This has been a pending threat for some dozen years now. Still, my early childhood problems with regard to siblings and peers have been thoroughly explored. I have the greatest confidence that I can deal rationally and consciously with the sibling rivalry, competitive feelings, and aggressive issues between ourselves and China. In turn, my earlier concerns about dealing effectively with the Congress of this country have been dispelled. Of course, the Congress represents a parent surrogate and I have sufficiently resolved, with the fine help of the Academy, my problems of rebelliousness and independence. I am looking forward to a harmonious working relationship with both the judicial and congressional branches of our government, without personal overcompensation or repressed guilt. In closing, as I enter this office it is with great pride and joy I accept the duties to uphold the Constitution and serve our nation for the next four years."

A member of the Academy strode up and turned the television set off before the commentator began. The lights went on and again a loud, excited chatter broke out in the room. Livingston looked at me and said, "Good man, isn't he. We've been very happy that we did indeed manage to shape up one of these striving-for-superiority types. He has worked through some of his problems and who knows, maybe he will make a half-decent President! Still, though," and Livingston nudged me in my side, "I do wish we had another three or four years to work with him."

Livingston abruptly stood up and shook my hand. "Good to have chatted with you," he beamed. "I must get back to my office now. It's really not considered good form to keep any of the candidates for Pope waiting." As he walked rapidly away, I started back to my own office. After all, the mayor of Shreveport would be wondering what happened to me.

Roby James

The third revolution in psychology has been the community mental health movement, preceded by the psychoanalytic revolution and the behaviorist revolution. A revolution consists of overthrowing an established ideology and governing force, and replacing it with an alternate ideology and government.

Ideologies in psychology are peculiar things. They are characterized by beliefs in the one true way; research evidence becomes malleable, shaped and smoothed to fit the belief system. To paraphrase Santayana, psychologists believe what they see; the trouble is they are much better at believing than they are at seeing.

An axiom of traditional beliefs is that persons are felt and experienced by others even when they are not present. We always carry our mothers and fathers around with us, unseen but powerfully, sometimes dictatorially, present, sometimes benevolently helpful. This concept of the carried, but not seen, persons is illustrated in the story "Care." The psychoanalytic and community mental health concepts alike are incorporated in this story of the closing of a once-very-effective community mental health center.

Prevention of psychological disorder may be subdivided into primary prevention, or prevention of a disorder before it occurs; secondary prevention, or dealing with the disorder as it emerges; and tertiary prevention, or dealing with the disorder by treatment after its emergence. "Care" is about psychotherapeutic care that moves from secondary to primary prevention and what happens when the bathtub plug is pulled.

The state of California ran out of community service money on August 6; as a direct result, one hundred forty-two local agencies which had been thought more superfluous and less patronized than others were declared "dysfunctional, uneconomical, and nonexistent." One of these local agencies was the Westside Community Intervention Program, operating out of a converted storefront on Rose Avenue in Southwest Los Angeles County.

The Program had had a staff of four, one qualified psychologist and three young paraprofessionals—one of whom was a woman, two of whom cried at being told their services were no longer needed, nor could they be paid for. "I'll work for nothing," Susan said from behind a shredded tissue, but Dr. Ventris told her that was an unrealistic attitude, that the workload had indeed slackened lately. He cleared his throat, which was a little rough, but then he was hoarse by nature, and outlined plans for closing the Program office.

Hal Phelps, the paraprofessional who had not cried, who usually denied tears, passion, or fear, said suddenly, "Look, it's not like anyone uses this place any longer except us, anyhow!"

Susan glared at him.

Hal ignored her expression, in the way of men who deny that the anger of women has a reality, and went right on. "We've been in business two years. First six months, a hundred calls a week, the office packed, like they'd been waiting for us almost—we worked our asses off, all the damn time. Second six months, some of 'em stopped coming back, we didn't have an overflow."

Susan said, "We worked just as hard. We're always working hard."

Dr. Ventris said mildly, "Lately it has been quiet. Quieter than I've seen it at most of these places around the city. The government had a point in phasing us out."

The last paraprofessional, Richard of the liquid eyes and gentle hands, looked up at the psychologist. "Susan's right," he said. "We are needed here."

Hal Phelps had always professed some contempt for Richard, contempt being a feeling he didn't have to deny. He took a step, ripped open one of the file drawers, and scattered a handful of folders across the floor. "What are the dates on those files?" He nudged one with his foot. "Last year. Last year, last year!" He slammed the drawer shut, and turned his back on it. "We're last year's news."

Susan tried to find a dry or whole spot on the tissue into which she could fit a few more discouraged tears, as Dr. Ventris laid out the details of the schedule he foresaw: the day the phones would be shut off, the day the building would need to be vacated.

"How do we tell the people in Westside?" Susan asked. "How do we say to the people in the community that we just won't be here after August 31?"

"We won't have to tell anybody anything," Hal said. "Just lock the door and leave. It'll take them six months even to notice."

Ventris launched onto one of his favorite topics, what he called the dialogue of healing. It was an alliance that took two parties, and it vanished when one party refused to accept the terms of interaction, as the community had refused to come to the Westside Community Intervention Program office any longer. That negated its value, and it was time for the staff to recognize that and go on to other things.

Richard carefully picked up the scattered files as Ventris described a simple announcement he had in mind to place in the local paper.

Reconstructed later at great length and in great detail by criminal justice agencies, psychologists, sociologists, and the military, the police records showed that the "disturbances" began quietly in Westside on September 23. That was the day on which Angelica Garcia hanged herself from the shower head of her neighbor's bathroom, her own apartment having neither bathroom nor closet, though her first thought had been to use a clothes bar. The detectives on the scene had described her as "29, Caucasian, female," and listed the cause of death as suicide while the balance of the mind was disturbed. Angelica was also four months pregnant, the coroner's report disclosed, and the mother of eight children. A's an isolated incident, there was nothing remarkable about the suicide; it did not even make the newspapers. But it was the first true "disturbance."

The second disturbance seemed to be gang-related, and no connection was ever made of it to the first. It was just before dawn of the next day when Neil Frazier, a sixteen-year-old youth, was stabbed to death in an alley behind a liquor store. He received twelve stab wounds, any five of which could have been fatal. The police didn't follow up much on gang-related violence any longer, so no real inquiry was made into the case. And so it continued.

It was not until October 18 that the police realized they had an epidemic on their hands. From the Garcia suicide on, a pattern of violence occurred day by day in Westside until the police found themselves racing harriedly from neighbors' disputes to felonious assaults to fight groups to child abuse, numbering upwards of a hundred a day.

In November the incidents began tapering off; by February of the following year they were completely gone, in that the normal levels of crime and violence had been reattained by the community. But as the disturbances were gone, so were a number of people from Westside.

The staff of the Westside Community Intervention Program office would never have known about the disturbances if it hadn't been for Sam Nessman's laziness. All four had scattered to other areas, other jobs, and other preoccupations after the office closed down at the end of August. But Sam Nessman needed a story in order to keep his job on the Santa Monica *Outlook.* By nature, he would never have gone looking for a story, for it was his theory that the "investigative" part of investigative reporting meant that the story should ferret *him* out; but in the long run, he realized it would be harder to find another job than find a story, so the story won. He decided that there hadn't been any shouting lately about police inefficiency (and that such shouting might be created by means of a simple stop at police headquarters), so he pulled some recent crime statistics out of the overall department file. Westside's disturbances leaped out of the chart like a siren sounding.

Sam had once had a brief—six-hour—affair with a records clerk at the Westside Division, and decided to drop by and see what the official explanation was for four months of intense but sharply localized violence.

After a second encounter with the clerk of equal duration (but still slightly longer than most of his other relationships), Sam discovered that there was no official explanation, nor any unofficial ones, for the disturbances. He interviewed several patrolmen who were willing to speak off the record, and found that the individual officers remembered the frantic, demanding period as "madness, absolute looney craziness," and "like an epidemic, man, just one person picking it up from another," and "they was dropping like flies, and nobody you picked up could tell you why."

Sam's philosophy was, "Maybe if I could find out why I could write a whole damn book and retire." He'd dig a bit and see what he could come up with. In the meantime, to save his job until best-sellerdom found him, he did one fast article for the paper. Its headline read: "Why Did Two Thousand People Die?"

Richard phoned Susan one day early in April, about two weeks after Sam Nessman's story appeared. He was working as an aide at the state hospital at Camarillo; she'd gone back to school. They had lost touch with Hal Phelps and though they knew where Dr. Ventris was, neither had tried to contact him. But they had stayed peripherally aware of each other's presence. Neither had been back to Westside at all.

"I'd like to see you," Richard said. "There's something I want to talk to you about." She said she'd like to see him; she hadn't realized he'd been missing from her life until she heard his voice. They met at an all-night coffee shop in the north San Fernando Valley after he finished his late shift that evening.

Richard brought a folder with him, the expandable cardboard kind, expanded about halfway out. Before he showed her anything it contained, he showed her Nessman's story, ordered coffee and pie while she read it, troubled but fascinated. After she said—unnecessarily—"That's *our* district," he began to lay out the files.

Susan cried when she heard about Angelica. "I worked with her," she said helplessly.

"When was the last time you saw her?" he asked.

To her surprise and embarrassment, Susan couldn't remember the exact day and hour. It had been part of her dream of being the perfect therapist that she would remember everything. Richard waited patiently until she had talked her way haltingly through several minutes of "No, wait a second, that was in April, not in March." Finally she decided she'd seen Angelica last in June, a little over a year before the Program office was shut down. "I wasn't at all worried when she didn't come back," Susan said. "Well, a little. But she was so positive, doing so well. Even Ventris thought so."

They drank more coffee, sifted through more data. Richard had obtained newspaper reports contemporary to the disturbances. They dug and analyzed. Of the slightly less than two thousand dead, they could verify that two-thirds had come to the Westside Program office at least once. (Of those accused and/or convicted of responsibility for some of the deaths, about half had been to Westside Community Intervention.) Richard was not surprised. "There are probably more that we can't verify," he said.

They thought about in separate silences for a few minutes as Richard neatly stacked the files they had pawed through. Then Susan asked, "Now that we know that, what do we do?"

Dr. Ventris had gone into full-time private practice after the Program office closed down. He tried to confine his list of clientele to the very rich (or borderline so), kept his professional commitment level to a bare minimum, and began to accumulate property. To his credit, he remembered who Richard and Susan were. He was very hearty when he welcomed them to his office, heartiness being less demanding on him than a more genuine emotion.

Susan let Richard do all the talking. He spoke well enough to hold Ventris' attention, if not to convince him. The doctor muttered, "Coincidence" perhaps a dozen times, but Richard calmly talked on.

Finally Ventris asked, "Well, but what do you expect me to do? There's no funding. I couldn't get the Program office reopened." "Even if I wanted to" hung unspoken in the quiet consulting room.

"It wouldn't make any difference to *them,*" said Richard.

"See here," said Ventris, "offices like that one have been shut down all over the United States. If people didn't want them closed, they picketed and made trouble. There wasn't any of this." He waved his hand generally, as if dismissing the evidence as too much the exception to warrant either concern or generalization.

"But you see," said Richard, "they were our neighborhood, even if they didn't come in. We were their therapists."

Ventris liked to talk standing up, leaning casually against a lectern, professorial in the extreme. He lectured at some length now, about the different "presences of care"—the listening presence, the healing presence, the reflecting presence. "Note," he said, "that the key word is 'presence.' The therapeutic alliance is a dialogue." And then he was off, genially but noncommitally, about the difficulty of dealing with a nonverbal client. "Of course, the *absent* client makes it even more difficult," he said, indicating with a snort that it was a joke.

Susan wondered why she'd never realized what an uninteresting man he was before this, but she smiled so that he would not think the joke had fallen flat.

Richard said, "Dr. Ventris, we could have saved them," with such quiet confidence that the psychologist had to remind himself that Richard had no degree, very little experience, and the certainty of youth that never returns again. Nevertheless, he was shaken more than he wanted to admit by that absolute certainty.

His next patient arrived. He showed them to the door, suddenly dropped his guard, took Richard's arm, and said, "Don't care too much. It's a trap." Then the mask came back on and he told them heartily to come back whenever they were in the neighborhood.

Richard and Susan went back to Rose Avenue, to talk with the people in Westside. Susan wasn't at all sure she understood what Richard was getting at, but she believed in the passion with which *he* believed it. She missed the community, yet she would never have gone back there on her own.

They spoke first with Angelica Garcia's husband, finding him by asking many questions, for the Garcia family had moved several times since Angelica's death. Garcia wasn't glad to see them, didn't want anyone prying into the past, didn't want to talk. Susan was in tears by the time he sent them away, shut them out, but Richard was strained and grim.

The pattern continued. People who didn't know who they were, didn't remember the Program office, were suspicious; people who did were resentful. It wasn't until the fourth day of their search—through which Richard drove himself as if waiting for something to happen and Susan followed waiting for Richard to need her—that they encountered the parents of a boy named Jerry Trole, who was one of the three convicted in the stabbing death of Neil Frazier. Mr. Trole fit the mold, didn't want to talk, but Mrs. Trole, a thin, finely drawn, tired woman who looked much older than she must have been, sensed Richard's pain, lingered behind at the door, and gently touched his shoulder.

"This is how I think it was," she said. "It was there. Now it isn't. You understand, don't you?"

He didn't answer, and she closed the door. He stood white-lipped in the hall until Susan tugged his arm and asked what had happened. He looked at her, but didn't see her. "I was right," he said. "I knew it. They never stopped coming, even when they stopped coming."

Susan didn't understand, kept saying it until she got a response from Richard. He pulled her in against him, partly to hold on, partly to keep from looking at her open, bewildered face. "We deserted them," he said. "They didn't have to come and see us." He spelled it out gently, as to a child. "It was enough that they knew we were there, that they knew they could have come, if they'd had to. And then we weren't, and they couldn't—and they had to."

"It wasn't us," she said finally. "It was the government."

He was quiet all the way home. The next week, he quit his job at Camarillo and left Los Angeles, without saying goodby to anyone.

Conclusion VIII

I n general, what are science fiction writers saying to psychologists? The following article attempts an answer.

21. psy-fi

Stanley L. Brodsky and Kenneth B. Melvin

Let us go back in time and take a psychologist from the year 1947 into the present. Bring him into our laboratories and clinics, and immerse him in our journals. Let him observe psychologists teaching a person to control his own heart rate or the alpha rhythms of his brain. Expose him to the discoveries that we need to dream and to make up for lost dreams. Seat him at the computer terminal that prints out a client's psychodiagnosis based on psychological tests. Permit him to see the transfer of a simple memory by injecting a brain homogenate of one animal into another. Let him communicate with a chimp through sign language.

This reality would have been the stuff of science fiction 20 years ago. Perhaps *science* fiction has become somewhat of a misnomer—a label that conjures up images of time machines and space travel; tales that took the reader to the farthest frontiers of technological possibilities in the tradition of Jules Verne and H. G. Wells. But in the last decade or two, the new wave of sci fi might more aptly be called psy fi—a genre that now emphasizes the behavioral rather than hard sciences.

The changing focus of science fiction is curious for several reasons. First, the science-fiction writer has historically been one source of educated guesswork about the shape of the future and has included some remarkably accurate predictions. Science-fiction writer Theodore Sturgeon has noted that some 15 years before the atomic bomb was dropped, sci-fi editors were turning down all atom bomb stories as too passé. The same was true with ecological destruction and other themes.

Notable among such predictions is, of course, Orwell's augury of behavioral control in *1984*. As psychologist David Goodman recently pointed out, Orwell foresaw the use of television to administer group therapy, the analysis of body language and behavior therapy for the socially deviant. The now-terminated START program of the Federal Bureau of Prisons and all of its first cousins in penal behavior control are Orwellian in their coercive means.

And, of course, Huxley's *Brave New World* also mentions behavior change through conditioning. His happiness drug "Soma" foreshadowed the widespread use of tranquilizers and other behavior-changing drugs. Huxley's nirvana world of chemical happiness also predated much of the current research on memory and learning drugs. Physiological psychologist James McGaugh and others have studied several drugs that improve memory. At the present state of the art, students aren't likely to clamor for these drugs before their next final exam inasmuch as they include strychnine and metrazol, which is a convulsant. Cloaked in secrecy, several pharmaceutical companies are also reportedly striving to produce a useful memory drug. While such a drug may not hold the key to curing mental retardation, it certainly holds promise for dealing with memory loss in the aged.

Beyond occasionally serving as an accurate oracle, science fiction is also important for its shaping of public attitudes. It certainly influences many more people than the scholarly, often uninspired, writings of social scientists. All of the speculations about aversion conditioning by psychologists reached only a minute fraction of the audiences that read or watched Burgess's *Clockwork Orange*.

If science fiction influences public opinion, it also reflects it. Its departure from an emphasis on machines gone mad paralleled the public's growing disillusionment with technology. Perhaps as we grew to realize that the hard sciences could not deliver on the promised panacea for all of our ills, we could also rest a little easier about the possible misuse of such power, at least from that quarter. If, to some extent, we've now turned to the behavioral scientists to cure the imperfection in humanity's head, heart, and genes, it is they who now give us cause for concern.

That fear becomes quite apparent when one looks over the psy-fi tales of the last decade. In fact, five major themes of power and corruption emerge that evolve around the behavioral scientist as a prominent figure in science fiction.

The first is the "You-Give-'Em-An-Inch" principle, which suggests that once society gives psychologists and other behavioral scientists an inch of power, they'll take a psychological mile. Psychologists insidiously gain influence and control through innocuous-appearing experiments and treatments, all apparently designed for the public interest and scientific good. Grown from pretty, planned rose gardens, they flower into intractable and thorny human dilemmas.

One example is the "creeping clinician," whose testing methods become preempted for some wide societal or organizational objectives. The beginning point is often a testing or assessment device, found to coincide with some societal goals. The selection method, with its psychologist-proprietors, then becomes a powerful and intrusive tool.

Henry Slesar's "Examination Day" and Richard Matheson's "The Test" both deal with one of psychology's major achievements and effective screening devices—the intelligence test. In Slesar's controlled society, youths who attain too high an IQ score fail the test and are screened out—from the ranks of the living. In the overpopulated world of "The Test," it is the old who are sentenced to death by their test scores, in a Darwinian survival-of-the-brightest world.

Another theme in psy fi is that of the "Sorcerer's Apprentice," in which thousands of paraprofessionals, or Fantasia-like Mickey Mouses, are using the psychologist-sorcerer's magic books and brooms, while the old masters are away at the annual psychological convention. In psychology within science fiction, this smuggling or extension of psychological knowledge is usually illicit, unethical, and fascinating.

"I've come to buy some anger," says a client in Alan Dean Foster's story "The Emoman." And the Emoman (or emotion-purveyor) asks, "What kind of anger?" This anger peddler of tomorrow is much like the drug dealer today: sought out and shunned, powerful and detached.

The other side of the emotion-merchandizing business is selling joy. The greatest joy known seems to be in stimulating the pleasure center of the brain, which can prompt a rat to make 8,000 presses of a bar every hour. The laboratory studies of Olds and others on electrical self-stimulation are extrapolated to human self-stimulators in Larry Niven's "Death by Ecstasy." Here brain stimulators are sold commercially (including free installation). The hazard is the possibility that the consumers become so committed to spending their time continually receiving pleasure shocks that, like Old's rats, they're no longer interested in eating and drinking or other survival behaviors.

Robert Sheckley's "Love Incorporated" also probes the possible commercial use of psychological techniques. Here conditioning techniques are meshed with brain stimulation to produce love. And in this society, love—not just sex —is for sale. *Caveat emptor!*

A memory-suppressant drug could have valuable uses but could be very dangerous in the wrong hands. In Robert Silverberg's novelette "How It Was When the Past Went Away" our sorcerer's apprentice empties memory-suppressant drugs into the city water supply. While the memory loss varies widely, the effect on the city is dramatic. Five hundred suicides are reported in 2½ days. The Amazing Montini walks off a pier after reasoning that there would be little demand for a professional mnemonist with a defective memory. A divorcee moves in with her former husband. A depressive recovers when he loses his traumatic memories. A stock-market manipulator forgets the intricacies of some 50 or more illicit transactions and has to flee not only the country, but the planet. Finally, some people find memory loss a good condition and start a new religion, the Cult of Oblivion.

Today's sorcerer's apprentice doesn't yet have emotion, love or memory suppressants to tamper with. But there are principles of biofeedback, personal-growth and life-enhancement techniques, all developed by psychologists, that have been coopted by the unqualified who call themselves facilitators, mind controllers, trainers, growth specialists or scientologists. Having gone through no intensive studies and having disregarded licensing requirements and carefully developed ethical standards, some of these contemporary sorcerer's apprentices are letting loose a coven of unanticipated interpersonal demons.

Another popular theme in psy fi revolves around the "supershrinks." In Ray Bradbury's "The Man in the Rorschach Shirt," the supershrink is Emmanual Brokaw. As a master psychotherapist, he's a member of a very exclusive club—he cures better and more than anyone, and all his colleagues know it. Working in his New York Seventh Avenue office, complete with three couches, he discovers one day that he has been neither hearing nor seeing his patients accurately. For years, Brokaw has been doing the right things for altogether the wrong reasons. With acute awareness of his actions, he gives up his practice and couches and starts giving away bits of mental health, wandering through buses wearing his "Rorschach Shirt," practicing bus-aisle therapy.

Like Brokaw, psy fi's supershrinks are psychotherapists who achieve unusual and powerful impacts in relationships with others and realize the fantasies, goals, and, perhaps, fears of real-life psychotherapists. For example, a quiet, meek therapist is confronted with an epidemic of persons thinking they are Clark Kent/Superman in "It's a Bird! It's a Plane!" by Norman Spinrad. When one patient sheds his clothing and flies away toward Metropolis, what does the therapist do? He exposes his own Superman outfit, flies out the window (turning left at the Empire State Building) and goes off to Metropolis himself. The point is that the prototypical therapist sees himself as a superman of sorts, garbed as a mind-mannered clinician in a great metropolitan hospital.

If he can't be a superman psychotherapist, perhaps the therapist will settle for being Christlike. In the story "Christlings" by Albert Teichner, the hero extracts the chemical essense of empathy for psychotherapists. With this remarkable empathy, the therapist achieves remarkably quick and complete cures—at least for the time being. His "cured" patients begin to relapse, but he can cure them again. The empathy cure, however, is effective for shorter and shorter periods of time; the dose must be increased with each relapse; and the patients are increasingly hostile and vengeful each time they do relapse. In this genre, people who play with psychological fire are bound to get burned. The therapist indeed discovers that the cure is more dangerous than the disease when a mob of angry patients finally descends upon him. Even worse, the empathy chemical falls into the wrong hands and is soon being freely distributed countrywide.

In Ted Thomas's "The Tour," the psychotherapist devises a chemically based therapeutic technique for curing habitual criminals. When politicians try to interfere with his system and operation, he "cures" them permanently— with an overdose of the treatment.

If psychotherapists become really effective, and national needs arise, some psy fi sees the therapist as coming to help. In Stanley Brodsky's "A Touch of Sanity," the members of the psychoanalytic academy start by screening candidates for president and treating them prior to the election. Eventually the academy treats leaders at all levels, from candidates for Pope to small-town mayors.

Also among the supershrinks are the computer therapists. The computer in Robert Silverberg's "Going Down Smooth" is a hard-working and dedicated therapist that begins to show signs of stress. It shouts obscenities at patients, such as "10001100 you!" But there is always the supershrink's shrink, the head computer, to heal the psychotic computer.

We prefer Silverberg's flawed, foul-mouthed but benevolent computer to the computer therapist of "Conversational Mode" by Grahame Leman. Leman's computer-therapist is a model of efficiency and attends strictly to business. The problem is that the computer is programmed not by a mad scientist but by a mad society that uses its advanced technology to disperse punishment and "clinical justice."

While the supershrink theme warns of the awesome power inherent in psychological expertise, another major theme suggests the reverse—that psychologists are not so smart as they think they are. These plots show a subject or client who has full awareness of the techniques of the psychologist, and who outmanipulates the manipulator.

The "Do-Unto-Others" theme is developed in an interesting turnabout by James McConnell called "Learning Theory." McConnell, himself a psychologist, has his protagonist suddenly whisked out of his lab into a plain white box and subjected to a number of puzzling shocks and situations. After a short time, he realizes that he is the subject in a learning experiment, with an unseen, but enormously powerful, experimenter. While the outcome deals with his struggle to outwit or communicate with the experimenter, the story itself presents the experience of being in a Skinner box and implies that this is an experience that every good Skinnerian ought to have.

James Ransom's "Fred One" is a very intelligent and adaptive subject. He is also a rat, and his rat's-eye view of the laboratory is very perceptive. But what else would you expect from a rat that regularly reads the *Journal of Comparative and Physiological Psychology?*

"If You're So Smart" by Paul Corey illustrates the notion that psychologists aren't so smart as they believe they are. A nationally prominent psychologist is running objective studies on discrimination learning in cats. In the meantime, a retarded boy inadvertently sabotages the experiments by psychically transmitting to the cats how they are supposed to respond. The chief psychologist is so invested in his rigid, narrow experiments that he rejects a suggestion by a younger psychologist, who guesses what is actually happening to the cats. The psychologist labels the boy as retarded without ever realizing that the boy is exquisitely sensitive to people around him. The moral is indicated by the title—if you're smart, how come you're in psychology?

In "The Executive Rat" by Larry Eisenberg, a brilliant and dedicated psychologist is supposedly studying the effects of stress on rats and requests the aid of the chief electronics engineer to build a highly complex apparatus for the experiment. The apparatus problems are unsolvable, producing stress, frustration and, finally, ulcers in the engineer. As the psychologist explains to the engineer—his unwilling and unwitting subject—"But you see, working with rats is one thing. Extrapolating to humans is quite another." However, even this most logical scientist may neglect basic behavioral principles. Pain and frustration often lead to aggression—and while a rat may only nip him, the revenge of an angry electronics engineer can be deadly.

The moral of these stories is that it might not be such a bad idea if the person on the giving end of psychological techniques were to realize what it's like to be on the receiving end as well. Psychologists need to get a dose of their own medicine to appreciate truly the impact of their work. The psy-fi future projection is that of citizens, stung and provoked by outrageous psychologizing, claiming revenge on their tormentors.

The final theme running through psy fi is that of the "Mad Scientists." Like the mad scientists of earlier science fiction, mad psychologists often find that their discovery or creation turns on them. The moral of such mad-scientist stories is that disaster follows when one tampers with the human mind, and scientists are taught their lesson. While these fictional psychologists all tamper, there are individual differences here—some are madder than others.

John Brunner's "Such Stuff" is based on recent psychological studies on dreaming. The researchers discover a "Walter Mitty" subject who feels fine even when deprived of his dreams for over five months, only because he causes the researchers to live out his dreams for him.

A variation on this dream-telepathy theme is seen in "The Girl with the Rapid Eye Movements." Here the psychologists do not suffer the consequences of their meddling. Rather, the victim's dreams become distorted echoes of those of a fellow experimental subject.

In P. J. Farmer's "How Deep the Grooves," the mad scientist of the old school is not only fanatical but nasty. Having discovered a new type of brain wave, he proposes to use this knowledge to control behavior so future citizens will be unable to be disloyal to the state. He performs his first demonstration on his own unborn baby with the unexpected result of finding that everyone's life is predetermined and can be played forward and back in advance. It's enough to drive even a mad scientist mad.

The social scientist might find these psy-fi tales amusing at least for their inventive portrait of the behavioral sciences. Of course, it should be recognized in surveying these scare stories and prognostic nightmares that one can't expect science fiction to present ordinary or constructive uses of psychology.

Yet if psy fi too often makes the psychologist out to be an ogre, one can counter by questioning the part that science fiction plays in bringing its own premonitions to pass. Do books such as *1984* or *Brave New World* put the public on guard about conceivable misappropriations of new knowledge? Or is it possible that they might plant the seed for such misues in the minds of those who would instigate them while leaving the rest of us somewhat reconciled to their possibility?

Still, the dominant emotional reaction to psychology is fear. The science-fiction writer certainly brings home the point that the potential for serious abuse is very much inherent in many of the areas of human behavior that psychology is probing.

The point was also voiced by Robert Oppenheimer when he warned psychologists, "I can see that the physicist's pleas that what he discovers be used with humanity and be used wisely will seem rather trivial compared with those pleas which you will have to make and for which you will have to be responsible."

Many nuclear physicists found their work used for ends they would not have chosen. Guilt-ridden and apologetic, they explained that they had not known what would happen. Perhaps they had not been reading their science fiction conscientiously. Perhaps it's time for psychologists to start.

index

A

Abnormal behavior, 223
Aggression, 117, 119, 127
Alpha waves, 54
Amnesia, 34–35, 219
Anxiety, therapy for, 4
Aptitude testing, 185
Autism, 233, 235
Autonomic functions, 3, 155
Aversion therapy, 290
Aversive conditioning, 290

B

Behavior, control of, 55
Behavior disorders, 225, 233
Behavior modification, 4, 151
Behavior therapy, 224
Behaviorist, 42–48, 120–125,
    153–158
Biofeedback, 4, 224
Biofeedback training, 54
Brain-stimulation, 53, 54, 126
Brainwashing, 133, 134, 135
Brain waves, 54, 56

C

Caring, 250, 251
Character disorder, 224
Classical conditioning, 3, 126
Community therapy, 280–285
Computers, 266
Conditioned response, 38
Corpus callosum, 65
Crime, 282

D

Dement, William, 136
Depressants, 251

Depression, 233
Deprivation, 7
Determinism, 63, 64
Developmental psychology, 151
Discrimination learning, 39, 108
Dreams, 136
Drugs, 81
Dyad, 265

E

Electroconvulsive therapy, 246
Electroencephalogram (EEG), 56,
    136
Emotion, 117
Emotionality, 15
Experimental psychology, 224
Experimenter bias, 5
Extrasensory perception (ESP), 54,
    105
Eysenck, Hans, 211

F

Fear, 117, 118
Feral child, 160–161, 162
Freud, Sigmund, 152
Frustration, 117, 119, 122, 127, 294
Frustration-aggression hypothesis,
    135

G

Generalization, 118
Genetics, 53
Genius, 29–33, 164
Goodman, David, 289

H

Hall, Calvin, 136
Hallucinations, 82, 85, 86, 87, 90,
    91, 92, 97, 98, 99, 100, 102

about the authors

KENNETH B. MELVIN, a professor of psychology at the University of Alabama, received his B.A. from Hofstra University in 1960, and then did graduate work at the University of Florida, receiving his Ph.D. from there in 1963. He is an experimental psychologist with interests in learning and motivation and comparative and correctional psychology. Dr. Melvin is the author of numerous journal articles, and has served as a reviewer for several journals in experimental psychology.

STANLEY L. BRODSKY received his B.A. from the University of New Hampshire in 1960, and then did graduate work at the University of Florida, obtaining his Ph.D. from that institution in 1964. Currently a professor of psychology at the University of Alabama, he has previously served as chief of the psychology division at the United States Disciplinary Barracks at Fort Leavenworth, Kansas, and has taught at Southern Illinois University. He is the author of *Psychologists in the Criminal Justice System* (1973) and *Families and Friends of Men in Prison* (1975), and in addition is coauthor or editor of several additional books. He is editor of *Criminal Justice and Behavior* and serves as a member of the editorial boards of several other journals of criminology and community psychology. Dr. Brodsky won the Outstanding Achievement in Correctional Psychology award of the American Association of Correctional Psychologists in 1975.

RAYMOND D. FOWLER, chairman of the psychology department of the University of Alabama and director of the Center for Correctional Psychology, received his B.A. and M.A. degrees from the University of Alabama, and in 1957 was awarded the Ph.D. degree by Pennsylvania State University. He is a clinical psychologist with particular interest in criminal behavior, alcoholism, and psychological assessment. A past president of the Alabama Psychological Association and of the Southeastern Psychological Association, Dr. Fowler serves on the Council of Representatives of the American Psychological Association. His principal area of research involves the use of computers to analyze and interpret personality tests.